Carnival Glass

The Magic and the Mystery

Glen and Stephen Thistlewood

Schiffer Publishing Ltd

**Revised and Expanded
2nd Edition**

4880 Lower Valley Road, Atglen, PA 19310 USA

Dedication

For Angie and Andrew

Other Schiffer books by Glen and Stephen Thistlewood:

The Art of Carnival Glass, ISBN: 0-7643-1963-9, $39.95

A Century of Carnival Glass, ISBN: 0-7643-1209-X, $39.95

Title page photo:
A magnificent blue STARBURST AND CROWN
water pitcher and tumbler by Riihimaki.

Designed by Bonnie M. Hensley and "Sue"
Type set in *Lydian Cursive BT/Zurich BT*

ISBN: 978-0-7643-2989-0
Printed in China
1 2 3 4

Published by Schiffer Publishing Ltd.
4880 Lower Valley Road
Atglen, PA 19310
Phone: (610) 593-1777; Fax: (610) 593-2002
E-mail: Info@Schifferbooks.com
website: **www.schifferbooks.com**

This book may be purchased from the publisher.
Include $5.00 for shipping.
Please try your bookstore first.
You may write for a free catalog.

In Europe, Schiffer books are distributed by
Bushwood Books
6 Marksbury Avenue
Kew Gardens
Surrey TW9 4JF England
Phone: 44 (0)181 392-8585; Fax: 44 (0)181 392-9876
E-mail: info@bushwoodbooks.co.uk

We are interested in hearing from authors
with book ideas on related subjects.

Contents

Acknowledgments

In writing this Second Edition of *Carnival Glass—The Magic & The Mystery*, we have been helped by many people including collectors and researchers. Mention must be made of certain people whose contribution to this Second Edition has been outstanding:

Marcus Newhall for his help and exceptional expertise in Czechoslovakian pressed glass

Professor F. F. Ridley for his astonishing archive and personal knowledge of Josef Rindskopf's Sons

Malcolm and Hilary Ross for sourcing the catalogs of the Hortensja factory in Poland

Joan Doty for her constant support

Bob Smith for his original research and enthusiasm

Siegmar Geiselberger for use of catalogs—see his website http://www.pressglas-korrespondenz.de/

Sincere thanks are also due to the following individuals and organizations who have provided us with information and support in so many ways:

Frank Andrews
Val and Bob Appleton
Claudia Avila, Registro y Colecciones: Museo del Vidrio, Monterrey, Mexico
Wilma and Neil Berry
Della Breukelaar
The late Lucile and John Britt
Nick Dolan
Dave Doty
Janet and Graham Dickson
Dean and Diane Fry, for the Butler Brothers catalogs
Rita and Les Glennon
Jeanette and Charles Echols
Ivo Haanstra
Martin Hamilton
Lance and Pat Hilkene
John and Frances Hodgson
Martin and Sue Hodgson
Tony Hodgson

Frank and Shirley Horn
Mahavir Jain, Director, Jain Glass Works (P) Ltd., Firozabad (no longer trading)
Wayne King, Fenton Art Glass Company
Annett van der Kley-Blekxtoon, Stitchting National Glasmuseum, Leerdam, Holland
Kaisa Koivisto, Curator, The Finnish Glass Museum, Riihimaki, Finland
Lois Langdon
Dietrich Mauerhoff
Janet and Alan Mollison
Tom and Sharon Mordini
Tammy Murphy
John and Loretta Nielsen
Dieter Neumann
Anthony Pike, Divisional Director Tableware International (formerly Pottery Gazette and Glass Trade Review)
Brian Pitman
Brian and Roni Randall
Karen and Allan Rath
Dave Richards
Howard Seufer
Lesley and Bob Smith
Carol and Derek Sumpter

And finally, sincere thanks to the Fenton Art Glass Company, Williamstown, West Virginia and the late Frank Muhleman Fenton in particular. In the mid 1990s, we were privileged to spend several days at Fenton, getting to know the processes in the factory and utilising the unique resources of the museum and the Fenton archives. We are grateful to both the company and to the late Frank M. Fenton for allowing use of archive photographs and the inclusion of some of Frank's early memories. The Carnival Glass world owes much to the dedication of Frank—it is a sadder place without him. (Frank Muhleman Fenton, 1915—2005).

All drawings are by Glen Thistlewood unless noted. All photographs are by Stephen Thistlewood unless noted.

Foreword

As a result of the authors' extensive and continuing research into the international production of Carnival Glass, a wealth of new information and up-to-date knowledge has been incorporated into this important and fully revised Second Edition of Carnival Glass—The Magic and The Mystery. Part Three, covering the production of Carnival Glass in Europe, Australia, South America, India and China has been re-written to reveal an astonishingly comprehensive coverage of manufacture of Carnival Glass in countries around the world from around 1915, or perhaps even earlier—much of it previously unreported. This early date is a revelation, showing that Carnival from Europe was first made at a time parallel with Classic Carnival production in the USA.

In the original First Edition of Carnival Glass—The Magic and The Mystery a range of puzzles and mysteries was included. In this revised Second Edition, the authors have solved many of those enigmas and in the process have uncovered much fascinating information. The manufacture of Carnival Glass in Poland, France and Brazil, plus the authors' discoveries of yet more Carnival makers in England, Czechoslovakia and Germany, overturns much old thinking and brings fresh knowledge to the fascinating world of Carnival Glass.

Throughout the book, value ranges are given for all items photographed in full, and only for the color and shape shown. Values can vary tremendously for different shapes and/or colors with the same pattern. The value ranges shown are based on auction prices and private sales (predominantly in the United States of America) and have been assessed on the basis that a piece has excellent iridescence and has neither flaws nor damage. Lower values would naturally be attributed to items with damage. Note also that iridescence, condition, color, availability, auction dynamics and subjective judgment all play a major part in determining value. The reader is referred to Tom and Sharon Mordini's Carnival Glass Auction Prices and similar guides to gain further pricing information.

For some exceptionally rare and unusual items, no price (NP) is given because the item concerned has not, to the best of the authors' knowledge, changed hands at a publicly disclosed price in the collectors' market. A speculative price category (SP) has also been used for items that may have been sold, but in such small numbers or in such a specialized market that attributing a value in the Carnival Glass collectors' market is speculative. Nevertheless, it is considered helpful to give an indicative value as a guide. Furthermore, the market for emerging sectors such as European and Indian Carnival Glass has not yet settled down and will no doubt fluctuate for some years yet to come.

Neither the authors not the publishers can be liable for any losses incurred when using the values attributed within this book, as the basis for any transaction, or for any other purpose.

The information presented in this book is based on the authors' research and current knowledge. Should you wish to contact the authors with comments, views or further information pertaining to the contents of this book, please visit the authors' website <http://www.carnival-glass.net> where you will find an email link for direct contact.

Three blue vases from Finland—left to right: WESTERN THISTLE (Riihimaki), SPINNING STARLET (Karhula) and STARLIGHT (Karhula).

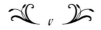

Part One
The Essentials of Classic Carnival Glass

Few Carnival Glass patterns are so universally recognized and loved as Northwood's *PEACOCKS*. The classic composition, the elegance of the design, the scintillating quality of its iridescence all combine to make this green bowl with a pie crust edge a truly outstanding item. $1200-$1750.

Chapter One

The Soul of Carnival: its Magic and its Mystery

Carnival Glass possesses a magic of its own. Imagine a rainbow, arched across the sky, deepest indigo, rich purples and pinks, soft greens, blues, even fragile gold, blending together into a shimmering, capricious, ever-changing hue. Or think of a soap bubble, its myriad of colors fleetingly captured in the blinking of an eye. Now imagine that captured on glass in the form of scintillating iridescence, an ever-changing sheen with many moods, the iridescence applied to carefully shaped glass on which are moulded exquisitely detailed patterns. Indeed, there are well over a thousand different Carnival Glass designs: spell-binding patterns featuring flowers, fruits, birds, animals, peacocks, geometric intricacies, and elegant imitations of lacework and embroidery. The total effect is sheer, breathtaking beauty, a shimmering dance of light and color.

Carnival Glass is also full of mystery. Looking at the history of its production is like holding up a mirror to the world. It reflects society's tastes and desires; it reflects commerce and industry; it reflects artistic and cultural trends. And in those reflections over time, there naturally lie many mysteries. The development of Carnival design and the influences that were behind it are fascinating. They reflect the era in which Carnival was produced and provide a unique way of discovering more about this splendid, captivating glass. But like all aspects of the past, there are elements that are unknown. Riddles to be reasoned, mysteries to be solved.

The purpose of this book is to give Carnival Glass its place within the framework of the decorative arts, to provide insights into its manufacture, to explain the origins and development of its pattern themes, and to show the many reflections it gives of societies and cultures the world over. The greater part of the book is devoted to the **original Classic Carnival**, which, for our purposes, we will define as **that which was produced in the United States of America from about 1907 to around 1925.** The final part of the book looks at the subsequent manufacture of Carnival as it echoed around the world from around 1915 (maybe even earlier) through the 1920s and 30s, and even lingering into the 1950s and beyond. Much original catalog and archive information has been used.

Memories

Carnival—the very word stirs up a kaleidoscope of images: traveling fairs, revelry, color, fun, and laughter. Yet the American factories that produced the beautiful glass that we now know as Carnival, way back in the early 1900s, were dark, hot, noisy, and fume-ridden. They were a true reflection of the might of the western world's industrialization, where working conditions were unhealthy and often dangerous. Out of all this rose the glory of Carnival Glass. Hand finished, mass produced glassware that took the world by storm when it was first made, Carnival Glass is repeating the process again today, as more and more people realize the unique history and artistry of this beautiful glassware, a true legacy of our past.

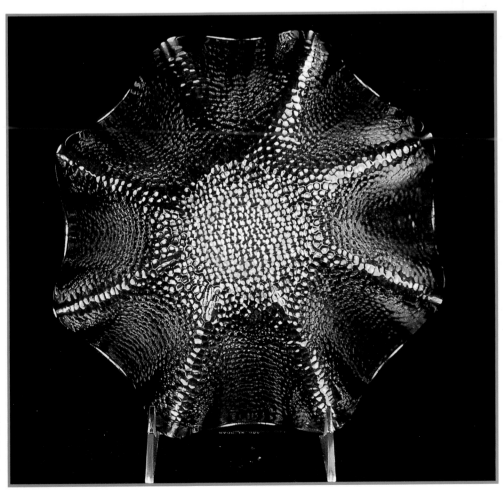

A simple abstract pattern, yet the Imperial Glass Company achieved an outstanding iridescent effect on a purple *COBBLESTONES* ruffled bowl. $250-$350.

Carnival Glass is an apt and colorful name—but it's a recent term. When Carnival was first produced in the United States during the early 1900s, a variety of descriptive names were used to advertise it. Such names, like "Pompeiian Iridescent," "Venetian Art," and "Mexican Aurora," have long since fallen out of usage, though they indicated that the new product was imitating imported iridescent glass. There were also odd names that seem to defy explanation, such as "Baking Powder Glass"[1] and "Nancy Glass."[2] Sometimes also termed "the working man's Tiffany" or "poor man's Tiffany," it was the pressed glass equivalent to the very expensive blown Art Glass. Its method of manufacture was cheap—the output was huge. Though the glass was press moulded, much of it was also hand finished. In fact, so much individuality was applied to each piece of glass in terms of its color, iridescence, or hand finishing, that it is really very difficult to find two pieces exactly the same in all respects.

The price of this mass produced glass was low; it meant that the ordinary folk could afford to buy beautiful, iridized glassware. Sales were good, it was cheap, and it sold through mail order catalogs, in dime stores, and in department stores, where it cost just a few cents apiece. Some were even given away as premiums with sales catalogs. It was also exported to countries such as Britain by the barrel load. This new, colorful, iridized glass brightened many dark and drab households back in the early 1900s.

Workers at the Fenton Art Glass factory circa 1907-1908, packing glassware into straw-filled barrels. They must have been very proficient at filling them, as they managed to pack six full water sets or four full punch sets into just one barrel. Smaller items fitted better. There were forty-eight regular sized compotes (or if the customer preferred, seventy-two standard sized vases) packed inside just one barrel. However, the prize for the fullest packed barrels must have gone to the assortments - ninety mixed items including bowls, compotes, vases, and bonbons all carefully packed into just one wooden barrel! *Photograph courtesy of the Fenton Art Glass Museum.*

The Fenton Art Glass Company made some wonderful Carnival Glass rivalling expensive Art Glass, such as this magnificent blue *PEACOCK AT URN* plate. $800-$1200. Note: a stunning example sold for $4250 at auction in April, 1998.

An early advertisement for Fenton's Carnival Glass as seen in a Butler Brothers catalog from October, 1909. Note that the iridescent range was called "Venetian Art" and that it was compared favorably with "expensive imported designs." The range of shapes was small; the patterns were simple. *COIN DOT* (top left and top middle), *STIPPLED RAYS* (top right, bottom left, and bottom right), and *BLACKBERRY BRAMBLE* (bottom middle) are the names by which these pieces are known today.

In addition, the magic of American-made Carnival had not gone unnoticed by glass manufacturers in other countries. From around 1915, countries such as Germany, Australia, England and Finland began to produce their own versions of Carnival Glass. Though it was similar to the Classic Carnival produced in the United States in some ways, the output of each country had its own distinct characteristics. Though often overlooked in the past, this Carnival Renaissance was responsible for some astonishingly beautiful glass. One of the aims of this book is to correct that oversight.

Fashions come and go and tastes change. Possibly due to unsold stocks or to poorer quality items swamping the market, whatever the reason, some of the iridized glass began to be given away at carnivals and county fairs in the United States and in countries such as the United Kingdom—hence its colorful sobriquet—**Carnival Glass**. A derogatory term, a bit of a "put down," and yet it works! **Carnival** sums up all the excitement, color, dynamism, and fizz of Carnival Glass collecting. It characterizes the incredible buzz, the electrifying thrill, when you find that special piece, as well as the kaleidoscope of color and the sheer beauty of the glass itself.

With the advent of the 1950s, a new era dawned for the Classic American Carnival. No longer a "give-away," it began to be seen as a collectible in its own right. The turning point came with what was probably the first authoritative article on Carnival Glass. It was written by Gertrude L. Conboy and published in *The Spinning Wheel* on January 10, 1952. Mrs. Conboy had fallen under the spell of Carnival ten years earlier, when she had come upon a furniture store sale and discovered a table full of the glass. She had purchased a deep purple, Northwood *ORIENTAL POPPY* tumbler which had become the impetus for her subsequent research into its background. Her article was a milestone for Carnival; the glass began to acquire an identity. Back in those early days of collecting, some amazing deals were offered. Contemporary reports indicate that it was so plentiful then, that it was usually sold at auctions by the basketful! One Pennsylvania dealer reputedly had a large table of "assorted pieces priced at ten cents each or three for twenty-five cents."[3]

Marion T. Hartung and Rose M. Presznick fueled the development of Carnival's rise to fame through the 1960s. Both issued pattern books on the glass based on their own research and collecting experiences. The Hartung series of pattern books are still considered a prerequisite for many collectors. Most of the Carnival pattern names in use today are those originated by Marion Hartung. Carnival Glass continued from strength to strength, boosted by the formation of collectors' clubs and associations on an international basis. The magic had spread worldwide both in manufacture and collecting interest.

So to the present. Carnival Glass is avidly admired and collected all over the world, not only as an item of great beauty and artistry, but also as an object of increasing value. Carnival Glass has a further quality to add to its overall beauty—that of durability. An item of glass made in 1907 or 1908 can look as if it were made yesterday. Fluid when molten, hard when cold, the Egyptians called glass "the stone that flows." While other artifacts may rust and decay, glass carries its years well. Though endowed with fragile beauty, glass remains resilient. The magic of Carnival Glass will surely endure. May the reader be the judge.

[1] "Baking Powder Glass" was probably used as a term for the glass we now call Carnival owing to the link with the Lee Manufacturing Company, who gave away iridized glass as premiums with their baking powder and similar products. See Part One: Chapter Five.

[2] "Nancy Glass" was probably used as a term for the glass we now call Carnival because of confusion between Carnival and the fancy art glass that came from Daum, Nancy in France. Possibly this confusion was also caused by the N mark on some Carnival (the Northwood trademark).

[3] O. Joe Olson, *God and Home, Carnival Glass Superstar* (Kansas City, Missouri: by author, 1976).

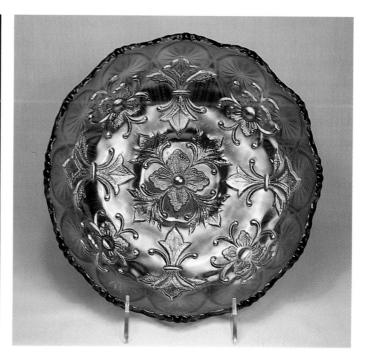

An exquisite peach opal *LINED LATTICE* squatty vase; Dugan/Diamond were masters of this Carnival Glass color. $400-$500.

A green *FLEUR DE LIS* ice cream shaped bowl by the Millersburg Glass Company. Although short-lived, they produced Carnival Glass of exceptional quality and design. $300-$600.

Chapter Two
The Production of Classic Carnival Glass

Carnival Glass was press moulded, made by a mechanical process that allowed for much greater quantities to be made than by the more laborious method of glass blowing. Indeed, Carnival was a mass produced glass that utilized industrial methods of production. While there was a lively debate in the trade journals of the time as to whether it was England or the United States that achieved the technological breakthrough, it is now a generally accepted fact that the art of pressing glass was perfected in the United States in the years leading up to 1820, although pressing by hand had been known in England prior to that date.

The Press Moulding Process

The first step in the glass making process is production of the glass batch—the mixture of raw materials from which all glass is made. The basic constituents of all glass are silica sand, soda ash, and lime, which are mixed together to produce the glass batch. (In fact, the availability of the purer silica sands coupled with a plentiful fuel source generally dictated the location of glass factories.) These raw materials plus various other substances such as glass cullet (broken glass) were mixed together and then heated in the furnace to a very high temperature—about 2500 degrees Fahrenheit—causing it to become a workable, molten, viscous fluid, sticky like hot taffy. This is the so-called "hot metal." A "gatherer" took up a lump (known as a gob or gather) of this hot metal on the end of a metal rod, while the lump was still molten from the furnace, and a sufficient quantity was then cut off with shears and dropped into the mould. The amount of hot metal was crucial and was gauged only by the experience of the glassmaker. Too little and the mould wouldn't be filled enough, too much and the glass would overflow the mould. The temperature of the iron mould had to be just right too. If it was too cold, the finished glass would be cloudy and imperfect. If it was too hot, the glass would stick to the mould. The viscous hot metal was dropped into the mould, and the plunger was pressed down into it, carefully squeezing the glass into all parts of the shaped mould.

Though pressing glass was essentially a simple procedure, the moulds into which it was pressed were relatively complex. The main body of the mould gave the basic shape of the glass object (for example a bowl or a tumbler) and its surface would usually have a pattern cut into it, this being the pattern which would appear, in relief, on the exterior of the glass. Moulds were usually hinged in two, three, or four places, so that they could be opened up in order to remove the finished glass item easily. A ring fitted around the top of the mould. This ring served three purposes: it held the body of the mould tightly closed, it created the shape of the top of the piece being pressed, and it allowed a plunger to be held exactly in position and pressed down into the center of the mould so that the molten glass evenly filled up the space between the mould and the plunger. Like the mould itself, the plunger would usually have had a pattern cut into it, which then came out on the interior of the finished piece. The mould also had a base or bottom plate—a disc which formed the bottom of the mould. It was possible, of course, to interchange plungers, moulds and base plates—thus giving rise to different permutations of the patterns. Cutting moulds was a meticulous and painstaking task, frequently undertaken with great skill and artistry. There are a multitude of different patterns on Carnival Glass, covering all manner of design motifs. Specialist mould-making companies existed, such as The Hipkins Novelty Mould Shop in Martin's Ferry, Ohio, which was known to have made the moulds for several of the Carnival Glass manufacturers.

After pressing, the piece was removed, technically "snapped up," with the tool known as a "snap," which was attached to the collar base of the glass item (the marie). At this stage, hand finishing could take place. The piece would be "warmed in" (re-heated) at a glory hole to make it pliable again. The glory hole is a very small furnace where the glass can be individually re-heated just enough to allow final manipulation to be made. Vases could be swung to give height and the edges of bowls were ruffled and crimped in a variety of ways to give individuality.

A Butler Brothers ad from April, 1912 for Fenton Carnival Glass. Back in 1908 and 1909, Fenton had offered a very limited iridescent range. By 1912, production had blossomed into a wide selection of fancy shapes, and exotic patterns in "floral, fruit, peacock and scroll embossing" were on display. Patterns shown include *ORANGE TREE, CHERRY CIRCLES, PEACOCK AT URN, PERSIAN MEDALLION,* and *RUSTIC*. The shapes illustrated include bowls, plates, rosebowls, loving cup, hatpin holder, puff box, sugar, creamer, bonbons, and more!

Once finished in this way, the glass could then be iridized by a process that is explained below. Finally, the finished items were annealed—that is, cooled to room temperature very slowly in an annealing lehr to ensure that any stresses in the glass that had been built up in the manufacturing processes were relieved gradually, which prevented cracking.

Characteristic Marks On Press Moulded Glass

The press moulding process gave rise to a number of characteristic marks that can frequently be seen on Carnival Glass. Such features should be considered as intrinsic to the method of manufacture and typical of all press moulded glass. Common examples of these are:

The horizontal mark above the design on the top of this green Fenton *TEN MUMS* bowl is a shear mark. It is intrinsic to the way the glass was made.

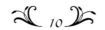

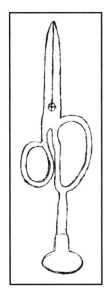

A glassmaker's shears, showing the dome shaped handle used for smoothing out shear marks. The dome shaped handle was added in the 1950s.

Shear marks. Shears were used to cut off the gob of molten glass as it was being dropped into the mould. Because the blades of the shears were relatively cool, the act of cutting the very hot glass resulted in a fractional cooling and resultant hardening of the surface of the glass at the point where it was cut. This is the shear mark (sometimes misleadingly called a "straw" mark). Usually—with skill on behalf of the presser—this mark could be hidden by the intricacies of the pattern, but if the design had large plain areas, the shear mark is often clearly seen. The iridescent surface may even emphasize the appearance of a shear mark.

Extra glass seepage between mould hinges. Marks were often left on the glass at points where the different pieces of the mould were hinged together. However skillfully the moulds were made, in the course of time the joints worked loose as a result of the expansion and contraction of the metal. The glass being pressed oozed into the loose spaces of the joints, and the surface of the finished articles thus displayed fine ribs of glass along the seam lines. This was sometimes overcome by actually designing the pattern in such a way that it would hide these seam marks as they developed.

Tool marks. These are indentations that sometimes appear on the surface of the glass where it has been pulled into shape by the glassmaker's tool. "Jack in the pulpit" shaping—where the front of a vase is pulled down and the back lifted up—may well exhibit this kind of mark.

Grinding chips on base. Glass items with a marie were gripped in a tool with clamp-like, spring loaded jaws called "snaps" while being finished off. This process was termed "snapped up"—these items have smooth, collar bases created by the shape of the mould. However, some pieces were made without a marie, and these were attached by the base to a hot metal punty rod after being extracted from the mould. The factory term for this was "stuck-up." After being finished, the glass item then had to be broken from the punty. This break left a rough base which had to be ground smooth, but often small chips remained behind. Examples of Carnival Glass with base grinding are *FOUR FLOWERS VARIANT* pieces, several Australian items, and Fenton *PANELED DANDELION* tumblers.

Variations in the Moulding Process

Articles which were wider at the bottom than at the top could not be pressed in the usual way, since the plunger had to be pushed into the mould and then withdrawn. Two methods for overcoming this problem were used in Carnival Glass making:

The "Cut Shut" method. Some pieces were pressed upside down (bottom up). Lips or projections sufficient to form the bottom were produced in the mould. The piece, after being pressed, was then withdrawn from the mould, the bottom was heated, and the lips were closed together with a tool.

Blow moulding. Instead of using a plunger, the hot metal was in some cases forced into the mould by blowing air into it. Many water pitchers and large bulbous vases were produced in this way.

An example of blow moulded (rather than press moulded) Carnival: a purple Northwood *GRAPE ARBOR* water pitcher. $400-$750.

Iridescence is the Essence.

So, how was the characteristic iridescence created? Once the glass had been fashioned into its final shape, it was re-heated and, while still hot, was sprayed with a liquid solution of various metallic salts. The liquid evaporated leaving a finely ridged, metallic film on the surface of the glass that can split ordinary daylight into the spectrum of colors in a rainbow effect. This iridescence is what distinguishes Carnival Glass from other press moulded, colored glassware. The name used in the factories for the iridescent spray was "dope," and it was usually mixed in a separate building called the "dope house." After doping, the hot glass articles were annealed.

Different chemical solutions produced different iridescent effects. Iron (ferric) and tin (stannous) chloride, or a combination of the two, were the most frequently used. Sometimes the glass was sprayed more than once, with varying metallic solutions, giving interesting effects. The temperature of the glass when it was sprayed also affected the outcome. If it was very hot, the iridescent effect would be matt or satin-like. If it was not quite so hot, the effect became shinier.

The notebooks of Harry Northwood (who became one of the best known manufacturers of Classic Carnival Glass) refer to the application of iridescence.[1] Northwood wrote; "Ordinary Chloride of Iron as bought at wholesale drug stores costs 3½ cents a lb....spray on glass when finished ready for lehr...glass must be fairly hot." He went on to observe: "Spray on glass very hot for Matt Iridescent and not so hot for Bright Iridescent," going on to mention that a spraying of iron chloride on hot glass, quickly followed by a second spraying with a tin solution, "gives beautiful effects."

Note that shaping took place before the glass was iridized. Further manipulation after iridization meant that minute breaks would occur in the surface of the iridescence. This was, however, intentionally done in certain instances, as it created the effect often termed "onion skin" iridescence that is found on stretch glass and some rare Carnival examples such as Fenton's celeste blue. The stretch effect was created by spraying hot glass with the metallic oxides that were used to give the iridescent effect, then briefly re-heating the glass in the glory-hole, the hottest part of the furnace. The spray, being metallic, didn't expand at the same rate as the glass, causing the iridescent effect to break into the onion-skin-like surface, producing a beautiful rainbow effect.

There were many variables involved in the iridizing or doping process. In addition to the chemical mixture which was applied and the temperature of the glass, another variable that altered the effect of the iridescence was the thickness of the glass itself. Some Carnival patterns are quite deeply moulded, and differences in the thickness of the glass resulted in differential cooling. The metallic salts in the iridescence were affected by this; consequently we can see different iridescent colors on the surface of the glass created by the pattern. Not all Carnival has this effect, but, seen at its best, a design composed, say, of plump grapes on a background of leaves may be seen with deep purple grapes against a greenish, purple

The Carnival Glass makers referred to the iridizing chemical spray as "dope," and they used various doping techniques. Many variables were involved in the process, which combined to achieve remarkable iridescent effects, as seen on this close-up of Imperial's *HEAVY GRAPE* pattern.

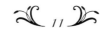

background.

Some Carnival Glass items, such as pitchers and tumblers, were often sprayed on the exterior only, while most bowls and plates were usually iridized both inside and out. It was, of course, necessary to hold the item while it was being sprayed. The snap was the tool used for the job and was clamped firmly onto the marie of the glass item with jaws of the correct size and shape for the piece. As the snap covered the marie during spraying, there was, obviously, no iridescence on the collar base of the glass. (This has an interesting sideline: modern reproduction items, and indeed some fakes, may well have iridized bases as their different method of manufacture allows for the iridescent spray to be applied to the marie as well.)

Iridescent Effects, Opalescent, and Ice Finishes

The incredible visual effect that iridescence has is caused by the light interference patterns produced by constantly shifting wavelengths. Certain iridescent effects have been given names by collectors. A matt effect is generally known as **satin** iridescence, while a multicolored, mirror-like effect is often called **radium**. A particularly desirable effect is **electric** iridescence. This is usually applied to blue shades (electric blue) but more and more collectors are extending the term to apply to other colors: electric purple, electric green (or strictly emerald green), etc. An electric effect is where the iridescence has a very brilliant, multicolored, indeed almost luminous quality. In fact, it almost gives the appearance of being connected to the power supply—it's so vibrant!

Different finishes can also be applied to Carnival; this then alters the named color. An **opalescent** or **opal** effect is created by re-heating glass (usually made from a batch containing bone ash) in the glory hole. The effect is seen as whitened edges, though it can sometimes be seen on thicker or protruding parts of the pattern as well. The opal effect on rare Fenton examples is usually light and fine, whereas the opal effect on most Dugan/Diamond examples is denser and broad. These contrasts were probably caused by the different methods of re-heating employed by the various Carnival manufacturers. Peach opal and aqua opal are the two main examples of opalescent finishes, but there are other rarer opalescent colors such as amethyst opal. Acid treatment (usually using hydrofluoric acid) causes an **ice effect** or **frosting** that can be felt as a kind of roughness on the surface; colors with this finish are often called pastels. Ice green, ice blue, and white are the main examples of the acid treated colors.

The final iridescent effect, therefore, could vary tremendously, and this sheer variety of the iridescence is one of the beauties of Carnival Glass. It may have a dazzling brilliance or a matt quality, it may be delicate and subtle or intense and vivid. No two pieces of Classic Carnival are exactly alike.

Electric purple iridescence on a Dugan/Diamond *CHERRIES* sauce. $120-$140.

On the left is a rare amethyst Millersburg *PEACOCK* 3 in 1 edge, 6" sauce with radium iridescence. Contrast this with the satin iridescence seen on the amethyst Millersburg *PEACOCK* sauce on the right ($150-$250). For the sauce on the right, possibly twice that for the 3 in 1 edge sauce.

A delightful *DAISY AND DRAPE* vase. The color is aqua opal—a Northwood specialty. $700-$750.

Peach opal Dugan/Diamond *DOUBLE STEM ROSE* plate. While this is a common pattern, the plate shape and marvellous opalescent effect combine to make this piece much more unusual. $300-$350.

Peach opal made by Fenton generally has less pronounced opalescence (and is rarer) than that made by Dugan/Diamond. The ruffled bowl on the left is *PEACOCK AND GRAPE* by Fenton ($450-$550), compared with a Dugan/Diamond *PETAL AND FAN* sauce ($50-$75).

A white Dugan/Diamond *WREATHED CHERRY* water pitcher which has additional decoration in the form of gilding around the rim and hand painted red cherries. $400-$450.

Colors in Classic Carnival Glass

"One color often shades into another and where we draw the line is usually in the eyes of the beholder."

—Don Moore, noted writer, researcher and collector of Carnival Glass (1917-92)

An outstanding pumpkin Northwood *POPPY SHOW* plate. Pumpkin is a particularly deep, rich shade of marigold, golden and glowing. Its iridescence is full of multicolored highlights that usually have many red tones. $2500-$3000. Marigold plate without pumpkin effect: $500-$1500.

Now that we have seen how the iridescent effects were created, we need to set out the amazing array of base colors that are generally recognized by Carnival collectors today. Regular glass color is usually clear; it's known as "crystal" glass in the United States and "flint" glass in Britain. However, naturally occurring elements in silica sands will give a colored tint to the glass, and glassmakers often add ingredients to the glass mix to produce extra clarity or brilliance.

Base Glass Color

The base glass color is determined by the mixture in the glass batch. It is the color of the glass itself without the iridescent effect. To determine the base glass color you need to hold the item up to a good, strong light source. Natural daylight is ideal (preferably on a sunny day, but don't look directly at the sun). Using a colored light source will obviously affect what you see—try to get as near to white light as possible. You will need to view the base glass at a point in the glassware that doesn't have iridescence. An uniridized part can usually be found on the collar base or, if the item possesses them, on the feet. The thicker the glass, the more intense the color will appear. **The color of the base glass is the Carnival Color.** Please be aware that the effect of the iridescence may change the appearance of the base color of items as viewed by the naked eye. Carnival Glass items that share the same base color may have a very different superficial appearance. This difference is generally caused by the iridescence.

Despite these varying appearances, the categorization of the color is classified according to the base glass. There are, however, a few exceptions, in particular, that of marigold, a beautiful golden orange shade and undoubtedly the most frequently seen Carnival color. The color marigold was actually created by the metallic spray applied to a *clear* base glass.

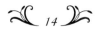

The golden orange color is imparted by the iridescent effect on the surface of the glass—hold the piece up to the light and you'll see that it's crystal clear. However, a large amount of Carnival Glass was also made from colored glass, the coloration being achieved by adding various metallic salts to the batch. After marigold, the deeper Carnival colors of blue, purple, green, and amethyst are perhaps most often seen. To produce green, for example, salts of iron or chromium are added. Adding cobalt produces a deep, rich royal blue shade, while copper gives a lighter mid-blue base glass. The addition of manganese causes the batch to be purple or amethyst while adding phosphate or bone ash (sometimes even arsenic) to the batch creates the effect of opalescence.

Then there are rare and sought-after "top dollar" colors like celeste blue, ice green, and aqua opal, as well as a series of unusual shades such as smoke, amber, and teal. An interesting and highly sought-after base glass color is red. Red was a difficult color to achieve. Shades of cranberry and ruby red had been created by adding gold to the batch, but this glass can only be blown, not pressed in the way that Carnival was made. The breakthrough came with the addition of selenium to the batch in the 1920s, which produced a bright cherry red color when the temperature control was exactly right. When selenium red is taken from the hot glass batch it is red. However, when it is then pressed in a mould, its color becomes yellow! Re-heating causes the yellow color to change back to red. The problem with selenium red was the difficulty in getting it to "strike." ("Striking" is when the crystalline structure of the coloring agent alters upon controlled re-heating.) When this happens, the color changes to red rather than remaining yellow. Amberina is the yellow-red shading that can often be found on red items.

As Carnival collecting has become increasingly sophisticated, more and more color variations have been defined. Coupled with the various effects caused by different kinds of surface application and other treatments, the variety is quite phenomenal. Sometimes it is very difficult to be absolute when defining a color; all the minor variations and nuances of color can be thought of as being on a sliding scale, rather than in strictly finite terms.

A different base color can make a major difference to the desirability of an item. Certain items may be easily found in some base colors yet be exceptionally rare in others. It's important to note, though, that the manufacturers would not have intended all these subtle shade differences. Carnival, though mass produced, was not always subject to the kind of quality control standards that apply today. Mixing the glass batch was often an empirical procedure, based more on judgment than precise measures. Naturally it resulted in non-standard colors. Many of the rare shades were probably factory experiments or even accidents. The search for rare colors certainly makes it interesting for today's collectors.

It is possible to categorize over sixty colors in Classic Carnival, subdivided into the broad color blocks of marigold, purple, blue, green, and so on. These are fully set out and defined in Appendix One.

[1] William Heacock, James Measell, and Berry Wiggins, *Harry Northwood. The Wheeling Years* (Marietta, Ohio: Antique Publications, 1991).

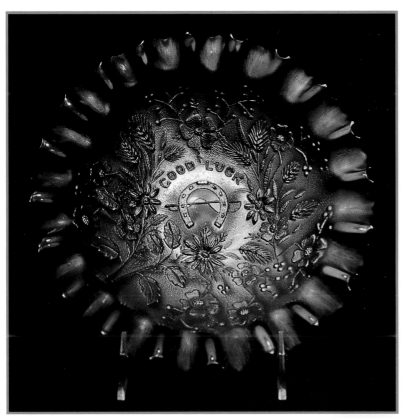

Cobalt blue, Northwood stippled *GOOD LUCK* pie crust edge bowl with electric iridescence. $600-$1000.

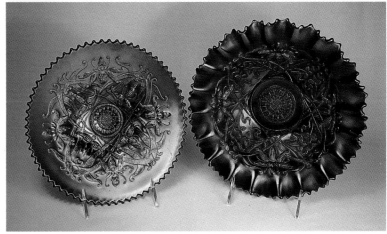

Two Northwood *WISHBONE* pieces. Both have the same purple base color glass, but the effect of the iridescence makes them look very different. The pie crust edged bowl on the right looks purple, while the footed plate on the left appears to be green. Bowl: $250-$300. Footed plate: $400-$600.

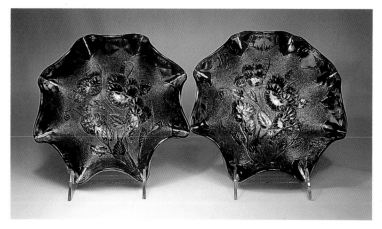

Two purple Imperial *PANSY* bowls showing effects of different iridescence. The one on the right shows vivid greens, pinks, and gold, while the one on the left has more purple and blue shades. $250-$450.

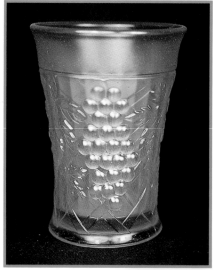

Rare ice green Northwood *GRAPE ARBOR* tumbler. $425-$475.

Ice blue Northwood *PEACOCK AT THE FOUNTAIN* tumbler; quite hard to find in this color. $200-$300.

Vaseline Northwood *CONCAVE DIAMONDS* tumbler glowing strongly under an ultra violet ("black") light. $175-$200.

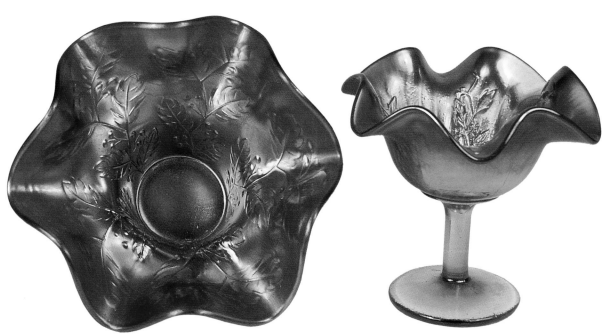

Red is a signature color of Fenton, very sought-after by collectors. On the left, a *HOLLY* ruffled hat ($350-$450). On the right, a *HOLLY* miniature compote with a typical amberina (orange/red) stem and base. ($400-$500).

The Northwood Glass Company produced Carnival Glass with magnificent designs and colors. One of their pastel colors is ice green, at its stunning best on a *PEACOCKS* plate. $500-$800. One sold in 2006 for $1200.

Another Fenton signature color is celeste blue. It is rare and brings top dollar prices. This is a *HOLLY* ice cream shaped bowl. $3500-$5000.

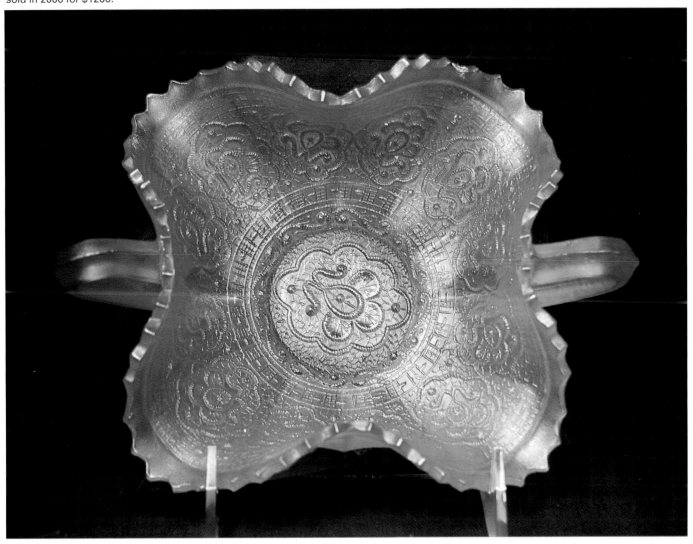

Rare celeste blue *PERSIAN MEDALLION* bon bon from Fenton. $1000-$2000.

A *PANSY* pickle dish in amber, a color often associated with Imperial. Such pieces usually have an incredible iridescence. $100-$150.

Various smoke effects on Imperial pieces. From left: *WINDMILL* sauce ($50-$75), *IMPERIAL GRAPE* wine ($40-$60), *RIPPLE* swung vase ($100-$150), *IMPERIAL GRAPE* sauce ($40-$60), *HATTIE* bowl ($300-$350), *IMPERIAL GRAPE* tumbler ($75-$100), *IMPERIAL GRAPE* decanter ($250-$300), *FASHION* tumbler ($100-$200), and *MORNING GLORY* small size vase ($100-$200).

A smoke Imperial *PANSY* oval tray. Made from the same mould as the pickle dish but not ruffled. $200-$250.

A *LOTUS AND GRAPE* ice cream shape bowl in Persian blue, which is a very unusual, semi-translucent color, exclusive to Fenton. $600-$900.

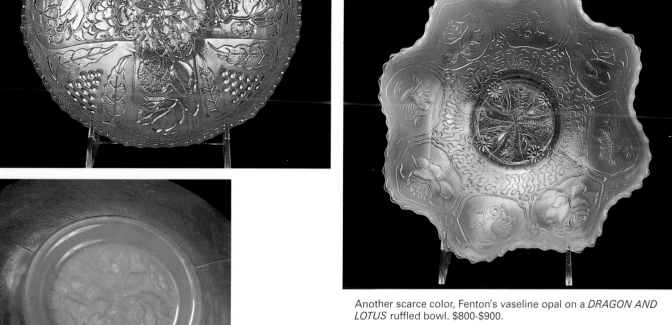

Another scarce color, Fenton's vaseline opal on a *DRAGON AND LOTUS* ruffled bowl. $800-$900.

The marie of the Persian blue Fenton *LOTUS AND GRAPE* bowl shows the base color very clearly.

Chapter Three

The Manufacturers of Classic Carnival Glass

Carnival Glass was "born" around 1907; the first known advertisement for it was in September 1908. The ad was in the Butler Brothers catalog and featured a "'Golden Sunset' Iridescent Assortment" which was described as having "entirely new, beautiful effects heretofore possible to produce only in the exclusive imported items." The imported items referred to in the ad were probably the iridized Loetz or Lobmeyer ware from Austria. Indeed, a 1906 Butler Brothers ad had shown iridized Loetz or "Loetz type" glass vases and bowls from Bohemia. Thomas Webb and Sons of Stourbridge, England had also produced free blown, iridized lustre ware in the late 1800s. They made a deep green glass, iridized in shades of purple, that they called "Bronze" glass, and later an iridized golden effect called "Iris." Queen Victoria herself bought some of Webb's iridized "Bronze" glass. Albert Revi[1] reported Queen Victoria's description of it. She wrote in 1878, "its purple bronze surface shines with the hues of the rainbow." In the United States during the late 1800s and early 1900s, Tiffany had produced his amazing iridized "Favrile" glass. Then Frederick Carder (also a Stourbridge man), who founded the Steuben Works, brought out the fabulous iridescent "Aurene" glass. However, these were all forms of expensive Art Glass: beautiful, exotic and desirable—but not priced for the masses.

The manufacturer of that "'Golden Sunset' Iridescent Assortment" advertised in the Butler Brothers catalog was the Fenton Art Glass Company, though that isn't noted in the ad. The color of the glass was marigold, the patterns and shapes of the items shown were simple and rather basic. But just look at the price—only eighty-five cents wholesale for a dozen items. Previous iridized ware from Bohemia had been priced at over five times that amount. This was glass the public could afford. It began to sell well in the ten cent stores. The December, 1908 edition of the *Glass & Pottery World* commented that, "it seems a pity that a glass so much like the Tiffany 'Favrile' product, save in weight, should find the counters of the cheap stores. However, these are days when a heavy bulk production is necessary to make even a light profit, and sentiment rarely outweighs dollars when pay rolls are to be considered."

This was just the beginning, the tip of the iceberg—over the next decade or so a multitude of shapes, patterns, and colors would explode onto the market. The new iridized glass would take not only the United States but also Europe and Australia by storm—spawning imitations that continue even to this day.

This Butler Brothers ad from September 1908 is one of the first to depict Carnival Glass. Early Fenton patterns *WATERLILY AND CATTAILS, BEADED STAR,* and *DIAMOND POINT COLUMNS* are featured. The "allover metallic iridescent luster in rich, rainbow blendings" is the color we now call marigold Carnival. *Fenton ad courtesy of Frank M. Fenton.*

The companies producing the glass were located fairly close to one another, in West Virginia, Pennsylvania, and Ohio. The Ohio River was of course a major focus, especially useful for transportation. Barrel loads of Carnival Glass, packed in straw, were loaded up and shipped out on the riverboats. The railroad took the rest. The proximity of essential raw materials, and, in particular, a major fuel source were also fundamental. The area also had the benefit of natural gas. Further, the supply of sand was of the best quality. Sand is, of course, the basis of all glass, but the very best must be as nearly pure silicate as possible. It must also be free from iron, as even a small amount will give a green tinge to the glass produced; fortuitously, some of the best silicate rock is found in Pennsylvania.

Barrels packed with glass, being loaded onto an Ohio riverboat back in 1907. *Photograph courtesy of the Fenton Art Glass Museum.*

Fenton Art Glass Company

"My particular work was in the matter of design and then I got the idea that if I could do this work for an employer, I could certainly do something for myself."

—Frank Leslie Fenton (1880-1948), co-founder of the Fenton Art Glass Company

Frank L. Fenton (1880-1948). *Photograph courtesy of the Fenton Art Glass Museum.*

This is one of Fenton's top dollar-beauties, a very flat, amethyst *CONCORD* plate. $2000-$3000.

Frank Leslie Fenton was born in Indiana, Pennsylvania, on January 24, 1880, the youngest son of James and Jennie Crawford Fenton. When Frank was fifteen he was hired by his uncle to help out behind the scenes in his uncle's restaurant and bakery. One of his tasks was to rise early, hitch up the "old gray mare," and deliver feed for the animals. Frank would spend the day delivering, then he would work in his uncle's restaurant until ten or eleven at night. At age seventeen, he graduated from high school and got another job—this time at the glass plant in his home town of Indiana. Within a year, Frank had become foreman; he was to stay there for three years, before moving on to Jefferson Glass in Steubenville, Ohio and then on to Bastow Glass at Couldersport, Pennsylvania. When Bastow Glass burned down (an ever present threat in the glass industry, dependent as it was on the use of so much raw heat), Frank Fenton went to Wheeling, West Virginia and entered the employ of Harry Northwood. But before too long, Frank realized his destiny. In his own words, "my particular work was in the matter of design and then I got the idea that if I could do this work for an employer, I could certainly do something for myself. So, with $284 capital, my brother John and I rented an old glass plant in Martin's Ferry and went into the glass business for ourselves." That was in 1905. The Fenton Art Glass Company was thus founded in Martin's Ferry, Ohio, by Frank L. Fenton and his elder brothers, John W. Fenton and Charles H. Fenton. Later, the other brothers, Robert C. and James E. Fenton, were to join in.

The first Fenton glass at the Martin's Ferry location involved the use of "blanks," plain glass items from other companies which the brothers then decorated themselves. Soon they moved to Williamstown, West Virginia, where they established their own glass plant. The company is still there—quite a success story.

The area around Williamstown has a rich and colorful history. Once settled by Indians, it saw the incursion of French explorers and traders followed by English settlement in the late 1700s. A fertile area, full of monstrous trees and wild animals, it was dominated by the Ohio River, which, in times of flood, became a raging torrent that quickly overflowed its banks and was to prove enticing for the location of the glass industry. Soon the Baltimore and Ohio Railroad embraced the area in its steel web. The discovery in 1860 of a vast oil field at nearby Burning Springs, followed by a gas well boom, made the area ripe for industrialization. Natural gas was particularly useful as a fuel source for the glass industry, for, besides being very cheap, the new fuel gave a uniform heat over the long periods which were necessary to melt a pot of materials. When the Fenton brothers arrived at Williamstown, though, it was pretty much underdeveloped despite its natural advantages—perfect for a new glass factory.

Carnival Glass was not the first ware to come out of the factory at Williamstown, but it is arguably the most famous. In 1907, Fenton were reported to be producing glass variously called "Iridie" or "Iridill" with a metallic lustre. This was **Carnival!** 1908 saw the first trade ad for their glass in the Butler Brothers catalog. Soon the trickle of Carnival became a flood. Just two years later, the same catalog was advertising almost fifty different iridized Fenton items—it was to continue this way for almost twenty years until the Depression. A contemporary account from 1916, recorded in the Fenton archives by one of their glass workers, Henry Snyder, gives an idea of what it must have been like to work in the glass industry: "When I first started they were making dope ware. They made crystal to put dope on the biggest part of it." "Dope," of course, refers to the iridescent coating. Snyder remarked that, when asked if he wanted to work at Fenton, he replied "yes, I would go, unless the place was hotter than hell." It seems that despite being assured that it was indeed very hot inside a glassworks, Snyder still took up a post! Lads were recruited from age sixteen upwards; wages were from $1.30 to $1.50 a day.

From 1907 through to the 1920s, the Fenton Art Glass Company produced an amazing range of Carnival Glass; in fact, it was their major product. The range included plates, bowls, vases, and novelties in all manner of colors and patterns. A few ads for Fenton's glass even appeared in the Butler Brothers catalogs in the early 1930s, overlapping with the Depression era. The company was very much a family concern and Frank's eldest son, Frank Muhleman, was eager to join the family firm. His memories of the early days spent there are fascinating, and give us a rare insight into those years.[2]

I remember that I was going to college back in the early thirties when we were in the depths of the great Depression. During summer vacation, I thought I'd like to get a job at the glass factory and get away from having to pull weeds while my mother stood over me telling me which were weeds and which were flowers. So, I asked my father if I could get a job at the factory. He said, no, there were too many people out of work who needed jobs. He didn't have anything for me. Then I went to my uncle Jim who was in charge of maintenance at the factory and asked him for a job. He said, "Sure, I'll give you a job, come to work next Monday." So I went to work the following Monday, and he put me down at the railroad siding pulling weeds. I think he probably had a great laugh about that.

Another memory of my early years was from the next summer. Uncle Jim again gave me a job up on the roof with a bucket of tar. I was to put a little bit of tar on every nail I saw sticking up through the roof. The roof leaked, but back in those days we didn't have enough money to put a whole new roof on. But I imagine I caused more leaks in the roof by walking on it than I fixed by patching the nails. So when people ask me if I started at the bottom and worked my way up, I tell them no, I started at the top and worked down.

The company held on through the years of the Depression; "Fenton Luck" held out as new lines were tried to aid diversification. The summer of 1940, however, was memorable for the company. One warm Saturday afternoon, heralded by a sound like a rifle crack, the entire, original, huge chimney stack collapsed in a pile of rubble onto the center of the hot metal works, destroying the roof as it fell. The opportunity to rebuild was seized, however, and a new plant was put into operation just a few months later.

Sadly, on May 18, 1948, Frank Leslie Fenton died from a heart condition, aged only sixty-eight. He had been highly revered within the glass trade, considered by many to have been that rare combination of employer and gentleman—with a heart filled with old fashioned goodwill and love for his fellow men. The company continued and indeed hung on through its lean years. In 1970, with Frank's sons at the helm, they successfully began to re-issue Carnival Glass. Fenton today is the only company of all the original manufacturers of Classic Carnival that is still in existence—quite an achievement! Today they continue to produce superb glassware, including Carnival. Frank Leslie Fenton's dream has been carried on down through the second, third, and fourth generations of the Fenton family. The family tradition continues. Their story is one of success brought about by hard work, dedication, flair, excellent marketing, and a good slice of "Fenton Luck!"

BOYS WANTED

16 Years or over

TO WORK FOR

FENTON ART GLASS COMPANY
Williamstown, W. Va.

Steady work at $1.30 to $1.50 per day.

Board furnished at $3.00 per week.

A good opportunity to learn a trade.

Ravenswood News Print

Recruiting workers for the Fenton Art Glass factory at Williamstown. Note that furnished board could have been arranged too, an attractive inducement. *Courtesy of the Fenton Art Glass Museum.*

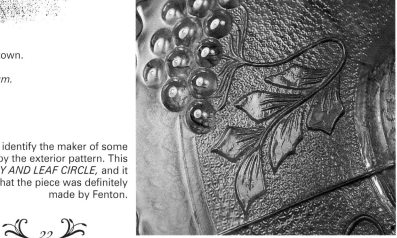

One way to identify the maker of some pieces is by the exterior pattern. This is *BERRY AND LEAF CIRCLE,* and it confirms that the piece was definitely made by Fenton.

A green Fenton *CAPTIVE ROSE* bowl with a very intricate, tightly crimped edge. $100-$150.

HOLLY is a favorite among Fenton patterns, seen to spectacular effect on a cobalt blue plate. $400-$500.

Signature Characteristics of Fenton Carnival Glass

Colors. Fenton made a very wide range of Carnival colors, but certain ones were their specialties. Red and celeste blue are distinctive Fenton colors that were introduced in the 1920s. Persian blue (a translucent, pale blue shade) is also characteristic of the company. Vaseline, too, is another unusual base color typical of Fenton. It is often difficult to spot, as a heavy marigold iridescence coats the light yellow-green base color. Many odd colors, possibly experimental or even accidental, were produced by Fenton. Amethyst opal and red opal are two off-beat examples. Fenton's opal edges are usually very light and delicate.

Shapes. Fenton made a broad range of shapes, but the detail and finishing are often a signature of the company. Fenton's plates, for example, are usually very flat indeed. Some plates have a twelve-sided effect. Edges on bowls, vases and water pitchers are sometimes frilled and tightly crimped, or fashioned into the candy ribbon (3 in 1) style. A scallop and flute edge is also typical of Fenton.

Patterns. Many Fenton designs have repeated motifs. *PEACOCK AND GRAPE* and *DRAGON AND LOTUS* are two good examples of that style. "Busy" type patterns often imitative of embroidery or lace work are also characteristic of Fenton. Exterior patterns by Fenton are *BEARDED BERRY*, which is fairly often seen on 8 and 9" plates and bowls, and *BERRY AND LEAF CIRCLE*, which is not too often seen and is always on smaller 7 and 8" plates and bowls. Fenton also enameled some of their Carnival Glass. Floral designs were painted on water sets and on very scarce table sets and berry sets.

Fenton's *BOUQUET* water pitcher in a typical shape and finish for that company. The pitcher is bulbous and blow-moulded. The top edge has the frilly crimping (also called a candy ribbon or 3 in 1 edge) that is characteristic of Fenton.

Northwood Glass Company

"WELL! Well! And whom have we here? Why yes, of course, Harry Northwood; known wherever glass is sold—and then some!"

—*American Pottery Gazette* (August 1908), on Harry Northwood (1860-1919)

Harry Northwood was born in the heart of England, at Wordsley, Staffordshire, in the area known locally as Stourbridge. The beauty of the surrounding countryside belies the industrialized nature of the area. Stourbridge was a region rich in the traditions of a glass industry that dated back to the 1600s, when Huguenot craftsmen, attracted by the availability of fuel and fireclay, first settled in the locality of Brierley Hill. They were to make the area famous for its crystal glass, their products known all over the world.

Harry, the eldest of ten children, was born in 1860, to a family that lived and breathed glass. His father, the celebrated John Northwood, was of course world famous for his artistry in cameo glass, having created

Harry Northwood (1860-1919). *Photograph courtesy of the Fenton Art Glass Museum.*

Surely one of Northwood's best. A superb, aqua opal stippled *THREE FRUITS* plate. $5000-$8000.

an amazing replica of the Portland Vase in 1876. At around the same time, the glass works of Thomas Webb and Sons—another Stourbridge glasshouse—were producing their iridescent lines known as "Bronze" and "Iris" glass. Harry, in his late teens at the time, was attending art school in the area and being trained in the glass trade by his father. Harry Northwood's skills were rooted in his childhood, nurtured by his father and enriched by an early intimacy with superb glass craftsmen. It's almost certain that he would have seen the amazing iridized ware that Webb's were producing at that time.

Harry Northwood emigrated to the United States in 1881 and his first job was as a glass etcher at the Hobbs Brockunier Glass Company in Wheeling, West Virginia. From there Harry moved to La Belle Glass Works in Bridgeport, Ohio, then to Phoenix Glass Company in Pennsylvania and back, yet again, to La Belle. In November, 1887, Harry (and other investors) bought the disused Union Flint Glass factory in Martin's Ferry, Ohio and re-named it—the first Northwood Glass Company had been founded.

However, by 1892, a decision had been taken to re-locate to a new factory at Ellwood City, Pennsylvania. Production was short lived, lasting only a few years. In 1895, Harry re-opened another disused glass factory, that of the Indiana Glass Company in Indiana, Pennsylvania, which was then re-named the Northwood Glass Company of Indiana. In 1899, the factory was sold to the gigantic National Glass Company and Harry Northwood returned to England as their London representative. Clearly, he missed the American scene. Within a couple of years he returned to the United States when the National fell on bad times. Quitting the firm, he bought the old Hobbs Brockunier factory in Wheeling, where he had first started twenty-one years earlier. The company was re-named Harry Northwood and Company and remained in production until its final closure in 1925.

It was at this Wheeling factory that Harry Northwood made Carnival Glass. In spring, 1908, the company issued their first iridescent glass called "Golden Iris." It is interesting to note that the name is very similar to that used by Webb's back in Harry's hometown, where thirty years or so earlier he had trained.

For the next decade, the Northwood works produced some of the finest Carnival Glass known in some of the most sought-after colors, shapes, and patterns. Sadly, Harry became seriously ill in 1918. He died quite suddenly in 1919 at only fifty-eight years of age. His death was recorded in the British *Pottery Gazette* (April 1,1919).

> Mr H. Northwood of Harry Northwood and Co. Wheeling, W.Va. USA, glass manufacturer, who passed away recently, was born at Wordsley, Staffordshire on June 30th. 1860, being the son of John Northwood, the famous artist in Cameo Glass. The deceased was educated at Stourbridge and was trained as a glassworker by his father. He went to America in 1881 and held successively the positions of designer and etcher for Hobbs Brockunier and Co., manager of the La Belle Glass Works, Bridgeport, Vice President and General Manager for Northwood Glass Co., Martin's Ferry, managing partner of Northwood Co., Indiana, Manager of the London office of the National Glass Co., and finally Vice president and General Manager of Northwood Glass Co. Mr. Northwood is survived by his widow, one son and a daughter.

Production dragged on at Wheeling for a while afterwards, but the guiding light was gone. The days of Northwood's Carnival Glass glory had ended.

Left: This April 1912 Butler Brothers ad for Northwood's Carnival Glass shows many collectors' favorites. *HEARTS AND FLOWERS* is seen in both the compote and ruffled bowl shapes. Also shown is a *PEACOCKS* (aka *PEACOCKS ON THE FENCE*) plate and two desirable vases: the *CORN VASE* and *DAISY AND DRAPE*. Other patterns include rosebowls or nutbowls in *BEADED CABLE*, *BUSHEL BASKET*, and *DRAPERY* plus a *FERN* compote.

Northwood made a number of novelty pieces. Two of their best known and very desirable ones are the *TOWN PUMP* (left: $700-$1200) and the *CORN VASE* (right: $500-$900). These examples are purple.

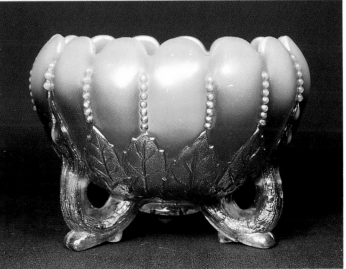

An aqua opal Northwood *LEAF AND BEADS* rosebowl. The iridescent effect is called "butterscotch" because of its rich, golden color. $350-$500. Note: a super, pastel example sold at auction for $850 in April 1998.

A Northwood *GRAPE AND GOTHIC ARCHES* tumbler in emerald green, a rare color for this pattern. $100-$200.

This is the exterior pattern on Northwood's *GRAPE LEAVES* bowl. Though known to collectors as *WILD ROSE*, it is more correctly identified as a variation of Northwood's *BLOSSOM AND PALM/SHELL*.

Left: A Northwood pattern not seen too often is *GRAPE LEAVES,* seen here on a ruffled purple bowl. This is one of the few patterns where the <u>N</u> trademark is incorporated in the center of the interior design. $150-$200.

Bottom left: Lettering is unusual on Carnival Glass, with the possible exception of the ever-popular *GOOD LUCK* pattern. This purple plate shows the wonderful Northwood design to great effect. $500-$700.

Bottom right: Northwood's *PEACOCKS* is considered by many to be one of the masterpieces of design in Carnival Glass. Here, in close-up, is a stippled blue plate. Such pieces are perennial favorites with collectors. $900-$1600.

Signature Characteristics of Northwood Carnival Glass

Colors. Northwood produced many colors, but there are some shades that are very characteristic of his factory. The "pastels," white, ice blue and ice green, were produced to very fine effect by Northwood. Aqua opal, however, was the one that Northwood excelled in over all others. Unusual in-between blue shades are also typical of Northwood: Renninger blue, sapphire, and teal are all good examples of the off-beat, blue-green colors produced by Northwood. Alaskan green is a strange mixture of marigold iridescence on green base glass. Not a popular color, it was probably one of Northwood's earliest. No true red was made by Northwood.

Shapes. A vast range of shapes was made by Northwood, both in the regular lines and in novelty shapes such as the *TOWN PUMP* and the *CORN VASE*. The finishing on bowls was sometimes very distinguishing, indeed, the pie crust edge shaping was only made by Northwood and can easily identify that factory (see Chapter Four on Classic Carnival Shapes for more detail on this characteristic edge treatment). Northwood's plates are also quite distinctive. They are often not at all flat, in fact the sides may slope up quite steeply. Only one large 10" plate shape (known as a chop plate) was made by Northwood. Known as the *PEACOCK AT URN*, examples are hard to find.

Patterns. Simplicity of design, quality, classic style, un-fussy, bold, elegant, and symmetrical are all words that come to mind when describing the characteristics of Northwood's patterns and overall style. Sometimes an Oriental feel is apparent on Northwood's designs; notice in particular the flowers and branches on *SINGING BIRDS*.

The Northwood Mark (<u>N</u>). Interestingly, the first appearance of Northwood's name on his glassware was back in the very late 1800s, before the advent of Carnival Glass. When Northwood introduced his "Pagoda" line (now known as "Chrysanthemum Sprig"), most of the items in the range bore the full script signature "Northwood." Later, we see this on rare examples of the *NAUTILUS* in Carnival Glass. *NAUTILUS* is known as a Dugan pattern, however, the likely explanation for Northwood's script signature on a Carnival item considered to have been produced by Dugan is straightforward. Tom Dugan took over the Indiana, Pennsylvania, glass plant from his cousin Harry Northwood. Some of the moulds remained; no doubt *NAUTILUS* was one of them. Eventually, Dugan removed the Northwood script signature. Northwood, too, did not continue with the lengthy flowing trademark. Instead, he opted for the simpler, characteristic <u>N</u> in a circle. Not all Northwood Carnival is marked with the <u>N</u>. The lack of a trademark doesn't hurt the desirability of the glass, but note that the presence of an <u>N</u> mark doesn't always guarantee authenticity either! An N mark (usually not underlined) is sometimes present on fake bowls in the Northwood patterns *GOOD LUCK, GRAPE AND CABLE,* and *PEACOCKS (ON THE FENCE).* These fakes are fairly easy to spot, and fortunately they aren't too plentiful. They are more brash in their iridescence than the genuine article, they are also heavier, and the overall design fills the face of the bowl too much. The N mark is big and coarse and the collar base (marie) may well be iridized over (a sure sign of a new item. Old Classic Carnival was virtually never iridized on the base).

Both L.G. Wright and Mosser Glass at one time produced Carnival items that had marks very similar to the Northwood <u>N</u>. In particular this can be seen on some *GRAPE DELIGHT* reproductions with the four, squared off feet (sometimes erroneously called *GRAPE AND CABLE*) and on some reproduction *GRAPE AND CABLE* butter dishes. These items were made by Mosser Glass in the 1970s in amber and ice blue, marked with what looks like an N within an almost complete circle. The American Carnival Glass Association (ACGA) went to court to stop the misuse of Northwood's famous trademark on pieces such as these. ACGA now owns the N mark in order to protect its use.

Millersburg Glass Company

"Speaking of real values in iridescent glass—have you seen Radium?"
—Advertisement for the Millersburg Glass Company, 1911

The *COURTHOUSE* is probably the most easily recognized Millersburg design. This amethyst ruffled bowl has a superb radium iridescence. There are also a few "unlettered" pieces known, where some of the wording was omitted. $600-$1000.

John W. Fenton, elder brother of Frank, had been the president of the newly founded Fenton Art Glass Co. in Williamstown. According to James Measell[3], John had had little to do with the everyday operation of the Fenton plant; "Frank L Fenton was the man in charge." John, it seems, was "impetuous and a bit on the extravagant side" and history seems to indicate that he was itching to set up by himself. Measell reports that a headline in the *Holmes County Farmer* (July 16,1908), the local newspaper for the Millersburg area, read "Looking for a Location." The associated story was about an officer of the Fenton Art Glass Company who was looking over the Millersburg area and talking to the local people. The officer, of course, was John Fenton. The local people were won over, the construction of a glass plant was discussed, land was sold in lots, investors were found, stock changed hands, and in September 1908, construction of a new glass factory began in the Amish town of Millersburg.

John W. Fenton (1869-1934), Millersburg Glass Company. *Photograph courtesy of the Fenton Art Glass Museum.*

The town of Millersburg is nestled deep in the heart of Ohio's early frontier, in scenic Holmes County, one of the world's largest Amish communities. Local place names are reminiscent of the early settlers' origins: Baltic, Berlin, Dutch Valley, Little Switzerland, and the Alpine Hills. Most of the Amish forefathers came from Germany and Switzerland, indeed, many were driven from their homes by religious persecution. Hundreds of them emigrated to the United States during a period of 125 years, starting soon after 1720. They have a simple lifestyle and believe strongly in a cohesive family structure.

Holmes County was an unusual choice for the location of a glass factory, away from the Ohio River, the major focus of the other glass works. It is a predominantly rural area, with plenty of local sand for glass making, though some was also imported from Michigan. In May, 1909, the *Holmes County Farmer* reported that the Millersburg factory was bringing in feldspar from Massachusetts, soda ash from Barberton, fluorspar from Kentucky, lime from Tiffin, and nitrate of soda from South America. In particular, though, there was an abundant local supply of natural gas and a good railway link. The works was situated near the C.A. & C. Railway with its own direct switch that entered between the two main buildings of the Millersburg plant—perfect for easy loading and unloading. Of course, there was also the delightful local scenery with its picturesque rolling hills, which may well have appealed to the romantic side of John Fenton. And there was plenty of local labor—friendly, helpful, and willing, typical of the local Amish people.

The Carnival Glass output from the Millersburg factory is highly sought after today. The short life span of the company meant that their beautiful glass did not have a long production time. John Fenton did not possess the business acumen of his brothers and the enterprise fell into debt. In 1911, he filed for bankruptcy. Samuel Fair bought the factory and opened the Radium Glass Company, with John Fenton as vice president and general manager. But this enterprise was also doomed to failure, closing its doors in 1912. In the short lifetime of the works, some of the most astoundingly beautiful Carnival Glass was produced.

Two geometric patterns on amethyst Millersburg tumblers: on the left is *MARILYN* ($150-$200) and on the right is *FEATHER AND HEART* ($100-$150).

A beautiful green Millersburg *MANY STARS* bowl with a 3 in 1 edge. $800-$1000.

In mid-spring 1911, this Millersburg ad appeared in the Butler Brothers catalog. It is incredible to think that the wholesale price was $2.10 a dozen. The *ROSE COLUMNS* vase alone has reached values of $5500 (Burns auction of the Spangler collection, February, 1996). An exceptionally rare blue *ROSE COLUMNS* at the same auction brought $12,000. Other patterns illustrated in the ad are *PEACOCK AT URN, CHERRIES* with *HOBNAIL* exterior, *VINTAGE,* and the scarce *DOLPHIN* compote with *ROSALIND* interior.

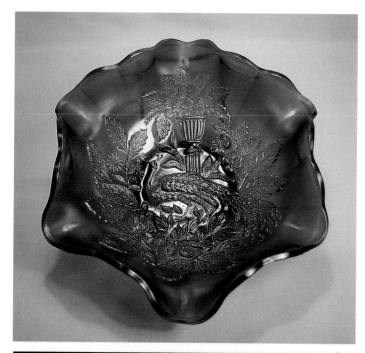

A green Millersburg *PEACOCK AT URN* ruffled bowl. Fenton and Northwood also made similar versions of the pattern. This one is $600-$650.

Signature Characteristics of Millersburg Carnival Glass

Colors. Millersburg produced three basic colors: marigold, amethyst, and green. Blue and vaseline were used only rarely, and are sought after "top dollar" colors. Radium iridescence is a particular signature of Millersburg Carnival. It's a very bright, mirror-like iridescence, high quality and multi-hued. They also produced Carnival with a satin-like, matt iridescence. Again, richly colored, but lacking the shiny effect that radium has.

Shapes. Millersburg were not in business for as long as most of the other Carnival manufacturers, hence they didn't produce such a wide range of shapes. Bowls—with a variety of interesting shapes and edge treatments—were the main shape that Millersburg made. Plates are very rare. Possibly the most distinctive shapes made by them were amazing and impressive vases. The *PEOPLES' VASE* and the *ROSE COLUMNS* vase are excellent examples.

Patterns. Millersburg frequently took a theme and made several different variations of it. There is a range of fruit patterns that have a different central motif. Also there's a variety of patterns that feature peacocks. The geometric exterior patterns produced by Millersburg are astounding in their complexity and beauty. Specifically matched with certain interior patterns, these are excellent signature characteristics of Millersburg's output. The list below matches up the Millersburg interior patterns with their geometric exterior patterns (interior listed first, exterior last):

RAYS AND RIBBONS and *CACTUS*
FLEUR DE LIS and *COUNTRY KITCHEN*
NESTING SWAN and *DIAMOND AND FAN*
PRIMROSE and *FINE CUT HEARTS*
WHIRLING LEAVES and *FINE CUT OVALS*
VINTAGE and *HOBNAIL*
Some *HANGING CHERRIES* have *HOBNAIL*
Some *HOLLY WHIRLS* have *NEAR CUT WREATH*
GRAPE LEAVES and *MAYFLOWER*
POPPY Compote and *POTPOURRI*
BERNHEIMER bowl and the *MANY STARS* have *TREFOIL FINE CUT*

A pattern not seen too often is Millersburg's *SEAWEED*, seen here on a ruffled, marigold bowl with a pretty satin iridescence. $250-$350.

A "must-have" for serious tumbler collectors: an amethyst Millersburg *PERFECTION* tumbler. $475-$525.

One of Millersburg's superb, geometric exterior patterns; this is *FINE CUT HEART*, an intricate, intaglio design exhibiting great craftsmanship. It was utilized as the secondary pattern on the outside of the *PRIMROSE* bowl.

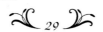

Dugan Glass Company (1904-1913) and Diamond Glass-Ware Company (1913-1931)

"A loss estimated at $100,000 was sustained when flames swept the plant of the Diamond Glass-Ware Company."

—*Indiana Evening Gazette* (June 29, 1931), on the disastrous fire which marked the end of Dugan/Diamond.

Though Dugan/Diamond made a lot of purple glass, the more subtle amethyst shades are not so common. This is a *PERSIAN GARDEN* two piece fruit bowl (the bowl and the base are separate) with great color and iridescence. $800-$1500. One sold in 2007 for $2600.

The Dugan and Northwood families were related by marriage. Harry Northwood and Thomas Ernest Albert Dugan were cousins, both coming from the West Midlands in England. Thomas emigrated to the United States in 1881, about the same time as his cousin Harry. They worked together for a while at Hobbs Brockunier Glass Company in Wheeling, West Virginia, and again at the Northwood Glass Company in Martin's Ferry, Ohio. The two stayed together through the Northwood re-locations, first at Ellwood City and then, in 1895, at Indiana, Pennsylvania, where Thomas Dugan became plant manager and his brother Alfred Dugan, plant foreman.

Thomas E.A. Dugan (1865-1944). *Photograph courtesy of the Fenton Art Glass Museum.*

Harry Northwood and Thomas Dugan went their separate ways in 1899. The Northwood factory at Indiana was sold to the gigantic National Glass Company. Harry returned to England as representative of the merger while Thomas remained behind as plant manager. Five years later, in January 1904, Dugan, along with sales manager W.G. Minnemayer, bought the Indiana, Pennsylvania factory and renamed it the Dugan Glass Company. Thomas Dugan's brother, Alfred, worked with him, the pair remaining there together until 1913, when the management of the factory changed in what appears to have been a fog of confusion. The works became known as the Diamond Glass-Ware Company. The Dugans moved on. Thomas first became involved with the Cambridge Glass Company in Ohio, then Duncan and Miller, and eventually Hocking in Lancaster, where he stayed until his retirement in the 1930s. Though Alfred had left the Indiana factory in 1913 too, he soon returned to the new Diamond Glass-Ware Company, becoming general manager (and continuing thus until the time of his death in 1928).

The Diamond Glass-Ware company continued throughout the decade and into the 1920s, producing Carnival Glass amongst other lines, until a disastrous fire—the ever present scourge of the glass industry—closed it in June 1931, just a few days after the opening of the Empire State Building in New York! The skyscraper became a symbol of American confidence despite the hard times of the Depression years, but the Diamond Glass-Ware Company was never to open its doors again. The factory had had a long history of Carnival Glass production. Thomas Dugan had been experimenting there with iridescent ware from the early 1900s: Butler Brothers catalogs in April 1931 carried ads for "Golden Glow Iridescent" glass known to be from the Diamond Glass-Ware Company.

All the movements between companies resulted in mix-ups over whose glass was whose! In the past, Carnival Glass writers and researchers attributed much of Dugan's Carnival output to Northwood. This was made more complicated by the fact that Dugan used moulds that Northwood had used previously. In fact, Harry's famous Northwood script signature can be found on one or two scarce examples of Dugan's

Carnival Glass! A company letterhead from December 1904 illustrates the situation perfectly. It read: "DUGAN GLASS COMPANY, successors to NATIONAL GLASS COMPANY, operating the NORTHWOOD GLASS WORKS, Indiana, Pa." Credit for sorting out the previous (understandable) mix-ups goes to the late William Heacock and Del Helman. Helman and his father dug and sorted shards of glass from the old Northwood factory, which became the Dugan/Diamond factory at the Indiana, Pennsylvania site. Heacock studied the shards and concluded "that Dugan and Diamond together were probably responsible for a full one-fourth of the Carnival Glass production in America."[4]

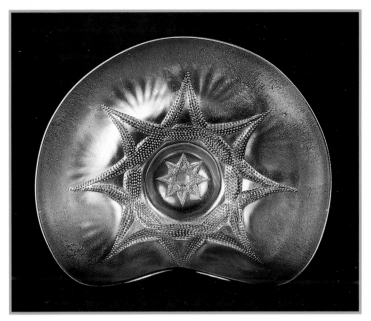

Dugan/Diamond made some spectacular Carnival Glass. This is a purple *SKI STAR* handgrip plate, with one edge turned up. $300-$350.

An exquisite, purple Dugan/Diamond *WISHBONE AND SPADES* 7" plate. Small plates are always popular with collectors as they show the patterns well, yet don't take up too much space! $250-$500.

A classic design, Dugan/Diamond's *FORMAL* vase in purple, with the Jack-in-the-pulpit shaped top (pulled down at the front and up at the back). $700-$750.

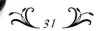

Dugan/Diamond's *GOD AND HOME* pattern is unusual in that it is lettered. This blue tumbler has a definite tilt, presumably because the glass had not quite set solid before the tumbler was set down on its base. $120-$200.

Signature Characteristics of Dugan/Diamond Carnival Glass

Colors. Marigold, amethyst, white, and peach opalescent are the usual colors found on Dugan/Diamond Carnival. Dugan/Diamond amethyst ranges from a deep, dense black amethyst through mid-purple, to a deceptive, ruby red color that is often termed **fiery amethyst**. This is a shade of amethyst that can appear to be deep red. The color is in fact a red-purple (and is not classified as a red shade). Blue was used for certain patterns quite frequently (such as *FANCIFUL, RAMBLER ROSE,* and *STORK AND RUSHES*), yet for other patterns, for example those found on most Dugan vases, it was very rarely used. Green is a rare color for Dugan/Diamond. Ice green and celeste blue are also Dugan/Diamond colors that are rarely found. An associated signature characteristic of Dugan/Diamond was their preference for not iridizing the exteriors of bowls and plates. This is particularly noticeable on the dark amethyst shades.

Shapes. Dugan/Diamond produced the usual range of shapes in Carnival. However, one of their most significant characteristics was in the shaping of the edges of their bowls. Exceptionally deep candy ribbon (3 in 1) edging or very tight crimping are Dugan/Diamond signature characteristics. Another characteristic feature was the use of a domed foot on bowls, rather than the ball or spatula feet used by most other manufacturers. On Dugan/Diamond plates, the edges frequently turn up a little, rather than being totally flat. Some plates such as *DOUBLE STEM ROSE* also have a domed foot.

Patterns. Dugan/Diamond produced an eclectic mixture of patterns. Indeed, it is quite difficult to pin down any specific characteristics. They were, however, the only company to enamel designs on peach opalescent bowls. Several different floral patterns were used in this distinctive way.

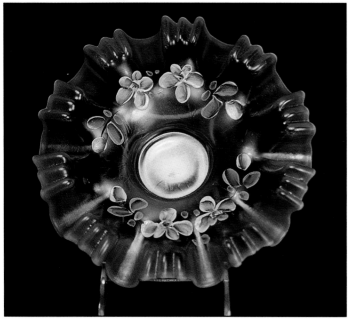

Dugan/Diamond were the only manufacturer to produce pretty peach opal bowls decorated with enameled flowers. According to contemporary advertising, the flowers on this bowl were meant to be roses. The deep 3 in 1 edge is typically Dugan/Diamond. $150-$200.

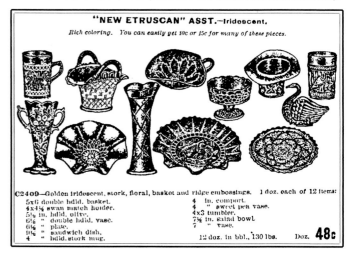

Unusual Dugan/Diamond shapes such as the *SWAN* salt and the two-handled *MARY ANN* vase were advertised in the spring of 1915. Other patterns shown include *STORK AND RUSHES, LEAF RAYS, VINING TWIGS* vase, *BEADED BASKET, MAPLE LEAF, PERSIAN GARDEN,* and the familiar *WINDFLOWER.*

A purple *NAUTILUS,* a popular novelty piece. Some (but not all) of these pieces have a Northwood script signature, though it is believed that they were, in fact, made by Dugan/Diamond using moulds left by Northwood at the Indiana, Pennsylvania plant. $175-$225.

Imperial Glass Company

Another great piece of Carnival Glass by Imperial: a purple *STAR OF DAVID* ruffled bowl. $200-$350.

The Imperial Glass Company was founded in 1901 by Captain Edward Muhleman, a one time riverboat captain turned investor. He had had experience in the glass industry, having previously been the general manager and then president of the Crystal Glass Company of Pittsburgh and Bridgeport, Ohio. With a capitalization of $500,000, Muhleman and a syndicate of investors began the Imperial Glass Company at Bellaire, Ohio, for the manufacture of pressed glass tableware, lighting fixtures, and gas and electric shades. Their aim, it seems, was to make it the most modern glass factory in America. In the 1880s, Bellaire had been known as "Glass City." Situated along the Ohio river with ample fuel and transportation available, the town, at one point, had had twelve different glass houses in operation.

On January 23, 1904, the first fires were lit in the furnaces at Imperial. In *Imperial Glass* by Archer,[5] it is noted that "Imperial's first sale was to the F.W. Woolworth Company." Soon they were also selling to retailers like McCrory and Kresge. The company was to become one of the main Carnival Glass producers and in 1910 their iridescent lines first appeared in trade catalogs. Carnival Glass became so popular that soon Imperial were selling it by the barrel and the boxcar load.

Edward Muhleman. *Photograph courtesy of the Fenton Art Glass Museum.*

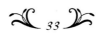
1881

A major export business also developed. Imperial shipped regularly to Europe, Central and South America, Australia, the West Indies, China, and India. Today's travelers might find that possibly the most available item of Carnival Glass, which has been reported all over the world, is the *IMPERIAL GRAPE* berry dish. Imperial also marketed their Carnival heavily in Britain as well as the home market. In March 1911, the first ad for Carnival appeared in the British *Pottery Gazette*. It was for "The Imperial Iridescent Glassware" and the ad featured a water pitcher in the pattern today's collectors call *IMPERIAL GRAPE*. An accompanying report on the wholesaler Markt & Co. (London) Ltd., stated that they had:

> ...introduced a range of iridescent glass, for which they claim several novel features. It is made in four standard colours, "Helios," "Azur," "Dragon Blue" and "Amber Flame." The "Helios" is a combination of green and silver, in which a striking iridescent effect is produced. The "Azur" gives a replica of the colours in a peacock's feather. In the "Dragon Blue" there is the beautiful iridescence of blue and green, while in the "Amber-flame" we have a rich fiery orange. The appearance of this iridescent glass is different from that presented by ordinary pearl like effects. The ware is made in bowls, plaques, jugs, vases, stands etc., a useful fruit stand on a pedestal is composed of two sections—one section forming by itself a bowl, and the pedestal serving the purpose of a flower stand. The ware is made in several entirely new designs, and we are informed the prices are such as to make them good selling lines.

The glass was all from the Imperial factory —the trade report on Markt & Co. was a fascinating, contemporary comment on the popular, new American import. Imperial continued to produce its Carnival right up to 1930, but the years of the Depression bit hard and the company faced bankruptcy in 1931. Fortunately, they hung on and just over thirty years later, in 1962, they were the first company to begin producing Carnival Glass again, in response to a growing interest in the old, Classic Carnival. However, the company was to face yet more financial problems, changing hands several times until, sadly, in the mid-1980s, production finally ceased. On April 11, 1985, Imperial's doors were closed and their moulds were sold. The old Imperial factory buildings were finally leveled in the summer of 1997 for a shopping mall.

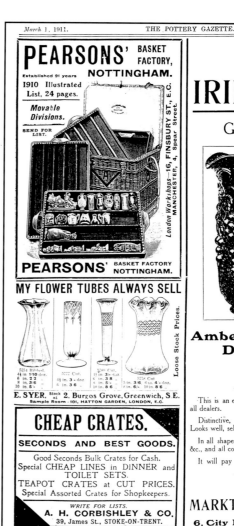

The British *Pottery Gazette* ran this ad for the *IMPERIAL GRAPE* water pitcher in March, 1911. It was the first Carnival Glass to be advertised in the United Kingdom and was described as "an entirely new line."

An amber Imperial *HEAVY GRAPE* 8" plate. $150-$200.

One of Imperial's top punch sets—the intricate geometric *BROKEN ARCHES* in scintillating purple. $1000-$2000.

Close-up of Imperial's
BROKEN ARCHES pattern
showing the superb detail
of the geometric design.

A purple Imperial *OPEN ROSE/LUSTRE ROSE* spooner with the stunning iridescence that was produced by multiple doping. $75-$150.

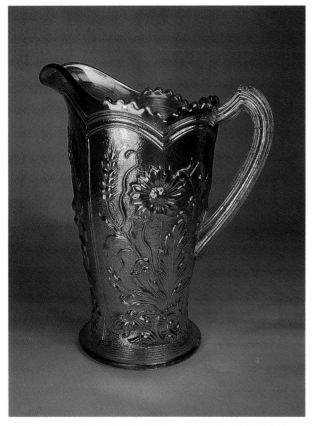

Marigold Imperial *FIELD FLOWER* water pitcher. $100-$150.

Signature Characteristics of Imperial Carnival Glass

Colors. Imperial produced a wide range of colors that include many offbeat and unusual shades. Primarily, they made marigold, helios (a distinctive silvery green), and a wonderful electric purple. Other characteristic colors include a rich brown amber, clambroth (a light yellow-ginger shade), smoke, and emerald. Even small amounts of red and vibrant vaseline were made by Imperial. They are renowned for producing high quality iridescence. **Shapes.** Many of Imperial's shapes were very functional—designed to be used. They rarely fashioned edges into anything more adventurous than simple ruffles. Imperial plates were very flat. Few bowls were footed, with exceptions such as *DOUBLE DUTCH* which has squared off feet. **Patterns.** Geometric designs were an Imperial favorite, using the "near-cut" moulds that they had previously used for crystal glass. A series featuring roses (Imperial's *LUSTRE ROSE* and *OPEN ROSE* patterns) and grapes (Imperial's *HEAVY GRAPE* and *IMPERIAL GRAPE*) were great favorites.

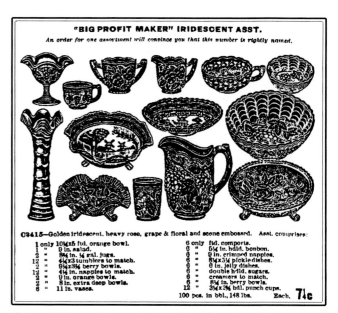

Spring 1915 saw this wonderful offering from Imperial. A range of shapes in *LUSTRE ROSE, PANSY, IMPERIAL GRAPE, DOUBLE DUTCH,* and *WINDMILL* plus a splendid *RIPPLE* vase.

Relationships between the Glass Families

There are many complex inter-relationships between the various Carnival Glass manufacturers. This was quite usual amongst the glass fraternity. Marriages frequently took place between members of rival glass firms, and sons would bear—for a middle name—the surname of the mother, thus joining two famous names. Inter-relationships such as this were no different amongst the Carnival Glass families. In one way or another, the five main producers were interlinked.

The family links between the Fenton and Millersburg companies have already been mentioned. John Fenton—who founded the Millersburg Glass Company—was brother to the Fentons who continued the Fenton Art Glass Company in Williamstown. The relationship between the Imperial Glass Company and the Fenton Company (and by extension, also the Millersburg Company) was due to Frank L. Fenton's marriage. In June 1907, Frank Fenton married Lilian Mae Muhleman, the niece of Edward Muhleman who had founded the Imperial Glass Company. Their eldest son was then christened Frank Muhleman Fenton. The Fenton Art Glass Company remains firmly in the safe hands of the Fenton family today.

The Northwood and Dugan families were also related. Thomas Dugan's father and Harry Northwood's mother, Elizabeth Dugan, were brother and sister. A second brother, Tommie, was uncle to both Harry and his cousin Tom. "Uncle Tommie" was also in the glass business, having emigrated to the United States when Tom and Harry were both lads. Subsequently, both Northwood and Dugan Glass Companies benefited from Uncle Tommie's financial help and expertise.

Jacob Rosenthal, a key employee at the Indiana Tumbler and Goblet Company, went to work for Fenton when the Indiana works burnt down in 1906. Rosenthal—a talented man and research chemist—was also a distant relative of the Fentons. Minnie Watson Kamm in her *Seventh Pattern Glass Book*[6] noted that Rosenthal "used his golden and grape-like lustres on countless thousands of objects" while at Fenton.

Links also existed through working relationships. Frank and John Fenton both worked for Harry Northwood; in fact, Frank's first job in the glass trade was at the Indiana Glass Company when Harry Northwood was in charge. Thomas Dugan also worked for Harry Northwood and was with him at three different factories. Alfred Dugan worked with his brother Thomas, at Indiana, Pennsylvania. At the time of his death in 1928, Alfred was general manager of the Diamond Glass-Ware Company where his son, Harold Nathan Dugan, had also learned the glass trade (before moving on to the Fenton Art Glass Company). There are also very interesting connections between Millersburg, Thomas Dugan, and the Cambridge Glass Company. The late William Heacock, in *Collecting Glass Volume 3*[7], put forward interesting evidence collected by Bill Edwards. The theory was that a glassmaker and chemist called Oliver Phillips (thought to have been the developer of radium iridescence at the Millersburg Glass works) subsequently brought his skills as well to the Cambridge Glass Company. Heacock quoted a trade journal report from October 1913 that said "Thomas Dugan, New York representative of the Cambridge Glass Co., is encouraged over the condition of business." Heacock suggested that the skills of Oliver Phillips, coupled with the arrival of Tom Dugan, were the stimulus behind the subsequent production of Carnival Glass at Cambridge.

There are even more, intricate inter-relationships noted by Heacock in the aforementioned *Collecting Glass 3*[7] journal. The Jefferson Glass Company was formed in 1900 and was located at Steubenville, Ohio, later moving to Fallansbee, West Virginia. The consortium that formed it consisted of Harry Bastow, George Mortimer, and D. J. Sinclair—all names that have loose connections with Carnival Glass. Harry Bastow and George

Mortimer had both previously worked for Northwood. Frank D. Sinclair, who was probably the son or brother of D. J. Sinclair, purchased the defunct and empty Millersburg factory on behalf of the Jefferson Glass Company. Old Jefferson moulds (*MEANDER, RUFFLES AND RINGS, FINECUT AND ROSES, VINTAGE* exterior) were purchased by Northwood and used in his Carnival Glass production. Further links, many of them quite complex, between Jefferson, Fenton, Northwood, and Mortimer can be studied in Heacock's *Collecting Glass 3*.[7]

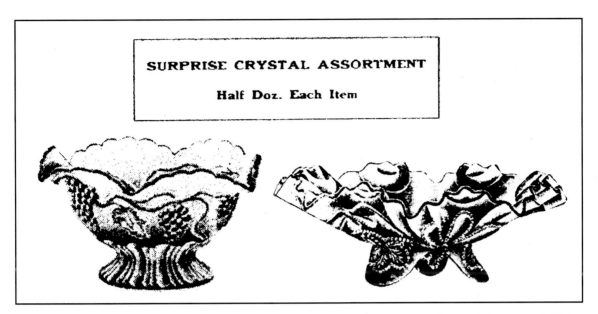

Two Jefferson patterns that were subsequently acquired by Northwood, shown in a Jefferson ad from around 1907. On the left is the *VINTAGE* exterior found on some dome footed *THREE FRUITS* and *STAR OF DAVID AND BOWS* bowls from Northwood. Occasionally, *THREE FRUITS* bowls may be found with a basketweave design overcut onto the grape pattern. On the right is *MEANDER*, found as an exterior on Northwood's *SUNFLOWER* and *THREE FRUIT MEDALLION* patterns. Note how this distinctive design extends onto the spatula feet.

Hipkins Novelty Mould Shop

The Hipkins Novelty Mould Shop in Martin's Ferry was begun by Stephen Hipkins, an Englishman, in about 1882. The company made many moulds for the glass factories; indeed, by the start of the 1900s, it was "the largest factory in the Ohio Valley, outside of Pittsburgh, devoted exclusively to making moulds for the numerous glass manufacturers of the Valley. Its reputation for fine designs and mould work was widespread."[6] Kamm further reports that sixteen highly trained artisans actually cut the moulds, while Stephen Hipkins and his eldest son, George, concentrated on the design work. Two other sons were in charge of bench work on the moulds.

Carnival Glass moulds were made there— Northwood, Fenton, and Millersburg are all known to have used Hipkins to design and make moulds for them. A glance at items such as Northwood's, Fenton's and Millersburg's *PEACOCK AT URN* patterns reveals many similarities that could well be due to them all being made by Hipkins. Other design links can be seen in patterns such as *GOOD LUCK* and *PEACOCKS* from Northwood and Millersburg favorites like *NESTING SWAN* and *FLEUR DE LYS*. Kamm, in her *Seventh Pattern Glass Book*[6] points out that "George Hipkins learned to etch and engrave glass from Harry Northwood, who had learned his trade in Brierley, England. George Hipkins designed glass for Northwood in 1898, but the exact patterns are not known. Indeed, he was also a shareholder in H. Northwood Co., and in fact became a pallbearer at Harry Northwood's funeral in 1919."

Moulds were expensive. Fenton records show that the Fenton Art Glass Company paid several thousand dollars to Hipkins (drawn on the German Savings Bank, Martin's Ferry, Ohio) over the period from August 1908 to March 1909. The link between Hipkins and John Fenton's Millersburg Company was sadly fraught with problems due to the huge sums of money that the moulds cost. Legal proceedings by Hipkins against the Millersburg Glass Company for non payment helped to bring about the bankruptcy and subsequent demise of the Millersburg factory in 1911.

Other Manufacturers of Classic Carnival

Carnival Glass was produced in those early years by several other manufacturers. The Westmoreland Glass Company, the United States Glass Company, and the Cambridge Glass Company all contributed significantly to the production of Classic Carnival. Several other companies, such as Fostoria, made small amounts too.

Westmoreland Glass Company

Westmoreland Glass began operating in 1889 as the Westmoreland Specialty Company of Grapeville, Pennsylvania. They built quite a reputation as the manufacturer of novelties and packaging glass, such as candy filled glass toys and glass containers full of mustard. These were sold via news stands and dime stores across the country.

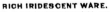

This 1910 Butlers Brothers ad for Westmoreland's "Rich Iridescent Ware" featured *FOOTED SHELL, SCALES, LOUISA, SMOOTH RAYS,* and the compote known as Westmoreland's #270.

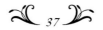

The 1908 Butler Brothers catalogs have an ad for Westmoreland's "Antique Iridescent Novelty Assortment," indicating that they were beginning to produce a type of Carnival at around the same time as Fenton. A landmark article by William Heacock in the *Antique Trader* (April 1982) stated that no less than thirty-five patterns and novelties were made by Westmoreland in iridized glass. Carnival colors typical of Westmoreland are teal, marigold on milk glass, blue opal, peach opal, and blue milk glass. They also produced a silvery amethyst shade. Westmoreland patterns tended to be fairly simple though many of their shapes, such as the *FOOTED SHELL*, continued the novelty theme.

Westmoreland continued to produce their Carnival Glass through the late 1920s, though the main period of production was 1908 to 1912, when Edward G. Minnemeyer was sales manager. In 1912, Minnemeyer moved to the Dugan works to join his brother, W.G. Minnemeyer, who was one of the founders of the Dugan Company. Many years later, in the 1970s, the company successfully reintroduced Carnival Glass. Sadly, however, on February 28, 1996, the Westmoreland factory burned down—another historic glass building had gone.

United States Glass Company

Fifteen individual glass companies associated themselves in the formation of the United States Glass Company in 1891—thereby creating the largest glass making organization of its time, in terms of its capacity. Its headquarters was in Pittsburgh, Pennsylvania. This was the era of corporate consolidations—many small companies had collapsed—and sound economics dictated the decision to merge. The different factories maintained their identities and were known by an identifying letter: for example, Bryce Brothers of Pittsburgh were Factory B while Hobbs Glass Company of Wheeling became Factory H. The biggest difficulty must have been the disparate locations of the factories which were spread over Ohio, West Virginia, and Pennsylvania while the head office was in Pittsburgh.

"RADIANT LUSTER" IRIDESCENT DINING SETS.
Big showy pieces that are always and unfailingly big profit winners.

C1673: Large pieces, attractive shapes, grapevine embossing and diamond and flor pattern, mother of pearl and golden finishes.
2 only 7 pc. water sets—½ gal jug, ground bottom tumblers,
2 " 7 " berry sets—8½ and 9¼ in. bowls, 4¾ in. nappies,
3 " 4 " table sets. 6 sets bbl., —— lbs. Set, **43c**

The United States Glass Company offered "big showy pieces" in "Radiant Luster" iridescence in this Butler Brothers ad from April 1912. The shapes illustrated are the water set, table set, and berry set. Two patterns only are featured: *PALM BEACH*, described as "grapevine embossing;" and *COSMOS AND CANE,* described as "diamond and floral."

Nevertheless, developments took place. In 1893, about 500 acres of land on the east bank of the Monongahela River was purchased and the town of Glassport, Pennsylvania was soon built, chosen because of its superb location near 438 gas wells! There were also excellent communication links. Soon foreign markets were explored. The new company was doing well.

Carnival Glass production by United States Glass Company (often known as U.S. Glass) is thought to date from around 1911. The *Pottery, Glass and Brass Salesman* reported in that year that "[their product, a] new iridescent line, is a marvel of color effects and graceful shapes." U.S. Glass Carnival is fairly limited in quantity. However, some of the rarest and most fascinating pieces in existence are believed to have been made by U.S. Glass. The company also exported heavily, in particular to the United Kingdom and Argentina—British Trade journals at the time featured ads though none actually specified iridized glassware. It's interesting to note that several U.S. Glass patterns turn up in Argentina more than anywhere else. The *RISING SUN* water set is a good example. A theory, as yet not proved, is that some moulds were sold by U.S. Glass to manufacturers in Argentina who then produced the items in Carnival.

Like Westmoreland, U.S. Glass Carnival is quite distinctive in its colors. Honey amber is considered to be primarily a U.S. Glass shade. White and marigold are more usually found, while very rarely seen are pastel blue, cobalt blue, and olive green. Familiar U.S. Glass patterns include *COSMOS AND CANE* and *PALM BEACH*.

From 1924 to 1938, the United States Glass Company suffered heavy financial losses. Twenty years later, they were sold to a New York group that had never engaged in glass manufacture, their prime interest being in resale—at a profit! It never happened. They attempted to sell in 1960, but three years later were forced to declare bankruptcy. The final ignominious demise came in 1963 when the Glassport factory was destroyed by a tornado. Frank M. Fenton tells[8] of wading around in the flooded basement of the building after the roof had been ripped off. He was able to purchase some of their moulds, in particular the "Alley Cat."

Cambridge Glass Company

The Cambridge Glass Company was born out of a conglomerate of about nineteen glass factories called the National Glass Company. In 1901, a new factory was built at Cambridge, Ohio and it took on the Cambridge name. Though it produced vast amounts of crystal tableware throughout its fifty or so year history, only very small quantities of Carnival Glass were made. They are distinctive in that virtually all the Cambridge Carnival patterns were imitation cut glass, intaglio designs executed to high standards. Their colors were green, amethyst, and marigold. Quite a lot of their Carnival items were trademarked NEARCUT; this famous mark was adopted sometime around 1906 to 1910 and used until 1920. Operations finally ceased at the Cambridge Glass Company in the 1950s when they were taken over by the Imperial Glass Company.

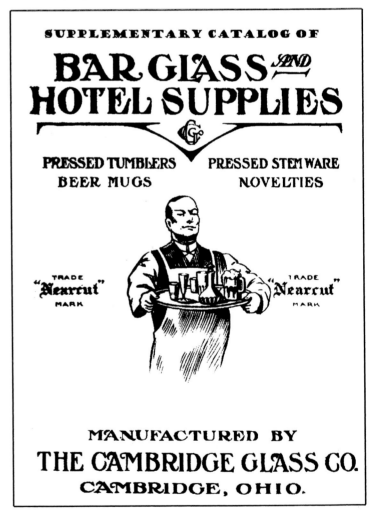

SUPPLEMENTARY CATALOG OF

BAR GLASS *AND* HOTEL SUPPLIES

PRESSED TUMBLERS   PRESSED STEMWARE
BEER MUGS   NOVELTIES

TRADE "Nearcut" MARK   TRADE "Nearcut" MARK

MANUFACTURED BY
THE CAMBRIDGE GLASS CO.
CAMBRIDGE, OHIO.

The Cambridge Glass Company issued a "Bar Glass and Hotel Supplies" catalog in 1910 that featured a number of iridized items, such as decanters, wines, and even a punch set in typical Cambridge "near-cut" patterns like *INVERTED FEATHER*.

Other Companies

Several other companies produced small amounts of iridized glass through the 1920s and into the 1930s.

The Fostoria Company began in Fostoria, Ohio in 1887, but moved to Moundsville, West Virginia when fuel supplies at the Fostoria location ran out. They are known for their Taffeta Lustre ware and the iridized Brocaded patterns. The Brocaded designs are especially distinctive with their acid cut-back patterns and unusual colors. Pink, ice green, and ice blue, often with gold edges, were typical of Fostoria's iridized colors. Edgar Buttome was the principal designer of the etched and cut-back glass.

The first iridescent glassware from Fostoria was introduced in 1915 and renamed "Mother of Pearl" in 1916. Fostoria issued a catalog (dated between 1920 and 1924) that was entitled "Beautiful Iridescent Glassware." All items were in this "Mother of Pearl" effect, described as being "rainbow tinted glassware" that was "constantly growing in popularity—perhaps due to the splendid results obtained in color effects, also because of its popular price." The shapes were simple: stemware, tumblers, vases, and so on, in plain panel or rib designs. Fostoria produced iridized ware until 1931.

The Jeanette McKee Glass Company produced iridized ware from around 1920. *HERRINGBONE AND IRIS* is one of their better known patterns in Carnival, though this is a "late" item, not considered to be Classic Carnival.

Jenkins is also recorded as having produced iridized "doped ware" toward the end of the 1920s and into the 1930s.

The Belmont Company from Bellaire, Ohio, produced a few iridized items around the same time. The *STORK ABC* plate is probably the one with which most collectors are familiar.

The Federal Glass Company included iridized and lustre treatments to its range in the 1920s.

The Central Glass Works at Wheeling, West Virginia is thought to have made some iridized glass.

[1] Albert Christian Revi, *Nineteenth Century Glass: Its Genesis and Development*, rev. ed. (Exton, Pennsylvania: Schiffer Publishing, 1967).

[2] Personal information courtesy of Frank Muhleman Fenton, past president of the Fenton Art Glass Company and currently the company historian.

[3] Marie McGee, *Millersburg Glass: As I Know It* (Marietta, Ohio: Antique Publications, 1995).

[4] William Heacock, "Carnival Glass by Dugan and Diamond," *The Antique Trader Weekly*, February 25, 1981, pp. 78-81.

[5] Margaret and Douglas Archer, *Imperial Glass* (Paducah, Kentucky: Collector Books, 1978).

[6] Minnie Watson Kamm, *A Seventh Pattern Glass Book* (Grosse Pointe, Michigan: by author, 1953).

[7] William Heacock, *Collecting Glass Volume 3* (Marietta, Ohio: Antique Publications, 1986).

[8] Newsletter of the Collectible Carnival Glass Association. September 1995.

United States Glass Co. was a large glass conglomerate, but their Carnival Glass output was not huge. The *COSMOS AND CANE* tumbler shown here is an unusual honey amber color. This particular example has advertising on its base: the moulded wording reads "J.R. MILLNER. CO. LYNCHBURG VA." The words are cut in reverse on the base, thus it can be read through the glass from the inside only. $150-$250 (less without advertising).

A white United States Glass Co. *PALM BEACH* butter. Note the distinctive handle shaped like a bunch of grapes. $200-$350.

Below: Cambridge Glass Company was another large glass conglomerate whose Carnival Glass output was very limited. Here are two purple Cambridge tumblers with clearly related patterns: *INVERTED STRAWBERRY* (left: $150-$200) and *INVERTED THISTLE* (right: $200-$300).

Westmoreland Glass produced a smaller amount of Carnival than most of the other big manufacturers. This is their *DAISY WREATH* ruffled bowl in an unusual blue opal color that is typical of Westmoreland. $175-$250.

"Practical items, floral, Persian, fruit cluster and peacock embossing, rich golden iridescent finish."

—Butler Brothers catalog ad for Fenton glass, April 1913

A spectacular, purple banana boat in Northwood's popular *GRAPE AND CABLE* pattern. It is one of the larger pieces of Carnival Glass and measures 13" in length. $250-$300.

"Practical items" said the "Aurora Golden Iridescent Glassware Assortment" ad. The items listed in that 1913 Butler Brothers ad for Fenton's glass were vases, bowls, salad dishes, massive footed orange bowls, jugs, nutbowls, rosebowls, bonbons, nappies, and mugs—all useful items. The main thrust was certainly to sell, sell, sell, and this, naturally, affected the kinds of shapes that Carnival was made in. Shapes had to be practical; they were called "popular staples." If possible, they ought to have multiple uses—and if they were decorative and ornamental as well, so much the better. Fenton had begun to export their Carnival to England in 1909, the sole agent for Fenton being Charles Pratt, who had showrooms in London. The British *Pottery Gazette* carried a report of the new iridized lines and stated that Pratts "were showing a most inclusive selection of fine pressed glassware for domestic purposes both useful and ornamental—the former principally."

An array of useful and practical shapes was offered by Fenton back in 1913. An extensive range of patterns was offered too: here are *BUTTERFLY AND BERRY, ORANGE TREE, DRAGON AND LOTUS, STAG AND HOLLY, PANTHER, BLACKBERRY BANDED, PEACOCK AND GRAPE,* and a *KNOTTED BEADS* vase.

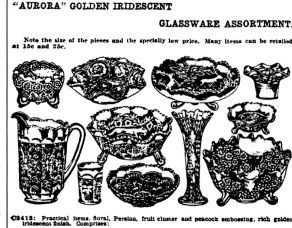

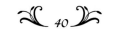

The shapes also reflected everyday life in the early 1900s: all manner of items for the dining table, dressing table sets for the lady's boudoir, vases for flowers to brighten up the house, and epergnes for impressive table centerpieces. The advent of the motor car gave rise to a demand for products that would adorn the vehicle—and so the glass makers produced automobile vases in Carnival Glass! And even though the International Paper Company had just developed the world's first "throw-away" waxed paper cup, it was still preferable to drink your beverage from a glass tumbler!

There are shapes in Carnival Glass for almost every purpose you care to think of. The main ones were bowls and plates, but there were also water sets, table sets, vases, bonbons, and compotes. Plus even more, including candlesticks, candlelamps, kerosene lamps, electric and gas shades, and magnificent Carnival lamp bases. Smokers were catered for too. Splendid tobacco humidors were produced—lucky is the collector who finds one of those today! Then there were spittoons—or more delicately—cuspidors! Toothpick holders, paperweights, and handled baskets, even a pickle castor and rare souvenir bells were also made. Sometimes whimseys were made—"one-offs"—unique and off-beat shapes, fashioned "on a whim." Regular shaped items also got the "whimsey" touch from time to time. Some rare pieces have irregular and unusual finishing that makes them stand out from the rest.

Bowls, Plates, and their Edge Treatments

There are probably more bowls than any other shape in Carnival Glass. They range from small berry dishes to huge "mammoth art shapes." Though mostly the intention was for them to be used for fruit, salad, nuts, or what you will, there's little doubt that many of the items were so attractive and ornamental that they would have been proudly displayed in a china cabinet or on hutch shelves. Some, perhaps given as gifts, were put away for the safe keeping of precious memories. Plates are harder for the collector to find today. It's possible that not many were originally made, as they required extra shaping and finishing. The plate was almost always formed from the bowl shape. The bowl would be attached to a punty rod and then spun; centrifugal force caused the hot glass to flatten and take on the profile of a plate. Bowls and plates would usually have a collar base or would be footed.

The following terms are useful when considering Carnival Glass shapes:

Marie: on a bowl or plate, it is the center of the base within the collar.

Collar base: the flat, circular base found on items such as bowls and plates.

Spatula feet: spade shaped feet found on some bowls and plates. Other items such as rosebowls may also have spatula feet.

Ball feet/ Scroll feet: these are round shaped feet that may sometimes actually be fashioned like claws. They are found on some bowls and plates as well as a number of other items such as rosebowls.

The following list classifies the types of bowls and plates that today's collector may expect to come across.

Berry set. This comprises a master berry bowl and six matching small berry bowls (sometimes called simply berries or nappies—names seemed to be fairly freely interchangeable!) Usually round in shape, but there are oval examples too. The pattern may be either on the interior, exterior, or both.

Salad or fruit bowl. Individual, round bowls—not sold as a set—in a range of sizes, the most common being about 8" in diameter. This is probably the most frequently found shape found in Carnival. The pattern may be on the interior, exterior, or both.

Orange bowl. An individual bowl, round in shape and usually footed and impressively large—often called "giant," "massive," or "mammoth" in contemporary ads. The pattern may be on the interior, exterior, or both.

Banana boat/bowl. An individual bowl, oval in shape and usually footed. Like the orange bowl, it is also large and showy and also may often have a pattern on both interior and exterior.

Ice cream set. Similar to the berry set in that it comprises a master bowl and six matching smaller ones. They were not called by this name in the original catalog ads—the use of the term has come along more recently. The ice cream set differs from the berry set in its flat shape and the fact that the pattern is always on the interior or upper face of the bowl. The late Don Moore described the true ice cream bowl as being "on a collar base...it comes out very flat from the center and then turns up sharply about an inch or so from the edge. The master ice cream bowl will measure from ten to eleven inches while the individual bowl will run some five and a half to six inches. We are not always precise to this definition these days, often using the term ice cream shape (ICS) to refer to round, non ruffled bowls in the standard eight and a half to nine inch size."[1]

Plate. There are three broad sizes of plates. Small plates run from 5 to 7" or so in diameter. Regular plates are around 9" in diameter and the large, impressive, showy chop plates measure around 10 or 11" or more. "Cake Plate" sets were sold that comprised an 11" dish (actually, what we now call a chop plate) plus six small 7" serving plates.

Plate variations. Sometimes the sides of the plate may be pulled up. If one side only is pulled up, the item is termed a hand grip plate, the curved-up edge designed so as to make it easier to grasp the plate. Two sides of the plate may be pulled up. This produces a shape that is sometimes called a banana boat shape. Rarely, three sides are pulled up; the item then becomes known as a tri-cornered plate.

This Dugan/Diamond cake plate set comprised a large plate, 11" or so in diameter (now known as a chop plate) plus six 7" plates. Patterns featured are a *FOUR FLOWERS* chop plate and matching small, serving plate; the other small plate shown is in the *WISHBONE AND SPADES* pattern.

What is a Plate? What is a Bowl?

How do you tell the difference between a plate and a bowl? It's a seemingly simple question, yet one which throws up a grey area for the Carnival Glass collector. The generally accepted definition of a plate in Carnival Glass terminology is that given by the late Marion Hartung and often referred to as the *two inch rule*:

Place the piece in question on a flat, bare surface such as a wooden table...the distance from the surface of the table to the top edge of the plate should not be more than 2" at the very most...a plate is round or square. If it is oblong, one has a platter or tray.[2]

Another way to determine whether a piece is truly a plate is to turn it upside down onto a flat table. Virtually all parts of the edge should touch the table without any ruffling or crimping. A further proviso is that the angle of the sides of the item should be nearly straight, with no curve on the outer edge. Some plates are very flat, others (typically those by Northwood) tend to have more steeply sloped sides. Plates may be collar based or footed. The feet may be spatula shaped, scroll footed, or even dome footed—generally the two inch rule will be overlooked if the plate is footed.

Plate profiles. Top left: collar based, flat plate. Top right: collar based with steeply sloped sides, typical of Northwood plates. Bottom left: dome footed plate, typical of Dugan/Diamond plates. Bottom right: spatula (or spade) footed plate, typical of both Fenton and Northwood. Note that feet can also be scroll (or knob) shaped.

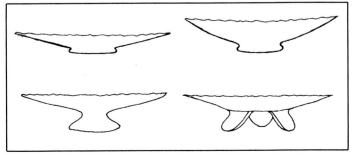

Edge Treatments on Bowls and Plates

Though Carnival was a product of the machine age and commercial mass production, it was, nevertheless, totally distinctive in that many pieces benefited from individual finishing. Nowhere is this seen more clearly than on the edges of many bowls and plates. Originally done by hand, crimping machines had really speeded up the process by applying what was sometimes called a "machine frill." The crimping operation required skill on behalf of the glassworker, to place the glass article (still attached to the snaps) centrally onto the crimper—otherwise the frilled edge would be wider on one side than the other. The crimping machine worked either by simple manual pressure or a mechanical foot pedal. Harry Northwood's father, John, had in fact patented a crimping mould in 1884. No doubt the splendid Northwood pie crust edge finish stemmed from Harry's desire to emulate his father's mastery of such techniques.

Edge treatments can be divided into those that are shaped by the top ring of the mould and those that are caused by individual finishing and shaping of the item's edge after it has left the mould.

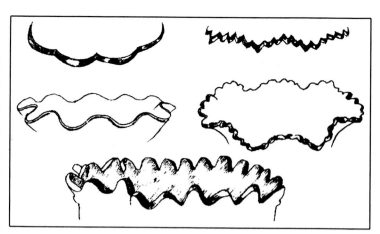

More edge variations. Top left: scalloped edge. Top right: saw tooth edge. Middle left: a ruffled, smooth edge. Middle right: a ruffled, fluted edge. Bottom: large flutes which are often called flames.

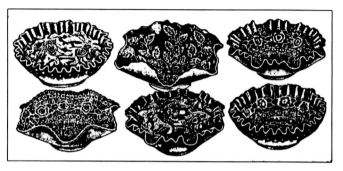

Shaping and finishing on bowls varied enormously. Top left: a continuous crimped edge, also called candy ribbon edging, on a *HEART AND VINE* bowl. Top middle: a ruffled bowl with fluted edge in the *HOLLY* pattern. Top right: a 3 in 1 (also called candy ribbon) edge on a *CAPTIVE ROSE* bowl. Bottom left: a ruffled, fluted edge on a *CAPTIVE ROSE* bowl. Bottom middle: a 3 in 1 edge on a *HEART AND VINE* bowl. Bottom right: a continuous crimped edge on a *CAPTIVE ROSE* bowl. All patterns are Fenton.

This purple Northwood *WISHBONE* bowl has an intricate pie crust edge. Such edges are susceptible to minor damage. $300-$500.

Mould variations on edges:

- Smooth or plain: the simplest edge of all, this is an edge with no shaping whatsoever. Found on plates more than on bowls.
- Flutes: these are small, gently pointed shapes. Seen on plates and bowls.
- Scallops: these are gently rounded half moon shapes. Seen on plates and bowls.
- Saw tooth: similar to flutes, but much sharper, jagged, pointed and better defined. Sometimes this edge is also called serrated. Used on both plates and bowls.
- Flames: these are much bigger projections, large flutes in fact, usually found on punch bowls or vases.
- Scallop and Flute or bracket edge: an interesting variation found on both plates and bowls.
- Bullet edge: seen on some Australian items, these are rounded, regular bumps which, from the side, look like a row of bullets.

Individual finishing variations on edges:

- Ruffles: are the wavy undulations around the edge of the bowl. Sometimes also called crimps.
- Pie crust: found only on some Northwood bowls, this delightful finish is so named because it is reminiscent of the finger and thumb pinched edging found on mom's home-made pies!
- Three in one (3-1): this is a very decorative edging found on some bowls. It's a ruffled edge that has one deep ruffle adjacent to two smaller ruffles. (Or indeed, three small ruffles sitting on top of the one larger one - it depends how you look at it.) Collectors also sometimes call this a candy ribbon edge or ribbon candy (often abbreviated to CRE).
- Tight ruffling or continuous crimping: also sometimes confusingly referred to as candy ribbon or ribbon candy edging, evocative of old style Christmas candy. This intricate edge is very tightly folded up. Found on bowls and occasionally on some small plates.

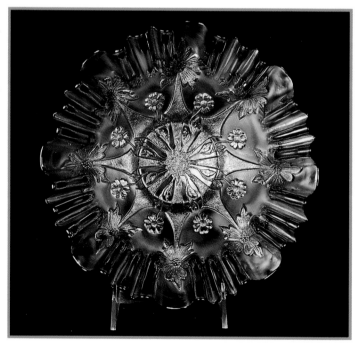

A green Fenton *LITTLE FLOWERS* bowl with a typical Fenton candy ribbon edge. $100 -$150.

A blue Northwood *WILD ROSE* bowl (it is the exterior pattern), with a very distinctive open edge of simplified heart shapes. The interior pattern is *RAYS.* $200-$250.

Three different water pitcher shapes. From left: blue Fenton *MILADY* tankard shape ($1000-$1200), marigold Fenton *APPLE TREE* bulbous shape ($200-$250), and blue Fenton *FENTONIA* standard ("as moulded") shape ($500-$900).

Blue Fenton *ORANGE TREE* four piece table set. From left: covered sugar, butter, spooner, and creamer. $600-$700 for the full set.

A relatively scarce, and very collectible, green Millersburg *LEAF AND LITTLE FLOWERS* miniature compote. $300-$400.

Compotes come in all shapes, sizes, and styles. From left: a purple Northwood covered *GRAPE AND CABLE* compote ($300-$400); a diminutive purple *AMARYLLIS* tri-cornered compote, possibly Dugan/Diamond ($300-$400); and a blue Northwood *HEARTS AND FLOWERS* stemmed compote ($400-$500).

A superb blue punch set by Fenton which shows the *ORANGE TREE* pattern very clearly. $400-$500.

Carnival Glass was made in a huge range of shapes for a lady's dressing table; here are just three. From left: green Fenton *ORANGE TREE* hatpin holder ($600-$900), blue Fenton *PERSIAN MEDALLION* hair receiver ($150-$200), and an amethyst Northwood *BANDED GRAPE AND CABLE* cologne bottle ($350-$400). The cologne is quite unusual: it is not the normal *GRAPE AND CABLE* pattern, but a variant where there is a plain band instead of the cable.

Dining Table Sets

Water or Lemonade sets were a typical domestic item back in the early 1900s. Six matching tumblers accompanied a large jug or water pitcher that generally held about two pints of liquid. The water pitchers were made in three basic shapes: tankard (tall and slender), bulbous (a "blown" shape), and standard (average size, straight sides). For the purposes of collecting, a matching pitcher plus *one* tumbler are considered acceptable as a water set. The handles on standard water pitchers were usually moulded in, but those on the bulbous and tankard pitchers were generally applied ("stuck" on). Caution should be used when handling water pitchers, as they are heavy items and are vulnerable to strain around the handle. Avoid picking them up by the handle—lift the whole item by the body instead.

Table sets were also designed for an obvious practical purpose and comprised a covered butter dish, a covered sugar bowl, an open spoon holder, and a creamer (cream jug). The sugar and spooner may have handles. (Later production in other countries gave rise to three part sets that omitted the spoon holder—spooners being a typical table item in the United States, but not much used in other parts of the world.)

Other table items. As well as the matching sets mentioned above, there were many other items intended to be used at the table. Two piece breakfast sets were made up of a matching unlidded sugar bowl and creamer. Stemmed compotes were very popular, ranging in size from cute miniatures, 3" high, to magnificent, showy specimens standing 8" and more. Some compotes were lidded—perhaps in response to a greater awareness of hygiene and the spread of disease. The United States Glass Company's ad in the June 1915 edition of the British *Pottery Gazette* emphasized the desire for covered glassware. There were nutbowls, sauce dishes, handled bonbons, and candy dishes too, as well as milk pitchers, open salts, biscuit barrels, and individual mugs. Decanter sets that comprised a whisky or wine decanter plus six shot glasses, small wines, or cordials were also produced in Carnival Glass. Larger goblets and scarce matching cup and saucer sets were available as well.

Punch Sets

Punch sets are magnificent and showy items—and probably the most expensive of all Carnival Glass pieces when they were first manufactured. The original wholesale price for the massive Northwood *GRAPE AND CABLE* banquet size punch set was $4.25 in 1910, compared with just ninety-two cents for a dozen large berry bowls. Punch sets were heavy too, possibly one of the most weighty items available in Carnival. Imagine the sheer physical effort involved in crafting, pressing, and finishing such a massive item. Standard sized sets were packaged three to a barrel, but the banquet set was so large that it needed to be packed by itself in a single barrel!

A punch set comprised a bowl and separate base plus six or twelve cups. Wire hooks were used to suspend the cups from the perimeter of the punch bowl. Most punch sets stand between 9 and 11" high, and measure from about 10 to 13" across. The largest set of all is the previously noted banquet size *GRAPE AND CABLE,* which stands 14" high and is 16.5" across. This pattern is the only one of all the punch sets that comes in three different sizes: small, mid size, and the banquet. All other punch sets come in one basic size, though there may be differences in the final shaping and finishing.

Punch sets had a multipurpose facility. The base—when inverted—could be used as a compote or a vase. The interior of most punch set bases are iridized to enhance the appearance should it be used in this manner. Punch cups could also be used as custard cups, while a punch bowl and base may have been used additionally as an "orange bowl."

Fenton's *WREATH OF ROSES* pattern is on this punch bowl, which also doubled as an orange bowl according to this 1911 ad.

This 1914 ad from John M. Smyth Merchandising Company, Chicago, featured two Northwood favorites, the *GRAPE AND CABLE* table set and the *GRAPE AND CABLE* water set.

Dressing Table or Bureau Sets

We know them today as dressing table sets, but the original Butler Brothers ads had them listed as bureau sets! Comprising various items for the lady's "toilette," we know these pieces today as hatpin holders, powder jars or boxes, pin trays, cologne and perfume bottles, large dressing table trays, and hair receivers. Sometimes they were issued in a matching set (as in Northwood's *GRAPE AND CABLE* items), other times they were sold separately. Either way, many of these are fairly scarce items.

Vases and other Flower Containers

"The concept of glass in motion is the fascination of swung vases."

—Joan Doty.[3]

No one writes more eloquently on swung vases than Joan Doty. Writing in *NetworK 6* [3], she says, "The vase shape is primarily functional, its purpose being to hold and display flowers. In general, most Carnival vases are fairly tall and slender, their mouths opening wide to fan out their floral contents to best effect. But within this broad generalization are many differences and, of course, there are other vase shapes that don't fit the 'tall and slender' description at all."

Swung Vases

The majority of vases produced by the American manufacturers during the Classic Carnival era were swung. Joan Doty describes the process thus: "In the creation process of a swung vase, the pieces were extracted individually from their moulds, clamped on the end of a snap, re-heated in a glory hole, then literally swung by the glassmaker while the glass was still pliable, to achieve their finished length." Joan also notes the differences in the type of *swing*. "There were easy pendulum swings, quick baton twirling swings, giant arc swings, and all in between. The centrifugal force lengthened the hot glass into slender, graceful shapes."

The variations in length would have reflected the elasticity and temperature of the glass and also the physical strength of the glassworker. Early in the shift, he would have been relatively enthusiastic and have given a good hearty swing, but later on in the day, tired muscles would have responded with less vigor, so producing a shorter vase. In Joan's words, "just as the camera freezes the dancer in motion, the swung vase captures glass in motion. This is the fascination of swung vases. All Carnival shapes have variation in pattern, in color and in iridescence; swung vases have a further dimension, variation in form."

Because height is dependent on how much a vase has been swung or stretched, vases are grouped according to the diameter of their base, irrespective of their actual height. There are four broad groups of swung vases according to size:

- Small (or miniature): base diameter of approximately 2.5"
- Standard: base diameter from approximately 3 to around 3.75"
- Mid size: base diameter ranging from around 3.75 to 4.75"
- Funeral: Northwood and Fenton funeral vases have base diameters of approximately 5.25". Imperial funeral vases run slightly smaller at 4.75 to 5".

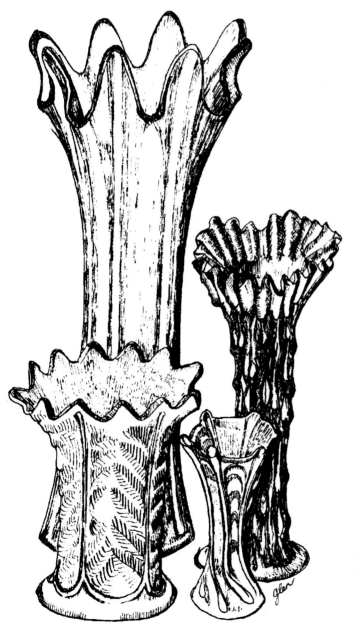

An exotic, almost writhing shape is presented by Dugan/Diamond's tiny *TWIG* vase. It's mouth has jack in the pulpit shaping (up at the back, down at the front) as well as being tightly crimped.

"Several ordinary vases, grouped together, can create a total sculptural shape that is much greater than the sum of its parts. Even commonplace flowers in the right vase can be breathtakingly dramatic." Joan Doty. These beautiful vases are Northwood's *THIN RIB* and Fenton's frilly edged *APRIL SHOWERS* at the back; Northwood's squatty version of *LEAF COLUMNS* and a diminutive 5" high example of Imperial's *THIN RIB AND DRAPE* at the front.

There is a tremendous range of height in swung vases. The small vases can be as tiny as 3" while the largest size, the impressive and truly magnificent funeral vase, can achieve the majestic height of 22" or even more, weighing 4 to 5 pounds. The standard sized vases generally are around 9 to 11" high, with unswung *squatty* versions measuring a fair bit less. Mid size vases can be swung up to almost 20", giving a tall, thin shape—yet they, too, may be unswung and end up around 7" high!

Some funerals have a further classification relating to height. A funeral vase that has not been swung is termed a "jardiniere." It is, of course, still a funeral vase, "jardiniere" being a rare type of funeral. Northwood *TREETRUNK* funerals have an additional unique height classification. A *TREETRUNK* funeral which was swung, but only to a height of 15" or less, is called an *elephant foot*. Thus, an elephant foot vase is a *TREETRUNK* funeral between 8 and 15" high. It was given this quaint and descriptive name by John Muehlbauer a good few years ago. He christened it thus because he said it looked just like an elephant's foot. Simple as that!

Many vases were given further shaping after they had been swung. One of the most attractive is the *jack in the pulpit* (JIP) shaping, which is imitative of earlier art glass examples from Tiffany and Quezal. (Quite possibly the JIP style was first developed at Harry Northwood's original workplace—Steven's and Williams in Stourbridge, England.) A JIP is pulled up at the back, and down and open at the front. Other vases were opened out and flared wide at the mouth—in some instances to a width even greater than the height of the vase. Other vases were crimped or ruffled around the rim. Some vases featured more than one type of finishing, having both crimping and JIP shaping. Joan Doty writes that "the *jester's cap* [authors' italics] is an unusual shaping in that it was applied to only one pattern, Northwood's *THIN RIB*. It is identified by one rib pointing up and eight ribs pointing down."

A massive, impressive, blue Fenton *RUSTIC* funeral vase. It is a magnificent 19" high and a full 8" across its flared mouth. Imagine the physical effort required to swing this piece! $700-$1500.

Two unusual blue vases. On the left is Dugan/Diamond's ice blue *BIG BASKETWEAVE* vase ($1000-$2000), on the right a rare celeste Fenton *FINE RIB* vase ($1000-$1700).

Two Fenton *916* vases which came from the same mould. On the left is a scarce, only slightly swung amethyst squatty vase that barely stretches to 7" (NP). On the right is a swung marigold example with a crimped candy ribbon edge that rises to a full 17" ($75-$125). Notice how clearly the pattern is defined on the squatty example.

Three jack-in-the-pulpit (JIP) shaped vases. From left: purple Westmoreland *CORINTH* ($40-$80), peach opal Dugan/Diamond *THIN PANEL* with its candy ribbon edge fashioned into a peaked JIP ($50-$100), and a mid size marigold Imperial *MORNING GLORY* ($50-$80). Note that the Westmoreland *CORINTH* vase can be identified by its twelve ribs.

Right: A contrasting assortment of vases. From left: green mid size Northwood *THIN RIB* rising to 13" in height ($300-$700); *TARGET* vase from Dugan/Diamond in blue, a scarce color for this pattern ($250-$300); two Imperial *MORNING GLORIES* that share the same base diameter of almost 2.5", the little, helios green one barely reaching 5" ($75-$250) while the taller, electric purple version was swung to nearly 9" ($75-$125); an immense, blue *RUSTIC* funeral vase from Fenton ($700-$1500); an unswung, squatty version of Northwood's *DIAMOND POINTS* in purple ($100-$250); and a tall, swung, blue Fenton *916* ($75-$100).

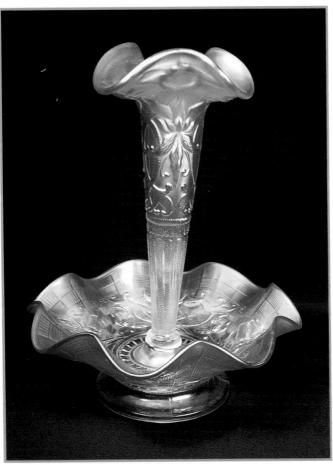

A distinctive shape—a marigold Northwood *WISHBONE* two piece epergne. The base of the lily sits in a circular moulded depression in the bowl. $350-$500.

An aqua opal Northwood *DRAPERY* rosebowl with a multicolored pastel iridescence, very much a favorite with rosebowl collectors. $200-$300.

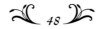

Two enameled decorated shades. Makers unknown, but quite possibly European. $50-$75 each.

Two more shades. On the left, a marigold Imperial *AUGUST FLOW-ERS* ($50-$75); on the right, a marigold on milk glass *DRAPERY* or *SQUARE PILLAR AND DRAPE* probably from Northwood ($50-$75).

A fragile and relatively rare shape: a green Northwood *GRAPE & CABLE* candlelamp. $600-$1000.

Moulded or Unswung Vases

Vases that were not swung when they left the mould but were "as moulded" are often called simply "unswung." They typically have little hand finishing yet still vary considerably in shape, size, and design. It is in this category that several exceptionally rare and desirable vases are found. These include vases such as the fabulous *PEOPLES VASE* and the *ROSE COLUMNS* vase from Millersburg, or the *LOGANBERRY* and *POPPY SHOW* from Imperial. Some unswung vases could not be made by the usual press moulding technique because of their wide and curvaceous shapes or their deeply sculptured patterns.

Instead, such vases were blow moulded. The size of unswung vases varies considerably, from the tiny to the statuesque. There is also a range of novelty vases that strictly fits into the unswung category. Northwood and Dugan/Diamond made several of these novelties, Northwood's *CORN* vase and Dugan/Diamond's *MARY ANN* being good examples.

Other Flower Containers

Rosebowls were very popular. The Carnival collector defines a rosebowl as any bowl which turns in at the top, whether it is footed or collar based. The purist rosebowl collector will also insist that the bowl is as wide as it is tall. (Note that nutbowls are similar in overall shape and size to rosebowls, but they flare out at the top instead of cupping in.)

Epergnes were *de rigeur* for the fashionable home in the early 1900s. The bowl would have contained a fruit display while the epergne lily (or lilies) would have held specimen blooms, the whole thing becoming a delightful table centerpiece. Ferneries, footed, deep, cupped

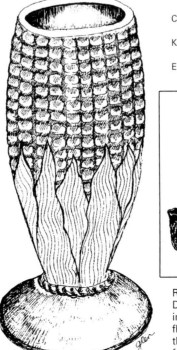

Northwood's splendid *CORN* vase was neither shaped nor swung after moulding.

in shape, and often sold with a removable glass or tin liner, were also popular. Then there were handled baskets for posies, wall pockets with moulded attachments and—sign of the times—automobile vases! (The latter doubled up for use in cemeteries! Its pointed base could either be popped into the holder fixed inside the car, or it could be driven into the earth at the graveside.)

Miscellaneous Shapes

A whole host of further different shapes were made, some useful and some purely decorative. The spittoon or cuspidor was a curious item—no doubt linked to the craze for chewing tobacco. The humidor, with its prongs for holding a damp sponge to keep the tobacco moist, is another relic from the days when smoking was more fashionable than, perhaps, it is today.

Lighting was catered for in a whole variety of ways. Candlesticks were produced by several Carnival manufacturers, and a candlelamp (a splendid combination of a Carnival candlestick and a delicate Carnival Glass shade) was made by Northwood. Glass shades were made for both electric and gas fittings. Magnificent "Gone With the Wind" oil lamps are also known in Carnival Glass.

[1] Don Moore, *Carnival Glass: A Collection of Writings* (Alameda, California: by author, 1987).

[2] Marion T Hartung, *Seventh Book of Carnival Glass* (Emporia, Kansas: by author, 1966).

[3] Glen and Stephen Thistlewood, *NetworK 6* (Alton, Hampshire, England: by authors, 1995).

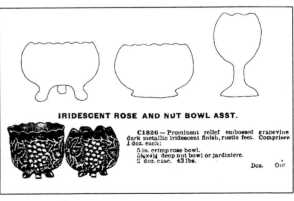

IRIDESCENT ROSE AND NUT BOWL ASST.

C1826 — Prominent relief embossed grapevine dark metallic iridescent finish, rustic feet. Comprises 1 doz. each:
5 in. crimp rose bowl.
5½x4¼ deep nut bowl or jardiniere.
2 doz. case. 43 lbs.

Doz.   Out

Rosebowls and nutbowls differ in their shaping: the Dugan/Diamond *GRAPE DELIGHT* rosebowl is cupped in (bottom right), while the nutbowl has a slight outward flare (bottom left). The three profiles across the top show the different forms that rosebowls may take. Left to right: footed, collar based, and stemmed.

Chapter Five
The Marketing Phenomenon of Classic Carnival

F.W. Woolworth, Sears Roebuck, and Butler Brothers all played a part in the colorful past of Carnival Glass. Frank Woolworth opened the first Woolworth store—effectively a "bargain basement"—in 1879 at Utica, New York. It was to be quite a success story. The Woolworth stores became known as the "five and dime" stores and Carnival Glass was one of their sales lines. Richard Sears and Alvah Roebuck operated in a different market—mail order—catering for the mainly rural population that couldn't easily get to the popular "five and dimes." They were hugely successful. In the years leading up to the advent of Carnival Glass, Sears Roebuck had grown so much that they employed over two thousand workers, processing over nine-hundred sackloads of orders a day. You could buy almost anything from the catalogs: a $25 road wagon, a $43 five piece parlor suite, or an eighteen cent box of roach powder. And yes...they sold Carnival Glass! Butler Brothers, Sommers and Co., and Sears Roebuck sold Carnival to merchants through their catalogs.

Butler Brothers

Probably the main wholesale marketing outlet for Carnival were the Butler Brothers catalogs. Charles, George, and Edward Butler, the men who laid the foundations of Butler Brothers back in 1877 when they opened a little wholesale store at 50 Arch Street, Boston, Massachusetts, had both vision and courage. At that time, the great American West was undeveloped—methods of production and distribution were crude. Retail merchants bought most of their goods on spring and fall trips to market, purchasing the remainder from traveling salesmen. Mail buying was unknown. Thus the development of the Butler Brothers system by the establishment of a major distribution house in each of the five "key" cities of the United States (New York, St. Louis, Chicago, Minneapolis, and Dallas) was truly far-sighted.

Butler Brothers concentrated on goods which they knew were popular and would sell. They bought direct from the manufacturers and sold to local merchants through the medium of their illustrated catalogs. The catalog—through which they successfully marketed a great deal of Carnival Glass and much else besides— was called *Our Drummer*. The choice of name reflects trading back in the late 1800s and early 1900s when a "drummer" was the name given to a traveling salesman. The catalogs certainly drummed up sales for Butler Brothers. Bargains were to be had, and ordering by this revolutionary form of mail order was so simple. A new catalog was issued every month and the goods packed up in barrel assortments at competitive prices, delivered right to the shopkeeper's door. As a further inducement, there was no package charge and no cartage charge. It couldn't fail.

Butler Brothers' key selling point was to charge the same price to all buyers—no matter who. "None of the magicians in fairyland (had such a place ever existed) could have done for you what we can do through our world-wide buying organization and our system of sample displays"—so went the persuasive text set out in a 1913 Butler Brothers catalog.

The centuries old custom of holding fairs and local exhibitions had been transformed by the British in 1851 when they invited all the nations of the world to the Great Exhibition held at the Crystal Palace in Hyde Park, London. This new trend continued into the early 1900s. The stage was therefore set for Butler Brothers to attempt their own version. So, on July 28, 1913, the formal opening of the "World's Exposition" took place on Broadway, New York City. But what did this Exposition have to do with Carnival Glass? Well, it was an exhibition of "holiday goods and general merchandise," set out for inspection for the retailers of the United States by the wholesale mail order giants, Butler Brothers, who described the Exposition as a place where the visitor "is literally transported from the single country where he does business to all the great marketplaces of the world." And set out amongst the merchandise—nestled between displays of lamps and jewelry, right opposite the aisles full of linen goods and hosiery—were tables *full* of Carnival Glass. Bowls, compotes, vases, water sets, punch sets, and much more besides.

The banner heading that can be found at the top of each Butler Brothers catalog.

This was the Butler Brothers New York building, located at 495-497 Broadway. On 28 July, 1913, it was the scene of "the greatest exposition of holiday goods and general merchandise ever collected for the inspection and use of the retailers of America." In one of the many sample rooms was a selection of glassware that, without doubt, would have included Carnival Glass.

Lee Manufacturing Company

Thanks to Lance Hilkene of New Jersey, another method of marketing involving Carnival Glass has come to light. Lance discovered a 1911 catalog for the Lee Manufacturing Company of Chicago, Illinois. They were importers and manufacturers of food and pharmaceutical goods; baking powder, tooth soap (sic), and the splendidly named "witch hazel and carbolic salve" were just some of their products. Their selling plan was mail order—but direct to the consumer through "lady agents"—with a "valuable present included in every assortment." And that "valuable present," guaranteed by company president John Magnus, was—for the lucky lady—Carnival Glass! What could sixty-five cents worth of baking powder, nutmeg, scouring soap, and stove polish have gotten you? Why, a Northwood *THREE FRUITS* saw toothed edge plate, sitting in a metal holder and marketed as a "cake basket." Premiums were also given for introducing new agents. Introduce five new agents and you would get $25 worth of premiums free. Lee Manufacturing advertised that they required no money in advance. "We furnish the capital and trust you. We ship all premiums with goods. We pay the freight and allow you time to deliver and collect"—persuasive stuff.

The Lee catalog carried a full page of testimonials from its lady agents, one of whom was Inez Holcomb Plum. A neat bit of detective work on behalf of Kathi and Galen Johnson (enthusiastic and knowledgeable Carnival collectors from Minnesota) revealed the following account of Inez' early experiences, as told by her cousin, Jo Campbell:

Inez Holcomb Plum was born December 18, 1907 in De Leon, Texas. She and her family moved to Mt. Pleasant, Texas, in 1912 when she was five years old. She related this story to me on March 2, 1995. I will try to write it in the "first person" so that none of the facts will be taken away.

"We moved to Green Hill Community around 1920. This was just a little way north of Mt. Pleasant. Me and my cousin would hitch up the horse and buggy and ride over to Argo (this was our territory) where we would take orders for the Lee Manufacturing Company. We would take our catalog from door to door and take orders on anything from Carnival Glass to enamel cooking ware. Lee Manufacturing carried practically anything for a general household. We would write the orders up and mail them off to Lee. In a few weeks we would get a mail order in from Lee. The merchandise would be packed in crates or barrels. It was then our job to get it delivered to the person who ordered it. We would collect the money for the merchandise and then mail it to Lee Manufacturing. In return for our work they would send us "premiums." These "premiums" included such things as Carnival Glass, sets of dishes, lamps etc. It was exciting work because the people were so anxious to

---

A *FLORAL AND GRAPE* water set was the premium gift offered by Lee Manufacturing Company for an extra $3.50 sale. *Catalog courtesy of Lance Hilkene.*

---

get the stuff they ordered—because we didn't get too much mail order stuff way back then."

Inez showed me a beautiful berry bowl and some other Carnival Glass pieces that she had received as premiums. She is a very knowledgeable, alert "young" eighty-eight year old lady who still enjoys life to the fullest. As I started to leave Inez' home, she told me that she could remember so well as children that they wore the cheapest shoes—often the wrong size—and that the shoes were so bad that they would rub a blister on your foot: carry on walking down the road and they would then rub the blister *off* your foot! She said that as she got older she vowed never to wear cheap shoes again. She then showed me three beautiful pairs of Italian leather shoes that she had received through the mail order from Niemans. She says that now she appreciates the finer things in life!

A selection of the agents whose testimonials for Lee Manufacturing Company appeared on the back page of the catalog. Many similar ladies must have received Carnival Glass from this source. *Catalog courtesy of Lance Hilkene.*

Baking powder, nutmegs, scouring soap, and stove polish for 65 cents—and take a dark Carnival, Northwood *THREE FRUITS* plate for free! Lee Manufacturing Company's "Plan No. 103" certainly offered a great deal back in 1911. *Catalog courtesy of Lance Hilkene.*

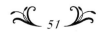

The Company Catalogs

The glass manufacturing companies also had their own catalogs. Special deals and assortments were offered to induce shopkeepers to buy the goods. In 1915, Imperial offered up "Spunk Rubigold Iridescent Deals" (a somewhat bizarre name) in order to sell. Of these "Spunk" deals, Imperial said:

This funny name describes the assortments correctly, because it took *spunk* on our part to offer them to you in this manner, and it will take *spunk* on your part to buy them...for you have to buy them like cats in bags. If you can muster up sufficient *spunk* to do this, they will do you a lot of good, especially when you use them for Bargain Sales. It is not such a dangerous problem anyhow because our reputation stands back of every word we say about them. Our object in making this special offer is to keep our stock clean by being able to ship every day the little lots of odds and ends which are developing every day in a factory like ours, where the vast majority of goods are marketed in solid barrel lots. Not more than three of any one of these *Spunk* deals sold to one dealer at one time.

And what did the shopkeeper get? Well, for example, in the "Spunk Nickel Iridescent Deal" he would have received twenty dozen iridescent pieces in assorted color, size, and quantity, all guaranteed to be regular goods and not seconds. A few years later the company offered "Lucky Lots," which were based on the same idea of moving stock rapidly and clearing out the packing rooms. Some great bargains must have been available. Who wouldn't take "Lucky Lot No. 1," which offered twenty dozen assorted iridescent pieces at forty-one cents a dozen? Or perhaps you'd have splurged and gotten "Lucky Lot No. 9"—the most expensive at $3 per dozen and containing three dozen assorted iridescent pieces. No doubt this one would have had water pitchers and similar larger items in it! Thirty-six items for $9—what a bargain!

Abroad: Britain and Australia

In the United Kingdom, the new Carnival Glass was popular with the general public. The London firm of Charles Pratt was the first to import Carnival Glass commercially to the United Kingdom. Pratt was an agent for Fenton, and the *Pottery Gazette* described the glass as being "Bright and cheerful without being gaudy." In March 1911, the London importers Markt and Co. announced that they too had introduced a range of iridescent glass. It was Imperial's Carnival and the colors were described in glowing terms. The first ad, picturing an *IMPERIAL GRAPE* water pitcher, appeared the same month. Later, Imperial were represented by Johnsen and Jorgensen and their first colored ad for Carnival Glass appeared in the British trade press in 1923. Northwood glass was probably marketed in the United Kingdom using Harry Northwood's position as the manager of the London office of the National Glass Company. Dugan/Diamond Carnival was also imported into Britain in quantity, probably through the British and American Glass Company. However, very little Millersburg glass is found in the United Kingdom.

In Australia, all you had to do was drink plenty of tea to get your fill of Carnival Glass! In 1923, the Bushell's Tea catalog #8 *All in the Glass* offered a wide range of mainly Fenton Carnival in exchange for tea packet labels. There were dishes and vases in several designs: *PANTHER, LITTLE FISHES, LEAF CHAIN,* and more. Several years later, in 1929, Bushell's began to offer home produced Carnival—Australian glass from Crown Crystal. It's enough to make you think of deserting your favorite brand of coffee!

Spunk nickel iridescent deal.

20 dozen pieces......$ 0.36	$ 7.20	
package	0.50	
SPECIAL!	$ 7.70	

20 dozen iridescent pieces, assorted in colors, assorted in sizes and assorted in quantities, which may be equal or not of the different articles.

All guaranteed to be regular goods, no seconds.

If bought in barrel lots regularly, none of the goods in this assortment would cost less than 40 cents per dozen, and many pieces would cost more, with extra package charge.

Lucky Lot No. 1	41 cents per dozen
20 dozen assorted Iridescent pieces, regular prices for barrel lots from 40 to 50 cents per dozen, special $0.38½	$7.70
1 barrel	$0.50
Not more than 2 dozen of any article.	$8.20

Lucky Lot No. 5	$1.26 per dozen
6 dozen assorted Iridescent pieces, regular prices for barrel lots from $1.10 to $1.30 per dozen, special $1.05	$6.30
1 cask	1.25
Not more than 1 dozen of any article.	$7.55

Imperial's "Spunk" (sic) deals and "Lucky Lots" offered cheap prices back in 1915.

Opposite page: This ad from the November 1925 edition of *The Pottery Gazette and Glass Trade Review* shows Fenton's Carnival Glass offered for sale in Britain. The advertising copy refers to it as "Iridescent Art Ware," emphasizing its worth, and continues to state that it is "the original iridescent glassware which still holds first place for beautiful colour effects." Marigold, green, purple, and blue Carnival were all on offer. Note that the *ORANGE TREE* item is called "1401 nut bowl," despite being the shape that today's collectors call a rosebowl. Another pattern shown is #922 *VINTAGE* fernery; additionally #1406 looks like a *CHERRY CHAIN* or *LEAF CHAIN* bowl, #32 is the *SWIRLED FLUTE* vase, and #1125 appears to be a *PANTHER* berry bowl.

IRIDESCENT ART WARE

NATIONAL GLASS Co Ltd

1 CHARTERHOUSE STREET, HOLBORN CIRCUS, LONDON·E·C·1

1401 NUT BOWL

922 FERN DISH

1406 9" DISH CRIMPED

82 9" VASE

1125 FLARED DISH

¶ THE ORIGINAL IRIDESCENT GLASSWARE, WHICH STILL HOLDS FIRST PLACE FOR BEAUTIFUL COLOUR EFFECTS—GOLDEN, GREEN, VIOLET AND ROYAL BLUE—HIGH GRADE QUALITY—AT MODERATE PRICES

¶ A VERY EXTENSIVE RANGE OF SHAPES AND DESIGNS MADE

¶ FOR CHRISTMAS TRADE WE CAN GIVE IMMEDIATE DELIVERY OF STOCK ASSORTMENTS COMPRISING DISHES, CAKE PLATES, NUT BOWLS, VASES ETC.

¶ WE CORDIALLY INVITE INSPECTION OF OUR WIDE RANGE OF TABLEWARE DESIGNS.

Part Two
Pattern Themes in Classic Carnival Glass

Carnival Glass patterns are like a mirror—they are a reflection of the social and design trends of their time. But what's their purpose? In the words of the British designer, William Morris, the function of pattern and design in our lives and our surroundings is "to beautify the familiar matters of everyday life." Why settle for plain ordinary when you can have true beauty?

One of the great attractions of Carnival Glass to collectors is its sheer range. There are over a thousand patterns in Classic Carnival alone (plus many hundreds from other countries), a myriad of different colors, and an extensive variety of shapes. This, together with individual hand finishing and the endless variety caused by the different effects of iridescence, creates a multitude of combinations and choices for any collector.

The vine was a popular motif used by artists and designers in the late 1800s and early 1900s. It is also often found on Carnival Glass patterns, excellent examples being seen on these three tumblers. From left: purple *IMPERIAL GRAPE* ($75-$100), blue Northwood *GRAPE AND GOTHIC ARCHES* ($50-$75), and an amethyst Northwood *GRAPE AND CABLE* ($75-$100).

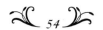

Chapter One

Inspirations and Influences

Social Background

So what would it have been like back in the early 1900s, at the advent of Carnival Glass? In the home, the tungsten light bulb was just becoming available, though candles and oil lamps were still in use. The vacuum cleaner had just been launched. Kellogg's Corn Flakes were the new *de rigeur* breakfast; Coca-Cola, Pepsi, and Jell-O were the new food fads; and pizza had just hit the New York food scene. In 1900, the Eastman Kodak Company put their "Box Brownie" camera on sale for just one dollar, making it possible for ordinary folk to become amateur photographers. A roll of six exposure film retailed for just ten to fifteen cents. An American photographer, Alfred Stieglitz, gave the hobby credibility, elevating it to an art form. The favorite children's tale was Frank Baum's *The Wonderful Wizard of Oz.*

Yet there were still indications of a blacker past: in 1905, 451 people died of mosquito borne yellow fever in New Orleans. This was an improvement; just over twenty years earlier, 4000 had died. Women were making inroads in society, getting jobs and breaking with tradition. The *Woman's Journal* (November 16, 1907) somewhat sarcastically remarked that women "have done nearly everything and the heavens have not yet fallen," yet only two years earlier a woman had been arrested for smoking in an open automobile on Fifth Avenue, New York.

Transportation was changing constantly. The railroads had forged across the country. Charles Francis Adams had described them as "an enormous force let loose upon mankind. Not many of those who fondly believe they control it, ever stop to think of it as the most tremendous and far reaching engine of social change that has ever blessed or cursed mankind." It certainly had an effect on Carnival Glass production. The transportation of raw materials to the glass factories as well as the distribution of goods and sales catalogs all over the country facilitated the commercial success of Carnival. The spread of the railway network meant mobility, communication, wealth, and progress. By 1900, over four thousand Americans owned

The price of either one of these stylish men's hats ($1.50) would have also bought you a green Carnival, Northwood *WIDE PANEL* epergne back in 1911. The *WIDE PANEL* epergne would cost you between $900 to $1500 today. Wonder what the hat would cost?

Fashions in 1908 included pin-tucking, embroidery, and soutache lace. Feathers, beads, ribbons, and ornamental fruits and flowers also adorned ladies' outfits.

cars, though the "Harley-Davidson" motorcycle was considered to be the fastest thing on the road. This, of course, was just the beginning. Automobile sales boomed, satisfied by Henry Ford's commercial credo "More cars, better and cheaper."

Transportation by sea had, of course, brought millions of people into the United States from other parts of the world. Immigrants had flocked in, carried by the steamships and the great ocean-going liners. It was the biggest movement of population ever to take place. From the early to the middle years of the nineteenth century, the United States welcomed all comers. By 1900, an estimated thirty-five million aliens had arrived from much of the civilized world, principally Europe. Many had brought skills, all had brought their own culture: both would be incorporated into the changing scene. The glass industry certainly benefited from the influx of skilled workers such as Harry Northwood, who was able to bring his experience of the glass industry in Britain. This no doubt helped to shape his future as one of the greatest producers of Carnival Glass.

Cultural Inspirations

The advent of Carnival Glass came at a time of changing fashion in art and design. The revolutionary Art Nouveau period was on the wane. The Arts and Crafts Movement had already spread its ideas. Many of the Great Exhibitions were past. The craze for Oriental style and eastern artifacts was a little passé in the chic circles. Tiffany had already delighted the world with his fabulous iridized glassware. So—what exactly inspired Carnival Glass? Where do we look for the background to the multitude of patterns seen on Carnival? The answer is, we must look to all of these trends and styles, for Carnival Glass was like a mirror, reflecting changing fashions and trends. Its style was truly eclectic—borrowing freely from various sources—a melting pot of all the different popular tastes. Its design was aimed at ordinary people in the ordinary home. And what's more...the people *loved* it!

All of these styles and trends, Art Nouveau, Arts and Crafts, and more, were reflected in Carnival Glass patterns and helped to create and shape Carnival—a little bit of this and a little bit of that! The patterns found on Carnival are very wide ranging—there is no *single* style, but there are many design sources. Yet there is one common thread: it was what the people wanted! It looked good in their homes: on their shelves or on their dining tables. This was "design" for the people.

The significance of Carnival Glass within the sphere of the decorative arts must be recognized. Carnival represents an eclectic fusion of design styles that echoed popular taste. It represents the meeting of "art" with ordinary things— familiar items that bear the traces of everyday life, not grand items of fine art that spent their days in the homes of the rich and famous or cocooned in dust, hidden away in museums and galleries. "The best design is one which...should become a commonplace."[1] Carnival Glass **is** that "commonplace;" it is the "art" that entered many homes, brightened up working lives, was admired by many, and continues to spread its magic today. It has a unique place in our history. It surely will continue to have a unique place in our future.

Below, we set out the various trends, fashions, and styles that helped to shape and determine the patterns that are found on Carnival Glass.

The Arts and Crafts Movement: William Morris

The Arts and Crafts Movement was a design style that grew out of the dissatisfaction following the Industrial Revolution. The growth of industry and its associated machinery, encroaching urbanization, and the subsequent rise in pollution caused distress to many. The movement had its beginnings in Britain, around 1830 in the writings of Augustus Pugin. However, the foremost name associated with the Arts and Crafts Movement in Britain was William Morris.

Morris was one of the major designers of his era: undoubtedly he revolutionized the art of pattern making and in doing so, altered the course of Western design. He took his inspirations from nature as well as medieval and Eastern designs. Many designs produced by his firm, Morris & Co., as well as others such as the Silver Studio, were widely available all over the United States and Europe. Morris wallpaper even adorned some of the first class suites on the ill-fated *Titanic*. In 1883, his firm exhibited at an International Trade fair in Boston. Morris's designs were very popular, in particular the "Peacock" and "Bird" patterns, and they had many imitators. It is fascinating to compare many of Morris's designs with Carnival patterns. One of the most strikingly similar designs is between Morris's "Orange Tree" patterned textiles and wallpapers and Fenton's *ORANGE TREE* design.

The Anglo-American Arts and Crafts Movement was enormously influential. Its ideas spread outward from a core of dedicated disciples to manufacturing industries such as those producing Carnival Glass. It was absorbed into their new designs as yet one more style. Hand embroidery and delicate lace work were important skills of the era. The Arts and Crafts Movement had fostered the idea of handiwork and it provided the platform from which had sprung many handicraft guilds. The revival of needlecraft was to prove an inspiration for many Carnival patterns. Delicate and intricate designs such as Fenton's *PERSIAN MEDALLION* and Northwood's *EMBROIDERED MUMS* are perfect copies of embroidery work.

The Studio

The Studio journal was the mouthpiece of the Arts and Crafts Movement. There was a free exchange of ideas and information between Europe and the United States in the years immediately before World War One (1914-18). Virtually everyone involved in the decorative arts in both Europe and the USA read *The Studio*. Its pages were full of design ideas. There were competitions, articles, and essays, plus designs, designs, and more designs—peacocks, irises, sunflowers, dragons, grapes, and other fruits. Any competent designer would surely have been able to pick up an idea or two from *The Studio* magazine. It's quite possible that the dragon in Fenton's *DRAGON AND LOTUS* and *DRAGON AND STRAWBERRY* patterns was inspired by a design first seen in *The Studio*, in 1894.

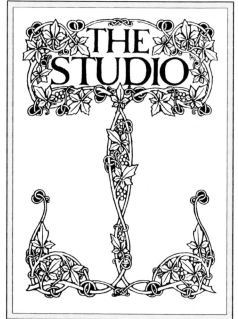

This cover from *The Studio* magazine #38, 1903, shows that the grapevine was a popular image of the era.

Below: *The Studio* magazine in 1894 portrayed the dragon (left)—note its four toes. This is a British style creature, very much like the Tudor dragon; Oriental dragons have only three toes. On the right is a detail from Fenton's *DRAGON AND LOTUS* pattern—again, four toes. Quite possibly it was from illustrations such as this in *The Studio* that the designer of the Fenton pattern got his inspiration.

The Aesthetic Movement

The Aesthetic Movement was something of an artificial invention, but has come to represent a taste for Oriental style and in particular, sunflowers and peacocks as ornament! While it might not find favor as a fully recognized design style, it nevertheless found favor with society. Fashionable stores such as Liberty sold imported Japanese goods. Their splendid fabrics soon became very popular in fashionable circles. The new style won many admirers. Sunflowers, Oriental artifacts, and peacock feathers were "hot" items for decorating the house. This was one late nineteenth-century fashion fad that certainly found favor with the Carnival Glass manufacturers. The peacock, in particular, was chosen for many Carnival patterns, and indeed, today, has come to represent the essence of Classic Carnival design.

The Style Book or Pattern Book

Style books were very popular through the latter part of the 1800s and the beginning of the 1900s. They supplied the decorative artist with an almost inexhaustible fountain of inspiration. One of the first style books was by Owen Jones, back in 1856. Called *The Grammar of Ornament*, it presented decorative motifs from a multitude of sources (Greek, Chinese, and Islamic to name a few). Jones believed that nature was the ultimate source of good design and inspiration and the effect of his influential manual on design and pattern lasted well into the twentieth century. The Greek key pattern, the fleur de lis motif—true classics found on Carnival designs—can be found within the pages of Owen Jones' great work.

Other Pattern books followed. Christopher Dresser, a successful commercial designer (who had produced designs for glassware) also brought out a manual on the decorative arts, entitled *Studies in Design*. Eugene Grasset, an exponent of Art Nouveau, also used the style book to give ideas for the adaptation of designs and motifs used on household items. Textiles and wallpapers as well as mundane everyday objects such as lamps, vases, and dishes were shown—transformed by the new design motifs. Grasset's influence was particularly strong in America due to the work of his pupil Louis John Rhead and his own celebrated covers for *Harper's* magazine.

The Audsley family produced several popular style books, which included *The Practical Decorator and Ornamentist*, that they believed "would prove of everyday value to the designer." These architectural style books from the Audsleys contained motifs from many different design styles ranging from ancient Egyptian, Greek, Roman, Moresque, Japanese, Arabian, French, and more. Their stated aim was "to supply the Decorative Artist and Ornamentist with an almost inexhaustible fount of inspiration." It is our opinion that these architectural style books with their many, easily copied design motifs were the source of quite a number of Carnival designs.

There were many other works intended to guide the artisan and student. Books and guides were available that showed how plant forms might be simplified and converted into ornament. There were many practical methods suggested for using such designs in different techniques, adapting a pattern for tableware, tiles, wallpapers, or embroidery. All were very useful material for the Carnival Glass mould makers and designers.

Orientalism—the Influence of the East

In August 1858, the British battleship, *HMS Furious*, was approaching Edo (today's Tokyo) in Japan. Lord Elgin, the British envoy, was on board, congratulating himself at having just signed a treaty that would open up trade with China. He was about to perform the same feat with Japan—an event that was to have far reaching repercussions not only on international commerce, but also on the culture and style of the United States and Europe during the late 1800s and early 1900s. In 1859, the American Commodore Perry also led an expedition to Japan. Trade between the West and Japan finally resumed again after centuries of isolation. With the opening up of the Far East and the subsequent spread of its culture and design, a phenomenon called "Japonisme" (a taste for things Japanese) took hold. Japanese art was first exhibited at the World Exhibition held in London in 1862. Many designers and manufacturers began turning to Japanese art as a new source of inspiration. In Carnival Glass, the Oriental influence is seen in the use of motifs popular at the time—in particular, the peacock and the butterfly—and in the style of various decorative floral elements.

Art Nouveau

Art Nouveau was a relatively short lived, though influential, artistic style. In a general sense, Art Nouveau is used to describe the great revival in the decorative arts that spread across Europe to the United States from around 1880, finally petering out around 1905. Art Nouveau itself was influenced by other forms of art—in particular that of the Orient and Japan. It's likely that it was also influenced by the slightly earlier British Arts and Crafts Movement. Art Nouveau style is characterized by flowing, sinuous forms inspired by nature. One of the features of the movement was the use of style books or pattern books of ornament (see above for more detail). These helped to spread design ideas. One of the classic portfolios was called *La Plante et Ses Applications Ornamentales* and was produced by Eugene Grasset and his pupil, Maurice Verneuil. Irises, sunflowers, waterlilies, dandelions, vines, and more were depicted. Though there are few **direct** examples of Art Nouveau style on Carnival patterns, it is easy to see a general influence and inspiration. In particular, note the similarities between the Carnival pattern *IRIS* and the Art Nouveau style illustration of the same flower.

A sunflower pattern by Art Nouveau designer Maurice Verneuil, this was one of the most popular motifs of the era. (The earlier Aesthetic Movement had also used sunflower designs.) On Carnival Glass it appears as the *DANDELION* pattern.

Architectural style books took their inspirations from many sources; in turn, they inspired other designs. The top pattern band is a detail from Fenton's *THISTLE* banana boat. The similar band below it could well have been its inspiration! Taken from Audsley's *The Practical Decorator and Ornamentist* (probably the most popular architectural style book of its time), the middle pattern band is based on Arabian interlaced ornament. The two motifs at the bottom are also from Audsley's book and could well have been the inspiration for another Carnival pattern, Northwood's *GREEK KEY*. They are in fact Oriental fret ornament (left) and conventional Greek foliage (right).

The Rococo Revival

The Rococo Revival began in Europe in the 1820s and was soon picked up as an international design trend. It was characterized by acanthus ornaments and curling 'C' and 'S' scrolls. Some Carnival patterns, such as the Millersburg *SEACOAST* pintray, Fenton's *FEATHERED SERPENT,* and Imperial's *ACANTHUS* design, have echoes of the Rococo style.

Louis Comfort Tiffany

Louis Comfort Tiffany was born in 1848, the son of a well-known New York jeweler. As a young man, he traveled to Europe and studied painting but gradually became more interested in the decorative arts. The Oriental and Middle Eastern styles, so influential in the contemporary Art Nouveau style, were particularly appealing to him. In 1879, back home in the United States, he set up a professional interior design firm—Louis C. Tiffany & Associated Artists. Probably his most famous works—and certainly the ones which have the most relevance here—are his wonderful, iridized glass designs in naturalistic forms of flowers and birds, particularly peacocks. His home, on East 26th. Street, New York, combined all the hallmarks of contemporary style. There were Moorish motifs over the doors, Japanese wallpaper, and peacock feathers everywhere. Though Tiffany's glass became one of the best known products of the Art Nouveau movement, he cannot be credited with the introduction of iridized glass in the late nineteenth century. The process of iridizing the finish is thought to have been first developed in Bohemia in 1856. A Viennese, Ludwig Lobmeyr, had also been experimenting in the 1870s with iridized glass; and indeed, such glass was exhibited at the Vienna World Fair of 1873 by Zahn and the Meyrs Neff Glassworks.[2] Tiffany's iridescent glass—known as "Favrile"—first appeared in 1894. It was hugely popular, with specialities like the peacock feather motif or the jack-in-the-pulpit vase. Soon others followed. Loetz of Bohemia acknowledged that its iridized wares were inspired by Tiffany. In the USA, Quezal, Durand, and Steuben followed suit, producing gorgeous iridized glass. Frederick Carder, of the Steuben Glass Works, first produced his "Aurene" range of iridescent glass in 1904, in shapes very similar to early Tiffany. Following this, Tiffany brought a lawsuit against Carder in 1913, but as iridescent glass was a well-known process, Tiffany could lay no claim to its invention, and the matter was settled out of court. Of course, Fenton, Northwood, Imperial, Millersburg, Dugan, and more were also producing it. Tiffany devoted much of his energy towards producing and distributing decorative arts destined to change the interiors of homes of wealthy buyers everywhere. It was high fashion. A true American entrepreneur, Tiffany not only created items of quality and technical innovation, he also attempted to make them accessible. However, though small tableware items such as cordial glasses could be purchased from about $1.00 to $1.50, it cost $150 to $175 for a vase—about a quarter of the price you could have expected to pay for a car! In fact, it would have taken the average worker almost two months' wages to buy such a vase. The availability of inexpensive glassware emulating the splendid Tiffany iridescence and with rich and decorative patterns was bound to please the buying public. The wholesale price of a dozen iridized vases from manufacturers such as the Fenton Art Glass Company was less than a dollar! In this way, Carnival Glass took the market by storm. In fact, in some circles it began to be called "poor man's Tiffany." In the words of Frederick Carder, founder of the Steuben Glass Works, "When the maid could possess iridescent glass as well as her mistress, the latter promptly lost interest in it."[3]

Imperial's *DIAMOND LACE* water pitcher in clear crystal glass—not Carnival—as illustrated in their 1909 Crystal catalog. Many pressed glass patterns were made in crystal, imitating the earlier cut glass. A good number of these moulds were then used to make Carnival Glass.

No. 434½ pitcher
packed 2 dozen in barrel.
barrel lots, $1.75 per doz.
smaller lots, 2.00 per doz.

Cut Glass and Pattern Glass

Cut glass, extravagant and splendid in execution, was very fashionable in the Regency era. Whole suites of glittering glassware adorned the wealthy household. Between 1851 and 1860, Stevens & Williams of Stourbridge in England recorded over a thousand cut glass designs in their pattern books.[4] Then, in 1867, at the Philadelphia Centennial Exhibition, Brilliant Cut Glass was introduced to America. The glassware was thicker, the patterns deeper, more reflective and more scintillating—intricate, geometric designs sparkling like diamonds. A glance through the Butler Brothers catalogs from the early 1900s shows how popular this type of glass was. It was also expensive to manufacture. However, the development and improvement of techniques for press moulding glass presented the manufacturers with a much cheaper alternative. Geometric designs—imitative of cut glass style, but made by press moulding intaglio patterns—were introduced. Called "near-cut," they were affordable and soon became hugely popular. The vogue for these imitation cut patterns was still very much alive when the first press moulded iridescent glassware caught on. Naturally, moulds already in use were utilized for production. It was successful—the geometric surfaces of the patterns adapted extremely well to iridized glass, catching the light and catching the eye.

Pattern glass was the early, press moulded glass (mainly tableware) that was produced in the United States from the 1830s on. As well as imitating the cut glass designs mentioned above, a different type of pattern also began to emerge, often featuring flowers, fruits, animals, and even peacock tails. These patterns were a product of the many design influences in evidence at the time. Many of these early patterns became a kind of springboard for the iridized glass that was to follow. They can be seen epitomized in the later Carnival Glass designs.

Close-up of the pattern on a blue Northwood *EMBROIDERED MUMS* bowl, clearly showing the influence of embroidery stitches on the design. $500-$800. An electric blue example sold in 2007 for $1300.

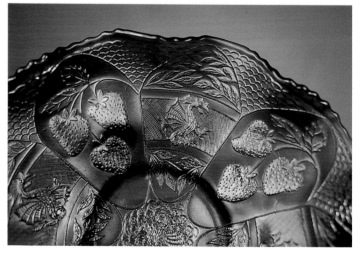

Close-up of the pattern on a green Fenton *DRAGON AND STRAWBERRY* bowl. $800-$2000.

Close-up of the luscious grapes on a purple *IMPERIAL GRAPE* water pitcher.

The Carnival Glass designers used a variety of source books to give them ideas for new patterns. Several such books featured the Greek key motif, in particular the popular architectural style books by the Audsleys. The motif is seen on Carnival Glass in this purple *GREEK KEY* tumbler from Northwood. $175-$250.

The Oriental influence can be seen on some Carnival designs. Here, for example, is a stylized version of the Japanese chrysanthemum seen in the center of a purple Northwood *WISHBONE* bowl.

A marigold Dugan/Diamond *QUESTION MARKS* compote which boasts two more patterns! *GEORGIA BELLE (PEACH)* is on the exterior and *PUZZLE* is on the foot. Sometimes this piece was flattened out into a stemmed cake plate. $75-$100. (There is a more common *QUESTION MARKS* two handled bon bon which has a plain exterior.)

Both the Aesthetic and Art Nouveau designers loved the sunflower motif. It can be seen on Carnival Glass too, though under a different name. Here it is on a marigold *DANDELION* tumbler by Northwood. The design is in reality a sunflower, which is how it was originally described in the contemporary Butler Brothers catalogs. $50-$70.

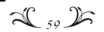

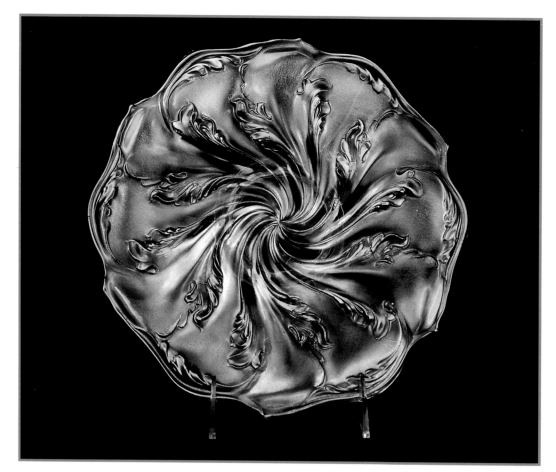

A marigold Imperial *ACANTHUS* plate with tremendous iridescence. The pattern design echoes the Rococo style. $150-$200.

Classic Carnival Harmony

Classic Carnival has no *one,* single style. It is a harmony, an interwoven blend. There are well over a thousand different Carnival Glass patterns. They fall naturally into just a few thematic groups, each of these groups picking up its characteristics from the decorative style or trend that inspired it. The use of pattern is truly eclectic. Carnival represents the popularization of a fusion of styles. Art Nouveau and the Arts and Crafts Movements were represented, Tiffany's wonderful glassware was emulated, intricate cut glass designs were copied. Carnival patterns reflect the style of the day—the wallpaper, the textiles, the crafts, the latest fashions. Carnival represents the people's aspirations and desires: to brighten a dull working class home with glittering iridescent glass; to own something that looked like Tiffany, which they never thought they could afford; to possess a delightful object. In the words of Walter Crane, a renowned artist and writer who died in 1915, "artists may take motives or inspirations from the past, or from the present, it matters not, so long as their work has life and beauty."[5] Carnival has that life and beauty. Carnival has a magical quality of its own.

The Carnival Glass patterns that are detailed and illustrated in Part Two all appear on Classic Carnival—that which was made in the United States from around 1907 up to around the mid 1920s. It is not an exhaustive list: not all patterns are covered. It would be outside the scope of this book to cover every single known Carnival pattern. Instead, patterns have been chosen that are representative of the popular contemporary themes—peacocks, fruit, flowers, and so on — forming a framework for the appreciation and identification of this unique decorative art form. Where relevant, the themed areas are split into patterns that are executed in a realistic manner and those that are stylized.

Each pattern is considered in terms of its design elements, shapes, and colors. The separate pattern index lists them all alphabetically. It should also be noted that not all shapes mentioned are known in all stated colors for that particular pattern. *We have listed known colors for the pattern in general and not for each individual shape.* Please also note that amethyst/purple is grouped rather than being noted separately. Similarly, blue is not qualified as being cobalt or the lighter copper blue. For a full definition of known Carnival colors, see Appendix One. The reader is referred to the Foreword for an explanation of the value ranges that have been assigned to the Carnival Glass items illustrated in color throughout the book.

Please note that where measurements are given they are approximate. Much Carnival had some element of hand finishing which makes absolute standardization of size very difficult. Measurements are in inches and, unless stated, usually refer to the diameter of bowls and plates.

A purple water pitcher and tumbler in Imperial's *DIAMOND LACE*, a Carnival Glass pattern that responded to the popular demand for cut glass. Such patterns take iridescence extremely well, producing scintillating results. $400-$600 for a set comprising a pitcher and six tumblers.

[1] W.R. Lethaby on the influence of the Arts and Crafts Movement. "Art and Workmanship." Number 1 *The Imprint.* January 1913.

[2] Robert and Deborah Truitt, *Collectible Bohemian Glass, 1880-1940* (Kensington, Maryland: B&D Glass, 1995).

[3] Larry Freeman, *Iridescent Glass* (Watkins Glen, New York: Century House. 1956, 1964).

[4] Charles R Hajdamach, *British Glass, 1800-1914* (Woodbridge, Suffolk, England: Antique Collector's Club Ltd., 1991).

[5] Walter Crane, *Of the Decorative Illustration of Books Old and New* (London, England: G. Bell & Sons. (Re-issue) 1972).

Another superb example of Northwood's *PEACOCKS*, an aqua opal ruffled bowl with an outstanding pastel iridescence. $1500-$3000. (Note that the golden-toned, butterscotch iridescence will usually command a slightly lower price.)

Carnival peacocks and their inspirations. Top left: a peacock "illuminated" letter *A* from *The Studio* in 1902. Top right: a peacock feather "illuminated" letter *P* from an early 1900s edition of *Art and Decorations Paris*. Bottom left: detail from Northwood's *PEACOCKS (ON THE FENCE)* design. Bottom right: detail from Fenton's *FLUFFY PEACOCK* design.

Where better to begin looking at Carnival patterns than with the peacocks? No image encapsulates the essence of Carnival more than the peacock. The ancient proverb "fine feathers make fine birds" epitomizes the glorious peacock, a favorite of artists and designers through the ages. As a motif, the peacock has an elegant, readily recognizable shape: a slender head, long neck, and splendidly arrogant and magnificent tail. When the tail is fanned out, it becomes an exquisite, repeating tracery of flowing fronds, thrown into relief by its many vibrant "eyes." According to ancient Greek legend, a giant named Argus boasted one hundred eyes, of which fifty remained open while the other fifty slept. After the giant's death, the goddess Hera distributed the eyes of Argus over the tail of her favorite bird, the peacock, thereby making its plumage so brilliant.

The peacock was a favorite motif in Japanese design dating back to the eighth century. As the Japanese style began to inspire the Arts and Crafts, Aesthetic, and Art Nouveau movements of the late nineteenth century, the peacock motif entered the repertoires of these movements. Peacocks (or their feathers) were everywhere—on magazine covers, on wallpaper and textiles, on art glass and lampshades. John Fenton, the founder of the Millersburg Glass Company, loved the birds. He is reported to have had a flock of peacocks that roamed at will in the vicinity of the Millersburg Glass plant. It seems that they also had a liking for the lawn of Millersburg's most famous public building—the Courthouse—and frequently terrified both pedestrians and horses with their raucous cries.

Most Carnival Glass manufacturers made patterns featuring the peacock or a motif representing its feathers. Sometimes the design was executed in a **naturalistic** way, the bird appearing lifelike and realistic, the design suggesting life and movement. Sometimes the design was interpreted in a **stylized** manner. (Stylization is where the artist portrays an image or a form in a recognizable, but not a naturalistic, way.) On the stylized peacock patterns we see a simplified interpretation of the peacock, often as a stiff and rather formal figure, with little portrayal of detail. Some designs took only the **idea** of the peacock feather and used an interpretation of it as the design.

Realistic/Naturalistic Patterns

PEACOCKS (ON THE FENCE)—Northwood

For many this pattern is the true essence of Carnival Glass. It is a harmonious and elegant composition, featuring two peacocks, one with a fanned out tail, upon a fence. The mould detail seen on the peacock feathers, the lattice work, and the flowers is superb. The background may be stippled—this adds to the iridescent effect and therefore, the value. These Northwood items usually have excellent iridescence, the multiple colors of which suggest the natural brilliant hues of the peacock. The exterior is usually ribbed but may sometimes be found with Northwood's *BASKETWEAVE* pattern. Ads for Northwood's *PEACOCKS* first appeared in the Butler Brothers catalogs in 1912.

Shapes: 8" bowls and 9" plates only. Ruffled edges or pie crust edges on the bowls. Plates are fluted. Both the plates and bowls are collar based.

Colors: marigold, amethyst/purple, blue, green, white, ice green, ice blue, and aqua opal. Rare and offbeat shades include horehound, lavender, smoke, lime, Renninger blue, and blue slag (sorbini).

PEACOCK AT URN—Fenton, Northwood, and Millersburg (also *PEACOCK*. Millersburg*)

This pattern is a masterpiece of flowing design and balanced composition. Look at the line drawing: focus on the peacock's tail feathers and allow your gaze to be drawn round the body of the peacock, up its stately neck and then, with the flowers and the leaves, to the urn at the top. The flower sprigs and leaves echo the movement around and the panels on the urn echo the plumes in the peacock's tail. It's beautiful—no other word will suffice. The mould work is astonishing and the final execution of the pattern in iridized glass with its changing hues is the "icing on the cake." *PEACOCK AT URN* was made by Fenton, Northwood, and Millersburg. Though the main, interior design is similar, there are distinct differences. The easiest way to tell them apart is to look at the exterior of the piece. Fenton's items are the only ones to have the *BEARDED BERRY* pattern and they have a plain marie (collar base). Northwood's *PEACOCK AT URN* has a *WIDE PANEL* exterior and there's usually an N in a circle trade mark on the marie. The Millersburg pieces can easily be spotted, as they usually have a many rayed star on the marie. Ads for Millersburg's *PEACOCK AT URN* first appeared in the Butler Brothers catalogs in 1911, Fenton ads followed a year later in 1912. Northwood probably made their version around the same time as Fenton.

*Note that the Millersburg version of this pattern where the urn is not beaded and there is no bee is called *PEACOCK*.

Fenton

Shapes: 8" bowls, 9" plates, and stemmed compotes. Bowls may have ruffled edges, candy ribbon edges, or may be round ice cream shaped. Plates have a fluted edge and are usually very flat indeed. Both the plates and bowls are collar based.

PEACOCK AT URN
by Northwood.

Colors: marigold, amethyst/purple, blue, and green. Rarer shades mainly found on bowls include red, white, vaseline, aqua, lime, moonstone, and Persian blue.

Northwood

Shapes: ice cream sets that comprise one large 10" bowl and six small 6" bowls. These bowls have scalloped edges and are unruffled. Usually sold as separate items. Seldom found are large ruffled bowls, small 6" plates, and the 12" chop plate. Both the plates and bowls are collar based.

Colors: marigold, amethyst/purple, blue. Harder to find are green, smoke, white, ice blue, lime green, and ice green. The most scarce colors are aqua opal, Renninger blue, and sapphire blue.

Notes: Northwood's *PEACOCK AT URN* items may also sometimes be found with stippling covering the central part of the background. Not all colors are found in all shapes. A variation in the tiara (horn-like projections on the peacock's head) has been found.[1] Some scarce examples of Northwood's *PEACOCK AT URN* have only two tiara on the peacock's head. Most examples have four tiara. There are also minor differences in the details on the bee. A further variant, with no bee, has been reported by Tom Mordini.

Millersburg

Shapes: large 10" and 6" bowls. Less often seen are medium sized 8" bowls. Edges may be ruffled, scalloped or, rarely, candy ribbon. Ice cream shapes are also found. Rare giant compotes, small plates, and whimsey shapes such as the rosebowl and chop plates are known. Both the plates and bowls are collar based.

Colors: marigold, amethyst/purple, green. Rarely seen are blue and vaseline.

Notes: there are many detailed variations to the pattern in the Millersburg pieces. The urn and beading vary, the bee may be present or not. For a full and detailed explanation of the varieties in this pattern by Millersburg, see Marie McGee's *Millersburg Glass*.[2]

PEACOCK AT THE FOUNTAIN—Northwood and Dugan/Diamond

A delightful design displaying an Oriental influence, *PEACOCK AT THE FOUNTAIN* is found in a range of shapes, including water sets and table sets. The floral element in particular is very Japanese in style. The pattern is on the exterior of the items. This is logical, as the shapes that *PEACOCK AT THE FOUNTAIN* were made in show the design better on the outside. Ads for Northwood's *PEACOCK AT THE FOUNTAIN* first appeared in the 1912 Butler Brothers catalogs. In 1914, Harry Northwood applied for, and was granted, a patent for this pattern. However, items in the *PEACOCK AT THE FOUNTAIN* water set are found that have been made by the Dugan/Diamond company. The design must have been very popular because a few years later, in 1918, it was also copied onto enameled "Nurock" kitchenware! The kitchenware items were made by "one of the best Rockingham factories" and boasted a "heavily embossed peacock and floral decoration" according to the Butler Brothers 1918 ad.

Detail from Northwood's *PEACOCK AT THE FOUNTAIN*.

The popularity of Northwood's *PEACOCK AT THE FOUNTAIN* can be seen by the fact that it was copied onto Rockingham "Nurock" kitchenware. This Butler Brothers ad from 1918 shows the range of kitchenware available. The pattern is virtually identical to the Northwood original.

Northwood

Shapes: full sets of this pattern were made, rather than individual items. Water sets (with a standard shaped pitcher), table sets, berry sets, and punch sets are those most often seen. Pieces from the set are often sold as individual items. Also known are rare compotes (where the pattern is on the interior), footed "orange" bowls, and a rare, whimsey spittoon shape. Almost all items are marked with the N trademark.

Colors: marigold, amethyst/purple, and blue. Other colors such as white, green, ice blue, ice green, and aqua opalescent are rare.

Dugan/Diamond

Shape: only the water set is known. The pitcher is the standard shape.

Colors: blue. Scarcer in marigold and amethyst/purple. Amber is very unusual.

Notes: it is easy to tell the Northwood and Dugan/Diamond versions apart. On the tumbler, look for the top row of beads on the fountain. There are eight beads on the Northwood fountain and only six beads on the Dugan/Diamond version. Some examples however, have seven beads. If in doubt, check the width of the mouth of the tumbler. The Northwood version is just over 3", while the Dugan one is just under 3".

Stylized Patterns

PEACOCK AND GRAPE—Fenton

A typical Fenton design characteristic is exhibited on this popular pattern—an alternately repeated motif, set in a panel type of frame. In this stylized peacock design, the simple motif is repeated four times. In between each peacock frame is one containing grapes. A stylized feather forms the wheel motif as a central focus to the complete pattern. It's a pleasing and well balanced design that was first advertised in 1913 and is probably one of the more easily found Fenton patterns. The exterior pattern found most frequently on *PEACOCK AND GRAPE* is *BEARDED BERRY*.

Shapes: 8" bowls and 9" plates are the only shapes known. They may have spatula shaped feet or may be collar based. Bowls may be ruffled, ice cream shaped, or have candy ribbon edging.

Colors: marigold, amethyst/purple, blue, and green. Less often seen are unusual colors such as amber, amberina, red, vaseline, vaseline opal, lime green opal, smoke, black amethyst, red slag, white, and moonstone. Bowls are found in the unusual colors.

PEACOCK AND DAHLIA—Fenton

Virtually identical in concept to *PEACOCK AND GRAPE* (though seen much less often), the grapes are replaced by a stylized, dahlia-like flower. This piece may have a plain exterior or may carry the more unusual Fenton back pattern *BERRY AND LEAF CIRCLE*.

Shapes: this pattern is distinctive in that it is found on smaller sized bowls than usual, 6 to 7" in diameter. They are ruffled or ice cream shaped. Scarce 7 to 8" diameter plates are also found.

Colors: marigold, amethyst/purple, blue, green, aqua, and vaseline. Plates are currently known only in marigold.

FLUFFY PEACOCK—Fenton

A highly stylized design in which the tail feathers of the peacock are minimized and exaggerated. Alongside the peacock is a large peacock feather, very similar in appearance to that used on Fenton's *PANTHER* design. As on the *PANTHER*, it is used here as part of the overall design concept and cleverly disguises the mould seams (which run along the spine of the feather). The design was first shown in the Butler Brothers catalogs in 1911.

Shapes: known only in a water set. The pitcher is bulbous and mould blown.

Colors: marigold, amethyst/purple, blue, and green.

NUROCK SPECIALTIES

Goods in demand every day in the week, every week in the year.

Extra hard body, highly glazed, prominently embossed. Made by one of the best Rockingham factories. All pieces except the bowls with heavily embossed peacock and floral decorations. Sold in any quantity.

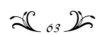

STRUTTING PEACOCK—Westmoreland

This is a distinctive design, the peacock's tail being rounded and simplified. The background has a stippled effect and the top edge of the piece has a characteristic "eyeball" design. This "eyeball" design is also found on Westmoreland's *SHELL AND JEWEL* sugar and creamer set. The pattern is also called "Victor." Chas West Wilson[3] claims that Westmoreland were the first to produce the "Victor" design. These items have been reproduced. Originals are believed to have uniridized lids.

Shapes: known only in a creamer and lidded sugar.

Colors: amethyst/purple and green.

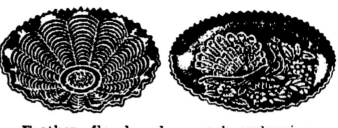
A contrast in styles seen on peacock patterns. Northwood's *NIPPON* (left) and *PEACOCKS (ON THE FENCE)* are featured in this detail from a 1912 Butler Brothers catalog.

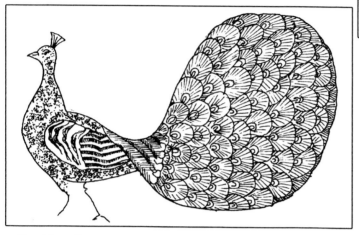

Detail from Westmoreland's highly stylized *STRUTTING PEACOCK*.

Inspired Patterns

These are patterns in which the artist took the idea of the peacock and its feather and used it to create a design that is reminiscent of the shape and concept of the bird and/or its feathers.

PEACOCK TAIL—Fenton

At first glance, this is simply a curvilinear design, fanning outward. Its name suggests, however, that the pattern is based on the concept of peacock feathers. The contemporary Butler Brothers catalogs called it a feather design. But is it? Could this simply be a classic rosette—a petal design—and not inspired by peacock feathers at all? Rose Presznick, the pioneering Carnival researcher and collector, decided to name the pattern "Flowering Almond," suggesting that she interpreted this as a stylized flower design. Whichever way previous observers may have interpreted the pattern—peacock tail feathers or stylized blossoms—it is undoubtedly a simple and effective design that took iridescence very well. The pattern was first seen in 1910 catalogs.

Shapes: bowls in various sizes. Edges may be ruffled, ice cream shaped, candy ribbon, square, or three-sided (tri-cornered). Small plates, compotes, hat shapes, and bonbons are also found.

Colors: marigold, amethyst/purple, blue, and green. Unusual colors include lime green, vaseline, lime green opal, and red.

Notes: can be found on the interior of some *APRIL SHOWERS* vases.

NIPPON—Northwood

Very similar to Fenton's *PEACOCK TAIL* in concept, the main difference in this pattern is the central motif, which is a stylized flower. It bears a close resemblance to the Imperial crest of Japan, the sixteen petaled chrysanthemum, hence its name *NIPPON* (meaning Japan). The chrysanthemum is the national flower of Japan. Like Fenton's *PEACOCK TAIL*, *NIPPON* could be seen as a floral design. However, contemporary Butler Brothers ads (April 1912) referred to this pattern as a feather design, which lends credence to the view that *NIPPON* was intended to be representative of stylized peacock feathers. The exterior may be ribbed or have the *BASKETWEAVE* pattern.

Shapes: 8" ruffled or pie crust edge bowls and rare 9" plates.

Colors: marigold, amethyst/purple, green, white, ice green, and ice blue. Unusual colors are lime green, lime green opal, and cobalt blue. Aqua opal is reported. Plates are more restricted in their color range.

FANTAIL—Fenton

Described in 1912 Butler Brothers ads as a "peacock feather" design, *FANTAIL* was undoubtedly inspired by the glorious tail feathers of that bird. Seldom found, this design is a simple radiating whirl. The peacock tail fan, complete with a multitude of "eyes," is repeated seven times around the design. The pattern is on the interior, *BUTTERFLY AND BERRY* being the exterior partner pattern.

Shapes: deep, footed bowls both ruffled and unruffled (ice cream shaped); very rare chop plate.

Colors: marigold and blue.

STREAM OF HEARTS—Fenton

STREAM OF HEARTS is similar in design to the *FANTAIL* pattern in that it is a radiating whirl of stylized peacock feathers. In this case, though, there are only four peacock tail fans and they are portrayed in closer detail, the "eyes" appearing as heart shapes. The exterior pattern on this scarce piece is *PERSIAN MEDALLION*.

Shape: the only known shape in *STREAM OF HEARTS* is the stemmed compote.

Color: the only known color is marigold.

Detail from Fenton's *STREAM OF HEARTS* pattern.

HEART AND VINE—Fenton

The stylized hearts are feathery tendrils of the peacock's tail. They entwine in a lazy necklace around the pattern. Introduced in 1911, it was a multi-purpose design: the blank middle area allowed the addition of an extra element—advertising! So, this basic design was also utilized for the scarce *SPECTOR DEPARTMENT STORE* advertising piece and the *COOLEEMEE* plate ("Souvenir of J.N. Ledford Company, Cooleemee, NC"). Furthermore, the replacement of the advertising with a horseshoe motif changed it into the rare *HEART AND HORSESHOE* pattern.

Shapes: 8" bowls and 9" plates. Bowls are ruffled, candy ribbon, or ice cream shaped.

Colors: marigold, amethyst/purple, blue, and green. Plates have not yet been found in green.

Notes: *SPECTOR DEPARTMENT STORE* and *COOLEEMEE* items are only found in the plate shape in marigold. *HEART AND HORSESHOE* is only found in the ruffled bowl shape, also only in marigold.

SCROLL EMBOSSED—Imperial

Forget the stereotype image of the peacock feather, and visualize—for a moment—the shape of the "eye" and the impression of the concentric circles of changing hues in the feathers above it. This is what *SCROLL EMBOSSED* is—an imaginative representation of the peacock feather. It is comparable to similar Art Nouveau illustrations. Rose Presznick named this pattern "Peacock Eye," implying that she also saw the link.

Introduced in 1911, Imperial's *SCROLL EMBOSSED* has a plain interior as well as several interesting geometric exteriors. The plates and some bowls usually have a plain exterior, though the *FILE* exterior is found on many bowls too. *EASTERN STAR* is seen on the outside of medium sized compotes, but the most unusual exterior pattern is *HOBSTAR AND TASSEL* that is found on the exterior of scarce bowls.

Shapes: 5, 7, and 8" bowls—mainly ruffled (sizes are approximate), 9" plates; medium sized, small and scarce miniature compotes are found.

Colors: marigold and purple in most shapes. Helios, smoke, amber, and aqua only on some of the shapes.

Notes: Sowerby in Tyneside, England copied the Imperial version of *SCROLL EMBOSSED* in the 1920s. It can be found on some small dishes and on the inside of the *DIVING DOLPHINS* bowls.

BEADED BULLSEYE—Imperial

It is not so easy to see this as a peacock's tail motif, but could it be the inspiration on this lovely vase? Concentrate on the bull's eye shapes at the top of the pattern, then follow them downwards. Upright peacock feathers? The bull's eye shapes are the "eye" in the feather.

Shape: vases from 6 to 14" high.

Colors: marigold, amethyst/purple, helios. More unusual colors are amber, smoke, lime green, blue, green, and vaseline.

RIBBON TIE/COMET—Fenton

Here is another pattern that could just have been inspired by the peacock's tail. Elongated fan shapes, radiating out from the center of the pattern, are the elements on this very simplified design. It's difficult to be certain what the inspiration was, but very possibly it was the peacock tail. It could, however, be a much used, classical pattern motif known as a skirl. Employed in designs spanning many centuries, the skirl is simply a rotating circle, intended to give an idea of circular motion.

Shapes: 8" bowls, ruffled or candy ribbon edged. Low bowls are sometimes considered to be "ruffled" plates.

Colors: marigold, amethyst/purple, blue, and green.

Even More Peacocks

Other patterns that feature the peacock tail motif, yet are scarce and seldom seen, are *PEACOCK TAIL AND DAISY* and *HEART AND TREES*, both rare Fenton bowls. In the latter, the peacock tail feather is used in a very stylized design. The "eyes" of the peacock's feather appear as heart shapes, circling around the pattern. Northwood's *TORNADO* vase has a motif that could well be a stylized peacock feather. Millersburg produced a pretty feather pattern, but although the name *PEACOCK TAIL VARIANT* suggests a link, it really has little to suggest the typical style of the peacock feather. Millersburg's *ROSALIND* is yet another possible peacock feather design. Other patterns incorporate the stylized peacock tail as part the overall design, rather than the main element; a good example is Fenton's *PANTHER*.

[1] In late 1997, a survey on Northwood's *PEACOCK AT URN* was carried out using the medium of the Internet, through the Woodsland World Wide Carnival Glass Association (www.cga). The aim was to gather information from as many collectors as possible on the variations spotted by club members regarding the peacock's tiara. It was established that about twenty percent of Northwood's ice cream set items (large and small bowls) in this pattern are the variant that has just two tiara on the bird's head. The remaining eighty percent of *PEACOCK AT URN* pieces, which included both large and small ice cream bowls as well as several chop plates, have the regular four tiara.

[2] Marie McGee, *Millersburg Glass: As I Know It* (Marietta, Ohio: Antique Publications, 1995).

[3] Chas West Wilson, *Westmoreland Glass* (Paducah, Kentucky: Collector Books, 1996).

The real essence of Carnival Glass for many collectors, Northwood's *PEACOCKS* pattern is brilliant in its design and an ever popular pattern. This blue plate is stippled, adding to the iridescent quality and to the value. $900-$1600. An electric blue, stippled plate sold in 2007 for $2600.

PEACOCK AT URN is a masterpiece of design. It was a pattern used by Fenton, Millersburg, and Northwood. This piece is a Persian blue ruffled bowl, a color only made by Fenton. $1000-$2000.

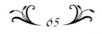

Close-up of a blue Fenton *PEACOCK AT URN* plate showing the exceptional quality of the mould work. There is a bee near the peacock's beak. The plate has a *BEARDED BERRY* exterior pattern that clearly identifies it as a Fenton product.

Close-up of a blue Northwood *PEACOCK AT URN* sauce (or small ice cream). Again, there is a bee near the peacock's beak. The exterior pattern is *WIDE PANEL,* which indicates Northwood was the maker. Normally these sauces are also N̲ marked. $100-$150.

Close-up of an amethyst Millersburg *PEACOCK* sauce (or small ice cream). There is no bee. The marie has a many-rayed star, indicative of Millersburg. $150-$200.

A glorious, ice blue Northwood *PEACOCK AT URN* master ice cream bowl. It has *WIDE PANEL* exterior and is N̲ marked. $800-$1200.

A purple Northwood *PEACOCK AT THE FOUNTAIN* butterdish ($250-375) and covered sugar ($200-$300). Although Northwood registered the design as "Garden Scene" at the United States Patent Office in 1914, it was actually copied by Dugan/Diamond to be used on their water sets.

Fenton's *PEACOCK AND DAHLIA* is very similar in concept to *PEACOCK AND GRAPE.* It's seen here on an 8" ice cream shape bowl in amethyst, a rather scarce color for this pattern. $300-$400.

Fenton's *PEACOCK AND GRAPE* was a popular pattern and is easily found. Some colors, however, are hard to find; this red slag ruffled bowl is one such example. $1000-$1500.

A highly stylized portrayal of the peacock is seen on Fenton's *FLUFFY PEACOCK* pattern. This is an amethyst tumbler. $70-$100.

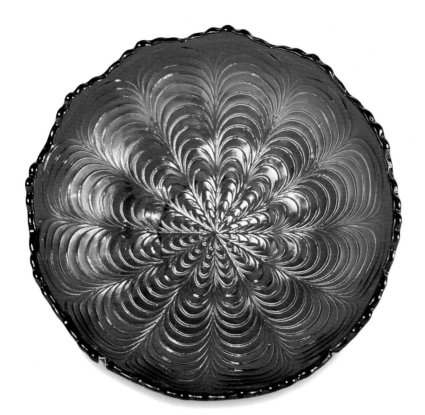

PEACOCK TAIL is a Fenton design that was inspired by the peacock feather motif. It is seen here on a highly desirable 6.5" red ice cream shape bowl. $1000-$2500

Another pattern inspired by peacock tail feathers—a blue Fenton FANTAIL bowl. $200-$500.

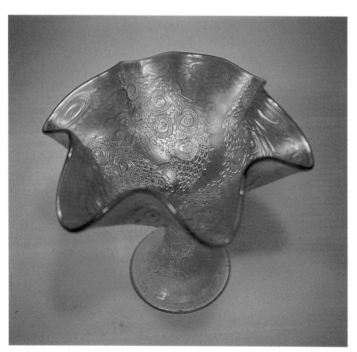

Fenton's STREAM OF HEARTS pattern represents stylized peacock feathers. It is only found on the marigold compote. Note the intentionally clear stem. $50-$125.

Imperial's *SCROLL EMBOSSED* is an imaginative representation of the "eye" of a peacock's tail feather and is similar to various Art Nouveau representations of the peacock's tail. It is truly spectacular on this vivid, electric purple plate. $450-$550.

Imperial also made this delightful and scarce *SCROLL EMBOSSED* miniature compote: it is only 3" high. $200-$300.

Three sizes of Imperial *BEADED BULLSEYE* vase. From left: purple vase with superb iridescence ($150-$200), rare vaseline that glows strongly under UV (ultraviolet) light ($400-$500), and marigold ($100-$150). All are from the same mould but were swung to different heights.

Fenton's *RIBBON TIE* seen on a blue ruffled bowl. Is this another representation of the peacock feather? $150-$200.

Three *TORNADO* vases. On the left is a marigold non-ribbed Northwood version ($300-$500) and on the right a purple ribbed version also by Northwood ($800-$1400). In the center is the much rarer marigold variant, maker currently unknown ($2000-$2500). The *TORNADO* vase was probably made to imitate Tiffany and Loetz vases, and the twisting "tornado" motif was very likely another representation of the peacock feather. Thomas Webb in England is a possible maker of the variant.

"Say it with flowers."

—Slogan for the Society of American Florists. Patrick O'Keefe (1872-1934), United States advertising agent.

Imperial's *OPEN ROSE* plate in rich amber. A very wide range of items was made in this delightful pattern. $300-$500. An example with magnificent iridescence sold for $1700 in 2005.

Flowers have been a natural source of artistic inspiration through the centuries. No one artistic movement can hold claim to their use. They have featured in the art of early Islam and Ancient Greece, in medieval and Renaissance art, in Elizabethan ornament, and Art Nouveau designs. During the decades leading up to the advent of Carnival Glass, the world had seen trade resume with Japan, after almost two hundred years of self-imposed isolation. The subsequent craze for the Japanese style and the use of Oriental design motifs—in particular the chrysanthemum and the sunflower—reflected the changes in world trade. The Japanese observation of nature and flowers, coupled with their subtle appreciation of decoration and form, caught the imagination and influenced the decorative arts arena. Floral designs and influences were all around: on wallpaper, textiles, and clothing. The dining tables of "society" were piled high with extravagant, floral centerpiece arrangements.

Craftwork and embroidery were very popular and pattern books containing hundreds of suggested designs were easily available. One in particular,[1] issued by Wm. Briggs and Co. Ltd. in around 1900 showed over five hundred motifs for craftspeople. Additionally, there were many familiar designs: pansies, poppies, roses, lilies, thistles, daisies, and much more. Indeed, several magnificent floral designs were produced in Carnival Glass that imitate embroidery stitches. These will be looked at later in Part Two, Chapter Nine.

The Carnival glassmakers pursued their art surrounded by these influences. What better way to bring beauty into the dark homes of an industrial age than to capture the magnificence of flowers on shimmering, iridescent glass? Floral designs on Carnival Glass range from naturalistic portrayals, executed in such a realistic manner that you feel you can almost touch the petals and smell the perfume, through fully stylized designs bearing only a slight resemblance to their source of inspiration. Well over a hundred patterns feature a flower or group of flowers as the main element of design. Many more utilize them as an integral and decorative part of the background. The threads of many design sources can be seen. A true hybrid of inspirational ideas produced the glorious, eclectic floral designs on Carnival Glass.

Realistic/Naturalistic Patterns

In the realistic flower patterns noted below, the portrayal of the flowers is very natural, the flowers can be easily identified. The development of the camera and its associated realism must have been something of a challenge to designers. Could they produce something that gave as natural an effect as the camera did? In 1900, Eastman Kodak had introduced the Box Brownie camera. Equipped with cheap six-photo rolls, anyone could produce a realistic image. Perhaps these superb floral designs were a response to the visual impact of the camera, with the added qualities of being both tactile and iridescent!

ROSE SHOW—Northwood

This is possibly the supreme Carnival floral design, breathtaking in its realism and exemplifying the very best in skilled mould making.

The rose petals on this pattern stand up as if they are sculpted, raised from the surface in deep relief. Great attention is paid to naturalistic accuracy—the whole design a harmonious grouping, simple yet full of detail. The background to the roses is a distinctive design known as *WOVEN WONDER*; it is also repeated on the exterior of the piece. These items are usually endowed with stunning iridescence and are rightly considered to be one of the most desirable of Carnival designs.

Shapes: 8" bowls and 9" plates only. The edges of both are scalloped; the bowls are ruffled.

Colors: marigold, amethyst/purple, blue, and white. Unusual colors are ice blue, ice green, green, aqua opalescent, and custard. Various rare opalescent shades are also known. Lime green and vaseline are reported for the plate.

Notes: there is a *ROSE SHOW VARIANT* that is attributed to Northwood: similar in concept to *ROSE SHOW*, but made of thinner glass and with a shallower design. Bowls and plates are known in marigold, blue, and Renninger blue.

Northwood's splendid *ROSE SHOW*.

POPPY SHOW—Northwood

The "sister" pattern to *ROSE SHOW* and equally as stunning, *POPPY SHOW* is a most desirable and sought after pattern. Again, the flowers are portrayed in great, naturalistic detail. The effect is three dimensional, the poppies standing out against the textured background. This distinctive background pattern is also repeated on the exterior of the piece and is known as *BARK*.

Shapes: 8" bowls and 9" plates only. The edges of both are scalloped; the bowls are ruffled.

Colors: marigold, amethyst/purple, blue, white, ice blue, ice green, and lime green. One bowl and one plate only are currently known in aqua opalescent. One plate is reported in ice green opalescent.[2]

POPPY SHOW—Imperial

Northwood made *POPPY SHOW* as an interior pattern on bowls and plates. *POPPY SHOW* from Imperial, however, was only made as an exterior vase pattern: an impressive and majestic piece, standing a full 12" high. The mouldwork on this item is outstanding, the densely packed poppy heads jostling with each other for attention. The detail is breathtaking; the overall effect can only be described as stunning. Imagine one of these magnificent vases full of flowers set on the table in a dark room back in the early 1900s. It would surely have brought a touch of gracious living.

Shape: vase only, as moulded and not swung.

Colors: marigold, amethyst/purple, helios, smoke, and rare amber.

OPEN ROSE/ LUSTRE ROSE—Imperial

As lovely and as realistic as Northwood's fabulous *ROSE SHOW* (but lacking the deep sculptured effect of that pattern), Imperial's *ROSE* designs are executed with attention to fine detail. The background to these lovely items has a fine stippled effect. This pattern was introduced around 1912, when a very wide range of shapes appeared in several Butler Brothers ads, described as "new designs and shapes, relief embossed roses ... the richest set yet." It continued to be advertised in Imperial catalogs right through to the early 1920s. Interestingly, it was referred to in those catalogs as "Rose design—American Beauty Roses." Carnival collectors have, in the past, confusingly established two names for this pattern. However, it seems that they were intended by the manufacturer to be a series in the same pattern. *LUSTRE ROSE* is often applied to the table sets and water sets. *OPEN ROSE* is more often applied to the bowls and plates.

Shapes: 5 and 10" bowls (berry sets), also 8" bowls and 9" plates (all collar based). Bowls may be ruffled or ice cream shaped. There are also footed bowls and centerpiece bowls, ferneries, nutbowls and rosebowls, table sets and water sets.

Colors: marigold, amethyst/purple, helios, amber, smoke, clambroth, aqua, and pale blue. Some items are known in vaseline. The fernery is also found in blue.

BASKET OF ROSES—Northwood

This pattern is very similar to Fenton's *WREATH OF ROSES* design—both are naturalistic interpretations, yet rendered in a far less sculpted manner than the *ROSE SHOW*. The design features a circle of roses, like a necklace, joined by a thorny stem. The background on some of these bonbons is finely stippled, which enhances the iridescence to great effect. The exterior pattern is *BASKETWEAVE. BASKET OF ROSES* is only known in the handled bonbon shape and is scarce. This shape may be confused with a similar Fenton piece. See notes below for differences.

Shape: handled bonbon only; stippled or plain.
Colors: marigold, amethyst/purple, and blue.
Notes: Northwood's *BASKET OF ROSES* has no center design. It usually has the N mark on the marie and carries the *BASKETWEAVE* pattern on its exterior. There are two other similar patterns, from Fenton and Dugan/Diamond respectively. Fenton's *WREATH OF ROSES* has a center design of leaves and rosebuds and does *not* have a *BASKETWEAVE* exterior. Fenton's *WREATH OF ROSES* is also found in a stemmed compote shape, as well as a stunning punch set. The Dugan/Diamond variant, *WREATH OF ROSES,* is known in a small rosebowl or nutbowl (marigold and amethyst) with a rose wreath design on the outside.

DANDELION—Northwood

This pattern was first advertised in the Butler Brothers catalog of February 1912. The ad was for a "Florentine Iridescent Lemonade Assortment." One of the two tankard water pitchers illustrated was what collectors now call *DANDELION*—at the time, however, it was actually called "Sunflower." It was an apt choice, for that's what the flower almost certainly was supposed to be. The sunflower was a much loved graphic symbol of the Aesthetic and Art Nouveau movements. The pioneering collector/researchers Rose Presznick and Marion Hartung differed on what the flower's identity was. Presznick called the pattern on the tankard water set "Sunflower" but Hartung dismissed the suggestion, insisting that "it is possible that some sort of wild flower was intended here, but we can certainly rule out the sunflower!"[3] Hartung's choice—*DANDELION*—became the accepted pattern name. The waters become a little muddied, however, when you realize that there are *two* different Northwood patterns both known as *DANDELION*.

DANDELION Water Set

This is a splendid tankard water set. The flower is face on, in high relief over a series of panels. The pitcher is mould blown and bell shaped at the bottom; the clear handle is applied. A rare variant of the tumbler, only known in ice green, has ribbing inside.

Shape: tankard water set only.

Colors: marigold, amethyst/purple, green, ice blue, ice green, and white. Tumblers only are reported in smoke, horehound, and lavender.

DANDELION Mug

As the illustrations clearly show, this is a completely different design from that on the water set. The flower actually resembles a dandelion, rather than a sunflower. It is viewed sideways on and is set against a stippled background. An interesting variant exists: the *KNIGHTS TEMPLAR* mug. This was a souvenir edition of the *DANDELION* mug, produced for the 1912 Knights Templar Convention. It has the emblem of the Knights Templar and the dates "May 27, 28, 29 1912" moulded into the base.

Shape: mug only known.

Colors: marigold, amethyst/purple, blue, green, aqua opal, and ice blue opal.

Notes: the *KNIGHTS TEMPLAR* mug is only known in marigold, ice blue, and ice green.

Detail from Northwood's *DANDELION mug.*

ORIENTAL POPPY—Northwood

Seen in the same 1912 Butler Brothers ad as the *DANDELION* water set mentioned earlier, *ORIENTAL POPPY* is a most attractive, realistic design. The flower is in high relief, full on, flanked by buds and leaves and set against a series of panels. The mould detail is astonishing. Poppies, of course, were another favorite of the Art Nouveau designers. The pitchers are mould blown and have an applied handle.

Shapes: tankard water set. Carl Burns reports a "one of a kind" 11" marigold bowl in this pattern.[2]

Colors: marigold and amethyst/purple. Harder to find colors are green, blue, white, ice blue, ice green, smoke, olive, and lime green.

Notes: only the tumblers are known in smoke, lime, and olive green.

PANSY—Imperial

In mid-spring 1911, "Golden Luster" salad dishes were advertised in the Butler Brothers catalog at a cost of seventy-five cents for a dozen. Here you would have seen Imperial's *PANSY* pattern: a delightfully simple, yet realistically portrayed design. Fortunately for today's collector, *PANSY* was a popular seller and it is still fairly easy to find an example in the more plentiful colors. The background to the flowers is finely stippled, which gives a highly iridescent overall effect. The exterior pattern on the bowls is *ARCS*. The exterior pattern on the nappies and oval dishes is the splendid *QUILTED DIAMONDS*. The handle on the nappy is most attractively fashioned in the "rustic" style, giving the appearance of a twig.

Shapes: 8 to 9" ruffled bowl, oval dish, one handled nappy, and breakfast set (comprising sugar and creamer).

Colors: marigold, amethyst/purple, helios, smoke, clambroth, amber, lavender, and aqua.

Note: Rare blue is reported for the oval dish shape only.

CHRYSANTHEMUM (NUART)—Imperial

This is a stunningly beautiful and naturalistic rendition; the single flower looks astonishingly real. Around the edge of the chrysanthemum motif is a distinctive Greek key border. The exterior has a rayed, fluted pattern. Some examples have the moulded word "NUART" at the bottom right of the interior.

The CHRYSANTHEMUM pattern was illustrated in Imperial's 1915 catalog; it was also shown in their catalog from the early 1920s. The only shape made in this pattern was a large chop plate, described in the catalogs as a "cake plate." The contemporary description of the CHRYSANTHEMUM plate and its "sister" plate, the HOMESTEAD, is fascinating. Imperial was obviously conscious of the sales potential of these attractive items for they were described as follows: "Real Novelties! These two plates have a rim on the back which makes it possible to hang them to the wall, just like a china plaque. If put in the proper light, these satin finished iridescent pictures form very beautiful wall decorations."

Shape: 10" chop plate only.

Colors: marigold, amethyst/purple, helios, smoke, amber, white, and blue.

Notes: examples in some of the above colors are very few in number.

DAHLIA—Dugan/Diamond

This pattern is executed in great detail, the flower bloom standing out proudly from the surface of the glass. The individual petals of the flower are executed in astonishing detail. The craftsmanship of the mouldmaker must truly be admired. The scrolls and the pattern around the flower are most interesting in that they are representations of popular contemporary motifs, such as those seen in W. and G. Audsley's pattern book of 1882.[4] Similar in style to an older, non-iridized Dugan pattern called "Fan," the shapes that DAHLIA is found in are virtually identical in form to those in which "Fan" appeared. Indeed, "Fan" is basically the DAHLIA pattern, but without the dahlias! There is also a DAHLIA VARIANT. It is similar in shape and pattern detail, but differs in the size of the dahlia flower, which is much smaller on the variant.

Shapes: water set, table set, and berry set. The DAHLIA VARIANT is found only in a very rare tumbler.

Colors: marigold, amethyst/purple, and white. The white may have gilding, or indeed other colors such as blue, silver, or red painted onto the flowers. The DAHLIA VARIANT is only known in purple.

Notes: all items except the tumblers are footed. The tumblers appear to have feet, owing to the trompe l'oeil effect of the design. They actually rest on a flat base.

DOGWOOD SPRAYS—Dugan/Diamond

Loosely identified as dogwood, these pretty sprays of blossoms and leaves are repeated opposite each other to make up a wreath. There is no exterior pattern.

Shape: 8 to 9" bowls with a domed foot. They may be ruffled or candy ribbon edged.

Colors: marigold, amethyst/purple, blue, and peach opal.

POINSETTIA AND LATTICE—Northwood

POINSETTIA AND LATTICE is a detailed and intricate design. The mouldwork is superb, giving the flowers a very realistic, almost three-

Dugan/Diamond's superb DAHLIA water pitcher.

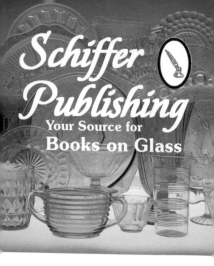

dimensional, effect. In the background, behind the flowers, is a lattice or trellis; its uniform rectangular grid contrasts with the flowing, organic effect of the flowers. The whole look is very evocative of William Morris's first, and very popular, wallpaper called "Trellis," which features flowers, leaves, and birds against a squared lattice background.

Shape: 8 to 9" bowls, ruffled and footed.

Colors: marigold, amethyst/purple, blue, green, white, lavender, ice blue, and aqua opalescent.

Northwood's *POINSETTIA AND LATTICE* design.

BLOSSOMTIME—Northwood

A wonderfully composed design, *BLOSSOMTIME* comprises interlaced arches of stylized branches and naturalistic, interwoven floral sprays. It has a satisfying symmetry that is softened by tiny leaf fronds and a fluid tracery of stems. It carries the *WILDFLOWER* pattern on its exterior.

Shape: stemmed compote only, the stem of which has an unusual spiral effect. *BLOSSOMTIME* is the only item known with this unique feature.

Colors: marigold, amethyst/purple, and green.

A purple Northwood *ROSE SHOW* ruffled bowl, with wonderful iridescent highlights in deep blue, purple, gold, and green. $500-$600.

The deep, sculpted mould work on this blue Northwood *ROSE SHOW* plate is a supreme example of the mould maker's skills. $1000-$2000.

Another outstanding example of Northwood's *ROSE SHOW*—a ruffled bowl in aqua opal, a sought after color. $1000-$2000. One sold in 2006 for $2200.

Close-up of a purple Northwood *POPPY SHOW* ruffled bowl showing the astonishing craftsmanship of the mould work.

The "sister" pattern to *ROSE SHOW* is Northwood's *POPPY SHOW,* seen here on a purple ruffled bowl. $600-$1000.

Northwood's *BASKET OF ROSES* purple bon bon seen here in the scarce, stippled version. $250-$400.

Is the flower on this elegant marigold tankard pitcher from Northwood a sunflower or a dandelion? Butler Brothers ads in 1912 described it as a "sunflower"—but today's collectors call the pattern *DANDELION*. $350-$400.

POPPY SHOW from a different manufacturer: this is Imperial's statuesque vase in marigold. $500-$1400.

Northwood *ORIENTAL POPPY* tumbler is purple, the iridescence has an attractive, predominantly green effect. $80-$100.

Detail from Northwood's *BLOSSOMTIME.*

This close-up of a *NUART CHRYSANTHEMUM* plate by Imperial shows the detailed mouldwork on the flower petals and leaves. Actually, this is taken from a modern version made by Summit Glass Company, using the old, original Imperial mould. Value of an original Imperial plate: $2000-$5000. (modern version: $100-$200).

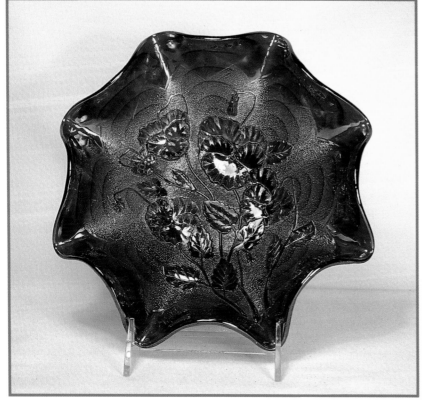

An outstanding, multicolored iridescence on a purple *PANSY* ruffled bowl from Imperial. $150-$450.

Northwood's *POINSETTIA AND LATTICE* ruffled bowl in an unusual and delicate shade of lavender. The whole look is very evocative of William Morris's first, and very popular, wallpaper called "Trellis." $800-$1000.

This detail from a cobalt blue, Northwood *POINSETTIA AND LATTICE* bowl clearly shows the intricate mouldwork and the contrast between the stippled background and the smooth lattice. $600-$1000. In electric blue, one sold in 2005 for $5500.

Stylized Patterns

A stylized design is one in which the floral motif is interpreted in a decorative and often simplified manner. The flower is derived from recognizable species, but it is then stylized to become part of the pattern itself. The ever popular floral patterns of William Morris that are seen on a variety of fabrics and wallpapers, as well as those of the Art Nouveau designers, utilized stylized flower forms. A particularly good example of a stylized floral design on Carnival Glass that undoubtedly derived its inspiration from Art Nouveau sources is Fenton's *IRIS* pattern. Compare it with the sketch of the iris done after the style of Maurice Verneuil.[5] The similarity of curves and sinuous lines is striking.

The iris motif was a popular one much used by Art Nouveau designers such as Eugene Grasset and Maurice Verneuil. This composite illustrates the similarities between Art Nouveau representations of the iris and the Carnival interpretations that they inspired. Both the long detail on the left and the border across the bottom are from Verneuil's "Iris" designs (1897). The single iris motif (bottom right) is by E. Hervegh (1897). The Carnival irises include detail from Fenton's *IRIS* pattern (top right), and detail from Dugan/Diamond's *HEAVY IRIS* (middle right).

IRIS—Fenton

This pattern made its first appearance in the Butler Brothers catalogs of 1910. As noted above, the elegant and effective design has its roots firmly in the Art Nouveau arena. It's a fluid, repeated, symmetrical composition that holds the eye and moves the gaze around the flowing pattern. The exterior is plain. The *BUTTERMILK* goblet is an item which has exactly the same shape as the *IRIS* goblet but a plain interior instead.

Shapes: only known in the stemmed compote and goblet shapes.

Colors: marigold, amethyst/purple, blue, green, and scarce white.

MIKADO—Fenton

In this pattern, the stylized flower is the Oriental chrysanthemum, beloved by many late nineteenth and early twentieth-century designers and decorators. The central flower motif is simplified to a sunburst, but is surrounded by slightly more recognizable chrysanthemums that have detailed stamens and petals. Interspersed between the three large flower heads are three lozenge shapes festooned with Oriental looking spirals and curlicues.

It's interesting to note that the exterior pattern on *MIKADO* is a combination of both realistic and highly stylized cherries. On the stem is a pattern that is similar to Fenton's stylized *CHERRY CHAIN,* while the exterior of the bowl features bunches of cherries portrayed in a very realistic manner—an intriguing blend of styles and patterns on one magnificent item.

Shape: only known in the large stemmed compote shape; these may be ruffled or smooth and round.

Colors: marigold, amethyst/purple, blue, and rare green. Red and white are reported.

MARY ANN—Dugan/Diamond

Mould drawings are known for this simple, yet effective floral design. It's virtually impossible to determine what the flower is meant to be—if indeed a particular species was in the mind of the mould maker. The vase shape that this pattern appears on complements the floral motif. The scalloped neck and base echo the curves of the petals. The curving handles and embellishments add to the overall flowing effect. "Mary Ann" was a family name for the Dugans; Thomas and Alfred Dugan's sister and mother were both called Mary Ann.

Shape: only known in a medium sized vase. The item usually has two handles, rare examples exist with three. On the three handled versions, the top is not scalloped; it is known as a loving cup. The regular, two handled version usually has eight scallops on its top rim. A scarce variant has ten scallops.

Colors: marigold and amethyst/purple.

WISHBONE—Northwood

A splendid design, its strikingly simple composition belies its intricate complexity. The symmetry of the pattern is easy on the eye, yet there is much detail within it. The design is highly stylized, borrowing from many sources including the decorative, ornamental designs of Christopher Dresser. The floral motif is often thought to be an orchid, but in fact is more likely to have been inspired by the lily. Intertwining leaves, altered beyond recognition, are seen as the "wishbones." On the bowls and plates, the center of the design has the familiar, Northwood symbolic rendition of the Japanese chrysanthemum also seen on *NIPPON*. The design is cleverly adapted to the shape of the item on which it appears. The exterior pattern on the medium sized bowls and plates is *RUFFLES AND RINGS*. This was an exterior mould design purchased by Northwood from the Jefferson Glass Co. Other bowls and plates have Northwood's *BASKETWEAVE* as the exterior pattern.

Shapes: 8 to 9" footed plates and ruffled or tri-cornered bowls; 9 to 10" ruffled or pie-crust edge, collar based bowls; 10 to 11" collar based chop plates; water set with a bulbous, mould blown pitcher; single lily epergne.

Colors: marigold, amethyst/purple, and green. Scarce shades are blue, white, ice blue, ice green, horehound, lavender, aqua, aqua opal, custard, and sapphire blue. There are probably others. Scarce colors are mostly known in the bowl shapes, though the epergnes are also known in white, ice blue, and ice green.

Northwood's *WISHBONE* pattern.

PRIMROSE—Millersburg

    PRIMROSE was advertised along with two other Millersburg patterns (*NESTING SWAN* and *WHIRLING LEAVES*) in the Butler Brothers 1910 "Santa Claus" catalog. A delightful and pleasing pattern, it is not, however, easy to be certain that this flower is the primrose. The design features four pairs of six petaled flowers, radiating from a central leaf motif. *PRIMROSE* is essentially simple in concept yet it is paired up with one of Millersburg's most intricate and complex designs—on the exterior is found the detailed geometric pattern *FINE CUT HEARTS*. Shapes: 10" bowl, which may be ruffled or have the scarce candy ribbon edge. Marie McGee reports both a rare 8" bowl and a whimsey banana boat shape with a tightly crimped edge.[6] Colors: marigold, amethyst/purple, and green. Blue and vaseline are exceptionally rare.

PANELED DANDELION—Fenton. This is a repeated pattern that lends itself perfectly to the shapes on which it is found. *PANELED DANDELION* features an indeterminate flower, accompanied by a distinctive dandelion leaf that is greatly exaggerated in length. The total pattern comprises six repeats of the dandelion and leaf motif. In a Butler Brothers ad from 1910, the *PANELED DANDE-LION* pattern was described as having "relief daisy embossed hexagon panels."

    Shape: only known in a tankard water set. The tumblers have a six-sided ground base. Colors: marigold, amethyst/purple, blue, and green.

SUNFLOWER—Northwood

    Northwood's *SUNFLOWER* is included here as a stylized pattern, despite it being an amazingly detailed rendition of that flower, with every petal finely stippled. The sunflower motif is the entire pattern—a huge and intricate flower head, like a sunburst. The petals are regular, almost regimented; the effect is one of harmony. The use of the sunflower was, of course, inspired by the craze for things Oriental. However, the significance of the design can't have been lost on the inhabitants of Kansas, for whom the sunflower is the state emblem. One wonders if this pattern sold more in the Sunflower State than elsewhere. (Certainly the "Sunflower" items made by the Phoenixville Pottery of Pennsylvania sold exceptionally well in Kansas.) The exterior pattern is Northwood's *MEANDER*, a pretty, curvilinear design that extends onto the spatula feet. This was another exterior mould design purchased by Northwood from the Jefferson Glass Co.

    Shapes: 8" spatula footed bowl. Exceptionally rare, footed plates are reported. Colors: marigold, amethyst/purple, blue, green, ice blue, Renninger blue, and teal.

TIGER LILY—Imperial

    This is the ultimate in stylizing—an imitation "near-cut" design, simply described in a 1912 Butler Brothers ad as a "floral" design. *TIGER LILY* is an intaglio pattern where the effect on the finished article is to imitate a design that has been cut into the glass. The large flower petals clearly exhibit the deep grooves associated with this type of design. The small, star-like flower heads that adorn the lower part of the pattern are deeply sunk into the surface of the glass. The tiger lily pattern is repeated three times, each section being divided by leaf motifs that cleverly disguise the mould seams.

    Shape: water set. Colors: marigold, amethyst/purple, helios, aqua, olive, blue, lavender, and amber. Water pitchers are not known in blue or amber.

    Notes: Riihimaki in Finland produced a version of this pattern in both tumbler and pitcher. There are distinct differences. For details see the relevant entry under Riihimaki.

COSMOS AND CANE—United States Glass Company

    COSMOS AND CANE first appeared in Butler Brothers catalog ads in 1912. It's an intaglio design that repeats alternate flower heads around the pattern. The "cane" is a rendition of the classic cane "near-cut" motif. As in *TIGER LILY* the petals have deep grooves; the leaves are also very similar. This pattern is unusual in that some bowls and rosebowls can be found with the *HEADDRESS* interior. *HEADDRESS* is a design that is also

known on various European Carnival items, in conjunction with several other patterns. The base of most items in this pattern has a distinctive floral design, however *COSMOS AND CANE* is also known on rare tumblers with the advertising slogan "J.R. MILLNER. CO. LYNCHBURG. VA" moulded on the bottom.

    Shapes: water set, bowl, berry set, rosebowl, breakfast set, and table set. Colors: marigold, white, honey amber, and scarce amethyst/purple.

FOUR FLOWERS—Dugan/Diamond

    Dugan/Diamond's *FOUR FLOWERS* was advertised in the Butler Brothers catalogs in 1911. The motif is made up of four flower stalks and four pincer-like "pods." Two exterior patterns are known: one is variously known as *DUGAN'S SODA GOLD* or *CRACKLE* (similar to Imperial *SODA GOLD*—just like the background effect seen on the Dugan/Diamond *MAPLE LEAF* pattern). The other is a type of *BASKETWEAVE*. There are two variations of this pattern: *FOUR FLOWERS* made by Eda Glasbruk in Sweden and Riihimaki in Finland, and the *FOUR FLOWERS VARIANT* (see Chapter Five—England). Shapes: 5 and 10" collar based bowls as well as 6 and 11" collar based plates. The bowls have various shapes including banana bowl and tri-cornered. They may be smooth or gently ruffled.

    Colors: marigold, amethyst/purple, and peach opalescent.

Dugan/Diamond's *FOUR FLOWERS* pattern.

FOUR SEVENTY FOUR—Imperial

    Almost a geometric design, *FOUR SEVENTY FOUR* features intricate hobstars as well as stylized flowers. The design is intaglio. Contemporary ads (from the early 1920s) show that Imperial called this their "Daisy" design. An ad from 1920 in the Butler Brothers catalog described the pattern as a "deep cut floral rosette and block diamond pattern." The current name of *FOUR SEVENTY FOUR* is derived from its original Imperial factory pattern number.

    Shapes: water set, punch set, and milk pitcher. Stemmed items are scarce to rare and include goblets, cordials, sherbets, and compotes (though the latter is perhaps more easily found, especially in marigold). Three sizes of rare pedestal vase are known (7, 10 and 14"). A rare ruffled bowl is reported.

    Colors: marigold, purple, helios, emerald, and olive. Stemmed items are found mainly in marigold and purple. Tumblers are found in a wider range including teal, aqua, blue, and violet. The pedestal vases are found in marigold, but a red one is reported in the small 7" size and we have had the pleasure of seeing a magnificent emerald green one in the large 14" size. The large vase is also known in purple.

Enameled or Decorated Carnival

    Enameled decoration was a well established technique in the United States glass industry prior to the period of Classic Carnival production. In late 1910, Butler Brothers ads showed that Dugan were producing peach opalescent enameled, iridized bowls. A year later, their catalogs featured ads that indicated Fenton and Northwood, as well as Dugan, were also producing Carnival Glass with enameled decoration. Daisies, forget-me-nots and crocuses, magnolias, freesia, and apple blossoms—a delightful floral bouquet was at the disposal of the decorator. The enameled decoration was usually applied to "blanks"—iridized items that may or may not have had moulded patterns. On the water sets, the pitcher usually features the full blown flower, while the tumblers usually show only the matching bud. The necks of some enameled water pitchers, for example *MAGNOLIA AND DRAPE*, also feature a matching bud. The style of painting is typically "broad brush" rather than delicate and intricate. There are many variations within the same basic enameled design. The decorator would have had a basic design to copy from, but each would have had his or her own style. Sometimes extra embellishments were added, giving individuality to the item. Fenton and Northwood mainly produced water sets, rare table sets, and rare berry sets. Dugan/Diamond, however, specialized in enameling peach opalescent bowls.

MAGNOLIA AND DRAPE—Fenton

The glorious, full magnolia flower is depicted on the side of the water pitcher in white enamel. These showy blossoms take up a large part of the items on which they are painted, making for a very spectacular effect. The flower centers are a pale creamy yellow, the stamens are picked out in deep brown. The leaves are creamy yellow green and there are tiny buds adorning the flower sprays. There is a moulded *DRAPE* pattern on the partly iridized interior of the water pitcher, while the tumbler has a moulded vertical ribbing on its interior. The bowls in the berry set have a moulded *STIPPLED RAYS* design inside (usually seen with a *SCALE BAND* exterior). A similar rayed design is moulded inside the table set items, but is not stippled.

Shapes: water set, with a bulbous and mould blown pitcher. It frequently has a tightly crimped, frilly top. Pedestal footed berry set comprising 5" berry bowl and 9" master berry bowl. The edge on the bowls has the typical Fenton scallop and flute. Table set with pedestal base. Items other than the water set are very scarce indeed. Color: marigold.

ENAMELED APPLE BLOSSOM—Northwood

This pattern is unusual in that the tumbler does not feature the bud of the full blown flower like most other enameled designs. The apple blossom flower on all items in this pattern is very similar—there are no buds depicted, all are full blown blossoms. These flowers are painted in shades of cream, pale blush pink, and white: their stamens are picked out in a rich brown, while the leaves are white, highlighted with strokes of green. The paintwork is typically very well executed. The table set and berry set items are very similar in shape to Northwood's *GRAPE AND GOTHIC ARCHES* pieces.

Shapes: water set with standard, straight-sided pitcher; berry set; table set. All items are very scarce indeed in this pattern. Color: blue.

ENAMELED CHERRIES AND LITTLE FLOWERS—Northwood and Fenton.

Both manufacturers made water sets enameled with a very similar cherry and floral design. Both feature an enameled pattern made up of a central bunch of cherries surrounded by leaves and an encircling wreath of little flowers. It's not too easy to tell them apart, but there are differences. The water pitchers are rarely (if ever) marked with the *N*, though some tumblers are—obviously these are the Northwood ones. Our extensive research into this pattern has revealed the following ways to distinguish Northwood's and Fenton's *ENAMELED CHERRIES AND LITTLE FLOWERS:*

Northwood

The water pitcher has a four-part mould and (usually) a paneled interior. There are eleven small flowers surrounding the central cherry cluster. The cherry decoration on the tumblers has three separate leaves coming from the separate cherries. Sometimes there is a moulded number on the base of the Northwood tumblers.

Shape: water set. The pitcher is bulbous and mould blown, with an applied handle. Colors: blue is most often found. Marigold and scarce amethyst/purple are known.

Fenton

The water pitcher has a two-part mould and either a *DRAPE* or smooth interior. There are usually nine small flowers (there may also be seven or eight) surrounding the central cherry cluster. The cherry decoration on the tumblers has two (sometimes even three) leaves coming from one single cherry.

Shape: water set. The pitcher is bulbous and mould blown, with an applied handle. Colors: blue is most often found. Marigold and scarce amethyst/purple are known.

IRIS (WITH PRISM BAND) aka BANDED IRIS aka BANDED DRAPE—Fenton

An elegant design that features a single open iris on the water pitcher (tumblers have the bud). The tumblers in this pattern are frequently confused with those from other enameled water sets, but they are easily distinguished by the fact that the double petaled blossom is to the right of the stem. There is usually a moulded diagonal band on the water pitchers. Matching tumblers have a moulded horizontal band. The first Butler Brothers ad for the enameled water sets was in 1911, a year after the peach opalescent enameled bowls from Dugan. The *IRIS* water set was one of the first advertised. Shape: water set only. Colors: marigold, amethyst/purple, blue, and scarce green.

ENAMELED LILY OF THE VALLEY—Dugan/Diamond

The delightful and easily recognizable lily of the valley can be found adorning several different kinds of Carnival bowls from Dugan/Diamond. Both the *STIPPLED FLOWER* bowls and *STIPPLED PETALS* bowls can be found bearing the lily of the valley enameled design. The bowls were advertised in Butler Brothers catalogs in 1910, while Thomas Dugan was still there, pre-dating the 1913 change in ownership to Diamond Glass Company.

Shape: bowl with candy ribbon or ruffled edge.

Color: peach opalescent only.

Notes: other similar enameled floral decoration (roses and forget-me-nots) can be found on the *STIPPLED FLOWER* and *STIPPLED PETALS* bowls. Dugan/Diamond's *CHERRIES* bowl is also found enameled.

The delightfully named "Santa Claus" edition of Butler Brothers catalog in 1910 featured this "Parisian Art" assortment. The items were all from Dugan/Diamond; their "pearl edges" were what we now call peach opal. The floral patterns were hand painted onto the bowls in enamel. From left, the designs are *LILY OF THE VALLEY* (on a *STIPPLED FLOWERS* bowl), *FORGET-ME-NOTS* (on a *STIPPLED PETALS* bowl), and *ROSES* (on a *CHERRIES* bowl).

Foliage

Not strictly floral designs, yet surely meant to be associated with them, the foliage designs provide an interesting selection that ranges from the astonishingly realistic to the highly stylized.

ACORN BURRS—Northwood

This is surely one of the most tactile patterns in Carnival Glass. Indeed it must also be one of the most realistic looking patterns, for the mouldwork is quite extraordinary. Leaves and plump acorn burrs stand out massively from the bark effect background, providing an astonishing example of the mouldmaker's skill. How difficult such items must have been to remove from the mould! Dating from about 1911, this design was described in a Baltimore Bargain House catalog in 1912 as a "New Chestnut Raised pattern"—so, maybe not acorn burrs after all! The design is exterior on all items. Pieces with handles are fashioned in a delightful, rustic, bark effect. The finials on the table set items are fashioned to give the appearance of an acorn burr surrounded by a twig.

Shapes: water set, berry set, table set, and punch set.

Colors: marigold, amethyst/purple, and green. The punch sets are also known in white, ice blue, ice green, lime green, and aqua opalescent. Punch cups have been found in cobalt blue, but so far, no punch bowl or base has been reported in that color.

MAPLE LEAF—Dugan/Diamond

Another pattern dating from around 1911, this one was advertised in the spring issue of the Butler Brothers catalog of that year, citing its "heavily embossed maple leaves." Like the *ACORN BURRS*, the leaves stand out proudly from the surface in a very realistic fashion. The background is an all over crackle effect that is sometimes called *DUGAN'S SODA GOLD*. Butler Brothers described the crackle background as a "jewel effect," while the 1912 Charles Broadway Rouss catalog said it was a "frosted background." The handles and finials on the water set and table set items are crafted to give the appearance of stemmed leaves.

Shapes: stemmed berry set, water set, and table set.

Colors: marigold, amethyst/purple, and cobalt.

A *MAPLE LEAF* assortment from Dugan/Diamond in the Butler Brothers mid spring 1911 catalog.

PINE CONE—Fenton

A highly stylized design dating from 1911, this pattern is composed of four repeated cone and foliage motifs in a satisfying overall composition. It is a good design, well thought out; the curves of the foliage echo the curves of the cones. The exterior is plain.

Shapes: 6" plate or saucer and small bowl; 7 to 8" plate.

Colors: marigold, amethyst/purple, cobalt blue, green, and amber.

Fenton's *PINE CONE* pattern.

Even More Flowers

There are many more floral patterns. They include Millersburg's lovely *POPPY* compote and their delightful little *COSMOS* bowl, as well as Fenton's *THISTLE,* their *BOUQUET* and *MILADY* water sets, and the rare *RAGGED ROBIN* bowl. Then there's Northwood's *WILD ROSE* and, of course, the ivy covered *TOWN PUMP,* plus Imperial's elegant, beaded effect *POINSETTIA* milk pitcher. Some others seem to fit into a "gray" area of being not quite realistic, yet not quite stylized. Imperial's *FIELDFLOWER* is a good example of a pattern that hovers between realism and style. It's a pretty floral design, known only in a water set. Similarly, both Dugan/Diamond's *RAMBLER ROSE*—another pattern exclusive to the water set shape—and their classic *FLOWERS AND FRAMES* are neither realistic nor fully stylized. Another foliage design is *WHIRLING LEAVES* from Millersburg, and from Fenton there's *AUTUMN ACORNS* and the similar *ACORNS,* plus of course the ever-popular *HOLLY.* Even more patterns feature flowers as part of the background design. Northwood's *GOOD LUCK* and the *PEACOCK AT URN* patterns are good examples.

[1] *Designs and Patterns for Embroiderers and Craftspeople* (Mineola, New York: Dover Publications, 1992). Retitled reprint of the original *Designs and Patterns for Embroiderers and Craftsmen*, a selection from the Wm. Briggs and Company Ltd., *Album of Transfer Patterns,* circa 1900.

[2] Carl O. Burns, *The Collector's Guide to Northwood's Carnival Glass* (Gas City, Indiana: L-W Book Sales, 1994).

[3] Marion Hartung, *Third Book of Carnival Glass* (Buckner, Missouri: HOACGA, 1962).

[4] W. and G. Audsley, *Designs and Patterns from Historic Ornament* (Mineola, New York: Dover Publications, 1968). An unabridged republication of the work originally published by Scribner and Welford in 1882 under the title *Outlines of Ornament in the Leading Styles.*

[5] Eugene Grasset, *Art Nouveau Floral Designs* (London, England: Bracken Books, 1988). A selection of plates from *La Plante et ses Applications Ornamentales* by Eugene Grasset, published by Lyon -Claesen, Brussels, 1897.

[6] Marie McGee, *Millersburg Glass: As I Know It* (Marietta, Ohio: Antique Publications, 1995).

Fenton's splendid *MIKADO* compote stands 8" high and measures almost 10" across its un-ruffled, marigold top. There are two different cherry patterns on the exterior. The stem is clear and uniridized. $200-$300.

Detail from Fenton's *MIKADO* showing the stylized Oriental chrysanthemum flower.

Northwood's *WISHBONE* pattern, seen here on a rich purple tumbler, is a highly stylized design. $100-$200.

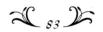

Dugan/Diamond's delightful amethyst *MARY ANN* vase has a most distinctive shape. $150-$200.

A tall amethyst tankard water pitcher in Fenton's stylized *PANELED DANDELION* pattern, originally advertised as a "daisy." $400-$500.

This amethyst, ruffled *PRIMROSE* bowl from Millersburg has a satin iridescence. Note the saw-tooth edge. $100-$250.

Seen in close-up, the amethyst Millersburg *PRIMROSE* bowl has highlights of blues and greens visible in its iridescence.

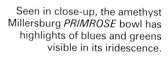

Two marigold tumblers from Imperial that feature stylized floral designs. On the left is *TIGER LILY* ($30-$50) and on the right is *FOUR SEVENTY FOUR* ($30-$50).

Cobalt blue is a scarce color for this excellent Northwood *SUNFLOWER* bowl. The design was possibly inspired by the craze for things Oriental. $450-$600. An electric blue example sold in 2003 for $1350.

A selection of Fenton's enameled pattern, *MAGNOLIA AND DRAPE.* The table set items (such as the covered sugar) are exceptionally hard to find. Tumbler: $40-$50. Pitcher: $100-$200. Covered sugar: $150-$200.

Three hard-to-find enameled tumblers. From left: Northwood's *SPRING FESTIVAL* in cobalt blue. Note the grooved base that helps to distinguish it from other enameled cherry patterns. ($75-$100); Fenton's *CHRYSANTHEMUM* in marigold ($50-$75); Northwood's sought after *APPLE BLOSSOM* in cobalt blue ($100-$200).

Fenton's blue, enameled *CHERRIES AND LITTLE FLOWERS* bulbous water pitcher and tumbler. $400-$500 for the full water set.

ROSE OF PARADISE tumbler. The enameling is exquisite, and the glass is slightly thinner than that usually found on enameled tumblers. The manufacturer is unknown. $125-$175.

Two Fenton *BANDED DRAPE* water pitchers in an elegant tankard shape. On the left is a scarce green example in the enameled *FORGET ME NOT* pattern, unusual for this pitcher ($1500-$2000). On the right is the delightful, enameled *IRIS* pattern that is more frequently seen on this shape of pitcher ($800-$1000 for an amethyst/purple example).

A Dugan/Diamond specialty—a peach opalescent bowl with the enameled *FORGET-ME-NOTS* design. $175-$225.

Described in a Baltimore Bargain House catalog from 1912 as a "Chestnut" pattern, Northwood's *ACORN BURRS* pattern (seen here on a purple water pitcher and tumbler) is a masterpiece of mouldwork. Pitcher: $600-$1000. Tumbler: $50-$100.

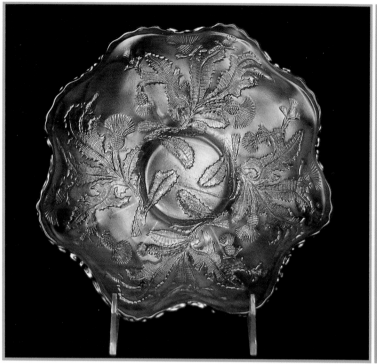

This ruffled bowl in Fenton's *THISTLE* is vaseline, an unusual color for this pattern. $350-$450.

A green *AUTUMN ACORNS* ruffled bowl from Fenton. $100-$150.

Dugan/Diamond's classic design, *FLOWERS AND FRAMES*, seen here on a purple ruffled bowl with an outstanding iridescence. $400-$500.

Chapter Four
Fruits

"Rightly thought of, there is poetry in peaches. . . . even when they are canned!"

—Harley Granville-Barker (1877-1946), British actor and dramatist

This green Millersburg *HANGING CHERRIES* ice cream shape bowl has an outstanding satin iridescence with magnificent coloring. $350-$400.

Fruits have been used in art and design through the centuries. They are found in medieval and Renaissance art, in Elizabethan ornament, and in Art Nouveau designs, to name just a few. They can be seen in still life paintings and photography, embroidery, tapestry, and wallpapers. The fashionable lady of 1908 was even wearing fruits on her head: the Sears Roebuck and Co. catalog for that year offered some quite amazing hats. One extravagantly constructed piece of headgear was described as "a pretty serviceable style, trimmed with cherries," and as extras they sold "a beautiful wreath of finest quality grapes, sprayed with natural foliage and stems. Enough to trim the entire brim of a hat."

The essence of a good design is that it should be suitable for its purpose as well as pleasing to the eye. The use of rich and opulent fruit patterns on Carnival Glass fulfilled that purpose. There are plump peaches, grapes, and cherries adorning berry bowls just waiting to be filled with a selection of tempting fruits, or perhaps to be piled high with oranges. Decanters are decorated with luscious bunches of grapes, ready to be

filled with wine. The pattern suggested the purpose. Glowing iridescence completed the picture and provided the household with a splendid, tempting display.

As with the peacock and flower patterns, Carnival Glass fruit patterns can be broadly classified as realistic or stylized. They range from natural looking portrayals, executed in such a realistic manner that they almost seem edible, to fully stylized examples bearing only slight resemblance to their inspiration. It's not always clear how to classify a pattern. Though the fruits themselves may be portrayed very realistically, the composition and the blending of the fruits with other elements takes them out of the realm of the truly naturalistic. Also, as with the floral patterns, a grey area lies between the two extremes, where the fruits are often quite realistic in portrayal but are part of an overall, repeated pattern that makes them lose some of their naturalistic impact. Where this is the case, it will be noted in the text.

Realistic/Naturalistic Patterns

IMPERIAL GRAPE—Imperial

Described by Imperial quite simply as their "grape vine design," this pattern had the catalog number 473 when it was first issued in around 1910. In March 1911, it became one of the first Carnival items to be advertised in the United Kingdom, where it took the buying public by storm. *IMPERIAL GRAPE* has a taste of opulence to it. The vine bunches standing out from the surface of the glass have a plump and luscious feel. When combined with deep purple iridescence, the grapes can look beguilingly real! Grapes, of course, were a popular motif at the time, as the illustration from *The Studio* shows.[1] Made in the widest range of shapes that Imperial produced, *IMPERIAL GRAPE* was a best seller.

There is a similar Imperial design, *HEAVY GRAPE*, which is distinguished from *IMPERIAL GRAPE* by virtue of the latter's scalloped border that appears on most items (though not all). *IMPERIAL GRAPE* is used as both an interior and an exterior design on many pieces (mainly bowls and plates), while others have a plain or ribbed interior. Items with handles are particularly attractive, as they have the rustic effect twig or bark design.

An interesting mismatch between actuality and catalog ad can be seen with regard to the *IMPERIAL GRAPE* decanter. The blown stopper of the decanter has a ribbed or fluted pattern. But check the stopper shown in the April 1912 Butler Brothers ad. It is not the same. It would seem that Imperial never put the one illustrated in the ad into production. Certainly later ads show the stopper as the ribbed one. Another mismatch is more recent. The *IMPERIAL GRAPE* water carafe, with a flared out mouth, was in fact originally advertised as a vase. Perhaps the intention was that it should be multipurpose. It certainly presented more selling opportunities that way.

Shapes: bowls ranging from 4 to 12" in diameter, 6 and 9" plates, rare nutbowl and rosebowl, punch set, water set, decanter and wine glasses, goblet, stemmed compote, water carafe or vase, cup and saucer, rare whimsey spittoon, handled nappy, and lamp shade.

Colors: Marigold, helios, and amethyst/purple are the most frequently found. Unusual shades include smoke, aqua, emerald, amber, cobalt blue, vaseline, teal, and clambroth.

In this April 1912 Butler Brothers ad, the *IMPERIAL GRAPE* decanter is shown with a matching grape design stopper. No such stopper is known in Carnival Glass. The "matching" blown Carnival stopper actually has a ribbed or fluted design.

HEAVY GRAPE—Imperial

This pattern may well have been intended as a "sister" pattern to the *IMPERIAL GRAPE* suite. It is, however, distinct in that the exterior pattern on *HEAVY GRAPE* items is Imperial's *FLUTE* pattern. *HEAVY GRAPE* also has a different catalog number (Imperial # 700), though it seems that this number actually refers to the *FLUTE* exterior. In contemporary Imperial catalog illustrations, the pattern is referred to as the "Colonial

grape" design. ("Colonial" was the name Imperial gave to their *FLUTE* type patterns). The *HEAVY GRAPE* pattern features a single, impressive bunch of grapes and leaves against a stippled background. Usually, there is also a quilt effect around the edge of the interior, though on some items this cannot be seen too well due to the secondary shaping of the piece.

A large, marigold *HEAVY GRAPE* bowl has the distinction of being the first Carnival item to be featured in color in the English trade press! An ad in the April 1923 edition of the *Pottery Gazette and Glass Trade Review* showed this splendid item.

Shapes: bowls in three sizes ranging from 5 to 10"; plates in three sizes ranging from 6 to 12". Also found are one handled nappies and a punch set.

Colors: marigold, amethyst/purple, helios, amber, and smoke. Unusual and off beat shades include cobalt blue, vaseline, white, aqua, and emerald.

Note: punch cups or custard cups are hard to find. Not all colors are found in all shapes.

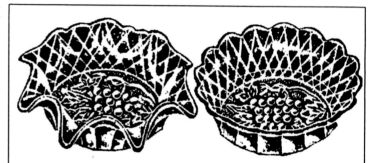

This ad for Imperial's *HEAVY GRAPE* bowls from mid spring 1911 clearly shows the diamond quilting effect around the inside of the pattern and the deeply moulded central grapes. Note that the ad called it "allover lattice pressing, relief grape centers."

LOGANBERRY—Imperial

LOGANBERRY is another outstanding Imperial pattern that looks good enough to eat! Deeply embossed clusters of berries cling to the sides of this splendid vase—the only shape known in the pattern. There is a background paneled effect and a stylized border featuring a floral and berry pattern around the neck. In concept, there are similarities between this pattern and Imperial's *POPPY SHOW* vase. It is a blow moulded shape, bulbous in the lower half, tapering at the neck and slightly flaring again at its mouth. Irregular, whimsied neck shapes are known.

Shape: 10" vase only.

Colors: marigold, amethyst/purple, helios, amber, and emerald. Rare smoke is reported.

PEACH—Northwood

Essentially very simple, *PEACH* is particularly effective in its portrayal of this plump and ripe fruit. On the smaller items, the design is composed of two heavy fruits hanging pendulously, twin leaves above them and a single leaf below. This motif is repeated on the opposite side of the item. On the larger items (especially the water pitcher) there are three fruits and the placing of the leaves is different: all three leaves are above the fruits. The background is paneled—a typical Northwood device. Bordering the paneling is a heavy, twisted cable design. Though this pattern is now known as *PEACH*, it is possible that the fruits were originally intended to be cherries.

Shapes: water set, berry set, and table set.

Colors: cobalt blue and white, which often has gilding on the fruits and cable. A few scarce items have been reported in marigold. Rare iridized blue slag (sorbini).

Notes: we were privileged to see an iridized, blue slag water pitcher at the Heart of America Carnival Glass Association 1997 Convention in Kansas City, Missouri.

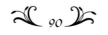

HANGING CHERRIES—Millersburg

The fruits and leaves are depicted in splendidly, realistic fashion. Each serration on the edge of the leaves is carefully and accurately portrayed. The main pattern motif is a random bunch of cherries and leaves, arranged differently according to the various shapes this pattern is found on. The contrast between the smooth surface of the fruits and the textured stippling of the leaves is very effective.

Some bowls are found with the rare *HOBNAIL* exterior pattern: this item can be clearly seen in a Butler Brothers 1911 ad for a Millersburg "Regal Assortment" (see Part One, Chapter Three on Millersburg).

Shapes: bowls in varying sizes from 5 to 10". They may be ruffled, ice cream shaped, or candy ribbon edged. Rare plates are known in 6 and 8" size, as well as a large chop plate. Also known are table sets, water sets, and a milk pitcher.

Colors: marigold, amethyst/purple, and green. Unusual shades of lavender and teal are known.

Notes: the regular tumbler has a collar base and a flared shape. There is also a variant that has a ground base and straight sides.

MULTI FRUITS AND FLOWERS—Millersburg

A bounty of fruits is found in this delightful yet scarce pattern. There are five fruits featured—cherries, apples, pears, plums, and berries—as well as dainty blossoms. The pattern of fruits forms a cohesive whole. *MULTI FRUITS AND FLOWERS* is an exterior pattern used on shapes, such as water sets, that don't usually display their interior. On a rare example of the very scarce *MULTI FRUITS AND FLOWERS* punch bowl however, there is an interior pattern that has been called *SCROLL AND GRAPE*.

Shapes: water set, punch set, and a stemmed sherbet dish (similar to a small compote).

Colors: marigold, amethyst/purple, and green. A few blue pieces are known.

Notes: all examples are very scarce. The punch bowl comes with both a flared out shape and a scarce, cupped in, tulip top shape. The base to the punch bowl can be used as a compote.

PALM BEACH—United States Glass Company

This pattern was shown as a four-piece table set in the United States Glass Company's domestic catalog for 1909-1910. It's a sumptuous portrayal of grapes, lush and full bodied. The vine leaves are large and showy, with fine stippling. Yet the overall effect is removed just a little from the truly realistic by the regular, interwoven pattern of the vine stems that criss-cross around the grapes. The finials on the covered table set items are shaped like grape bunches; the handles on the water pitcher, sugar, and creamer are fashioned in a rustic, twig effect. The bases of *PALM BEACH* items have a grape and leaf pattern. *PALM BEACH* is an exterior pattern; bowls may be found with the delicate *GOOSEBERRY SPRAY* design inside

Shapes: water set with a distinctive, squat pitcher; table set; vases (both as moulded and whimsied as the spooner shape); and small bowls (often whimsied as banana boat shapes or rosebowls).

Colors: marigold, honey amber, amethyst/purple, and white. Scarce lavender examples are known, also white with a silver band.

THREE FRUITS (and its variations)—Northwood

This is a well balanced design featuring a wreath of leaves against which are set a pair of peaches (or perhaps apples), a trio of cherries, and two pears. The symmetry and evenness of the pattern, coupled with the fact that the leaves, though realistic in appearance are identical for the three different fruits, takes this design out of the realm of the truly naturalistic patterns. The cherry trio is repeated in the center of the design. There are several variations on the design, and the pattern changes according to the different shapes that *THREE FRUITS* is found in. Confusingly, there is a very similar pattern from Fenton (see below). Also, Northwood added flower blossoms to the overall design concept and created another similar pattern called *FRUIT AND FLOWERS*.

Shapes:
•Collar based 8" bowls and 9" plates. The bowls may have a pie crust edge or be ruffled. The exterior pattern may be *BASKETWEAVE, RIBS,* or plain. The background to the pattern may be stippled or plain. On the sought after stippled items there is a triple ring around the outer limit of the stippling.

•Spatula footed 8" bowls. The pattern fills much less of the face of the bowl than on the collar based items. A spray of three leaves takes the place of the three central cherries found on the collar based pieces. The background to the pattern may be stippled or plain. The exterior pattern is a stylized curvilinear motif called *MEANDER* (an old Jefferson Glass Co. pattern). This version of *THREE FRUITS* is usually called *THREE FRUITS MEDALLION*.

•Dome footed 8" bowls have a similar, but somewhat tighter pattern, more like that on the *THREE FRUITS MEDALLION*. In the center of the design is a spray of three leaves. The exterior is interesting in that it may have either *BASKETWEAVE* or a *VINTAGE GRAPE* pattern. Some examples have a version of both together—the grape design being visible through the basketweave. *VINTAGE GRAPE* was a mould purchased by Northwood from the Jefferson Glass Co.

Colors:
•Collar based bowls and plates are found in a very wide range of colors: marigold, amethyst/purple, lavender, blue, green, white, ice blue, ice green, and aqua opalescent. Unusual shades such as custard, sapphire, clambroth, olive green, smoke, horehound, teal, and aqua are also reported.

•Spatula footed bowls are found in marigold, amethyst/purple, blue, green, white, ice blue, ice green, and aqua opalescent. Unusual shades of lime green, Renninger blue, pearl, ice blue opalescent, and ice green opalescent are also reported.

•Dome footed bowls are found in marigold, amethyst/purple, blue, green, white, and ice green. Horehound is reported.

Notes: A further variation has been noted [2] in the arrangement of the fruits on the collar based items. There appear to be two distinct and very different arrangements. On one version, when the central cherry bunch is hanging straight down, the other three fruit clusters are arranged in a Y shape. This is the most common arrangement found. A very rare variation seems to be found only on stippled plates. In this arrangement, when the central cherry bunch is hanging straight down, the other three fruit clusters are arranged in the totally opposite way, in an upside down Y shape.

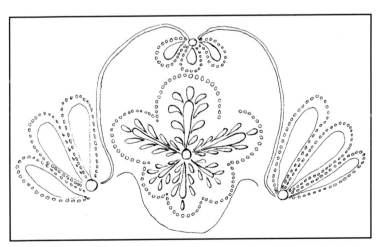

Northwood's *MEANDER* design (an old Jefferson mould) found on the exterior of *THREE FRUITS MEDALLION* items.

United States Glass Company's *GOOSEBERRY SPRAY* pattern found on the interior of some *PALM BEACH* bowls.

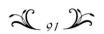

FRUITS AND FLOWERS—Northwood

The main difference between this pattern and *THREE FRUITS* is in the addition of tiny flowers amongst the leaves. The stemmed bonbons may be found with background stippling. On most items there is no central cherry cluster or leaf bunch—there may instead be an <u>N</u> mark. The pattern is interior. On the exterior, *BASKETWEAVE* is usually found.

Shapes: the stemmed and handled bonbon is the shape most often found. Also found are berry sets comprising a master berry (which may have more fruits in the clusters) and small bowls, as well as 7 to 8" plates (which may have one side turned up in the "handgrip" shape or two sides turned up in the "banana boat" shape).

Colors: marigold, amethyst/purple, blue, and green. The stemmed, unstippled bonbon is known in a wider range of colors, which includes white, lavender, ice blue, ice green, and aqua opalescent.

THREE FRUITS (Variant)—Fenton

An almost identical, collar based plate in the *THREE FRUITS* pattern was made by Fenton. It is differentiated from the Northwood version in that it has a distinct twelve-sided edge. There is no exterior pattern.

Shape: 9" plate with collar base.

Colors: marigold, amethyst/purple, blue, and green.

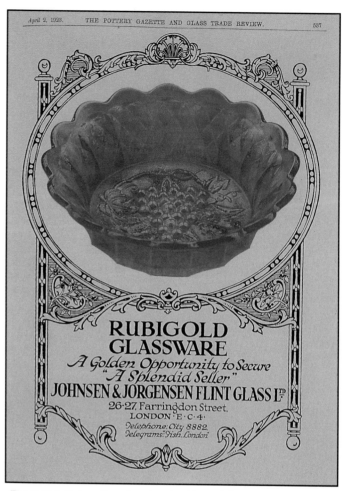

This purple *IMPERIAL GRAPE* decanter with stopper has a scintillating, multicolored iridescence. The mouldwork on these items is superb, the grapes stand out in deep relief. $200-$400.

The British *Pottery Gazette* advertised Imperial's *HEAVY GRAPE* bowl in 1923. It was the first color ad for Carnival to appear in the British trade press.

Imperial's *LOGANBERRY* vase has splendid, realistic-looking fruits. This example is in amber, a "signature" color of Imperial. $600-$1000.

The *IMPERIAL GRAPE* carafe seen here in purple was originally sold as a vase, according to contemporary ads from 1911. $200-$250.

A stunning, purple *HEAVY GRAPE* chop plate from Imperial with an electric iridescence. $400-$700. One sold in 2007 for $1900.

A favorite among tumbler collectors, North-wood's *PEACH* tumbler in blue. $100-$200.

Three tumblers featuring the vine. From left: black amethyst Dugan/Diamond *VINEYARD* ($100-$150), honey amber United States Glass Company's *PALM BEACH* ($100-$150) and blue Fenton *LATTICE AND GRAPE* ($40-$60).

This *PALM BEACH* whimsey banana boat shape is 7.5" long. It is from United States Glass and has a strange honey amber base color, yet the iridescence causes it to appear almost amethyst. $100-$150.

Northwood's characteristic pie crust edge is seen on this stippled, emerald green *THREE FRUITS* bowl. $900-$1000. A stunning example in emerald green sold in 2007 for $2500.

A variation on the *THREE FRUITS* pattern theme from Northwood is this *THREE FRUITS MEDALLION* ruffled bowl in cobalt blue. $350-$600.

Two shapes in Northwood's *FRUITS AND FLOWERS* pattern. On the left is an amethyst plate with "two sides up" ($150-$200). On the right is a regular green 7.5" plate ($150-$200). The pattern is very similar to *THREE FRUITS* but has the addition of tiny flowers.

This green plate shows Fenton's version of the *THREE FRUITS* pattern; it is distinguished by having an unusual twelve-sided edge. $150-$200.

CHERRIES—Dugan/Diamond

This is seen most often as a familiar, rather deep bowl, easily recognized by its three, distinctly shaped feet. The design features leaves and fruits in a realistic, pendulous arrangement. It may be found with the CHERRIES pattern on the exterior as well, in the case of the three footed bowls. It is sometimes also found on smaller items that carry the Dugan/Diamond pattern JEWELLED HEART on the outside.

Shapes: three footed 8" bowls, 5 to 6" plates, and small bowls. The edges may be ruffled, tightly crimped, or candy ribbon edged.

Colors: marigold, amethyst/purple, and peach opalescent.

STRAWBERRY—Northwood

A "sister" to Northwood's THREE FRUITS pattern (and indeed, illustrated alongside it in a 1910 Butler Brothers ad), this design features just the one type of fruit. It's a naturalistic portrayal of detailed, plump strawberries and leaves that are almost identical to the leaves on THREE FRUITS. This pattern also can be found in stippled and non stippled versions—the stippled have the same encircling triple ring as on the stippled THREE FRUITS items. (Sometimes the stippled version is called STRAWBERRY VARIANT.) The exterior may be plain, ribbed, or have the BASKETWEAVE design.

Shapes: 8" collar based bowls and 9" plates. Smaller 7" handgrip plates are also known.

Colors: marigold, amethyst/purple, and green. Bowls are known in blue; a blue stippled plate has been reported in Australia. The bowls only are also known in a wider range of colors including white, ice blue, ice green, smoke, horehound, lime green, peach opalescent, and Renninger blue. A single example of an aqua opalescent bowl is currently known.

WILD STRAWBERRY—Northwood

Yet another "sister," this time the family is the STRAWBERRY pattern. WILD STRAWBERRY differs from Northwood's STRAWBERRY pattern in that there are delicate strawberry blossoms sprinkled around and there are more leaves overall. BASKETWEAVE is the exterior pattern.

Shapes: collar based 5 and 10" bowls and 7.5" handgrip plates.

Colors: marigold, amethyst/purple, and green. Bowls only are also known in white, ice blue, and ice green. Lime green is reported for the large bowl.

BLACKBERRY/STRAWBERRY/GRAPE WREATH (and Variants)—Millersburg

We have grouped these patterns together as they are almost identical in their basic design. Minor differences give rise to a different pattern name. The broad concept is a naturalistic treatment of a square shaped wreath made up of berries, leaves, and curling tendrils. In each case,

the fruits and leaves are very similar. All items have a plain WIDE PANEL exterior and a multi point star base on the marie.

BLACKBERRY WREATH.

Right in the center of this design is a blackberry motif, with three large leaves. A rare variation exists which has a different shaped berry in the center with four (not three) leaves.

Shapes: ruffled and candy ribbon edged bowls ranging from 5 to 10". Rare 6 and 8" plates are known, as are rare chop plates. A spittoon whimsey is also reported.

Colors: marigold, amethyst/purple, green, and rare blue. Not all colors are known in all shapes.

GRAPE WREATH.

This name is strictly assigned to the pattern with a central motif that features a four pointed "feathery leaf." However, a range of interchangeable motifs can be found on the center of this design—these are called GRAPE WREATH VARIANTS.

The three other central motifs are:
• Eight point star or multi star motif (like a spider's web)
• Peacock eye and feather motif, also described as clover and feather
• Square and plume motif, also described as star and bars

Shapes: ruffled and candy ribbon edged bowls in varying sizes from about 6". Unusual tri-cornered bowls are also known.

Colors: marigold, amethyst/purple, and green.

STRAWBERRY WREATH

This name is assigned to the berry wreath pattern that has no central motif, just a tiny dot (sometimes called the jeweler's bead).

Shapes: ruffled and candy ribbon edged bowls in varying sizes from about 6". Tri-cornered and square shaped bowls are known, as is a compote.

Colors: marigold, amethyst/purple, green, and rare vaseline.

GRAPE LEAVES—Millersburg

This pattern is very similar in overall concept to the above mentioned Millersburg WREATH patterns, but the major difference here is the exterior pattern and the central motif. The splendid Millersburg near cut pattern MAYFLOWER is the exterior design. On the marie there is no star, instead there is a complementary motif. The central motif is a large berry surrounded by four symmetrically placed leaves.

Shapes: large 10" bowl and a scarce 8" bowl.

Colors: marigold, amethyst/purple, green, and rare vaseline.

Notes: there is a Northwood pattern with the same name that is quite different from the Millersburg item.

WILD BLACKBERRY—Fenton

WILD BLACKBERRY is a delicate, intricate, interwoven pattern composed of berries, leaves and fronds. The distinctive four leaf motif in the center helps to identify the pattern. It's a curvilinear design that draws the eye around, the style very similar to Fenton's IRIS pattern. The exterior is Fenton's WIDE PANEL.

Shape: 8" bowl only, with either a ruffled or, less often, a candy ribbon edge.

Colors: marigold, amethyst/purple, and green.

Notes: WILD BLACKBERRY is also known with "Maday" advertising. On the marie, the words "H. MADAY AND Co. 1910" are moulded into the glass.

VINTAGE—Fenton

A simple, natural looking grape and leaf design, VINTAGE is used extensively over a wide range of shapes and colors. The pattern alters according to the shape on which it is portrayed. As these shapes are substantially different, the elements and proportions of the pattern do change from one piece to another. The exterior pattern to VINTAGE when it is used on plates and bowls is usually WIDE PANEL. On some items, such as the epergne lily, VINTAGE is used as an exterior pattern itself. It is also found on the inside of some beautiful WREATH OF ROSES punch bowls and cups. (PERSIAN MEDALLION is used instead of VINTAGE on other examples of the WREATH OF ROSES punch set items).

The variety of central motifs found on Millersburg's GRAPE WREATH and GRAPE WREATH VARIANTS. Clockwise, from top left: eight point star motif (spider web); the feathery leaf motif found on the GRAPE WREATH; peacock eye and feather motif (clover and feather); square and plume motif (star and bars).

Fenton's *WILD BLACKBERRY* pattern.

Shapes: 5 to 10" collar based bowls. Their edges may be ruffled, ice cream shaped, or candy ribbon. Rare 7 to 9" plates are also known. Other shapes include a footed fernery, small epergne, and a compote.

Colors: marigold, amethyst/purple, blue, green, amberina, vaseline, red, Persian blue, aqua opalescent, and celeste blue.

VINTAGE (Variant)—Dugan/Diamond

Very similar to the Fenton version of this pattern, the Dugan/Diamond *VINTAGE* is usually identified easily by its domed foot. Though the basic pattern is very similar, it is slightly smaller and more compact than Fenton's. The range of shapes is much smaller.

Shapes: dome footed 8" ruffled bowls and 9" plates.

Colors: marigold, amethyst/purple, blue, green, white, and celeste blue.

Notes: a mug, as well as a very scarce pitcher and tumblers, is known in a similar pattern called *VINTAGE BANDED*. It differs only in that it has a lattice band around the top and bottom. A powder jar is also known in marigold, purple, powder blue with marigold iridescence, and white.

VINTAGE—Millersburg

The three large bunches of grapes coupled with realistic leaves are enough to distinguish this pattern from the other manufacturer's versions of *VINTAGE*. But, just to make sure, the exterior has the very distinctive *HOBNAIL* pattern, plus a many rayed star on the marie.

Shapes: 9 to 10" bowls and small 5" sauce dishes. Edges may be ruffled, candy ribbon, or ice cream shaped.

Colors: marigold, green, rare amethyst/purple, and rare blue.

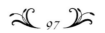

GRAPE AND CABLE—Northwood

Here we have bunches of grapes and leaves, neatly arranged in a balanced composition. A cable motif encircles the design. The candle lamp in the *GRAPE AND CABLE* pattern is an interesting item. It's very possible that Harry Northwood got his inspiration from a similar item made in England. A decorated "vine wreath foot candle lamp" was made in the area near Harry's Stourbridge home[3] and could well have been seen by the young man before he emigrated to the USA. Also, a similar pattern was used at Hobbs Brockunier where Harry Northwood first worked in the United States' glass industry. Northwood's *GRAPE AND CABLE* pattern was introduced in 1910 and became the company's widest range of shapes in the same design. The arrangement and size of the grape bunches and the leaves alters according to the shape on which it is portrayed. Described in early advertising as a "Vineland" pattern, an amazing number of different shapes were made. It was indeed popular! So popular that Fenton produced their own version. *GRAPE AND CABLE* is used as both an exterior and an interior pattern. It is also used in conjunction with other exterior designs such as *MEANDER* and *BASKETWEAVE,* or the exterior may simply be plain or ribbed. Further variations are given by stippling the background and by using plain bands instead of the cabling on a few scarce items. Stippled items are more scarce and sought after. The iridescence is often heightened by the stippled effect.

Shapes: an amazing range—collar based and spatula footed bowls, berry sets, plates in four different sizes, handled bonbon, one handled nappy, sherbet dish, banana bowl, centerpiece bowl, orange bowl, breakfast set, and table set. There are two sizes of water sets, three sizes of punch sets, a whiskey decanter with shot glasses, a dressing table set (comprising a hatpin holder, powder jar, large and small trays, and cologne bottle with stopper), candlelamp, cracker jar,

tobacco humidor, fernery, sweetmeat compote, plus large compotes both open and covered

Colors: marigold, amethyst/purple, green, blue, white, ice blue, ice green, and aqua opalescent. Not all items are available in all colors. For example, no cobalt blue water sets or tumblers are known. Some shapes are fairly easy to find in certain colors, while other shapes are very scarce in the same color. A good example is green. The collar based bowls and plates are reasonably available in green, while punch sets in green are very hard to find indeed. Most shapes are more available in marigold, yet the large covered compote and the sweetmeat compote are rare in marigold. The only known aqua opalescent punch set (small size) is one of the rarest and highest priced shapes in Carnival. It changed hands in 1996 for around $95,000.

Notes: there is a variant called *BANDED GRAPE AND CABLE* where the usual cable is replaced by a plain band. Another variation is that "Old Rose Distillery" advertising lettering can be found on the back of some green *GRAPE AND CABLE* plates.

Harry Northwood's *GRAPE AND CABLE* candle lamp. It may be found in marigold, amethyst and green: marigold is the scarcest of the three colors. It is hard to find the shades—quite possibly many were broken during use, as they balance on top of the fitment in a rather delicate manner. Heat, too, must have played a part in causing damage.

1910 saw the introduction of Northwood's *GRAPE AND CABLE* pattern—and what a splendid range of shapes it became known in. Here are just a few, all of them impressive and showy items. Three different kinds of large footed bowls are illustrated, as well as the stemmed open compote and the lidded cracker jar. Note the vase on the right of the ad. This is not *GRAPE AND CABLE,* instead it is Northwood's *TREETRUNK* funeral sized vase, described in the ad as a 19" "mammoth rustic embossed vase."

This candle lamp was designed by Messrs. Blews of Birmingham, England, and Richardson's, the famed glass manufacturer of Stourbridge, England, for the Great Exhibition at the Crystal Palace in London, 1851. The glass shade is festooned with grape vines in much the same way as the Northwood version of the *GRAPE AND CABLE* candle lamp. It's quite possible that the young Harry Northwood, whilst living and working in the Stourbridge area himself, may have seen such a lamp.

GRAPE AND CABLE—Fenton

This pattern is very similar to the Northwood version. Indeed, it can be very hard to tell the difference between the manufacturers. There are ways, however, to distinguish between them. Fenton made fewer shapes in *GRAPE AND CABLE* and also made colors that were not in the Northwood line. Quite a lot of the Northwood pieces are trademarked with the N. A full explanation of how to differentiate between the Fenton and Northwood versions of *GRAPE AND CABLE* is set out below.

Shapes: collar based and scroll footed bowls and plates. Also found are orange bowls with scroll feet (some have *PERSIAN MEDALLION* interior).

Colors: marigold, amethyst/purple, blue, green, aqua, moonstone, vaseline, blue opal, amberina, red, and celeste blue.

"New Aurora" Iridescent Assortment
Sparkling iridescent glass, embossed bird, floral and fruit designs.

ler Brothers catalogs in the 1920s. This one, in 1924, was for Fenton's *GRAPE AND CABLE* footed orange bowl with the beautiful *PERSIAN MEDALLION* interior.

Differentiation Between Northwood and Fenton GRAPE AND CABLE

The main confusion is with the 8" and 9" bowls and plates, which are common to both Northwood and Fenton. Some distinguishing characteristics **for these two shapes only** may help to sort out the confusion:

- Scroll feet are usually Fenton. Both Northwood and Fenton made pieces with spatula feet and collar bases.
- Pie crust edge is Northwood.
- Scallop and flute edge is Fenton.
- N mark is—of course—Northwood.
- Colors: vaseline, red, amberina, moonstone or celeste blue are Fenton. Ice blue, ice green, and aqua opal are Northwood.

If the above characteristics have not already determined whether it's Fenton or Northwood, then you most likely have a plain backed bowl or plate with no clues from the edge or color as to the manufacturer. At this point, it's necessary to count the grapes! Fenton's pieces usually have four bunches of grapes neatly arranged rather like "pool balls in a rack." There are usually fourteen grapes per bunch (though fifteen in one bunch is also possible). Northwood's bunches usually have more grapes to the bunch (twenty-one to twenty-four) and the grapes are more randomly set out, in a more naturalistic manner.

GRAPE AND CABLE—Dugan/Diamond

Not to be outdone, it seems that Dugan/Diamond also tried out their hand at this pattern. Shards of what appeared to be a *GRAPE AND CABLE* perfume bottle were discovered at the old Dugan site in Indiana, Pennsylvania. The perfume bottle (just 4.5" high) is probably the only example of Dugan's version of this pattern. Virtually identical in design concept, there are, however, significant differences from Northwood's *GRAPE AND CABLE*. There is no cable—instead there are beads! The stopper on the little bottle is quite unlike the stopper on the Northwood cologne bottle: it has a flatter shape and paneled mouldwork on its lower section. Northwood's examples have the grape design all over the stopper.

Shape: perfume bottle. Color: amethyst/purple.

A splendid, tightly crimped edge is seen on this black amethyst Dugan/Diamond *CHERRIES* 6" plate. $200-$400. One sold in 2004 for $510.

Northwood's *STRAWBERRY* pie crust edge bowl is seen less often with a stippled background. Green, as shown here, is an unusual color. $400-$800.

Northwood's *WILD STRAWBERRY* 7.5" handgrip plate in green. $150-$200.

Northwood's *WILD STRAWBERRY*, seen here on an amethyst berry bowl, can be identified by the presence of tiny flowers amongst the fruits (The flowers are absent on the *STRAWBERRY* pattern.). $40-$60.

A rare, blue Millersburg *BLACKBERRY WREATH* ruffled bowl. $1000-$1500.

This amethyst *GRAPE WREATH VARIANT* ruffled bowl has a typical Millersburg radium iridescence. $150-$200.

A display of *GRAPE AND CABLE* in a wide variety of shapes. Top row from left: marigold tobacco humidor ($250-$350), green hatpin holder ($400-$500), amethyst 9" plate ($150-$200). Bottom row from left: purple sweetmeat compote ($250-$300), purple perfume ($500-$800), purple powder jar ($175-$325), and marigold 11" ruffled bowl ($75-$125). All by Northwood except the perfume bottle, which is from Dugan/Diamond.

Fenton's *VINTAGE* is easily found in the bowl shape, but this 9" flat plate is very scarce indeed. $1000-$2000 in marigold.

Stylized Patterns

The line between realistic and stylized fruit patterns is thinly drawn in many cases. In some patterns, however, the fruits are so detached from reality that it is difficult to recognize them.

In the language of flowers, the orange tree stands for generosity. It is one of the most prolific trees and is an ancient symbol of fertility. Long associated with love and marriage, the blossoms will often be carried by a bride at her wedding. The British designer William Morris, and many of his contemporaries, produced a rich variety of popular patterns that featured the orange tree in the late 1800s and early 1900s. The symbolism of the tree and its fruits and flowers was not lost on these designers, many of whose patterns bear an amazing resemblance to the later *ORANGE TREE* designs produced by Fenton that were clearly reflecting popular taste. Three distinct, stylized *ORANGE TREE* designs were made by Fenton. In each, the orange trees are very much alike, though the background pattern of leaves or scrolls varies.

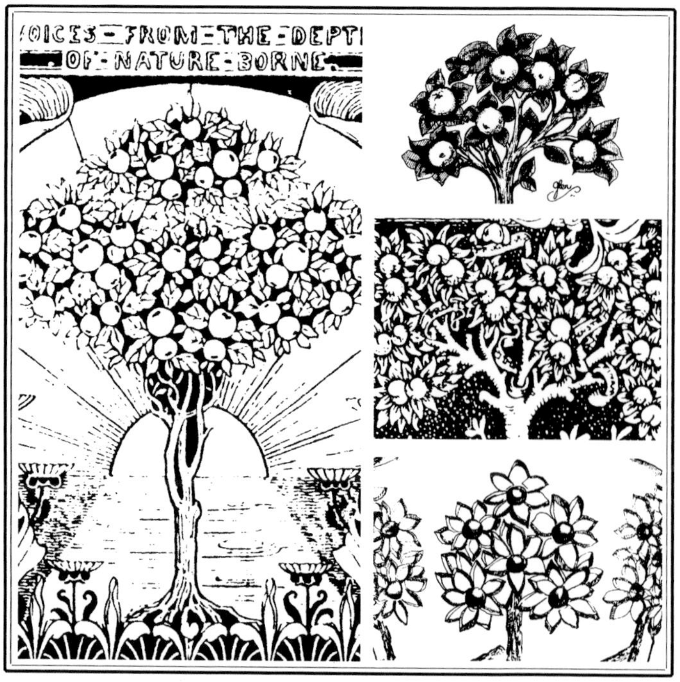

ORANGE TREE aka *FOOTED ORANGE TREE or SMALL ORANGE TREE*—Fenton

The most well known of the orange tree designs from Fenton, this pattern was produced from about 1911, in the widest variety of shapes they ever issued. It was produced as both an interior and exterior pattern. The main pattern motif is a stylized orange tree, its branches laden with plump, round fruits that are themselves surrounded by leaves. The fruits and leaves look a little like flowers themselves: the round fruit being mistaken for the center of the flower head and the leaves being mistaken for the surrounding petals. On the *ORANGE TREE* rosebowl or nutbowl shape, the effect is of flowers rather than trees and this has led to the pattern on those items often being called *FENTON'S FLOWERS*. *ORANGE TREE* is distinct in that many items (but by no means all) in the pattern have squared off feet that carry a leaf design. The exterior pattern on some bowls and plates is *BEARDED BERRY*.

Shapes: the water set, berry set, table set, and hatpin holder are all square footed. The centerpiece or orange bowl

The orange tree was a popular motif (symbolic of love and marriage) and was much used by designers and illustrators in the late 1800s and early 1900s. The orange tree with the rising sun shown on the left of this composite is from an early edition of *The Studio* in 1894. Top right is a detail from Henry Dearle's "Orange Tree" tapestry, from around 1900. (Dearle, who was a student of the noted designer William Morris, also designed a popular wallpaper that is almost identical to this.) The illustration at middle right is from *The Studio* in 1910. Bottom right is an interpretation of the orange tree motif on Carnival Glass: this is a detail from Fenton's *ORANGE TREE ORCHARD* design, introduced in 1911.

has scroll feet while the 8" bowls and 9" plates are collar based. Other items are the breakfast sugar and creamer, punch set, puff or powder jar, and distinctive two handled, loving cup. Also known in *ORANGE TREE* are the wine glass and goblet, two sizes of mugs, a sherbet dish, and a nutbowl and rosebowl, both of which have three distinctive, curving, twig feet.

Colors: marigold, amethyst/purple, blue, green, white (sometimes with gilding), aqua, teal, vaseline, amber, moonstone, celeste blue, red, and rare aqua opalescent.

Notes: the centers of some 9" plates and 8" bowls vary. Some have a "treetrunk" variation where the trunk of the tree extends into the outer portion of the center of the plate. This variant is sometimes referred to as "stylized flower center." A rare variation to the tumblers and pitchers is known. On the regular pattern there is a cable band and an embroidery motif of overlapping stitches (correctly described as needle lace, though sometimes called a "scale filler") near the top of the items. The variant has neither cable nor embroidery motif.

ORANGE TREE SCROLL aka *ORANGE TREE VARIANT*—Fenton

Whereas *ORANGE TREE* was known in a huge variety of shapes, this pattern was extremely limited in its range and color. It features a very similar orange tree motif, but this is bordered above and below by a curvilinear, scroll design.

Shapes: water set (pitcher is tankard shaped).

Colors: marigold and blue. White, amethyst/purple, and green are reported but we cannot confirm.

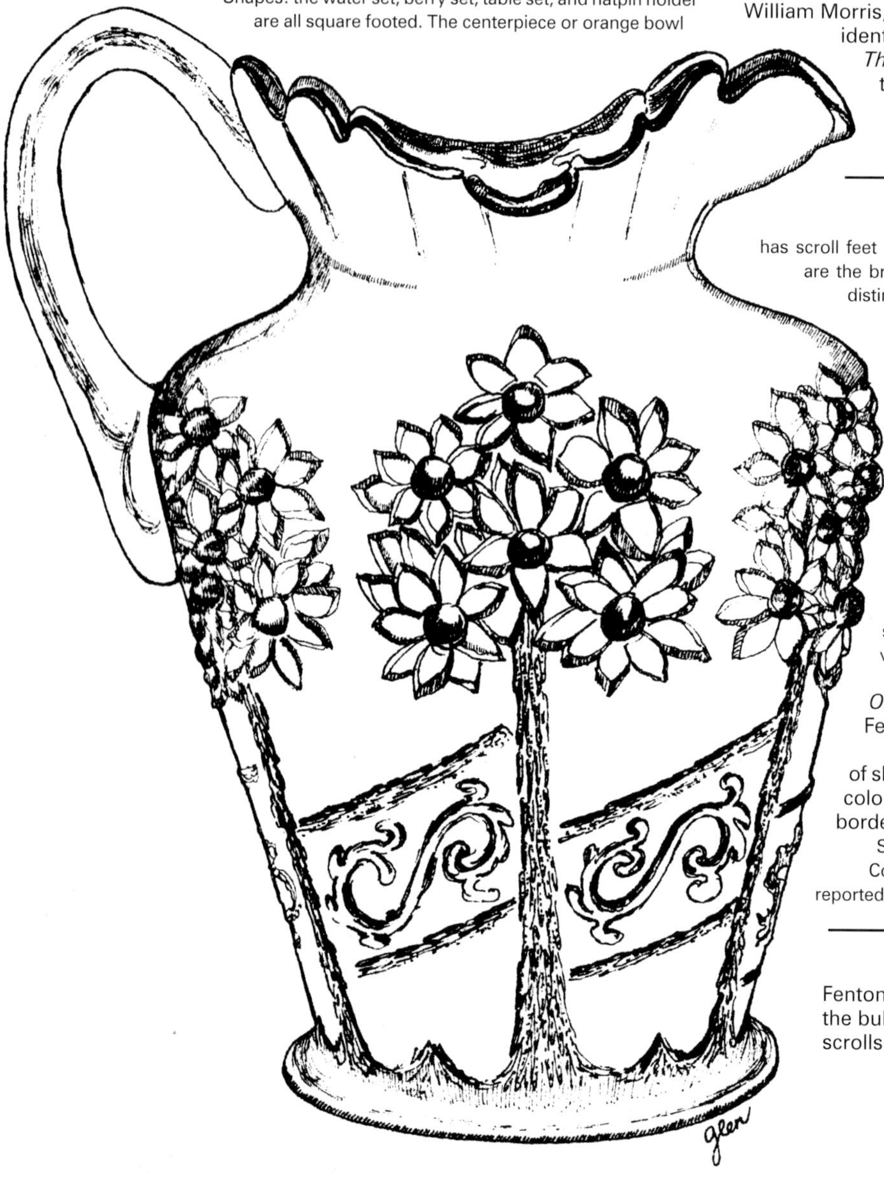

Fenton's *ORANGE TREE ORCHARD* design as seen on the bulbous water pitcher. Note the fancy rococo type scrolls between the tree trunks.

ORANGE TREE ORCHARD aka *ORANGE TREE AND CABLE*—Fenton

Introduced in 1911, this pattern also enjoyed only limited shapes and colors. It is distinguished from the other two orange tree designs in that it has a line of cabling above the orange trees on the tumblers as well as a Rococo spiral (or arabesque) design below. The bottom of the pattern is bordered by a scalloped motif that joins together the trunks of the orange trees.

Shapes: water set (pitcher is bulbous). Colors: marigold, blue and white. Green and amethyst/purple are reported but we cannot confirm.

WREATHED CHERRY—Dugan/Diamond

"A handsome design of cherries and leaves" was how the 1917 catalog of the John M. Smyth Merchandise Company described this stylized pattern. Cherry clusters are neatly "wreathed" by leaves, creating a medallion effect on this attractive design which was introduced by Dugan/Diamond around 1911. A stylized fan motif separates the wreaths further. The design also lent itself to the application of enameled paintwork. On some of the white Carnival examples, therefore, the cherries were picked out in red, the leaves in gold.

Shapes: berry set (oval shaped bowls), water set (tankard shaped pitcher), and table set. Colors: marigold, amethyst/purple, and white (enameled).

Notes: the master berry bowl, being oval, is sometimes called a banana boat. The butter dish base has been reported bearing a D in a diamond trademark.

BLACKBERRY BLOCK—Fenton

An interesting combination of elements makes up this elegant design. A sharp contrast is formed between the informal, natural looking, leafy sprays of blackberries and the angular, squared off background design. The overall effect is akin to blackberries growing on a trellis. The squared off "blocks" are delineated by a cable or rope effect. There is a fine diagonal hatching behind alternate rows of blocks. It is interesting to note that the design as shown in a contemporary 1911 Butler Brothers ad had very different leaves to the ones seen on the actual *BLACKBERRY BLOCK* items themselves.

Shapes: water set (bulbous pitcher, often with crimped edge).

Colors: marigold, amethyst/purple, cobalt blue, green, rare white, and vaseline.

This Butler Brothers ad from mid-spring 1911 showed three fine Fenton water sets. From left they are *MILADY, FLUFFY PEACOCK,* and *BLACKBERRY BLOCK*. Note that the description below referred to the patterns having "butterfly and grape embossings." The ad must have been hastily put together, as that description does not refer to any of these three patterns. The compositors also managed to spell "assortment" wrong too! (Note the double R). But who was bothered about accurate descriptions and spelling at prices like this? 65 cents for a full water set!

INVERTED STRAWBERRY—Cambridge

This design is unusual in that it is one of the few intaglio (or near cut type) patterns that are not geometric. Highly stylized—owing to the nature of the intaglio mould work—the strawberries are deeply embossed into the surface of the glass. Leaves and blossoms complete the overall design.

The design is exterior on all items including bowls. The words NEAR-CUT are often found on the interior of items in this pattern. The marie has a distinct flower and leaf pattern. There is also a "sister" pattern called *INVERTED THISTLE*.

Shapes: berry set, water set, milk pitcher, table set, compote, candlestick, powder jar, cuspidor, and celery.

Colors: marigold, amethyst/purple, blue, and green.

STRAWBERRY SCROLL—Fenton

The composition of elements on this superb design is carefully executed. It is almost symmetrical and very carefully balanced. The central motif is a curvilinear scroll that snakes its way around the pattern. Above and below it lies a straight cable. Above and below that are the strawberries and leaves, thoughtfully placed to create a balanced whole. There is a very similar "sister" pattern called *LILY OF THE VALLEY.*

Shapes: water set (pitcher is mould blown and very distinctive).

Colors: marigold and cobalt blue.

Exaggerated Stylizing

Some patterns are stylized to a great extent, the fruits becoming extremely simplified. One such is *CHERRY CHAIN*, an intricate design imitative of detailed stitchwork. Though named for the fruits it incorporates, *CHERRY CHAIN* is primarily classed as an "embroidery" pattern. A variation of the *CHERRY CHAIN* is featured on the stem of Fenton's *MIKADO* compote. The stylized "embroidery" patterns will be considered in Part Two, Chapter Nine.

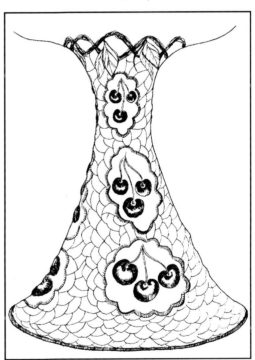

This is a variation of the stylized pattern *CHERRY CHAIN*, as seen on the pedestal stem of Fenton's *MIKADO* compote.

These truly realistic looking cherries seen on the outside of the *MIKADO* compote bowl are in complete contrast to the stylized cherries (*CHERRY CHAIN* variation) seen on the compote's stem.

FENTONIA FRUIT—Fenton

This scarce design is simplified down to a basic diamond pattern. Alternate diamonds are filled with a needle lace embroidery motif ("scale filler") and a stylized cluster of fruits, probably cherries. Each diamond shape is separated by a cable type line. *FENTONIA FRUIT* has a more easily found "sister" called *FENTONIA* in which the fruits are replaced by a "spider web" embroidery motif. A careful study of the diamond shapes that contain the fruits on *FENTONIA FRUIT* reveals traces of the "spider web" motif as an underlying pattern. It would seem, therefore, that *FENTONIA FRUIT* is from the original *FENTONIA* mould that was cleverly re-cut to extend its life.

Shapes: water set (standard pitcher), and berry set.
Colors: marigold and blue.

FANCIFUL—Dugan/Diamond

A little bit of imagination is needed to interpret this pattern as stylized strawberries—yet that is surely what is intended. The fruits, however, are far removed from reality, reduced to a heart shape filled in with a diamond block effect. The central portion of the pattern, however, appears to emulate embroidery work. All in all, it is a curious mixture of styles verging on the abstract, bearing great similarities to another Dugan/Diamond design, *ROUND UP*. The exterior design to *FANCIFUL* is *BIG BASKETWEAVE*.

Shapes: collar based 8" bowls and 9" plates.
Colors: marigold, amethyst/purple, blue, and white.

Even More Fruits

There are many more delightful fruit designs, including several that successfully blend together fruits with other motifs. *PEACOCK AND GRAPE* and *DRAGON AND STRAWBERRY* are particularly good examples of this. Fenton's *TWO FRUITS* pattern, only known in the divided bonbon shape, features pears and apples. In addition, the rare *STRAWBERRY EPERGNE* from Dugan/Diamond, Northwood's *RASPBERRY*, the *STRAWBERRY* bonbon from Fenton, as well as the exceptionally rare *PLUMS AND CHERRIES* items from Northwood all fit into this category.

[1] *The Studio.* Issue number 38. London, England, 1902.

[2] This variation to the regular *THREE FRUITS* pattern by Northwood was first noted and researched through the medium of the Internet Carnival club, Woodsland World Wide Carnival Glass Association (www.cga). The unusual nature of the Internet, with its instant communication and wide accessibility, meant that many collectors could contribute to the 1997 survey conducted by the authors as Education Coordinators of the club and later reported on the World Wide Web. Similar educational articles are always available at the Woodsland web site and educational resource.

[3] The bronze and brass "vine-wreath foot" candle lamp was designed by Messrs. Blews & Sons, Birmingham, England. The leaves and fruit were colored to stand out. The glass shade, also decorated with vines, was made by Messrs. Richardson of Stourbridge, England. Circa 1851.

Three blue Fenton tumblers with a multitude of names! From left: *ORANGE TREE SCROLL* aka *ORANGE TREE VARIANT* ($75-$125), *(FOOTED) ORANGE TREE* ($75-$125), and *ORANGE TREE ORCHARD* aka *ORANGE TREE AND CABLE* ($75-$125).

Two Dugan/Diamond *WREATHED CHERRY* tumblers. Marigold on the left ($40-$70) and a white tumbler decorated with red cherries and a gilt rim on the right ($75-$100).

This close-up detail of Fenton's *BLACKBERRY BLOCK* tumbler shows that the leaves are very different from those illustrated in the Butler Brothers 1911 ad.

Close-up detail of the orange tree in Fenton's pattern of the same name. An extremely wide range of shapes and colors was produced in this pattern over many years, from 1911 through the late 1920s. The example shown here is on a blue punch bowl.

The iridescence on this marigold *RASP-BERRY* pitcher by Northwood is superb. $175-$225.

At first glance you might think this was the regular blue Fenton *FENTONIA* design. In fact, it is the seldom seen *FENTONIA FRUIT* pattern—note the cherry bunches which have replaced the "embroidery stitches" found on the regular *FENTONIA* pattern. $300-$500.

Stylized strawberries are the featured motif on this blue, Dugan/Diamond *FANCIFUL* plate. $600-$850. Note: a superb example sold for $1700 at auction in April 1998. *Courtesy of Rita and Les Glennon.*

Two similar Fenton tumblers. On the left is *STRAWBERRY SCROLL* ($200 -250) and on the right is its "sister" pattern, *LILY OF THE VALLEY.* ($275-$350).

Butterflies

"When I was a small child .. I thought that success spelled happiness. I was wrong. Happiness is like a butterfly which appears and delights us."

Anna Pavlova (1881-1931), Russian ballet dancer

A massive piece of glass, Dugan/Diamond's purple *BUTTERFLY AND TULIP* square shaped bowl never fails to impress. $2000-$4000.

Close-up detail of Northwood's *SINGING BIRDS* pattern on a green tumbler

For the lover of Carnival Glass, the delight of the butterfly is less ephemeral: its beauty firmly fixed on the glass, its scintillating colors captured by the shimmering iridescence. Ancient civilizations believed the butterfly was a reflection of the soul. To the Chinese, it represented happiness and joy. In Japan, it was one of the most popular insect designs. The favorite literary themes for the Japanese were also the favorite design themes. Butterflies—popular in Japan—caught on in the western world too, as part of the general trend for Oriental design. Most of the Classic Carnival designs represent butterflies in a somewhat stylized manner. They are part of a pattern and are portrayed as simplified and conventionalized. They are decorative and visually attractive design motifs. In Carnival Glass, butterflies have their day in the sun.

BUTTERFLY AND BERRY—Fenton

One of Fenton's most popular designs, *BUTTERFLY AND BERRY* features a typical device for that company—a repeated, alternate pattern. The stylized butterfly motif is set alongside bunches of berries, the overall effect being that of a paneled pattern. The berries are often thought to be grapes—not so! They were originally intended as blackberries. The shape and size of the berry cluster as well as the distinctive shape of the leaves all confirm this. Further, when the pattern was introduced in 1911, Butler Brothers ads described the pattern as having "embossed blackberry and butterfly panels." It's easy to see how the blackberries came to be thought of as grapes, though. A few years after the 1911 ad, the pattern was no longer described as having blackberries; instead, the more anonymous terms "berry" and "fruit" were used. Gradually, the fruit lost its initial identity. *BUTTERFLY AND BERRY* was a popular line for Fenton and was still selling well into the early 1920s. (The advertisers stretched the imagination somewhat by calling the pattern a "**new** embossed design.") Butler Brothers ads for the pattern in 1924 described it as having an "embossed butterfly and grape design." Undoubtedly, though, the motif was originally intended to be a blackberry.

BUTTERFLY AND BERRY is mainly used as an exterior pattern. On the tall items, the paneled design is lengthened to the extent that the butterfly becomes a totally different shape. Long and thin, it is a somewhat odd caricature of the squatter version seen on the bowls. When found on bowls, it is in combination with a variety of interior designs. One of these is the *BUTTERFLY AND BERRY* pattern itself. As an interior pattern it is no longer paneled, and in fact has a more realistic feel. The butterfly is placed centrally and is surrounded by a blackberry wreath. Other interior patterns that are sometimes combined with *BUTTERFLY AND BERRY* on footed bowls are *PANTHER*, *FANTAIL*, and the rare *HEARTS AND TREES*. The pattern adapts for use on a variety of very different shapes.

Shapes: a very wide range was produced, which included footed berry sets and individual bowls with 5, 8 and 10" diameters. Other shapes are the fernery, water set, footed table set, and hatpin holder. Whimsey shapes include a cuspidor fashioned from a sugar bowl and vases pulled up from the tumbler shape. Colors: marigold, amethyst/purple, blue, and green. Rare in white and red.

Notes: the footed items have very distinctive ball and claw feet. *FANTAIL* bowls are only known in blue and marigold. There are rare chop plates in *FANTAIL*.

Fenton's *BUTTERFLY AND BERRY* pattern was introduced in 1911. It must have been a "best seller" since it was still being advertised in the 1920s, as this Butler Brothers ad shows. The items illustrated in the 1924 "Golden Glow" Dining Set Assortment were the water pitcher and master berry bowl as well as the covered butter dish, covered sugar, and creamer from the table set. Marigold was the only color offered at this time.

HEARTS AND TREES is known in marigold and maybe other colors. *PANTHER* is known in most colors including the rare Nile green.

BUTTERFLY AND FERN/PLUME—Fenton

This is one of Fenton's earliest Carnival water set patterns, seen in ads from 1911, where it was described as "all over butterfly and leaf embossed." Another repeated design, this attractive pattern is comprised of open winged butterflies framed by stylized leaf fronds. There are three butterflies around the tumblers and six around the pitchers.

Shape: only known in the water set. The pitcher is mould blown and usually has a tightly crimped, almost frilly looking top. Colors: marigold, amethyst/purple, blue, and green. Notes: there is a variant tumbler. The only significant difference is that the variant has a collar base and is slightly taller than the regular version, which has the ground base.

Two Fenton water pitchers seen in a Butler Brothers ad from 1910. On the left is *BUTTERFLY AND FERN*, also known as *BUTTERFLY AND PLUME*. On the right is the *PANELED DANDELION* tankard pitcher.

BUTTERFLY—Northwood

There is only one central butterfly on this design from 1910. One's eye is immediately drawn to it, pulled in by the background design of rays that focus onto the center of the motif. It is a simple, yet extremely effective design. Found only in a handled bonbon dish, this item usually has a plain exterior. It is sometimes found, however, with an unusual pattern of concentric circles on the exterior. These circles are part of the press moulded pattern and imitate an earlier glass making technique. The concentric circles are intended to look like "threading"—a popular style of winding fine glass filaments around glass objects as an applied, decorative technique. Harry Northwood's father, John, had used the technique in England (he worked at Stevens and Williams, the famous glassworks in Stourbridge, England). In 1885, John Northwood patented a machine to improve the application of glass threads, making it easier and more uniform. True to the spirit of mass production, Harry converted the manually applied threading into his machine, press moulded Carnival Glass.

Shape: two handled bonbon only.

Colors: marigold, amethyst/purple, blue, and green. Rare in ice blue (threaded exterior only) and smoke (plain exterior only).

BUTTERFLY AND TULIP—Dugan/Diamond

This item is extremely impressive due to its immense size and the magnificent, sheer simplicity of its decorative effect. It is a massive heavy piece, weighing in at three and a half pounds. The design is dominated by a huge stippled butterfly, behind which are three stylized tulip flowers and curling, stippled leaves. The exterior pattern is *FEATHER SCROLL*, aka *INVERTED FEATHER AND FAN*.

Shape: four footed bowl only.
Colors: marigold and amethyst/purple.

Even More Butterflies

There are several other attractive butterfly designs: Fenton's *BUTTERFLIES* bonbon, only known in that two handled shape; United States Glass Co.'s exceptionally rare *BIG BUTTERFLY* tumbler; the rare and delicate *BUTTERFLY ORNAMENTS* made as "give-aways" by Fenton; and the exceptionally rare *BUTTERFLY AND CORN* vase, considered to be by Northwood. Various other patterns also feature butterflies; Northwood's *SPRINGTIME* design is one example. The Australian manufacturer Crown Crystal produced several delightful Carnival patterns featuring butterflies, which will be discussed in Part Three.

BUTTERFLY AND BERRY was a very popular Fenton pattern that was in their line from 1911 through the early 1920s. This blue covered butterdish is part of the four piece table set. $100-$300.

Fenton's *BUTTERFLY AND FERN* aka *BUTTERFLY AND PLUME* water set. The pitcher is blow moulded. $400-$800 for a full water set in blue comprising pitcher and six tumblers.

Three tumblers featuring butterflies. From left: green Fenton *BUTTERFLY AND FERN* ($60-$130), purple Northwood *SPRINGTIME* ($100-$140), and blue Fenton *BUTTERFLY AND BERRY* ($30-$40).

There's a classical simplicity, typical of Northwood's designs, on this purple *BUTTERFLY* bon bon. $75-$100.

Close-up of the butterfly motif on Northwood's purple *BUTTER-FLY* bon bon.

Birds

"You can picture my father going out in the early morning and watching the rascally thrushes at work on the fruit beds and telling the gardener—who growls 'I'd like to wring their necks!'—that no bird in the garden must be touched."

—May Morris, daughter of the British designer William Morris (1834-1896)

Carnival patterns featuring birds took their inspiration from various sources—for example, Oriental designs and the various, decorative bird motifs in the Art Nouveau style books. It is also possible to see links in the splendid bird patterns that were the work of the British designer, William Morris. These patterns were seen on wallpaper and fabrics as well as in the trade journals. Further, at the International Trade fair in Boston in 1883, Morris's "Bird" designs were popular and sold well. He took his inspiration from nature (the thrushes in his garden, in particular) as well as medieval and Eastern sources. A glance at Morris's patterns such as "The Strawberry Thief," "Bird," and "Brer Rabbit" will show similarities with some of the bird motifs seen on Carnival Glass.

SINGING BIRDS—Northwood

Possibly the most easily recognized bird pattern, *SINGING BIRDS* has a strong Oriental feel to it, shown especially in the look of the flowers and branches. It is an elegant, stylized design that has a paneled effect. The background to some of the mugs in this pattern is also stippled, which enhances the iridescent effect. (Sixty cents was the cost of a box of twelve such mugs in 1912, according to a contemporary Butler Brothers ad.) *SINGING BIRDS* is an exterior pattern.

Shapes: water set (the pitcher is the standard shape), berry set, table set, and mug.

Colors: marigold, amethyst/purple, and green. Small berry bowls and mugs are also found in blue. A wider range of colors is known for the mugs, including ice blue, white, lavender, and aqua opal.

This detail from Northwood's *SINGING BIRDS* has an Oriental "feel." The stylized flowers are particularly evocative of Japanese design.

ROBIN—Imperial

This Imperial design is reminiscent of Morris's "Bird" patterns. The floral decoration is highly stylized, the background has a fine stippled effect that picks up light very effectively. *ROBIN* has the distinction of being the only Imperial design that features a bird—indeed it is the only Imperial design pattern that predominantly features any kind of fauna.

Shapes: water set (the pitcher is the standard shape); mugs are also known.

Colors: marigold for the water set and mug. Rare smoke tumblers and mugs are known. Odd shades of light green with marigold or smoky iridescence are sometimes found on the mugs.

The British designer William Morris produced a range of designs featuring birds. Interestingly, Imperial's *ROBIN* is in a very similar style to them.

BIRDS & CHERRIES—Fenton

A simple yet most effective design, with more than a hint of an Oriental feel, this pattern had been introduced in a 1911 Butler Brothers ad that (somewhat confusingly) described it as both "Venetian" and "Oriental!" The birds are very reminiscent of those drawn by William Morris in his "Strawberry Thief" pattern. This is a stylized design, carefully adapted to the shapes on which it is featured. A central motif made up of leaves provides the focus for the design. Branches radiate out from the center, connecting up with the outer encircling "wreath" of birds, berries, and blossoms.

Shapes: compote, handled bonbon, scarce large and small bowl, and very rare chop plate.

Colors: marigold, amethyst/purple, blue, and green. It's possible that vaseline examples may exist.

Another bird pattern with an Oriental "feel" to it, this is a detail from Fenton's *BIRDS AND CHERRIES* pattern.

STORK & RUSHES—Dugan/Diamond

Here is another design that has an Oriental influence. Though it was referred to in contemporary ads as a "Bird design," *STORK AND RUSHES* should perhaps have been named "Crane and Rushes." The crane design was one of the most popular bird designs in Japan. Not only did its graceful figure appeal to the imagination of the Japanese artists, but it was also a powerful symbol of longevity in their culture. In *STORK AND RUSHES* the bird is depicted against a background of reeds and shallow water. The motif is repeated around the pattern, with alternate birds looking in different directions. In many ways, this is an attempt at a naturalistic interpretation: consider the foliage on the water's edge, the elegant stance of the birds. *STORK AND RUSHES* is an exterior design, and has a distinctive band of beads (usually) or lattice bordering both the top and bottom. There is also a paneled effect to the pattern. The total design concept is very reminiscent of Northwood's

PEACOCK AT THE FOUNTAIN pattern.

Shapes: water set (the pitcher is the standard size), berry set, mug, and punch set. Colors: marigold, amethyst/purple, and blue.

Notes: only tumblers and mugs have so far been found with a lattice design. No mugs have yet been found with the beaded border. It is thought that the base to the punch set is the *SUMMER DAYS* vase, though not all collectors agree.

HERON MUG—Dugan/Diamond

This pattern is very similar to the *STORK AND RUSHES* design and possibly also an attempt at realism. There is only one bird (and it is different, its beak is much larger) and the foliage is not the same. But there is also a border—in this case a rope effect. In a 1913 Butler Brothers catalog it was called a "Stein" and the design was described as "Embossed Stork and Tropical Plants."

Shape: mug only. Colors: scarce marigold and amethyst/purple.

Notes: the motif is only on one side of the mug. Its "sister" pattern is the

FISHERMAN'S MUG. These items are thought to have been used as food containers, and sold in that fashion (i.e., full of some type of foodstuff).

NESTING SWAN—Millersburg

Regal and stately, this is a stylized design of great elegance. An interior pattern, it is always coupled with the magnificent, geometric exterior pattern

DIAMOND AND FAN. The single swan is central in the design. Its foot dips into the water as flowers, rushes, and leaf sprays radiate outward. The design has coherence and an effective sense of harmony. The eye focuses on the swan, drawn in by the converging pattern of leaves.

Shapes: 10" bowls, ruffled, candy ribbon edged, or tri-cornered. A rare 8" bowl is reported. Also known are a single marigold rosebowl and a single green spittoon whimsey.

Colors: marigold, amethyst/purple, and green. Rare (currently single examples) blue and vaseline bowls are known.

BIRD WITH GRAPES—Dugan/Diamond

This was a later pattern, described in the Butler Brothers catalog for 1927 as "New in design." Its shape is unusual and distinctive, for this pattern is only found on a triangular shaped wall vase (or wall pocket). The back is pierced with two holes for easy hanging. The stylized design is on the facing side only and features a single bird against a backdrop of grapes and leaves. The background is deeply stippled, which enhances the iridescence well.

Shape: wall pocket/vase only. Color: marigold.

A 1913 Butler Brothers ad for Dugan/Diamond's *HERON* mug, described as a "Stein." Note that the caption refers to the design as an "embossed stork and tropical plants."

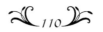

Even More Birds

Birds feature in other ways on Carnival. The famous Dugan/Diamond *FARMYARD* bowl, of course, features a rooster and two hens. Swans were fashioned into salt dips, in the style of the older British examples (originally posy holders) from Burtles and Tate. There are also several splendid bird designs from Crown Crystal in Australia and Sowerby in England, but these will be discussed in Part Three.

Millersburg's splendid *NESTING SWAN* ruffled bowl, seen here in green. $200-$400.

Close-up showing the excellent mould detail of Millersburg's *NESTING SWAN*.

Three items featuring birds. From left: marigold Imperial *ROBIN* tumbler ($40-$60), blue Fenton *BIRDS AND CHERRIES* handled bonbon ($75-$100), and blue Northwood *SINGING BIRDS* mug ($150-$200).

Two versions of Dugan/Diamond's *STORK AND RUSHES* tumblers, with the lattice band version on the left ($75-$100) and the beaded band version on the right ($40-$60). Both are blue.

An unusual item, this is a marigold *BIRD WITH GRAPES* wall pocket from Dugan/Diamond. $75-$120.

"A Horse! A Horse! My Kingdom for a horse!"

—William Shakespeare (1564-1616)

Dugan/Diamond's *PONY* bowl in deep purple with a superb iridescence. $150-$200.

Animals in various forms are the dominant feature of several Carnival Glass patterns, most of which were produced by Fenton. The manufacturers of Early American Pattern Glass had utilized many popular animal motifs back in the 1800s. There were lion patterns from Gillinder and others, deer or stag patterns from McKee, and a "Farm Yard Assortment" of covered animal dishes produced by Challinor, Taylor and Co. At the same time in Britain, during the Victorian era, the animal motif had also been a prominent artistic theme (largely inspired by a group of French sculptors called the "Animaliers"). It was the height of fashion for the Victorian household to be decorated with various artistic forms of animals such as horses, lions, stags, and bears. Such images were often full of drama and movement, though at other times they were portrayed in a gentler, more coy manner. Animal designs were also used in the Art Nouveau movement of the late 1800s, as "nature" was their ultimate source.

Nursery rhyme and book illustrations were another source of inspiration. Previously, books had never been so available to the general public. Their illustrations, particularly in the children's sector, enjoyed much international popularity. The endearing images portrayed by Kate Greenaway, Walter Crane, and Beatrix Potter were treasured by many. Potter's *Peter Rabbit* was a huge success in the early 1900s. Toy glass, featuring cute animals such as kittens and made specially for children, was popular too.

Semi-Realistic/Naturalistic Patterns

The animals in many designs are portrayed in a realistic manner, with an obvious intent to convey the essence of the beast. In most of these patterns, although the animals look natural (and indeed wild), the overall effect, particularly the background, tends to have a stylized feel to it. For that reason, we have classed this group as semi-realistic, rather than fully realistic.

STAG AND HOLLY—Fenton

There's a majestic feel to the splendid stag that stands so proudly between the holly sprays. The antlered animal motif is repeated four times around the design which focuses on a central, stylized chrysanthemum type flower. *STAG AND HOLLY* had a lasting quality: it was advertised in Butler Brothers catalogs from about 1913 and was also seen in Sears Roebuck ads as late as 1927.

Shapes: 8" ruffled or ice cream shaped bowl and 9" plate, both with spatula feet; 10" ruffled or ice cream shaped bowl and 11" chop plate, both with ball feet. There is also a rosebowl.

Colors: marigold, amethyst/purple, blue, green, smoke, aqua/ teal, vaseline, amberina, and red.

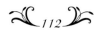

Fenton's *STAG AND HOLLY* pattern.

Detail from Fenton's *PANTHER*. Note the stylized peacock feathers that provide the "foliage" in the background.

LIONS—Fenton

First seen in Butler Brothers ads in 1916, this design features a roaring lion, mouth wide, with full, flowing mane, surmounted upon a rocky outcrop. The lion motif, interspersed with trees that look very similar to Fenton's orange trees, is repeated four times around the design. The center has a pattern made up of eight stylized daisies. The exterior is *BERRY AND LEAF CIRCLE*.

Shapes: 7" ruffled or ice cream shaped bowls and 8" plates only. Both the plates and bowls are collar based. Colors: marigold and blue.

PANTHER—Fenton

There's a splendid contrast in this pattern between the realistic, fearsome panther and the stylized peacock feathers that masquerade as jungle foliage in the background. The panther motif is repeated only twice, in a kind of reverse mirror image either side of the mid line. The exterior pattern is *BUTTERFLY AND BERRY. PANTHER* was advertised in the Butler Brothers catalogs in 1913. The following year, another of the Butler Brothers ads described the pattern as having "Tiger and Palm" embossing.

Shape: berry set only, comprising small 5" and large 9" footed berry bowls. Colors: marigold, amethyst/purple, blue, green, white, olive, red, and Nile green.

Notes: Only one example of Nile green is known (a 9" bowl).

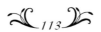

HORSE MEDALLION (HORSES' HEAD MEDALLION)—Fenton

Back in the 1960s, the author and Carnival Glass expert, Sherman Hand, wrote about the inspiration for this splendid design. As a young lad, Hand had earned his first wages selling "Cloverine Salve" at twenty-five cents a box, to receive only a dollar for the effort! As well as the money, he had also been presented with the gift of an art print—the picture was by John F. Herring (a British artist) and was entitled "Pharoah's Horses." Sherman Hand noted the astonishing similarity between the painting and the Classic Carnival design. More recently, a similar, remarkable likeness was spotted on a powder flask, fashioned in copper and brass, by an eagle-eyed Carnival collector in the United Kingdom. The flask bears a medallion motif that is surely the twin of Fenton's *HORSE MEDALLION*. It pre-dates the Carnival example and is identical even down to the rope effect encircling the medallion shape. It makes you wonder, did one of the Fenton employees—or maybe Frank Leslie Fenton himself—have a similar powder flask?

The Carnival pattern is composed of five medallion shapes, each containing three horses' heads, their manes flying free. Radiating out from the center and filling all the available intervening space are tiny stippled petals, similar to those used on the *STAG AND HOLLY* design. The *HORSE MEDALLION* pieces have either a plain exterior or the *BERRY AND LEAF CIRCLE* pattern.

Shapes: 7" ruffled, ice cream shape and jack in the pulpit shaped bowls. Also known are 8" plates, rosebowls and nutbowls. The items usually have three ball feet, though they may also be collar based.

Colors: marigold, amethyst/purple, blue, green, aqua, vaseline, smoke, amberina, red, and celeste blue. Not all colors are known in all shapes.

PONY—Dugan/Diamond

This is a familiar design and essentially very simple in concept. A realistic and tame looking horse's head, complete with bridle, dominates the center of the pattern. A classic, circular frame in a Greek key motif encloses the pony. On the underside of the bowl, the mouldwork for the pony's head can be felt in reverse. The edge of the bowl usually has distinct and sharp scallops and tiny flutes.

Shape: 8" bowl. The number of ruffles varies.

Colors: marigold, amethyst/purple, rare aqua and ice or pale green.

TROUT AND FLY—Millersburg

TROUT AND FLY and its "sister" pattern, *BIG FISH*, are two sought after patterns from the short-lived Millersburg factory. They are very similar in concept. Confusingly, the fish is actually smaller in the *BIG FISH* design. Not surprisingly, there is a fly (near the fish's mouth) on the *TROUT AND FLY*. Other than that, the designs are very close. The fish curves around, as if leaping from the water, against a background of stylized flowers. There is no exterior pattern, though the marie has the typical Millersburg multi-pointed star.

Shapes: 8" bowls with a wide variety of shaping and edge finishes. A rare 9" plate is also known.

Colors: marigold, amethyst/purple, green, and rare lavender.

Note: the *BIG FISH* is so far only known in the bowl shape. It is found in rare vaseline as well as the colors mentioned for the *TROUT AND FLY*.

SEACOAST—Millersburg

SEACOAST is a distinctive, realistic and unusual design found on a similarly distinctive shape. It is only known in the form of a petite pintray. There are no matching items. The design features a leaping fish, very much like the trout in *TROUT AND FLY*. The background portrays a detailed seascape of rocks, a lighthouse, and a rising sun. The edge of the pintray is exquisite, being intricately shaped in the form of long, curving leaves and scrolls, reminiscent of the Rococo Revival style. A similar pintray, *SUNFLOWER*, was also made by Millersburg.

Shape: pintray.

Colors: scarce marigold, amethyst/purple, and green.

ELKS—Dugan/Diamond, Fenton, and Millersburg

These rare items were made as souvenir items for the Benevolent Protective Order of the Elks (B.P.O.E.), possibly to be sold or given away at their various functions.

Dugan/Diamond's version of the *ELKS* design is the simplest. The animal's head and antlers are proudly displayed against a plain background. The elk faces the left.

Shape: one handled nappy only: its shape is similar to the familiar Dugan/Diamond *LEAF RAYS* nappy.

Color: amethyst/purple.

Fenton's *ELKS* designs were produced in 1910, 1911, 1912, and 1914, according to the wording on the items themselves. The elk's head and antlers face right, and on the bowl and plate shape there is an encircling background of twelve, five pointed stars. A banner winds behind the elk. The wording on the banner varies according to the item. On the 1910 souvenir, it reads "1910 DETROIT B.P.O.E." On the 1911 souvenir, it reads "1911 ATLANTIC CITY B.P.O.E.," and on the 1914 souvenir it reads "1914 PARKERSBURG B.P.O.E." On each there is a clock above the elk's head. The exterior pattern is *WIDE PANEL*.

A souvenir bell was also made—on this the overall design concept varies. The animal's head is seen against the background of an enlarged clock face. The lettering is around the top section of the bell while the stars circle around the rear section of the bell. The handle has a threaded effect. Bells are known for the Atlantic City and the Parkersburg Conventions. So far only one bell is known for the 1912 Portland Reunion. These are exceptionally rare items.

Shapes: ruffled and ice cream shaped 6" bowl, 7" plate, and bell.

Colors: marigold, amethyst/purple, blue, and green. Not all colors are known in all shapes. The bells are only found in blue.

Millersburg's *ELKS* always face the left and the design on the bowls is quite different from the Fenton version. The lettering is not enclosed within a banner, and the background has a full design of leaves. Like the Fenton items, however, a clock features in the design, behind the elk's head. A rare paperweight is also known (which has been reproduced). The only year that the Millersburg *ELKS* items were produced was 1910, for the Detroit convention.

Shapes: ruffled and ice cream shaped 7" bowls and a rare paperweight.

Color: amethyst/purple. The paperweight is also known in rare green.

Stylized Patterns

Some animal designs are totally removed from reality, either by virtue of the subject itself (dragons, for example) or because of the way in which the animal is portrayed (such as dancing, laughing bears).

DRAGON AND LOTUS—Fenton

Dragons, of course, don't exist, but in Carnival Glass they certainly had their "day in the sun." As noted and illustrated earlier, Fenton's wonderful dragon is very similar to a motif presented in *The Studio* magazine for 1894. An immensely popular design, it first appeared in Butler Brothers catalogs in 1913. The dragon is a repeated motif, separated by stylized lotus blossoms. There is a "sister" pattern, *DRAGON AND STRAWBERRY*, in which the lotus flowers are replaced by strawberries.

Shapes: ruffled, candy ribbon, and ice cream shaped 8" bowls, and 9" plates (they can be either spatula footed and collar based). A collar based nutbowl is also known.

Colors: marigold, amethyst/purple, blue, green, aqua, amber, lavender, vaseline, moonstone, lime green opalescent, peach opalescent, vaseline opalescent, amethyst opalescent, amberina, red, red opalescent, and aqua opalescent. The widest range of colors is found on the bowls.

Notes: *DRAGON AND STRAWBERRY* is a larger piece than the *DRAGON AND LOTUS*. It is only found in footed or collar based bowls, both ruffled and ice cream shaped. The colors are marigold, blue, green, and amethyst/purple.

FROLICKING BEARS—United States Glass Company

This has long been regarded as one of the mysteries—and indeed one of the great rarities—of Carnival Glass. However, catalog pages from the United States Glass Company clearly show a crystal water pitcher and tumbler in this pattern (described as a "Novelty 3-Pint Jug and a Novelty Table Tumbler"). It's a quixotic design, whimsical and amusing. Bears skip and tumble around the design against a backdrop of sharply peaked mountains. What could have inspired such a pattern? Where did the designers get their idea from? A very poor reproduction from an old United States Glass Co. ad[1] may have given us the answer. The ad is for a "Teddy Bear plate." The plate measured 7 by 10" and was priced at eighty cents a dozen. The design on it was a central medallion containing a portrait of Theodore Roosevelt. At the top of the plate is an eagle motif, and the bordering pattern is of bears frolicking, skipping and tumbling around the design—the very same bears that are seen on the Carnival pitcher and tumbler. Here, surely, is the origin of the *FROLICKING BEARS* pattern.

The design of the "Teddy Bear plate" must certainly be connected with the much reported bear hunting incident that involved Roosevelt in 1902. Kamm suggests that the date of the ad is 1898, but this is too early. Roosevelt was sworn in as the twenty-sixth President of the United States on September 14, 1901. The term "teddy bear" was coined in 1902. Theodore ("Teddy") Roosevelt was especially fond of bear hunting and while visiting the southern States to settle a boundary dispute between Mississippi and Louisiana, he took time off to hunt. After a pretty uneventful day, a bear cub was captured and brought to him. Roosevelt's subsequent refusal to shoot

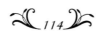

Fenton's scarce *DRAGON AND STRAWBERRY* pattern, sometimes called *DRAGON AND BERRY*. An exceptionally rare variant of this design is known without the dragons, called (unsurprisingly) *ABSENTEE DRAGON*.

the defenseless animal became the subject of a cartoon that appeared in the *Washington Post* on November 16, 1902. An enterprising New York shopkeeper used the cartoon to push sales of his soft toy bears. The label alongside the bear read "Teddy's Bear. " The toy was an overnight success. The "teddy bear" name was destined to become a firm favorite. So, the "Teddy Bear plate" from United States Glass Co. was no doubt an attempt to cash in on the same success story. In fact, the description in the ad stated "we have made ample preparations to meet an enormous demand for this article, as it is sure to prove the most popular, consequently the fastest selling, glass novelty ever placed on the market." The Carnival Glass items, of course, lack Roosevelt, as by 1908 William H. Taft had taken over the presidency for the Republicans. But the bears were obviously too good to waste! Around the base of the *FROLICKING BEARS* items a trailing vine pattern was added and the rare Carnival Glass examples were produced.

Shapes: water pitcher and tumbler.

Color: smoky olive green.

Notes: exceptionally rare!

PETER RABBIT—Fenton

"Once upon a time there were four little Rabbits, and their names were—Flopsy, Mopsy, Cotton-Tail and Peter." Beatrix Potter, October 1902.

A favorite—if you can find one—for this is a rare item. The vogue for nursery rhymes and children's book illustrations was almost certainly the inspiration behind this whimsical design. In the early 1900s Beatrix Potter, the English writer, produced a hugely popular, delightfully illustrated, series of books, the first of which was entitled *The Tale of Peter Rabbit*. The little creature was used by others too: in the 1920s "Peter Rabbit" was a popular cartoon character seen in the *New York Herald Tribune*. *PETER RABBIT* is not the best composed Carnival Glass design. The pattern is around the outside, the center is left devoid of any focus. The stylized rabbits circle in a pattern band, interspersed by small trees. Either side of the rabbit band is a characteristic motif that Fenton also employed on their *CORAL* and *LITTLE FISHES* patterns. Reminiscent of stylized starfish and seaweed, the motif looks strangely out of place with the rabbits. Despite all the negative aspects of the design, this remains a much sought after and well-loved piece. Interestingly, most *PETER RABBIT* items have been found in the United Kingdom. This isn't surprising in light of the character's origins. It probably indicates that they were exported to satisfy a demand following the success of Potter's books.

Shapes: 8" ruffled bowls and 9" plates. Both are collar based.

Colors: marigold, blue, and green.

[1] Minnie Watson Kamm, *A Sixth Pattern Glass Book* (Grosse Pointe, Michigan: by author, 1970).

Fenton's *HORSE MEDALLION* 8" plate in marigold. $275-$375.

Fenton's *LIONS* 7" ruffled bowl in blue. This pattern was only made in these smaller sized bowls and plates. $250-$400.

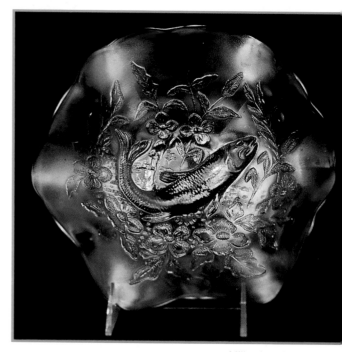

Millersburg's *TROUT AND FLY* ruffled bowl, seen here in the rare and exquisite shade of lavender. $1300-$1900.

The design on this copper and brass powder flask is very reminiscent of Fenton's *HORSE MEDALLION* pattern. *Courtesy of Alan Mollison.*

Detail of the powder flask design. *Courtesy of Alan Mollison.*

The *SEACOAST* pin tray from Millersburg was made in only three colors—
marigold, amethyst, and green. Though
all are scarce, the marigold one is the
hardest of all to find. $600-$1200 in
green. A spectacular green *SEACOAST*
pin tray sold for $2300 in 2007.

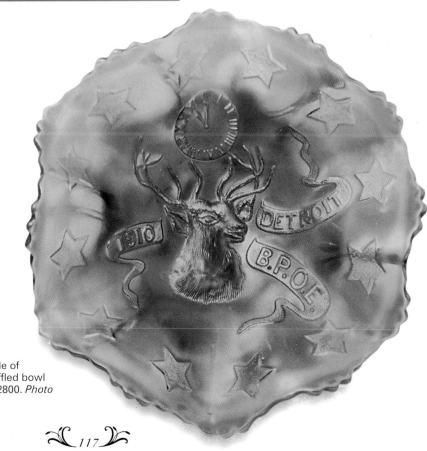

A truly outstanding example of
Fenton's *DETROIT ELKS* ruffled bowl
in emerald green. $2600-$2800. *Photo
courtesy of David Doty*.

Millersburg's version of the *DETROIT ELKS*
seen here in an amethyst, ice cream shaped
bowl. $2000-$4500. *Photo courtesy of David
Doty.*

The wonderful Millersburg *ELKS* paperweight, seen here in
rich purple. $1500-$3000. *Photo courtesy of David Doty.*

Fenton kept the dragon theme but replaced the
lotus flowers with strawberries on their *DRAGON
AND STRAWBERRY* pattern. This is a footed,
ruffled bowl in green. $800-$1000.

Close-up of Fenton's whimsical pattern, *PETER
RABBIT.* A scarce item, it's seen here on a green
plate. $5000-$6500. *Photo courtesy of David Doty*.

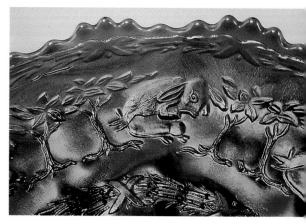

Aqua opal was a rare color for Fenton. Note the delicate opal edge on this *DRAGON AND LOTUS* ruffled bowl. $2800-$3200.

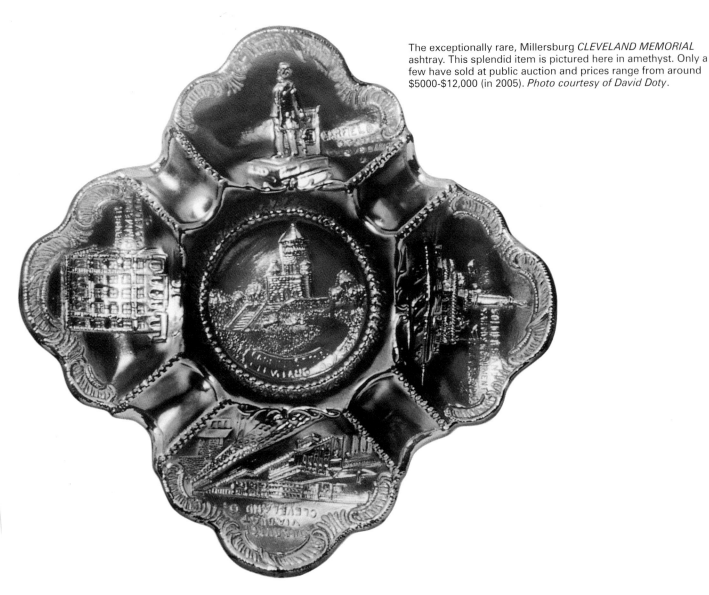

The exceptionally rare, Millersburg *CLEVELAND MEMORIAL* ashtray. This splendid item is pictured here in amethyst. Only a few have sold at public auction and prices range from around $5000-$12,000 (in 2005). *Photo courtesy of David Doty.*

Examples of architecture, seen in familiar structures as well as imposing public buildings, appear on Carnival Glass patterns. They give us a fascinating opportunity to glimpse the civic scene back in the early 1900s. By their very nature, because they are portraying specific buildings and must therefore be recognizable, many of the patterns featuring buildings are realistically portrayed. Others, though, are stylized and rather sentimental versions of types of buildings—windmills for example.

Realistic/Naturalistic Patterns
HOMESTEAD (NUART)—Imperial

This is a design that epitomizes the early years of pioneering settlement. It was a Golden Age, embodied in the Homestead Act of 1862 that granted Americans the right to claim 160 acres of land provided they had farmed it for five years. Within forty years of the Act, over half a million small farmers had been granted land. Possibly this design was meant to symbolize this major social change. It does, however, have a European "feel" to it. Maybe it was designed by one of the many immigrants that are reported to have worked for Imperial. Glass making in Europe was an old, traditional industry and no doubt some of the immigrant workers would have had those skills. Realistic in its overall style, *HOMESTEAD* is essentially a nostalgic, rural landscape. Trees frame the scene, there's a

stream with a wooden bridge, a water pump, and a cozy cottage. It's a reassuring and tranquil portrayal. The "sister" pattern to *HOMESTEAD* is the *NUART CHRYSANTHEMUM*. They were both illustrated in Imperial's 1915 catalog and also shown in a catalog from the early 1920s. The only shape in this pattern was a large chop plate, described in the Imperial catalog as a "Cake plate." The contemporary description indicates that they were intended for use as decorative wall plaques. The exterior is rayed with a fine fluted pattern.

Shape: 10" chop plate only.

Colors: marigold, amethyst/purple, helios, rare blue, rare emerald green, amber, smoke, and white.

Notes: hard to find. Examples in some of the above colors are known in very small numbers indeed.

Commemorative and Advertising Patterns
At the other end of the spectrum from the nostalgic and familiar items like *HOMESTEAD* are the group of commemorative and advertising items that feature buildings. On these, the structures depicted are grand and monumental, meant to impress and inspire. American cities in the late 1800s were growing at a rapid

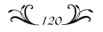

pace. The idea of town planing was in its infancy, but growing. The great Colombian Exposition at the Chicago Fair in 1893 gave impetus to the City Beautiful Movement, the aim of which was "The City Monumental." City after city built its civic center or its cultural center—the aim was to achieve "Grand Effect." Grandiose buildings constructed in classical Renaissance manner brought grand vistas and imposing civic memorials. The rich and monumental style captured the imagination of city planners and the public alike.

Of course, not all the advertising pieces featured buildings, some simply bore moulded trade logos or advertising slogans such as "We Use Broeker's Flour" or "Campbell and Beesley Co. Spring Opening 1911." Extensive research has been undertaken on these items by John D. Resnik and we refer the reader to Mr. Resnik's publication for further information.[1] Other items didn't have specially produced designs, but utilized existing moulds instead. On these, the base plate could be changed and a new one bearing the name of a store could be substituted. A good example of this is Fenton's *OPEN EDGE BASKET,* which bears advertising for John Brand Furniture Store. Unfortunately, the advertising isn't seen unless the item is turned over to view the base. Some souvenir items even had place names stenciled on them in enamel, possibly to catch the tourist trade. However, only those items featuring buildings will be considered here.

CLEVELAND MEMORIAL ASHTRAY—Millersburg

During its heyday, Cleveland's vast iron and coal supplies made it one of the world's most important steel and shipbuilding centers. John D. Rockefeller and many others made their fortunes here. Founded in 1796, Cleveland, Ohio, was one of the cities that invested in monumental structures.

This rare and beautiful Carnival Glass item depicts five of them. They are: the Garfield Statue, the Soldiers and Sailors Monument, Superior Viaduct, the Cleveland Chamber of Commerce, and Garfield's Tomb. It's a scenic tribute to the city that also provokes questions about the city's history. Why should a viaduct be considered worthy of inclusion? The answer lies in the fact that Cleveland is nearly divided into two parts by the winding Cuyahoga River as it flows into Lake Erie. The Superior Viaduct was one of several similar, immense engineering feats, constructed to join the parts of the city together.

> Shape: ashtray only.
> Colors: marigold and amethyst/purple.

BROOKLYN BRIDGE— Dugan/Diamond

A tremendous feat of engineering, the construction of the Brooklyn Bridge began in 1870. The bridge was finally opened for traffic on May 24, 1883, taking over from Robert Fulton's steamship service, which had previously carried passengers between Brooklyn and Lower Manhattan. The original cost of the bridge was ten million dollars. It was, in its day, a technological quantum leap. It towered above the low brick structures around it, and until the early 1900s was the world's largest suspension bridge, as well as the first to use steel cables. Indeed, for many more years it remained the longest single span bridge. During the time when Carnival Glass was actually being made, an estimated one million people passed over the bridge daily. On the *BROOKLYN BRIDGE* bowl, there is an airship (blimp) above the bridge and two tug boats underneath, rather a delightful touch. The letters "BROOKLYN BRIDGE" are moulded below the blimp. Rare unlettered examples exist. There are suggestions that the Carnival item was issued to commemorate an anniversary of the bridge. It is interesting to note that this item is found in the United Kingdom rather more than in the USA. One wonders why, as the British public wouldn't really have appreciated the relevance of the Brooklyn Bridge. Perhaps unsold stocks were sold off cheaply.

> Shape: 8" bowl that may have 6, 8, or 10 ruffles.
> Color: marigold.

ILLINOIS SOLDIERS AND SAILORS HOME: QUINCY, IL—Fenton

The monumental structure of the building, flag flying, dominates

Dugan/Diamond's *BROOKLYN BRIDGE* pattern. It's interesting to note that many of these items have been found in the United Kingdom. Back in the 1960s, a British dealer, the late Sam Williams, equipped himself with a set of Marion Hartung's Carnival Pattern books. On the books' pages, Sam noted the prices (in pounds sterling) that United States' buyers would pay him for each item. The *BROOKLYN BRIDGE* bowl was annotated with the price of fifteen pounds—about $45 at that time. Later Sam acquired the Hartung Price Guides for 1971 through 1973. He must have noted that the price estimate for the bowl was $250 to $300, as his original note of fifteen pounds was crossed through and fifty pounds (about $200 at that time) added instead!

---

this design. It's a detailed portrayal of the Soldiers and Sailors Home, that would surely have been instantly recognizable to the Civil War Veterans who inhabited it. Lettering, as in the given name of the design, also covers the face of the pattern. The exterior carries the *BERRY AND LEAF CIRCLE* pattern.

> Shape: 8" plate.
> Colors: blue and marigold.
> Notes: very rare. There are two other similar items from Fenton that feature buildings and monuments in Indiana. They are the *INDIANA STATE HOUSE* and the *SOLDIERS AND SAILORS MONUMENT, INDIANAPOLIS.* All three of these designs share the same exterior pattern *BERRY AND LEAF CIRCLE.* All three have lettering. These last two are known in "single figure" numbers.

BIRMINGHAM AGE HERALD—Fenton

Similar in style to the *ILLINOIS SOLDIERS AND SAILORS HOME: QUINCY, IL,* this rare advertising item differs in that it comes from a larger mould and does not have the *BERRY AND LEAF CIRCLE* exterior. The imposing building depicted in this design is the head office of the Birmingham Age Herald newspaper. It still stands in Birmingham, Alabama. The exterior pattern is Fenton's *WIDE PANEL.*

> Shapes: 9" bowl and 9.5" plate. Color: amethyst/purple.

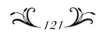

COURTHOUSE—Millersburg

A splendid item, this depicts the imposing Holmes County Courthouse building that stands to this day, in the town of Millersburg, Ohio. The mould work is impressive in its quality and detail. The lettering on the design reads: "Millersburg Souvenir; Courthouse, Millersburg, Ohio." There are rare "unlettered" bowls. (They actually do have some but not all of the lettering.) They simply read "Millersburg Souvenir." Nostalgic tales connected with the Courthouse abound: tales like that of John Fenton's peacocks, which roamed the Courthouse lawn, strutting about and frightening the horses; tales that these pieces were given to the local people who had helped John Fenton build his glass factory. The exterior has a *WIDE PANEL* design, while the marie has a multi point star.

Shapes: ruffled, candy ribbon, or ice cream shaped 7" bowls.

Colors: amethyst/purple and rare lavender.

Semi-Realistic/Naturalistic Patterns

WINDMILL—Imperial

The initial approach to this pattern is realism—the finished effect, however, with the addition of a daisy border, gives the pattern a distinctive style. It's a landscape, undoubtedly European in origin, with the windmill dominating the scene. A feeling of nostalgia pervades. *WINDMILL* often confuses as it comes in several different landscape variations according to the size and shape of the item it is found on. The elements in the scene vary, however:

There's always a windmill (though the shape of the roof varies

and the sails are in different positions).

• There are always trees (they vary—sometimes all deciduous, but on one bowl there's a conifer).

• There may, or may not be, a church.

• There's always a bridge, but it varies as to whether it's in the background or the foreground.

• The fabric of the bridge varies—it may be stone or wood.

The main pattern element that determines *WINDMILL* is the single windmill. All variations of bowl, dish, and tray have a stylized daisy pattern above and below the landscape. On the jugs and tumblers the landscape motif is within framed medallion shapes, each separated by stylized daisies.

Shapes: various sizes of bowl, oval dishes and flat trays, water sets, and two further sizes of jug. The *WINDMILL* pattern varies according to the shape it is found on. (Its original pattern number in earlier catalogs was #514.)

Colors: marigold, helios, amethyst/purple, clambroth, smoke, aqua, and emerald. Tumblers are also known in lavender, olive, and blue (water pitchers also in blue). Large and medium sized bowls are also known in marigold on milk glass.

DOUBLE DUTCH—Imperial

Similar in concept to *WINDMILL*, this pattern differs in the extra elements that appear in the landscape. There are two windmills and a boat as well as trees, a bridge, and so on. The stylized floral border is there again, but only around the sides and at the bottom. The exterior pattern is *FLORAL AND OP-*

The *MILLERSBURG COURTHOUSE* bowl depicts the Holmes County Courthouse building. It still stands to this day, a nostalgic reminder of John Fenton and the beauty of Millersburg's short-lived Carnival Glass production.

TIC. Note that there are three distinctive, squared off feet on this piece. *DOUBLE DUTCH* had the same original factory number as *WINDMILL* (#514) and was undoubtedly intended to be in the same pattern range. In fact, *DOUBLE DUTCH*, *WINDMILL*, and *HOMESTEAD* all made their appearance together in 1915, suggesting that they are all variations on a theme.

Shape: 8 to 9" footed bowl, ruffled or round (ice cream shaped).

Colors: marigold, amethyst/purple, and smoke. Also reported are helios, emerald, and amber.

Stylized Patterns

CHRYSANTHEMUM— Fenton

Despite the name, this design features windmills! (Rose Presznick called it "Windmill and Mums.") It's a highly stylized pattern that was first advertised in Butler Brothers catalogs in 1914. Though the center of the design is dominated by stylized chrysanthemum heads, the rest of the pattern features windmills, boats, buildings (that seem to be churches), and oddly shaped trees. It's a strange mixture of elements that really don't seem to go together—and yet it works!

Shapes: 8" collar based and 10" footed bowls, ruffled or ice cream shaped.

Colors: marigold, amethyst/purple, blue, green, powder blue, black amethyst, vaseline, and red.

[1] John D. Resnik, *The Encyclopedia of Carnival Glass Lettered Pieces* (Nevada City, California: by author, 1989).

An advertising piece from Fenton, this is the *BIRMINGHAM AGE HERALD* plate in amethyst. $2500-$3500. *Photo courtesy of David Doty.*

A purple *WINDMILL* tumbler from Imperial; the iridescent effect accentuates the design. $100-$150.

Another commemorative, this is a blue Fenton *ILLINOIS SOLDIERS AND SAILORS* plate. $2000-$2500. *Photo courtesy of David Doty.*

Imperial's *DOUBLE DUTCH* pattern is distinguished from its "sister" pattern *WINDMILL* by the presence of **two** windmills (instead of just one as on *WINDMILL*). $200-$700 for a purple bowl.

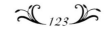

Chapter Eight
Geometric

"Massive Brilliant Assortments"—"Crystal Beauties"

—Extracts from Butler Brothers catalog ads in 1907

Geometric patterns, by their very nature, are stylized designs. They are composed predominantly of lines, circles, triangles, and diamonds. They are not executed freehand, but are drawn with the aid of technical instruments. Usually they are intaglio—impressed into the glass rather than raised up from the surface. They are frequently referred to as "near-cut" or "imitation cut glass."

Cut glass, extravagant and splendid in execution, was very fashionable in the 1800s. Whole suites of glittering glassware adorned the wealthy household. At the Philadelphia Centennial Exhibition in 1876, Brilliant Cut Glass was introduced. It was thicker, more reflective, and more scintillating than the previous cut glass. The intricate geometric designs sparkled like diamonds. But of course, it needed much skilled craftsmanship and hours of labor. The subsequent imitation of expensive cut glass in press moulded designs not only cut costs but also enabled greater quantities to be available for the buying public. These intaglio, press moulded patterns became known as "near-cut." Though initially utilized in the production of clear crystal glass, the "near-cut" designs were also used for Carnival Glass production as the geometric surfaces of the glass adapted very well to iridescence.

An ever present difficulty with "near-cut" geometric designs is recognition. All those hobstars and files can seem very much like each other. We attempt in this chapter to give "identifiers"—pattern indicators to aid the recognition of some of these complex designs. It's easy to mistake one geometric pattern for another, especially when they have very similar elements. The Imperial designs *CRABCLAW, HOBSTAR FLOWER,* and *BLAZE* have been mis-identified and mixed up over time owing to their many similarities. These three patterns are described and identified below. Another frequent confusion concerns the pattern found on the exterior of the Imperial *SCROLL EMBOSSED* large compotes, which is frequently mistaken for the *CURVED STAR* pattern. It is actually Imperial's *EASTERN STAR. CURVED STAR* is a different pattern entirely and is found only on European Carnival Glass.

Millersburg Exterior Patterns

Millersburg are renowned for their intricate, imitation cut, geometric exteriors. In many cases, the exterior pattern combines with just one specific interior design. For example, *FINE CUT HEART* is the geometric pattern on the exterior of *PRIMROSE* only. *TREFOIL FINE CUT* is found on the outside of the rare Millersburg *BERNHEIMER* bowl and the *MANY STARS* patterns. Millersburg's geometrics are unusual in that they often have a detailed design on the marie that reflects elements of the full pattern. They are intricate and are the product of superb craftsmanship. Though these patterns are primarily exterior designs, their sheer magnificence and complexity warrants a separate listing and appreciation within this text. Two examples have been chosen as representative of these lovely designs.

Millersburg's amazing intaglio design *TREFOIL FINE CUT* is found only on the exterior of the *MANY STARS* and *BERNHEIMER* items.

FINE CUT OVALS—Millersburg. Exterior of *WHIRLING LEAVES*.

Seen in the Butler Brothers catalogs in 1910, this is a complex, imitation cut, geometric design found only as an exterior pattern to *WHIRLING LEAVES*. The drawing illustrates the detailed intricacies of this press moulded design. Primarily composed of diamonds and fine file, the overall effect is of six large ovals. The marie is highly detailed and very distinctive.

Shape: 9 to 10" bowl. The shaping varies and may be ruffled, ice cream shaped, tightly crimped, square, or tri-cornered. A diamond shape is also reported.

Colors: marigold, amethyst/purple, and green. Rare blue and vaseline examples are known.

Identifiers: look for six large ovals. Within these ovals is a cross shape with four diamonds above the center and nine diamonds below the center. Also look for the very distinctive marie featuring two interlocking ovals.

This is a detail from Imperial's intricate *EASTERN STAR* design, found on the exterior of some *SCROLL EMBOSSED* compotes. It is sometimes confused with a superb European design called *CURVED STAR*. The two are quite different, as the illustrations in Part Three (see *CURVED STAR*) show.

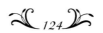

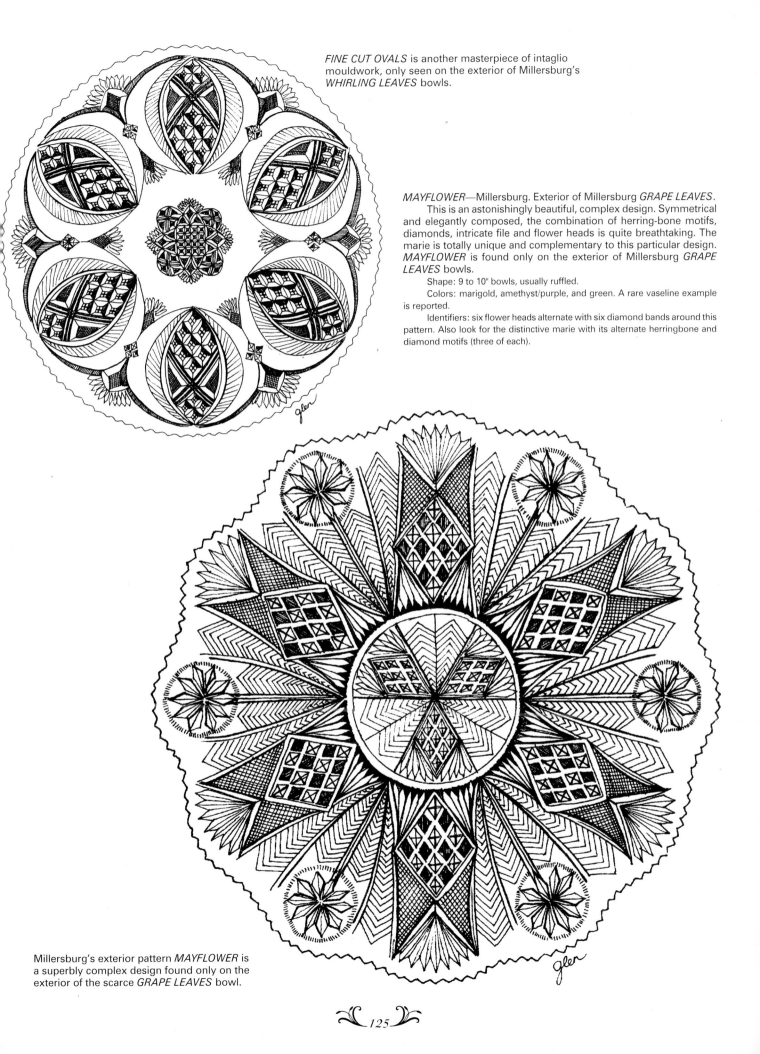

FINE CUT OVALS is another masterpiece of intaglio mouldwork, only seen on the exterior of Millersburg's *WHIRLING LEAVES* bowls.

MAYFLOWER—Millersburg. Exterior of Millersburg *GRAPE LEAVES*.

This is an astonishingly beautiful, complex design. Symmetrical and elegantly composed, the combination of herring-bone motifs, diamonds, intricate file and flower heads is quite breathtaking. The marie is totally unique and complementary to this particular design. *MAYFLOWER* is found only on the exterior of Millersburg *GRAPE LEAVES* bowls.

Shape: 9 to 10" bowls, usually ruffled.

Colors: marigold, amethyst/purple, and green. A rare vaseline example is reported.

Identifiers: six flower heads alternate with six diamond bands around this pattern. Also look for the distinctive marie with its alternate herringbone and diamond motifs (three of each).

Millersburg's exterior pattern *MAYFLOWER* is a superbly complex design found only on the exterior of the scarce *GRAPE LEAVES* bowl.

Other Geometric Patterns

FASHION—Imperial

Imperial are well known for their imitation cut designs. *FASHION* is possibly one of the best known and most easily recognized of Imperial's geometrics. It is probably most easily found in the punch bowl shape, many of which have been found in the United Kingdom. It was issued in crystal before iridized versions were introduced. Imperial's January 1909 catalog of table glassware, lamps, and tumblers shows many items in the pattern we know as *FASHION*, then simply identified as number 402½. Many of the same items were still being advertised in their catalog over ten years later.

Shapes: 9" bowls, both ruffled and ice cream shaped. Also found are the punch set, water set, breakfast set, rosebowl, and large compote.

Colors: marigold, amethyst/purple, helios, smoke, and clambroth. Not all shapes are known in all colors. A red punch cup is reported, though no other shapes have yet been found in red.

Identifiers: the most characteristic motif of *FASHION* is a hobstar that closely resembles a flower on a stem. Above the "flower" is a notched arch that helps to make this pattern recognizable.

No. 402½ pitcher.
packed 2 dozen in barrel.
barrel lots, $1.50 per doz.
smaller lots, 1.75 per doz.

In January 1909, the Imperial Glass Company issued a general catalog of crystal glass items. The *FASHION* pitcher illustrated was depicted there. It was later also produced in Carnival Glass.

DOUBLE STAR—Cambridge

The specialty of the Cambridge Glass Company was undoubtedly their imitation cut glass. They marked such glassware with the moulded trademark NEAR-CUT. Many of their imitation cut Carnival was marked in that way, though almost no *DOUBLE STAR* examples were. It's an intricate, expertly designed and executed pattern that is possibly the most easily found of all Cambridge's Carnival. There is also a pattern known only in a cruet, which collectors have called *BUZZ SAW*: in reality it is the *DOUBLE STAR* pattern.

Shapes: water set (the tumbler is easier to find than the pitcher); spittoon whimsey. There are two sizes of *BUZZ SAW* cruet.

Colors: marigold and green.

Identifiers: look for the large whirling stars. On the tumbler, there are two such stars—back and front, separated by a smaller hobstar and a cane type panel. A large whirling star is also on the base of the tumblers.

CHATELAINE—Imperial

This is an elegant, streamlined design that was illustrated in the 1909 Imperial catalog as number 407½. It was not as long lived as many of the other Imperial designs and was not shown in many later catalogs.

CHATELAINE is a stunning design that is, sadly, seldom found.

Shape: water set only.

Color: amethyst/purple only.

Identifiers: the most significant elements of the design that will aid recognition are the tall, upright shapes that are really rather reminiscent of an Art Deco skyscraper. There are four such elongated shapes on the tumbler. The pitcher has a deeply notched handle.

MARILYN—Millersburg

Here's a Millersburg "near-cut" that *isn't* on the exterior of a bowl. *MARILYN* is a stunningly impressive example of intaglio mouldwork, intricate and yet balanced. It was produced in crystal prior to Carnival in about 1909. The Carnival examples are very limited, though in crystal Millersburg produced a wider range of shapes. It is not coupled with another pattern, but stands alone.

Shape: water set only.

Colors: marigold, amethyst/purple, and green.

Identifiers: the main feature of this pattern is the hobstar with an arch above it and an elongated cross below it. Between the hobstar motifs are vertical sections that contain four diamonds on the tumblers, five diamonds on the pitchers. The center of the cross below the hobstar has a sunburst effect.

MEMPHIS—Northwood

Northwood made very few geometric patterns. There is the exceptionally scarce *NORTHWOOD'S NEAR-CUT* and the *DIAMOND POINTS BASKET* (*thought* to be Northwood). However, *MEMPHIS* is probably Northwood's finest geometric design—indeed, it is probably the only one known to most collectors. In common with many of the other "near-cut" patterns, *MEMPHIS* was first produced in crystal before being utilized in the production of Carnival. A very wide range of crystal items was offered, many of them being multipurpose or interchangeable in their use. *MEMPHIS* is a stunning and massive looking pattern that makes one feel somewhat in awe of the mould makers who produced it.

Shapes: punch set, berry set, fruit bowl and base. It's possible that a table set exists, but only a sugar has been reported so far. A rare compote is reported.

Colors: marigold, amethyst/purple, green, white, ice blue, ice green, and rare blue. Not all shapes are known in all colors, the widest range being found in fruit bowl and base, and punch set. Ice green, ice blue, and cobalt blue are rare colors for *MEMPHIS*. (Fruit bowls are the only shape currently known in blue.)

Identifiers: the most striking feature is the oval shape containing an intricate hobstar. The rest of the design has a checkerboard effect composed of hob-nails.

CRABCLAW (1), HOBSTAR FLOWER (2), and BLAZE (3)—Imperial

These are three distinctly different Imperial patterns, yet all three have been confused with each other at some point by collectors. A close study of the Imperial 1909 catalog, however, has enabled them to be individually identified as three, clearly different patterns. All three have hobstars and a curving file pattern. The shapes that each occurs in, however, helps to differentiate the three patterns.

Three Imperial patterns that are frequently confused—the detail drawings here should help to sort out the muddle. Top left is a detail of the *CRABCLAW* design, only found on water sets. Bottom left is a detail of Imperial's *BLAZE* design, only found on bowls. On the right is the *HOBSTAR FLOWER* pattern as seen on the decanter that has been mistakenly called the *CRABCLAW CRUET*.

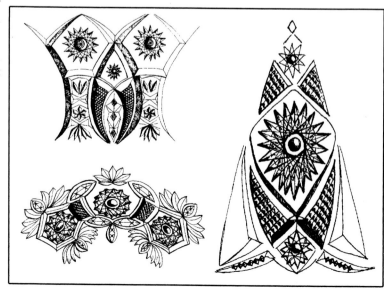

CRABCLAW (1)—Imperial

This had the pattern number 409 in the Imperial catalog. It is found *only* in the water pitcher and tumbler shape. Confusion has crept in because the cruet called *CRABCLAW* is actually the *HOBSTAR FLOWER* pattern (see below).

Shape: water set only.

Color: marigold.

Identifiers: look for the tapering, pincer-like curves on the file sections that almost meet near the bottom of the item. The lower section of the pincers is filled with a cross-hatched file pattern. Note that the tumblers have a ground base and no collar.

HOBSTAR FLOWER (2)—Imperial

This had the pattern number 302 in the Imperial catalog. Currently it is known in the compote shape. There is also a decanter, previously called the *CRABCLAW CRUET*, which is in fact *HOBSTAR FLOWER*. This decanter does not have the pincer-like file motifs that are characteristic of *CRABCLAW.* The Imperial catalog clearly shows this decanter with the pattern number 302 (which is *HOBSTAR FLOWER*).There may well be more shapes in this pattern that have not yet come to light.

Shapes: compote and decanter (often called a cruet).

Colors: marigold (decanter only in marigold), helios, amethyst/purple, and emerald.

Identifiers: there is a large hobstar and a bordering file motif—but no pincer-like shapes. The cruet has a notched handle and may well have a blow moulded *OCTAGON* stopper that was matched up at the factory.

BLAZE (3)—Imperial

This pattern was identified by Rose Presznick, (though Marion Hartung confused it with *CRABCLAW)*. It has the Imperial pattern number 347. *BLAZE* is found in large and small bowls only. There may well be more items in this pattern that have not yet come to light.

Shapes: large and small berry bowls, ruffled or ice cream shaped.

Colors: marigold, amethyst/purple, helios, and smoke. Cobalt blue is reported for the small bowl.

Identifiers: *BLAZE* is differentiated from *CRABCLAW* in that it does not have the pincer-like file motifs but does have a very distinctive marie pattern on the base. The marie design will identify *BLAZE*, as it is the only pattern with this unique characteristic.

The marie of Imperial's *BLAZE* pattern is very distinctive, and will serve to identify the design.

Three geometric design tumblers. From left: purple Imperial *CHATELAINE* ($200-$350), green Cambridge *DOUBLE STAR* ($50-$75), and purple Imperial *FASHION* ($250-$500. However, note that a purple *FASHION* tumbler sold at auction in 2002 for $970).

No. 409 pitcher.

Imperial's *CRABCLAW* pattern, as illustrated in their 1909 crystal catalog.

There are few Northwood geometric patterns. *MEMPHIS* is the most familiar one. $50-$75 for a green punch cup.

Imperial's *CRAB CLAW* tumbler in marigold. $30-$60.

Within this section are the patterns that, though grouped by a common theme or design, occur only in small numbers. Also in this section are the abstract patterns that are difficult to fit into any particular group.

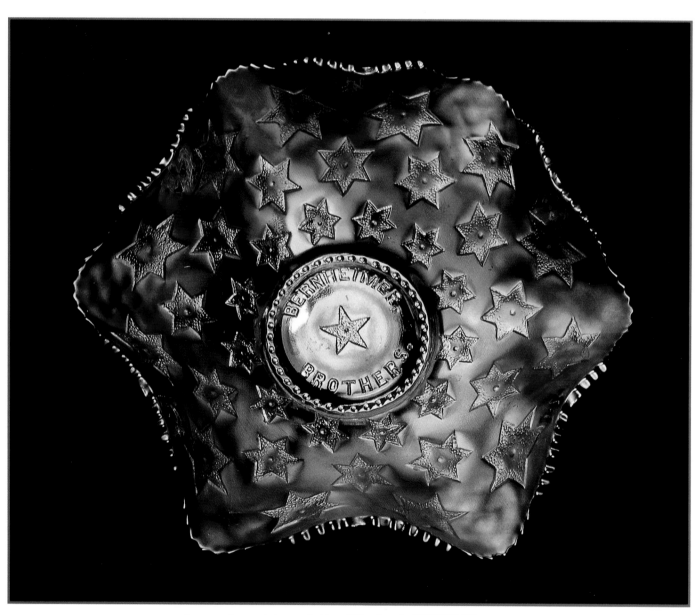

A scarce item only known in blue, Millersburg's *BERNHEIMER BROTHERS* 10" bowl utilizes the *MANY STARS* pattern for its advertising. $2000-$3250.

Embroidery and Lace Work Patterns

In the late nineteenth century, many craft guilds were established. Embroidery and lace work were particular favorites. Sometimes the Carnival mould makers chose to reflect the popular craft of embroidery in their designs. Indeed, following a close study of patterns such as Fenton's *PERSIAN MEDALLION* and Northwood's *HEARTS AND FLOWERS*, various types of stitches can be identified. The skill of the mould maker in emulating detailed stitches through the medium of an iron mould must be admired. It is the unique quality of glass—plastic when molten and able to be moulded in fine detail—that allows the intricacy of embroidery to be reproduced in such a lasting manner. Further, when the shimmering colors and light catching qualities of Carnival Glass's iridescence are added, the overall effect is magnificent, allowing all the minute details to be appreciated.

CAPTIVE ROSE—Fenton

The "captive" roses appear to be crafted in embroidered satin stitch in this highly stylized, floral design. They are repeated in a wreathed effect around the design, joined together by yet more imitative "stitches." Indeed, the whole pattern gives the impression of having been delicately stitched by hand! Quite an achievement. It's an intricate, highly complex design that takes iridescence very well indeed. *CAPTIVE ROSE* appears in Butler Brothers catalogs from Spring 1911.

Shapes: 8" bowls, ruffled and candy ribbon edged. There is also a 9" plate, handled bonbon, and stemmed compote. Colors: marigold, amethyst/purple, blue, green, and white.

Fenton's intricate *CAPTIVE ROSE* design: a breathtaking portrayal of detailed embroidery stitches captured on glass.

The heart shapes are picked out in an imitation of satin stitch on Northwood's *HEARTS AND FLOWERS* pattern.

HEARTS AND FLOWERS— Northwood

This is another design that imitates embroidery stitches. Again, it's essentially a highly stylized floral pattern. The "hearts" are crafted as to appear as if they have been embroidered using satin stitch. It's a complex and beautifully composed design made up of repeated motifs. The total effect is very sophisticated and elegant. As with most embroidery designs in Carnival, *HEARTS AND FLOWERS* takes iridescence very well. The pattern first appeared in the shape of a bowl and a compote in the Butler Brothers catalog ads in 1912. On the compote, the *HEARTS AND FLOWERS* pattern is repeated down the stem.

Shapes: 8" bowl, ruffled and pie crust edged. There is also a 9" plate and a stemmed compote. A white, stemmed whimsey plate is reported.

Colors: marigold, amethyst/purple, blue, green, white, aqua, lime green, ice blue, ice green, vaseline (plate only), and aqua opalescent. The compote is also known in Renninger blue, ice blue opalescent, and marigold on custard. The plate shape is also known in sapphire blue.

PERSIAN MEDALLION—Fenton

PERSIAN MEDALLION was clearly a popular design as it appears in Butler Brothers catalogs from 1911 through 1922. It is a splendidly intricate pattern that uses repeated motifs reminiscent of Islamic designs. This stylized pattern also has mould work that looks like satin stitch, as well as several other types of stitchwork. One common motif, typically used by Fenton as a background, has previously been thought to be representative of overlapping scales. However, an authority on needlecraft[1] has informed us that the "scale filler" is actually a perfect rendering of "needle lace." This same lace work motif can be found on many Fenton patterns such as *FENTONIA, ORANGE TREE, LEAF CHAIN,* and *CHERRY CHAIN,* as well as being the main pattern on many other items. The *PERSIAN MEDALLION* pattern was also used as the interior design on some *WREATH OF ROSES* punch sets and some *GRAPE AND CABLE* large, footed orange bowls.

Shapes: 5, 8, and 10" bowls that can be ruffled, candy ribbon, or ice cream shaped. Also found are 9 and 11" plates, two sizes of compote, rosebowls, hair receivers, and handled bonbons.

Colors: marigold, amethyst/purple, blue, green, white, celeste blue, aqua, black amethyst, moonstone, vaseline, and red.

Notes: the larger of the two sizes of compote usually has a candy ribbon edge. The *PERSIAN MEDALLION* pattern is on the interior and exterior of the large compote.

HATTIE—Imperial

At first glance, *HATTIE* owes more to geometry than embroidery. It's an intricate and complex design that certainly seems to have been drawn up with the aid of mathematical instruments. But look more closely and you will see that the "spider's web" motif that is repeated all over the design is, in fact, imitative of embroidery stitchwork. *HATTIE* pieces are distinctive in that they have exactly the same pattern on both interior and exterior: indeed, sometimes (perhaps by coincidence) the two are in perfect register!

Shapes: 8" bowls and 11" plates. A rare rosebowl is also known.

Colors: marigold, amethyst/purple, helios, smoke, clambroth, amber, and emerald.

Patterns that Feature the Human Figure

Carnival Glass designs featuring the human figure are rare and sought after. Though the classical style was in vogue in the late nineteenth century and early twentieth century, it obviously wasn't a popular theme for the Carnival mould makers and designers. Only four items in Classic Carnival that feature the human figure are reasonably well known. They are all exceptionally rare, yet the patterns are easily recognized.

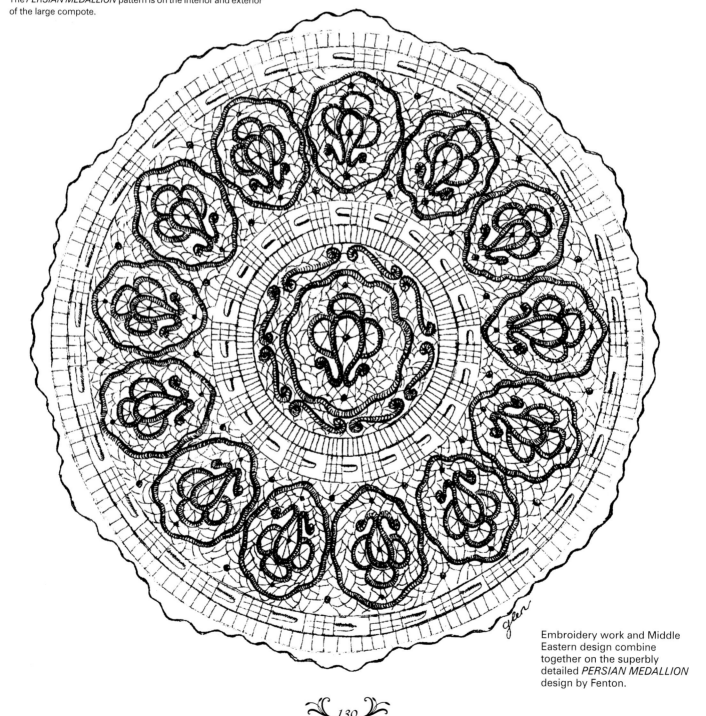

Embroidery work and Middle Eastern design combine together on the superbly detailed *PERSIAN MEDALLION* design by Fenton.

Imperial's *HATTIE* combines stylized floral motifs with embroidery style "spider-web" motifs.

PEOPLES' VASE—Millersburg

PEOPLES' VASE is truly a legendary item of Carnival Glass. Possibly every collector's dream is to find one tucked away in an old barn! There are very few of these magnificent items known—less than ten in fact. The *PEOPLES' VASE* is a massive, heavy piece of glass that stands about 11" high. The pattern depicts a group of six people dancing, with an onlooker leaning on a staff. Legends abound. It is thought that it was made in appreciation of the Millersburg Amish community, who had helped John Fenton set up his glass factory in their town. The inventory of Millersburg glass that was made after the factory went bankrupt in 1911 showed an item called the "Holland Vase." It is interesting to speculate that this might have been the *PEOPLES' VASE*, and that the figures may indeed have been modeled on the many Dutch immigrants who lived in the Holmes County area. The people featured on the cobbled ground certainly do have a European look about them.

Shape: vase (press moulded, not swung) in a cylindrical shape. The top may be ruffled or unshaped.

Colors: marigold, amethyst/purple, green, and blue.

Even More People

Other rare items featuring the human form include the splendid *GODDESS OF HARVEST* bowl and the delightful *DANCE OF THE VEILS* vase, both made by Fenton. Imperial's only contribution (not including the tiny figures seen on the *DOUBLE DUTCH* and *NUART HOMESTEAD* patterns) was the *CRUCIFIX* candlestick, which depicts the figure of Christ on the Cross.

Detail of the intricate pattern on Fenton's *CAPTIVE ROSE*—seen here on a green bowl with a tightly crimped edge. $100-$150.

Several patterns were executed in a style imitative of embroidery. This is an amethyst 9" plate in Fenton's *CAPTIVE ROSE* design. $300-$600. One sold for $900 in 2004.

One of Northwood's embroidery style patterns—*HEARTS AND FLOWERS*—on a stunning lime green plate. $3000-$3500.

Close-up detail of the complex design of Northwood's *HEARTS AND FLOWERS* pattern.

Detail of Fenton's *PERSIAN MEDALLION*.

PERSIAN MEDALLION is an elaborate, embroidery style design which works well on this cobalt blue bon bon. $50-$100.

Fenton's *LEAF CHAIN* pattern, seen here on a blue plate, also incorporates imitation embroidery stitches. $500-$2000. One sold in 2006 for $2500.

Abstract Patterns

This is a "catch-all," intended to include all those indefinable patterns that don't seem to fit into any particular category. Many vases can be included here, with their ribs, swirls, and hobnail effects. There are also some patterns that don't quite fit the "Geometric" description, being too free flowing, so are included here instead.

PLAID—Fenton

Called "Granny's Gingham" by Rose Presznick, PLAID is a simple design composed of lines radiating from the center, broken by irregular concentric bands. The pattern's attraction comes from the way in which the iridescence refracts off the many different lines; the overall effect is akin to a sun-ray effect. Surprisingly, PLAID doesn't seem to appear in any Butler Brothers catalogs until 1924, towards the latter part of the Classic Carnival era. This may account for its color range and the relatively few examples that are found.

Shapes: 8" ruffled or ice cream shaped bowl. A plate shape is known, though it turns up slightly at the outer edge.

Colors: marigold, amethyst/purple, and blue. Rare celeste blue and red.

ROUND UP—Dugan/Diamond

ROUND UP is a strange whirling design that was once called "Spinning Feathers." It acquired its present name due to the unusual characters that encircle the center—it seems that they look a little like the old western brands that were burned onto the hide of cattle. However, for a more likely inspiration it's necessary to look back at classical design sources. The type of motif is a skirl (a kind of rotating circle), intended to indicate circular motion.

Shapes: 8" bowl, ruffled, ice cream shaped, and candy ribbon edged. A 9" plate is also known.

Colors: marigold, amethyst/purple, blue, white, and peach opalescent.

Fenton's CHERRY CHAIN in a blue 6" plate. $100-$150.

One of Millersburg's most evocative Carnival Glass items, the PEOPLES' VASE. A perfect amethyst example sold at auction in June 1996 for $43,000. A cracked one sold at the same auction for $13,500. In 2007, an amethyst PEOPLE'S VASE sold for $65,000. A blue PEOPLE'S VASE sold in 2006 for a record $100,000. Photo courtesy of David Doty.

These abstract motifs are amongst some of the oldest known. They have been used throughout the centuries in different interpretations of the same basic design by different civilizations. At the top is the skirl, a kind of spinning circle, that probably originated in ancient Greece or ancient Egypt. It forms the basic design concept of Dugan/Diamond's ROUND UP pattern. Bottom left is the spiral or whorl, also called a looped S; its origin also, was possibly ancient Egypt. Bottom right is the Dugan/Diamond interpretation of the looped S motif as seen on their S REPEAT pattern. Dugan very likely copied a pattern called "Snail" that was issued by George Duncan and Sons in pattern glass around 1890.

S REPEAT—Dugan/Diamond

Another classical motif, this one is a spiral—the particular type being known as a whorl (or "S"). On the S REPEAT items, the motif is repeated continuously. It is a simple yet very effective design that was first used in 1903 when Thomas and Alfred Dugan were managing the Northwood Glass Works of the National Glass Company at Indiana, Pennsylvania.[2] It was made in crystal glass at that time and was called "National." Fewer items in the range were made in Carnival Glass. S REPEAT was used as the exterior design of a compote, with CONSTELLATION on the inside. Oddly enough, the S REPEAT pattern is usually referred to as SEAFOAM when it is found on this compote, though it clearly is S REPEAT.

Shapes: the punch set, though rare, is the most well known shape. Tumblers are also known and a spittoon is reported.

Colors: marigold and amethyst/purple. Amber is reported.

HOBNAIL and SWIRLED HOBNAIL—Millersburg

The "hobnail" motif was used in cut glass patterns and was later copied by many pressed glass manufacturers. A very large number of pressed glass articles were made in the late 1800s and early 1900s featuring many varieties of hobnail effects. Millersburg used the HOBNAIL pattern alone and also with a wavy, swirled effect in the background (SWIRLED HOBNAIL aka HOBNAIL SWIRL), which heightens the overall effect of the iridescence. Fewer shapes are known in the SWIRLED HOBNAIL pattern. HOBNAIL was also used by Millersburg as an exterior pattern on bowls, coupled with their distinctive VINTAGE design on the inside. It is a scarce pattern; complete table sets and water sets are very rare. Shapes: swung vase, spittoon, rosebowl, water set, and table set (only the vase, rosebowl, and spittoon in SWIRLED HOBNAIL). Colors: marigold, amethyst/purple, green, and rare blue. Not all colors are known in all shapes. Notes: the vase is from the same mould as the rosebowl and spittoon.

RUSTIC—Fenton

Only known in the vase shape, RUSTIC is a variation of the hobnail effect. The vase varies greatly in size. Base diameter ranges from just under 3.2" on the smallest examples, right up to 5.25" on the immense funeral vase size. (It is the diameter of the base, not the height, that determines whether a vase is a funeral.) As the vase is swung, the hobnails are stretched out, changing from their round shapes to elongated ovals. There are no markings between the hobnails on RUSTIC.

Shape: only known in a vase with varying heights and base widths. The tallest vases can have been swung to reach 23" in height.

Colors: marigold, amethyst/purple, blue, green, white, vaseline, red, lime green opalescent, amethyst opalescent, and peach opalescent.

Notes: the number of rows and columns of hobs varies according to the size of the vase. RUSTIC standard size vases have a base diameter of just over 3". Mid size vases have a base diameter of just over 4". Funeral size vases have a base diameter of 5.25". There is a variant to the funeral which has a band at the base. There is an unswung jardiniere shape that stands only 7.6" high. The mid size variant has the same hob configuration as a reported "Millersburg" vase called HOBNAIL VARIANT. However, the attribution has not been proven at this point; indeed, illustrations in Fenton catalogs suggest that the HOBNAIL VARIANT is actually a Fenton item.

APRIL SHOWERS—Fenton

These vases frequently get confused with Fenton's RUSTIC and Northwood's TREETRUNK. Indeed "Rustic" seems to have been the name Butler Brothers gave to all vases that had hobnail effects. These vases all have similarities, but there are sufficient differences for identification. APRIL SHOWERS has the hobnail effect, though they tend to be elongated into protruding ovals. It also has a very distinctive background pattern, rather like raindrops or paint drips. Joan Doty comments on the perfect choice of the name APRIL SHOWERS:

Streams of raindrops. How appropriate for a flower container. These streams of raindrops are in the nine wide panels around the exterior. The bottom of each panel forms an indented scallop; in the center of each scallop is a raindrop, or small hob, seemingly in a set of parenthesis formed by two stream ends. It is the scallops on the top of the base that provide a quick identification of APRIL SHOWERS vases from all the other vases with hobs.

A feature of APRIL SHOWERS is the interior pattern. Joan Doty's description of this effect is impossible to improve on. She says:

APRIL SHOWERS is the only vase with a PEACOCK TAIL interior, although that can't always be used as a means of identification. In some cases it is very sharp and distinct; in others all that can be seen are concentric circles of scallops on the interior of the base which seem to echo the nine scallops of the Wide Panels. Then there are others where the PEACOCK TAIL can be only barely discerned in the patterns of the iridescence

on the interior of the top. Occasionally an APRIL SHOWERS will appear to have a smooth interior.

Shape: vase ranging in height from unswung "squatty" versions of about 5" up to swung versions that reach 15". All have a 3.5" diameter base.

Colors: marigold, amethyst/purple, blue, green, teal, white, vaseline, amethyst opalescent, and red.

Notes: may have tightly crimped edging around the neck. Note that APRIL SHOWERS is not found in the range of base widths and heights of RUSTIC and TREETRUNK vases.

TREETRUNK—Northwood

TREETRUNK is yet another hobnail type of pattern that is found only on vases. It differs from the others in that there are small curving lines in the background of the pattern. Unlike APRIL SHOWERS, these lines do not join together. The N trademark may well be present on these vases. A wide range of sizes was made in TREETRUNK and there is a further variation known as an "Elephant Foot." See Notes below for details.

Shape: vase. Sizes detailed in Notes below.

Colors: marigold, amethyst/purple, blue, green, white, lime, sapphire, teal, marigold over custard, horehound, Renninger blue, ice blue, ice green, and aqua opalescent. Not all colors are known in all sizes. Some of these colors are exceptionally rare.

Notes: TREETRUNK has various size categories:[3]

Squatty or stubby: base diameter 3.5". Height less than 7". There is a variation with a star on the base.

Standard swung vase: base diameter also 3.5". These are swung to over 7 but under 12" high.

Mid-size swung vase: base diameter over 4.5". These are swung to over 12 but under 15" high. A variant exists that has a band around the base.

Funeral vase: the base has a band and must have a diameter of over 5". These are swung to over 15" and may even be greater than 20".

Elephant Foot: the base has a band and a base diameter of over 5" but they are swung to less than 15" in height.

PANELED TREETRUNK—Dugan/Diamond

This is another abstract pattern that has a rustic effect. This one, however, is so scarce that few collectors will have had the privilege of seeing one. PANELED TREETRUNK is found in a squat, yet very wide vase shape arund 6-8 inches high, as well as a taller version swung to around 11 inches. On the squat versions, the immense wide mouth flare stretches to nearly 9 inches across. There are eight flames around the neck opening and eight panels to the body of the vase. The base has a diameter of 4.9" with a forty point star in a flat dome on the marie. Joan Doty explains that the marie is very significant on this vase since it strongly indicates the manufacturer to be Dugan/Diamond. The "Dugan marie" has a plain outer edge about three-eighths of an inch wide with a recession before the rays of the star begin.

Shape: vase. Color: black amethyst (other colors reported are peach opal, marigold, and green, but we cannot confirm)

RIPPLE—Imperial.

RIPPLE is only found on vases. It was first seen in the Butler Brothers catalogs in April 1912 when it was described as a "spiral embossed" pattern. It continued to be advertised through to 1929, when it was described as a "flared optic pattern vase." RIPPLE can best be described as a series of seventeen concentric circles running from top to bottom. There is a fine vertical ribbing on the interior. The overall effect is different on almost every piece, as the amount to which the vase has been swung alters the spacing, distortion, and appearance of the ripple circles. Each vase has an individuality that is further enhanced by variations in the iridescent effects. There is a star on the base which has either sixteen, twenty or twenty-four points according to the size of the vase base.

Shape: vase. Sizes detailed in Notes below.

Colors: marigold, amethyst/purple, helios, green, smoke, amber, aqua, clambroth, teal, lavender, white, blue, experimental red shade, and vaseline.

Notes: five base sizes have been identified [4]—note that the largest size is considered to be a funeral vase, though it is smaller than the size that determines TREETRUNK and RUSTIC funerals. The five base diameters are: 2.5, 2.9, 3.4, 3.9, and 4.75". The vases range in height from approximately 4" up to 20".

LINED LATTICE—Dugan/Diamond

An abstract composed of interlocking diamond shapes, each lightly ribbed, LINED LATTICE takes iridescence very well indeed. The vase was originally produced by the Northwood factory in opalescent, non-iridized glass at the Indiana, Pennsylvania factory. This pre-Carnival vase was called "Palisades" and though frequently elaborately shaped, it was not swung. Joan Doty, writing in NetworK 4,[5] noted the reason why:

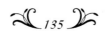

It's easy to see why they weren't swung, there is no collar base on which to clamp the snap for swinging. Obviously Dugan devised some method for swinging the iridescent vases, for they are all found anywhere from 4.75 inches up to 16 inches tall. Inexplicably, there were three entirely different moulds for these vases. One, with triangular feet, has the mould seam through the centers of three of the nine feet. These vases tend to rest solidly on the flat base, with the little feet projecting out. Another mould, also with triangular feet, has the three mould seams between the feet. The lattices on these often project down and the vase rests just on the points of these lattices. Yet another mould, this one requiring its own exclusive marie, has rectangular feet. These rectangular feet are similar to the ones on Dugan/Diamond's *GRAPE DELIGHT* rosebowls, although *GRAPE DELIGHT* has six feet and *LINED LATTICE* has nine. These vases with rectangular feet, sometimes referred to as square toes, are larger and heavier vases than the smaller, more delicate, triangular footed vases. It is unusual to see a *LINED LATTICE* with triangular feet taller than about 12 inches, but it is these larger, square toed vases that are usually found in the 11 to 16 inch height range.

Shape: vase, details as above. Colors: marigold, amethyst/purple, black amethyst, white, and peach opalescent. A pale, smoked amber example is known. A blue one is reported.

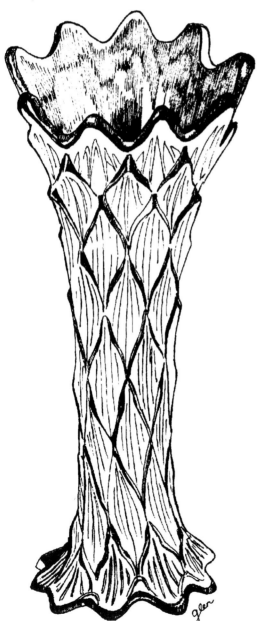

Dugan/Diamond's *LINED LATTICE* with distinctive triangular feet.

ZIGZAG—Millersburg

A mesmerizing design that radiates out from the center, *ZIGZAG* is pure abstract. Composed only of lines and stippling, it is at its best when found with scintillating iridescence. The overall effect is a form of stylized sunburst.

Shapes: 9 to 10" bowls, ruffled, candy ribbon edged, ice cream shaped, or tri-cornered. A rare 6" bowl and a card tray are reported.

Colors: marigold, amethyst/purple, and green.

DIAMONDS—Millersburg

DIAMONDS is essentially a very classic and simple design that could also be categorized as geometric. It doesn't, however, have the mathematical "feel" of a geometric interpretation.

Shapes: water set, rare punch bowl and base (no cups known), and a rare spittoon whimsey. The pitcher is quite small compared with others, standing a fraction more than 7" high.

Colors: marigold, amethyst/purple, and green. Aqua is reported.

FEATHERED SERPENT—Fenton

This is an abstract pattern that is actually a series of Rococo scrolls, which in turn was a development of an old pattern motif—the spiral. The 1910 Butler Brothers ad for this pattern correctly described it as a "scroll" design. The exterior pattern is *HONEYCOMB AND CLOVER*.

Shapes: large 9 to 10" and small 5" bowls, ruffled, candy ribbon edged, or tri-cornered shaped. Colors: marigold, amethyst/purple, blue, and green.

Notes: a rare spittoon whimsey is reported.

BERNHEIMER BOWL—Millersburg

A gem amongst advertising pieces, this scarce beauty utilizes Millersburg's *MANY STARS* pattern. (*MANY STARS* is an interesting item too, reminiscent of the design for the 1907 Great Seal of the State of Oklahoma.) In the center of the *BERNHEIMER BOWL*, replacing the large star, is a tiny star surrounded by the words "Bernheimer Brothers." According to John Resnik,[6] Bernheimer was "one of the first discount stores in America." Based in Baltimore, it seems that they enjoyed using catchy advertising ploys—no doubt this bowl was one of them. Note that this bowl is only known in blue, a rare color for Millersburg.

Shape: 10" ruffled bowl only. Color: blue.

[1] Betty Laker, past Chairperson of the Embroidery Guild, Petersfield (UK) branch.

[2] William Heacock, James Measell, and Berry Wiggins, *Dugan/Diamond: the story of Indiana, Pennsylvania, Glass* (Marietta, Ohio: Antique Publications, 1993).

[3] George Thomas, *Texas Carnival Glass Club Bulletin ("Ranger")*, October 1991.

[4] Ken Oppenlander, *Texas Carnival Glass Club Bulletin ("Ranger")*, July 1992.

[5] Joan Doty, "Collector's Facts: Lined Lattice Vase." *NetworK* 4 (Alton, England: Glen and Stephen Thistlewood, 1994).

[6] John D Resnik, *The Encyclopedia of Carnival Glass Lettered Pieces* (Nevada City, California: by author, 1989).

Millersburg's *BERNHEIMER* bowl. The design is based on the *MANY STARS* pattern.

An unusual shape, Millersburg's *SWIRLED HOBNAIL* (aka *HOBNAIL SWIRL*) spittoon in amethyst. $700-$950.

Opposite page: Dugan/Diamond's *S REPEAT* pattern on a purple punch cup. $50-$75.

Fenton's *PLAID* ruffled bowl in celeste blue combines a rare color with a seldom seen pattern. SP $5000-$6500. One sold at auction in 2006 for $10,000. Reportedly, it had a small chip (typical of celeste blue).

Fenton's *RUSTIC* vases in various sizes. From left: green mid size 15" high ($100-$400); blue funeral 19" high ($900-$1500); green standard 10" high ($50-$80); another green mid size 13" high ($100-$150).

An exceptionally rare vase, this beauty is *PANELED TREE TRUNK* in deep purple. Thought to be from Dugan/Diamond. Examples have sold for $5200 (in 2002) and $2600 (in 2007). *Courtesy of Alan Henderson.*

Two patterns that are sometimes confused. From left: Northwood's *TREETRUNK* standard vase in rich, cobalt blue ($200-$1200); purple 6.5" squatty *TREETRUNK* ($100-$300); green, standard size *APRIL SHOWERS* from Fenton with a tightly crimped top ($75-$100).

Imperial's popular *RIPPLE* vases were made in five different base sizes, three of which are shown here. From left: 12" high purple *RIPPLE* with a 3.4" base ($150-$250); 8" high electric purple *RIPPLE* with the smallest of the base sizes, 2.5" ($100-$150); another *RIPPLE* with the mid sized 3.4" base, but only slightly swung to reach 8" ($150-$200); and an olive green vase, 12" high, with a wide 3.9" base ($150-$200).

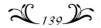

Dugan/Diamond's purple *LINED LATTICE* vases. From left: the square toed version ($150-$400), the more frequently seen triangular toed version ($100-$300), and a splendid squatty example ($350-$450). *Courtesy of Rita and Les Glennon.*

The outstanding iridescence heightens the sunburst effect on this crimped edge, tri-cornered shaped, amethyst *ZIG ZAG* bowl from Millersburg. ($700-$1000).

Millersburg's *DIAMONDS* standard water pitcher and tumbler in green with a pretty, satin iridescence. Pitcher: $300-$500. Tumbler: $40-$100.

Millersburg's *LITTLE STARS* 8" ruffled bowl in green. $300-$500.

Note the attractive, tightly crimped edge on this Fenton *FEATHERED SERPENT* bowl in amethyst. $80-$125.

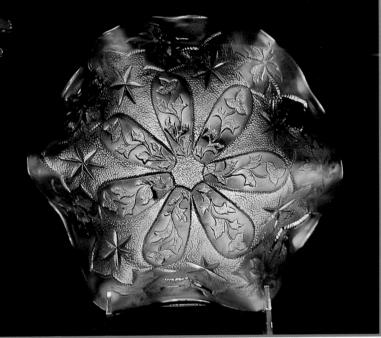

Part Three
Carnival Echoes Around the World

This is a much traveled pattern, *SUNK DAISY* is known as *AMERIKA* in the Nordic countries (where this blue example was made in the 1920s or 1930s, either by Riihimaki or Eda: $100-$300). Prior to that, it was made by Cambridge in the USA, but not in Carnival. In mid-2008, the authors and John Hodgson revealed further fascinating history of this pattern: it appears in the 1901 catalog of the Portuguese maker, Marinha Grande, along with an illusttration of the *THEBES* candlestick. Confirmation of iridised glass from Marinha Grande has been given by the curator of the glass museum there, although the production time is not yet known for certain. Our research further found that the *THEBES* candlestick was also made at Bayel-Fains in France—where it appears iridised production might possibly have taken place prior to 1900. Our research continues on this intriguing story. *Courtesy of Ann & David W. Brown.*

Chapter One

Introduction

Uncovering the Mysteries

Part Three of this book is the embodiment of the authors' extensive research into the production of Carnival Glass around the world. It contains an exceptionally comprehensive coverage of manufacture in countries outside the USA from around 1915, perhaps even earlier. In the first edition of this book a range of puzzles and mysteries was included—in this second edition, the authors have solved many of those enigmas and have uncovered much fascinating information. Further revelations include the manufacture of Carnival Glass in Poland and Brazil, plus the authors' discoveries of other Carnival makers in England, Czechoslovakia and Germany.

Classic Carnival was produced in the United States of America from around 1907. In the past it was thought that the other countries, for example Germany and Czechoslovakia, didn't make their own versions of Carnival Glass until two decades later—around the mid 1920s. However, we now know that to be wholly incorrect. Proof absolute in the form of a 1915 Brockwitz catalog, shows that marigold iridised pressed glass was being made at Brockwitz at that time. Items in *CURVED STAR* and *ROSE GARDEN* are shown in Carnival Glass (described as *GOLDIRIS* and having fired on iridescence). This means that Brockwitz were making Carnival Glass at the same time as Northwood, Fenton, Dugan and Imperial. To refer to Brockwitz as "Secondary" Carnival is incorrect. They began at least as early as 1915 (which is the date of the first currently known catalog) and may well have been making Carnival several years prior to that. And they weren't the only European factory to have been producing Carnival at that time; we believe that Josef Inwald's Rudolfova Hut was most likely making it from at least as early as 1914.

Soon afterwards, other glass makers began to produce Carnival too. Hot on the heels of Brockwitz and Inwald came Eda Glasbruks in Sweden, Sowerby in England and Crown Crystal in Australia. Others followed and over the next decade or two, Carnival Glass was either being made, or had been made, in almost every part of the world. There were many influences on the spread of Carnival, some were obvious and direct, others were less straightforward. Sometimes, patterns were copied; sometimes old moulds were brought out from storage, dusted down or re-tooled, and re-used, but in the main, excellent and well designed new moulds were made (often in a dedicated mould shop at the factory) ready for iridized glass production.

ROSE GARDEN and *CURVED STAR* were two of the earliest Carnival patterns made in Europe. Vases in these two patterns were shown in Brockwitz 1915 catalog, described as having *eingebranntem Lüsterdekor*—fired on iridescence. On the left is a 9.5 inch cylinder vase in *CURVED STAR*, in the center is the mid size *ROSE GARDEN* oval or letter vase while on the right is a 9.5 inch *ROSE GARDEN* cylinder vase (SP $200-$400 for the *CURVED STAR* vase and SP $400-$800 for the *ROSE GARDEN* vases).

A *PINEAPPLE* sugar from Sowerby in a scarce and unusual color—Vaseline Carnival. NP

Signature characteristics of European and Scandinavian (Nordic) Carnival Glass

Though the history is complex, much of the Carnival Glass produced was simply stunning. From intricate geometrics to classic Art Déco, and with iridescence of the highest quality, European Carnival has a scintillating magic of its own.

One common characteristic is that the patterns are frequently only on the exterior. On plates and bowls, the inside is often plain, possibly to facilitate use. Bases are often (not always) ground flat and may have tiny grinding chips present due to the way they were made (i.e."stuck up").

Carnival colors are not quite as wide as Classic USA Carnival. Marigold was the most common color, with blue also being used in the Nordic countries and Germany as well as some scarce examples of blue from England. Amethyst and purple Carnival was made in the Nordic countries and England. Other shades include: aqua, amber, green, smoke, pink, black, vaseline, opaque white and brown slag.

Shapes are exceptionally varied, often functional, and include a wide variety of rather unusual tableware items. Lighting, including candlesticks and shades, was also made. Vases and other flowers containers, including massive and showy epergnes, are avidly collected. A few examples of some of the tableware shapes follows: **Celery vases**—tall, cylindrical containers, often on a pedestal foot, known as a *traubenspuler* in Germany, these items were also used for washing fruit, especially grapes, at table. The **flower-bowl** or *blumenbowl* was also a popular item. It is shaped rather like a squat, wide vase and comes complete with a metal grille to hold the blooms in place. **Footed cake stands**, *tortenplatten* or salvers displayed gateaux well. **Table sets** comprised only a covered butter dish and a sugar and creamer—Europeans didn't use spooners. Larger covered **cheese stands** or German *kaseglocken*, are also known, and may be mistaken for the butter dish, which is quite a bit smaller. The **two piece fruit stand** or *fruchtshale* was an imposing item, comprising an upturned stemmed sugar (compote) with a large bowl on top. These, of course, were multi-purpose, as the two items that made up the fruit dish were used in their own right. **Jardinieres**—large oval fruit or flower bowls—were popular shapes. **Table centres**, known as *tafelaufsatze* in Germany, were the splendid epergnes that decorated the center of the dining table.

Signature characteristics of Australian Carnival Glass

One factory alone is considered responsible for Carnival Glass production in Australia—the Crown Crystal Glass Company (previously Crystal Glass Ltd.,) who were located in Sydney, New South Wales. This splendid glass has some easily identifiable characteristics.

Australian Carnival was primarily made in two colors—marigold and "dark" (which ranges from purple to a dense black amethyst) both typically with excellent, rich iridescence. Rare examples of aqua base glass with marigold iridescence are known and pale pink is also claimed.

Distinctive Australian flora and fauna are often depicted—for example, kookaburra, kingfisher, kangaroo and wattle garlands.

Shapes generally found are bowls (both large and small) and compotes or cake stands, while other shapes, for example, swung vases, water sets, sugars and creamers, are found less frequently.

Signature characteristics of South American Carnival Glass

Argentina, Brazil and Mexico produced Carnival that often has a vibrant style, however the characteristics of their glass are rather diverse.

Carnival colors are mainly marigold and blue with rarer examples of green, purple and amber.

Shapes include an interesting selection of ashtrays, often with advertising logos and lettering. Water sets were also a favourite tableware item.

Signature characteristics of Indian Carnival Glass

In recent years our knowledge of Indian Carnival has grown tremendously—possibly the most surprising revelation has been the number of factories that produced it.

Carnival colors are limited to marigold (sometimes with frosting) and occasionally a pale blue.

Shapes are dominated by vases and water sets.

Quality control was most likely not a priority and rather a lot of Indian Carnival is not of high quality. There are exceptions—some of the older vases and tumblers are beautifully made and splendidly iridized and even decorated (frosted).

Format

It is not possible to link the Carnival production that was made outside the United States by pattern themes in the same way that was done in Part Two for Classic Carnival production, thus, we have adopted a region by region approach. The scope of this book does not allow the authors to list all the known patterns for each maker, thus a selection of representative patterns has been chosen and where appropriate, recently discovered items have also been recorded.

A close-up look at a delightful piece of Australian Carnival—Crown Crystal's *KOOKABURRA* master bowl in dark (black amethyst) in a rare ice cream shape. Surrounding the kookaburra are wattle sprigs, waratahs and flannel flowers. This example is one of very few known in the ice cream shape and it sold in 1999 at auction for $1950.

Brockwitz

This three-part epergne from Brockwitz is a breathtaking centerpiece that stands 18 inches high. The pattern is *CURVED STAR*, a complex geometric design—the color is marigold, the only color known in the epergne shape. A rare piece, it has seldom been offered for sale at auction. $1000-$1500

The first pieces of glass were poured in the Brockwitz glass factory on the very first day of January in 1904. Three hundred workers were employed at the factory when it began. In ten years the number of workers had doubled. That number was to double yet again to a staggering twelve hundred workers by 1927, just twenty or so years after the factory was established—a phenomenal rate of growth. Typical German efficiency and skill, coupled with clever investment and a naturally good location, had resulted in a rapid rise in growth and output. The glass works was massive: located on the bank of the River Elbe in Saxony, it had great transport links as well as a cheap, local supply of fuel—lignite, otherwise known as brown coal. Tax free and easy to excavate, the lignite was converted into gas to power the eight melting furnaces at the factory.

In the past it had been assumed that Carnival production from countries outside the USA began in the 1920s, however, the discovery (by German glass researcher, Dieter Neumann) of a Brockwitz Pattern Book from 1915, overturned conventional thinking. Carnival from Brockwitz was made much earlier than originally thought. Items in that 1915 catalog in the *CURVED STAR* and *ROSE GARDEN* patterns are shown in Carnival Glass, described as *GOLDIRIS* and mit. eingebranntem *LÜSTERDEKOR* (fired on iridescence).

Brockwitz were making Carnival Glass at the same time as the main producers in the USA. We have clear evidence that they were producing marigold Carnival in 1915 (at the height of the First World War) and it is highly probable that they actually introduced it some years earlier, possibly just prior to the War. A covering letter that accompanied the 1915 Pattern Book advised customers that delivery times would be longer than usual due to the ongoing war and that all glass ware would be costlier because of the political situation. It was surely not the time for them to be experimenting with new techniques—it was much more likely that they were using existing ones.

Brockwitz Carnival is greatly sought after today, on account of its magnificent iridescence and artistry of design. They had a huge engineering and mould shop, which also made moulds for other glass works, such as Eda Glasbruks in Sweden. Typically Brockwitz created complex, intricate patterns cut into soft cast-iron moulds—indeed they perfected and patented a method by which the moulds were coated (post-cutting) with chromium to prevent wear. On most items the patterns are exterior and intaglio ("near-cut") and the bases are ground flat, sometimes with tiny flakes resulting from the grinding process. The jewel-like appearance of these imitation cut designs allows for the iridescent effect to be maximised on all the "cut" surfaces. A wide range of shapes was produced, including tableware, vases, lighting and boudoir items—usually the items were "as moulded" however some pieces are found with crimped edges. Carnival colors from Brockwitz are blue and marigold, usually with excellent iridescence.

The combination of the Great Depression and World War Two was not good for Brockwitz. During the War the factory had been pretty much turned over to the production of glass for military purposes—there was a 1941 catalogue, and there was still some domestic glass output, but it was small. After the war, Brockwitz was in the Russian controlled part of East Germany and all materials and tools were taken away to the USSR. There were a few attempts to revive the plant, but nothing really worked, and a fire in the 1960s razed what was left of the buildings to the ground. The glory that was Brockwitz was at an end. Their legacy lives on in some of the finest Carnival Glass in existence.

Reports of previously unknown items continue to come in—for example, both the *BOND* vase and the *CATHEDRAL ARCHES* comport are now reported in blue as well as marigold. Further fresh information can be read below.

ASTERS originally **MARGUERITE**—Brockwitz

ASTERS is an exterior, intaglio, stylized floral pattern—all examples have a distinctive star on the base, while bowls and plates feature an unusual scallop and flute edge. The SUNFLOWER AND DIAMOND vase (see below) was actually part of Brockwitz' ASTERS pattern range, but this was not appreciated until catalog illustrations were studied (hence the separate pattern name). Shapes: bowls (round and in a rare, square shape), rose bowls and plates. Sizes range from a diminutive 3.5 inch diameter bowl to a full sized 11 inch chop plate. Salvers (footed cake stands) in various sizes and a rare, small size, oval vase are also known.

Colors: marigold and blue (but note the salver is only known in marigold so far)

The truly magnificent iridescence on this marigold ASTERS chop plate makes it a most desirable piece. $200-$400

BREMEN—Brockwitz

A full range of other shapes was illustrated in Brockwitz' catalogs including a decanter, vases of various sizes, celery, stemmed sugar, jardiniere, handled bonbon, bowls, oval platter and a covered punch bowl and ladle with custard cups. Two fruit set "marriages" are also shown; one comprises a large fruit bowl with an upturned celery beneath it, the other comprises a fruit bowl with an upturned sugar bowl beneath it. Only a handful of shapes are currently known in Carnival but it is very likely that any of those other items may also have been made in Carnival.
Shape: wine glass, decanter, oval fan vase
Color: marigold

Brockwitz BREMEN pattern is seen here on a most unusual, fan shaped vase in marigold. This is the only known example of this splendid item, and thus we are unable to speculate on a value. NP
Courtesy John and Frances Hodgson.

CHRISTUS (JESUS) CANDLESTICK—Brockwitz

Brockwitz' CHRISTUS candlestick is a seldom seen beauty. There are two versions of the candlestick illustrated in Brockwitz catalogs: one with a square base (standing 10 inches high) and one with a round base and scroll feet (standing 12 inches high). Only the square base version is so far known in Carnival Glass, and marigold is the only colour currently reported. A similar MARIA (aka SAINT) candlestick was also made and like the CHRISTUS, is shown in the catalogs with both types of base. Again, only the square base version of MARIA has been reported in Carnival (marigold). The word "rare" is often over-used with regard to Carnival, but these marigold items really are rare, the number reported being in single figures. These items were shown in Brockwitz' catalogs as early as 1915 (and possibly before). They continued to appear in them right through to the early 1940s—no doubt the design had a constant appeal.

In 2004 and again in 2008, a handful of "fake" Christ and Maria candlesticks appeared in mainland Europe and the UK. They seem to have been cold iridized (painted on iridescence) and the candlesticks that were used were old Fenne originals in clear glass. Fenne's Christ and Maria candlesticks are very different in appearance to the Brockwitz ones and can be easily distinguished. The iridescence on these "fakes" is light and spotty and comes off very easily indeed.
Shape: candlestick
Color: marigold

The CHRISTUS candlestick was made by Brockwitz and this example stands 10 inches high. It is an exceptionally rare item and has not changed hands at auction in recent years. SP $4000-$8000

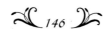

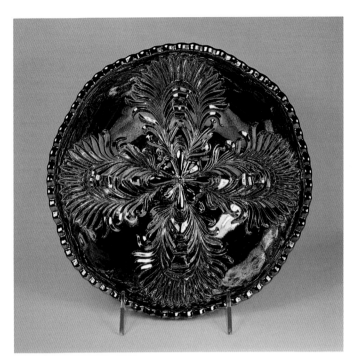

This massive, covered, marigold powder jar in the *CURVED STAR* pattern is the first one reported. It stands almost 7 inches high and measures nearly 8 inches across. SP $300-$600

CURVED STAR originally *ZURICH*—Brockwitz
 This is a complex, intaglio design combining a variety of geometric motifs which differ according to the shape of the finished item. Because of this, various shapes have (in the past) been thought to be different patterns when in fact they are simply part of the extensive range of items made by Brockwitz in the *CURVED STAR* design. The rose bowls, for example, have been called *FLOWER BLOCK*, while the celery vase (which is distinguished by "blackberry" prunts) has been called the *CATHEDRAL CHALICE*. As noted below, the jardinière in this pattern has been called *SUPERSTAR*. All are shown in the Brockwitz catalogs as part of their *ZURICH* pattern suite.
 This pattern was one of the earliest ones iridized. The cylinder vase (three heights were noted —approx. 7, 9 and 11 inches) was depicted in the Brockwitz 1915 catalog; the explanatory text showed that all three were available in Goldiris (marigold Carnival). The pattern featured in their catalogs for the greater part of the ensuing three decades—it was undoubtedly one of Brockwitz' main sellers and must have been very popular at the time. Although both Eda Glasbruk in Sweden and Karhula in Finland both made a slightly altered version of *CURVED STAR*, their production of it was much smaller than that of Brockwitz and examples of them are scarce and very seldom seen.
 Colors: marigold and blue
 Shapes: bowls in a very wide range of sizes (measuring from as little as 3.5 inches across) and shapes (including a square bowl and an oval bowl), plates in various sizes up to a chop plate, epergne, creamer, cylinder vase (three sizes; approx. 7, 9 and 11 inches high), stemmed celery, stemmed sugar (compote) in two different shapes, covered stemmed sugar, fruit stand, pitcher, small salt, butter dish (two versions—pattern inside the lid and outside the lid), cheese dish, covered powder jar

HEADDRESS—Brockwitz
 The main pattern motif on *HEADDRESS* is a feathered plume, repeated four times around a central stylized floral motif. Interestingly, there are several different variations of the pattern; the position of the curling tendrils and the presence (or lack) of stamens on the central flower, may all vary.
 Though this pattern does not, to our knowledge, appear in any Brockwitz catalog, we are attributing it to this factory as it is found on the interior of several known Brockwitz patterns: *CURVED STAR, NUTMEG GRATER*, and *EUROPEAN POPPY* (a confirmed Brockwitz pattern on account of its appearance in the company's 1915 catalog). *HEADDRESS* is also found teamed with *COSMOS AND CANE* (made by the United States Glass Company). It seems that the pattern was simply copied by the European designers in much the same way that they copied several other patterns, such as Dugan's *FOUR FLOWERS*.
 Shapes: bowls and compote (stemmed sugar)
 Colors: marigold and blue

The interior pattern on some *CURVED STAR, NUTMEG GRATER* and *EUROPEAN POPPY* pieces is *HEADDRESS*. Here it is shown on a blue *CURVED STAR* bowl. $100-$200

PATRICIA—Brockwitz
 This pattern is known in one shape only—the lidded pickle jar. The elongated diamond and fan design is repeated in miniature around the tall lid. Unusual for Brockwitz, this geometric design is cameo (rather than intaglio)—the diamond shapes swell up from the surface, catching and reflecting the light.
 Shape: lidded pickle jar
 Color: marigold

A delightful, lidded pickle jar from Brockwitz standing almost 7 inches high—this has been named *PATRICIA* by collectors. None have been sold at auction and so the value is speculative. SP $100-$350

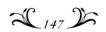

This stunning chop plate in Brockwitz *ROM* pattern shows off the intricate design to great advantage. Only a handful of items are currently known in this pattern, so the value is impossible to gauge. NP. *Courtesy Martin Hamilton.*

ROM—Brockwitz

The exquisite mouldwork on this magnificent design is unusual in that it is a complex mixture of intaglio and cameo. The pattern was shown in Brockwitz catalogs through the 1920s where it was called *ROM* (meaning Rome). Bowls and plates in various sizes were shown, along with a covered butter dish and a large cheese dish.

    Shapes: small bowl and large chop plate
    Color: marigold

STIPPLED CLOVER AND GOTHIC—Brockwitz

Only one shape was apparently illustrated in Brockwitz' catalogs in the *STIPPLED CLOVER AND GOTHIC* pattern—a lidded butter dish. It can be seen in the 1915 catalog, but no others (as far as currently known). The pattern is rather formal and stiff, featuring a repeated triple motif. The same motif is found on the inside of the lid and across the entire underside of the dish. But the main question is what do the motifs represent? They could be three leaved clovers or they could be crosses—two smaller crosses flanking a larger central one, as in the Crucifixion of Christ. Each of the main motifs is framed, the bottom line of the frame being curved upward, like the top of a hill. Perhaps it is indeed supposed to be the hill of Calvary.

    Shapes: butter dish
    Color: marigold

The repeated motifs on the *STIPPLED CLOVER AND GOTHIC* butter dish might possibly represent the three crosses of Calvary. This is the only shape known in the pattern and indeed, the only example currently reported. NP.

SUNFLOWER AND DIAMOND—Brockwitz

This is actually the cylinder vase from a suite of shapes made by Brockwitz in the pattern known as *ASTERS* (see above). The intaglio pattern is a blend of stylized daisies and file-filled diamonds and the vase was made by Brockwitz in three sizes—approx. 6 inches, 8 inches and just over 9 inches (the Brockwitz sizing in metric is 16 cm., 20 cm., and 24 cm.). All three sizes are known in marigold Carnival, though it should be noted that only the largest size is easily found—the others are exceedingly rare. Eda Glasbruks made a version of this cylinder vase, but it can be distinguished by having a coarser file pattern on the diamond shapes, and a height of 7 inches.

    Shape: cylinder vase in three sizes
    Colors: marigold and rare blue (blue currently only known in the large 9-inch vase)

Three *SUNFLOWER AND DIAMOND* vases from Brockwitz. On the left is the 6 inch vase in marigold, while on the right is the 8 inch version, also in marigold. Both these sizes are exceptionally rare and examples are known in marigold only. SP $600-$1200 for either one. In the middle is the 9 inch vase in blue—a rare color for this item. SP $800-$1200

SUPERSTAR—Brockwitz

The name *SUPERSTAR* only applies to the jardinière shape, which is actually part of Brockwitz' *CURVED STAR* range (see above). Some of the familiar *CURVED STAR* pattern elements are not present on the jardinière and thus when the item was first recorded, collectors mistakenly thought it was a different pattern altogether. The design was, of course, adapted to fit the shape of the low, oval boat. This shape may be referred to as a banana boat today, but it was actually termed a jardinière in the Brockwitz catalog—its purpose being to hold potted plants, probably displayed on a window ledge.

    Shape: jardinière
    Colors: marigold and blue

Brockwitz *SUPERSTAR* jardinière is actually part of their *CURVED STAR* range. Shown here in blue. $200-$350

TRIPLE ALLIANCE—Brockwitz

This pattern is only known in the form of a magnificent covered cookie or cracker jar (biscuit barrel). The style is typical of Brockwitz—an intricate intaglio design featuring a combination of stylized floral and geometric motifs. The *TRIPLE ALLIANCE* cookie jar was shown in the Brockwitz catalogs through the 1920s and 1930s and was clearly a popular and functional item. The scarcity of these cookie jars today, especially the matching glass lids, suggests that many were broken during use. Some jars have been found with metal lids, but these were not originals.

    Shape: covered cookie jar
    Colors: marigold and blue

This magnificent, blue cookie jar is Brockwitz' *TRIPLE ALLIANCE*. A scarce item that is sometimes found either without the matching lid or instead, occasionally with a metal replacement lid. SP $550-$850

August Walther and Sons later VEB Säschenglas

August Walther and Sons were contemporary with Brockwitz—in fact they were located not far away from them in Ottendorf-Okrilla near Dresden in Germany. Walther merged with Sächsische Glasfabrik Radeberg in 1932 and became Sächsische Glasfabrik August Walther and Sohne, Aktiengesellschaft, Ottendorf-Okrilla and Radeberg. After World War Two the glass works was nationalized and became VEB Säschenglas, Ottendorf-Okrilla. A small amount of Carnival was produced, along with their many other pressed glass lines: their first period of production was in the 1930s and then again (after World War Two) a second period in the 1950s and 1960s after they were nationalized. Walther also made their own version of Davidson's Cloud Glass which they called Oralit. They're also well known for their fabulous deco style table centrepieces, flower figurines and dresser sets, though none of these are currently reported in Carnival.

The title page of the 1936 catalog from Sachsische Glasfabrik August Walther & Sohne AKT, shows their glass works at Otterndorf-Okrilla bei Dresden. *Courtesy Siegmar Geiselberger and Dietrich Mauerhoff.*

BRILLIANT—August Walther and Sons

A full suite of items in the *BRILLIANT* pattern was shown in Walther's 1932 Export Catalog (courtesy Seigmar Gieselberger and Dietrich Mauerhoff) however only a footed sugar bowl can currently be confirmed in Carnival. A wide range of shapes was shown in the catalogs, however, and any of these might possibly be found in Carnival. Thanks to John Hodgson for tracking this one down.

    Shape: pedestal footed sugar bowl or basin (compote)
    Color: marigold and yellow

The footed sugar basin on the right of this 1932 Walther Export catalog illustration, is known in yellow base Carnival with a marigold iridescence. As you can see, Walther called this pattern *BRILLIANT*. *Courtesy Siegmar Geiselberger and Dietrich Mauerhoff.*

CIRCLES AND GROOVES originally *PISA*—VEB Säschenglas

This pattern features large circles and intervening "grooves"—hence the name. We called the giant marigold vase in this pattern *CIRCLES AND GROOVES* when we first found it, not realizing that it already had a pattern name (*PISA*) given by the maker. We also thought that it might have been a Rindskopf item. Not so—we now know the manufacturer was VEB Saschenglas (originally August Walther) as it is illustrated in their catalogs from the 1950s and 1960s.

    Shape: large vase
    Color: marigold

This large, marigold *CIRCLES AND GROOVES* vase by VEB Saschenglas, is a tall and weighty item made in thick glass. SP $100-$150

HOBSTAR AND SHIELD originally *GERTRUDE*—August Walther and Sons

We originally thought this was a Karhula pattern because a bowl with the same design is shown in their catalogs—but that was before we saw the pattern on a water set in the 1928 Radeberg catalog and again on a creamer and sugar set in Walther's catalog (dated after the Walther merger with Radeberg in 1932). We now believe that this pattern was made in Carnival (on water sets) by August Walther shortly after the 1932 merger using Radeberg moulds. The Radeberg name for this pattern was *GERTRUDE*.

    Shapes: tumbler and water pitcher
    Colors: marigold and blue (water pitcher only)

JOSEFS PLUMES—August Walther and Sons

The *JOSEFS PLUMES* vase is illustrated in early Walther catalogs from the 1920s. It has a ground base and all examples we have seen have boasted scintillating iridescence. The same vase is also shown in a catalog for the Bernsdorf glass company (a German glass maker contemporary with Walther) however we do not believe that the Carnival versions were made by them.

    Shape: vase
    Color: marigold

The iridescence on this *JOSEF'S PLUMES* vase from Walther is breath-takingly lovely. One sold at auction in 2004 for $1,200.

This blue *HOBSTAR AND SHIELD* water pitcher by Walther is the only one we are aware of in this color, though several marigold ones are known. SP $500-$900

PILLNITZ—VEB Säschenglas

Illustrated in the 1950 and 1958 VEB Saschenglas (originally August Walther) catalogs, this is currently known in the form of a large, 11 inch master bowl. The pattern is cameo on the exterior and features four panels of roses on a diamond background. The pattern was called *PILLNITZ* by Saschenglas. Smaller, individual bowls were also illustrated and are likely to have been produced in Carnival.

Shape: master (footed) bowl
Color: marigold

This 11 inch master bowl in the *PILLNITZ* design from VEB Saschenglas is pictured here upside down so as to better illustrate the little scroll feet and the interesting design on the marie. SP $50-100. *Courtesy Frank and Shirley Horn.*

TAURUS aka *HERZ*—August Walther and Sons

It is important to note that the *TENNESSEE STAR* vase (see the information on Riihimaki's *TENNESSEE STAR* vase for further details and illustration) was also illustrated in Walther's catalogs in the 1920s and 1930s. A wide variety of shapes were shown in this pattern that Walther called *TAURUS* (and earlier *HERZ*). The *TENNESSEE STAR* vase is considered to have been made by Riihimaki of Finland. Examples sourced in Finland are almost certainly from Riihimaki and Carnival versions in blue or rare amethyst are also undoubtedly by Riihimaki, but it is not wise to totally rule out the possibility that Walther might have made this vase in marigold.

Shape: not confirmed
Color: not confirmed

TAURUS SERVICE

All Prices quoted are Shillings per 144 PIECES, **not** per 100 PIECES

FLOWER VASES

Number				437	438	439
Size in height to millimetres				180	210	290
Size in inches				6¼	8¼	10⅜
Number in case				300	183	112
Gross weight of case kilogramms				145	155	180
Nett weight in kilogramms				100	106	130
Size of case				II	II	I
Price per gross				80 -	122 -	184 -

This illustration is from Walther's 1928 catalog and features a vase in a pattern they called *TAURUS*. This is the cylinder vase known to Carnival collectors as *TENNESSEE STAR* that is considered to have been made by Riihimaki of Finland. It is not currently possible to confirm production of this item in Carnival by Walther.

WALTRAUT—August Walther and Sons and VEB Säschenglas

A cameo rose design features on this pattern which is shown in Walther's catalogs over both periods of production. Bowls in this pattern have little feet that are ground quite flat.

Shape: bowls (cupped in and flared out)
Color: marigold

A pretty, little rose bowl from Walther in a pattern that they named *WALTRAUT*. SP $30-$60

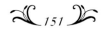

Leinauer Glaswaren (LGW)

Some years ago we came across examples of vividly iridized glass with a strange smoky base color. On one was a label that read: LGW *Pfauenauge* and *Kaleidoskop*. We asked fellow researcher, Siegmar Geiselberger, for help and he uncovered the fascinating background to the production of this unusual iridized glass by Lleinauer Glaswaren (LGW) in Bavaria. The date of production seems to have been fairly recent—into the 1980s—and was carried out by vacuum iridising glass blanks brought in from other makers (for example, Cristal d'Arc or Annahutte). Marcus Newhall reports an LGW piece made using a plate that was designed by Jírí Brabec for the Rosice factory of Sklo Union, around 1980.

The blanks were iridized using a novel method that involved suspending the glass in a high vacuum cage and, characteristically, only the outside of the items was iridized. Geometric style vases, ashtrays and chandelier pendants were made (the latter for firms such as Swarowski) and quite a lot was exported. The words *Pfauenauge* and *Kaleidoskop* on the label refer to the iridescence—meaning shimmering, ever-changing and peacock-like. We have also seen labels with the words *Pfauenage Bleikristal* (crystal glass). Although these items are fairly recent we are including them here as they often cause confusion when found. The very vivid iridescence and the often smoky base glass (or silvery metallic appearance) are characteristics that will aid identification.

LGW SHELLS—Leinauer Glaswaren

These are round, shell-like hors d'oeuvres dishes, 6 inches in diameter, with an incredibly vivid iridescence. The underside has an opaque silver color. One of these dishes known has a paper LGW label.

Shape: small dish
Color: silver base with multi-colored iridescence

CUBIST Vase—Leinauer Glaswaren

A delightful contrast in textures on the surface of this unusual vase, standing 7.5 inches high—the smooth rectangular shapes showing up well against the stippled background. The base glass has a typical smoky effect.

Shape: vase
Color: smoky grey base with multi-colored iridescence

This unusual, square shaped *CUBIST* vase, iridized by LGW, features a contrast of both texture and color. It is the one of two examples currently reported. SP $50-100

BAVARIAN ETCHED LEAVES and BAVARIAN ETCHED FLOWERS— Leinauer Glaswaren

Various shapes of drinking glasses and stem ware are known featuring an etched design that provides a splendid contrast on the iridescent surface. Typical LGW vivid coloration and a smoky base glass are the key characteristics on these items.

Shapes: tall tumbler, juice, liqueur and cordial glasses, straight sided and flared
Color: smoky grey base with multi-colored iridescence

The startling, vivid iridescence on these three items from LGW make them easy to recognize. On the left is a delicate *BAVARIAN ETCHED FLOWERS* liqueur glass; in the middle is an *LGW SHELL* hors d'oeuvres dish with a paper label that reads LGW Pfauenauge Kaleidoskop; on the right is a *BAVARIAN ETCHED LEAVES* cordial glass. SP for any one $25-$50 each.

At the end of World War One, the Treaty of Versailles proclaimed the creation of Czechoslovakia. In this country, about the size of the state of New York, there were over three hundred glass factories already in existence—their beginnings were centuries earlier in Bohemia for glass-making is a long-standing traditional industry here. From 1919 through to the start of World War Two in 1939, the Czech glass industry prospered and exported vast amounts of glass; in fact during that period "the biggest export contingent of glass in any year to one country was that to America from Czechoslovakia in 1927" (source Dr. Ing V. Čtyroký, Director of the Glass Institute, Hradec Králové, writing in 1931). Technical and artistic training in specialist glass schools and institutes ensured high standards and by 1936 the region was producing 40% of the world's glass. World War Two, however, was to have a devastating effect on Czechoslovakia. War damage and subsequent political upheavals changed the face of the country's industry. In 1958 and again in 1965, Czechoslovakian glass production was reorganized and the glass factories collectivized—the era that produced Carnival Glass in Czechoslovakia was over. In 1993, Czechoslovakia split into its two ethnic components, the Czech Republic (which contained Bohemia) and Slovakia.

Our continuing research has uncovered factories in this region that were previously not known to have produced Carnival. To the already well-known name of Inwald we add Rindskopf as a major producer, but there are others too, that produced smaller amounts and these names can now be added to the growing list. Marcus Newhall, the Sklo Union researcher and writer, has been of great help to us in our research and we are very grateful to him.

Josef Inwald

Josef Inwald's head office was in Vienna, but they made glass at various locations with Rudolfova Hut (Rudolfshutte) being their main location for pressed glass and Carnival. Lying to the north-east of Prague in Teplice, this was a major glass "hut" (facility for the production of hot glass) and was the main Bohemian factory to make an international name for itself in the production of pressed glass. Founded in 1884 as a sheet metal factory, Josef Inwald had bought Rudolfova Hut in 1905 and converted it to glassmaking the following year. In the beginning the works blew household glass, but soon they began to produce pressed glass and at the height of production, over a thousand glassworkers were employed there. The plant was modernized considerably between the independence of Czechoslovakia in 1918 and the beginning of the 1930s. Following the introduction of new machinery and technologies, it ranked among the leading producers of pressed glass. The Czech writer, Alena Adlerova, notes that "the first successful efforts not to treat pressed glass simply as a cheap substitute, are to be attributed to the company Inwald" (translation courtesy Marcus Newhall). Their sales were facilitated by warehouses and showrooms located in a number of countries and they exported much glass to other parts of Europe, the USA, Argentina and Australia. After World War Two, the company came under state control and later, became part of Sklo Union. Today, the company is owned by Avirunion, a subsidiary of Owens Illinois, and makes container glass.

Inwald's Carnival was produced at Rudolfova Hut from (we believe) as early as 1914. Scarce Carnival examples of patterns that are seen in Inwald's early catalog are known—*BRILLANT MEDALLIONS* aka *LOOP DE LOOP, FLOATING HEN, RUSSISCHE STEINEL* and an *INVERTED PRISMS* tea warmer are all reported. The Carnival made at Rudolfova Hut is of consistently excellent quality and most examples exhibit a mirror-like polish on the ground base. The "golden years" for Inwald's Carnival are from the mid 1920s through the mid 1930s and it usually boasts superb iridescence that can be a shimmering multi-hued pastel or a rich deep pumpkin marigold.

Inwald's catalogs from 1914, 1924, 1928 and 1938 have been very useful for allowing us to identify items. The wholesaler, Markhbeinn (who marketed a large amount of Inwald's glass) also issued catalogs in 1928, 1933, 1934, 1935 and 1936 that actually depicted some Inwald items

in color—marigold—and described them as *irisé* (iridized). In fact two specific terms were used: *irisé* and *ambre irisé*: it seems very possible that the *irisé* term refers to the lighter, shimmering marigold that is shot with gold, lime, pink and aqua and that the term *ambre irisé* refers to the deeper more intense, pumpkin marigold that is shot with raspberry, turquoise and jade.

Furthermore, it is possible that some blue Carnival from Inwald may also exist, as we have seen two pieces in a 1936 catalog in "azurite irisé" which means iridized blue. Neither of the two shapes in that catalog is known in marigold Carnival (although a marigold vase in one of the patterns—*AIGLON*—is known), nor have they been reported in blue, but this does suggest that some blue Inwald Carnival may exist—for example, the *DIAMOND CUT* jardinière (see below).

Rudolph Schrötter—"The Master"

Thanks to recent groundbreaking research done by Marcus Newhall, the importance of Rudolph Schrötter within the field of Pressed Glass in general, and Carnival Glass in particular, is beginning to be understood. Schrötter was born on 3rd April, 1887 in Freital u Drážd´an. He was well educated and technically trained and he was employed by Rheinische Glashütten Aktiengesellschaft, Köln- Ehrenfeld, between 1904 and 1912, starting there when he was just seventeen. Eight years later, with his drawing and design skills honed to perfection, Schrötter went to work at Inwald's Rudolfova Hut on July 1st 1912 where he was the company's first (indeed their **only**) "in-house" designer. He continued to work for Inwald until August 1st 1958 when he officially retired, however his enthusiasm was not diminished by age, for he continued to help out with new designs even after he retired. Over those forty six years, Schrötter is believed to have designed some 6500 different glass shapes in many hundreds of different patterns.

Few Carnival patterns can be fully attributed to a specific designer—their names, along with those of the skilled mould makers, artists and other craftsmen involved, are rarely known. In the case of Inwald, how-ever, we know that all their Carnival was designed by Rudolph Schrötter. *JACOBEAN* (originally known as *LORD*) was first designed by him in 1921 in a vast range of different forms.

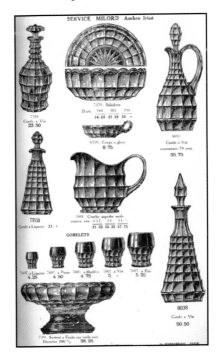

This color ad in for Inwald's *JACOBEAN* glass appeared in Markhbeinn's wholesale catalog in 1928. Note that the glass is described as Ambre Irisé (pumpkin marigold Carnival) and the pattern name is shown as *MILORD*. Inwald referred to this pattern as *LORD* and the first pieces in the pattern were designed by Rudolph Schrötter in 1921. Many more shapes were to follow—all designed by Schrötter.
Courtesy Siegmar Geiselberger and Dieter Neumann.

Schrötter's output and creative force were phenomenal and his work was a masterly blend of functionality and aesthetic simplicity with a strong hint of Art Déco style. He has been referred to as "The Master" on account of his astonishing ability to both understand and command the medium of glass in the context of its design. For it wasn't just patterns on the glass that Schrötter created—he also designed a multitude of shapes and forms to best fit the functions required. His vases in particular are simple and practical yet also stylishly magnificent and visually breathtaking. Schrötter was undoubtedly a genius, a true master of design, with a rare ability to adapt pattern themes to a multitude of different forms and functions.

This fascinating information on Rudolph Schrötter is courtesy of Marcus Newhall and Miroslav Grisa (*Rudolfova hud´v Dubí*: Teplice, 2006—translation from original Czech text by Marcus Newhall).

Discoveries

As well as recently discovered items, our research has also uncovered several patterns made by Inwald that appear to have also been produced by a newly discovered Carnival maker in Poland—Hortensja. Read more about this in the chapter below on Polish Carnival Glass.

Other fresh information has revealed the original pattern names of some familiar Carnival designs, for example; *BANDED DIAMONDS AND BARS* was originally called *CARTHAGE*; *BOHEMIAN OVALS* was originally called *OLIVETTES TUDOR*; *DECORAMA* was originally called *SPHINX* and *FLEUR DE LYS* was originally called *SIGURD*.

BAY LEAVES—Inwald
Only one shape in this pattern is known—a slender, pedestal footed vase. The design comprises a series of horizontal bands, featuring an encircling ring of stylized bay leaves on alternate rows. It was illustrated in the 1928 Inwald catalog with the pattern number 8080 (introduced in 1922). The foot of this vase is wide and heavy, while a glance underneath will reveal the polished, mirror-shiny ground base.
Shape: vase
Color: marigold

CIRCLE SQUARED—Inwald
Illustrated in a 1938 Inwald catalog , this vase was given the pattern number 9045, which actually dates its introduction back to around 1922. It has a pedestal base with the typical Inwald polished bottom. The vase is unusual in that the body is actually square-sided, tapering down to a domed pedestal base. The moulded pattern features a series of linked circles.
Shape: vase
Color: marigold

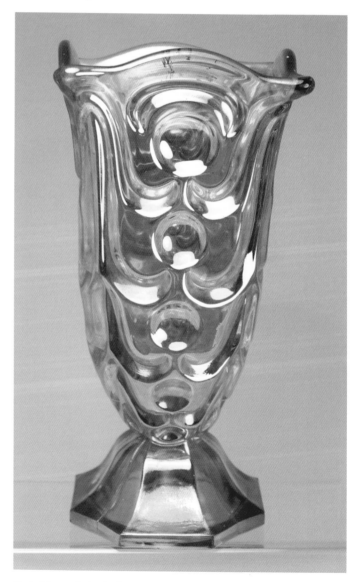

Standing 8 inches high, this *BAY LEAVES* vase has a breathtaking iridescence, shimmering with lime, fuschia pink and turquoise tones, that is typical of Inwald's peacock marigold. SP $350-$600

Probably made in the late 1930s, this *CIRCLE SQUARED* vase from Inwald has a most unusual design. SP $100-$200

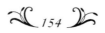

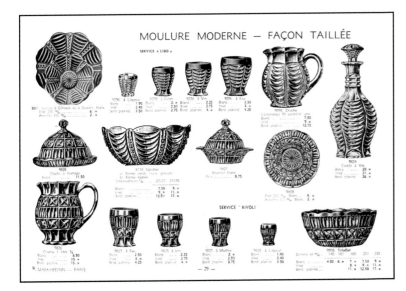

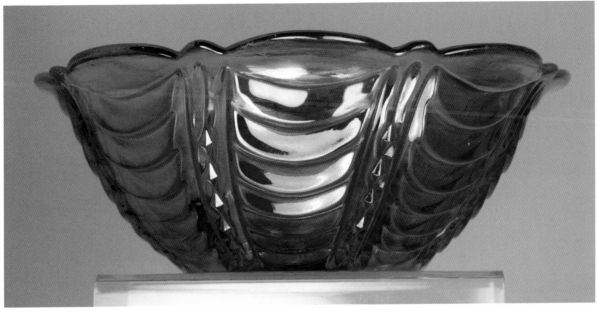

DIAMOND CUT—Inwald

This intaglio design features a fan motif and cross or diamond shapes (the interpretation depends on how you view it). A large cylinder vase, which is known in marigold Carnival, was shown in a 1938 catalog from Inwald in which it was given the pattern number 7731, dating its introduction to 1922. Nine further shapes in this pattern (mainly bowls in various shapes and a stemmed compote) were illustrated in Inwald's 1928 catalog but we cannot currently confirm any of those shapes in Carnival. The exact same cylinder vase shape was also shown in the catalogs of Hortensja in Poland (for illustration of the vase and further information see the chapter on Poland below). Bowls in the *DIAMOND CUT* pattern were also made by Crown Crystal of Australia.

Blue *DIAMOND CUT* jardinières have been found in Argentina. Could they have been made by Inwald and exported to Argentina? A substantial amount of Inwald's Carnival has been found there, along with many other European items. Or could the jardinière have been a copy that was actually manufactured in Argentina? We believe that it is possible that Inwald may have made some blue Carnival (see above). Our research continues to try and solve these puzzles.

    Shape: cylinder vase and possibly the jardinière

    Color: marigold and possibly blue

DRAPERY VARIANT originally LIDO—Inwald

This pattern was previously attributed to Riihimaki as the tumbler was shown in their 1929 catalog. The authors, however, have long suspected that the maker could indeed be Inwald. Our feelings were based on the polished mirror grind often found on the base (which is an Inwald characteristic) plus the fact that examples are often seen in the UK (Inwald's

Carnival is frequently found in the UK whereas Riihimaki's Carnival is hardly ever sourced there). Furthermore, the *DRAPERY VARIANT* water set is shown in the South American Piccardo catalog with the name "Checo"—a sure hint of the Czech origin. Our suspicions were borne out when 1928 and 1934 Markhbeinn catalogs of Inwald's glass were found (courtesy Dieter Neumann and Siegmar Geiselberger) depicting a full range of *DRAPERY VARIANT* items (called *LIDO*). These items were described in the catalogs as *irisé* (iridized—Carnival) and they were shown alongside other known Inwald items such as *JACOBEAN*. It is possible that Riihimaki made some items, of course (although there's no proof they were iridized), but undoubtedly most (if not all) *DRAPERY VARIANT* in Carnival was made by Inwald.

We know now that the pattern was introduced by Inwald circa 1924 and it is likely that it was first made in Carnival around that time too. It is similar to Northwood's *DRAPERY*, differing mainly in the fact that there are fewer lines in the drapes. The iridescence is outstanding on every piece in this pattern that we have handled—an amazing marigold, shot through with pinks, limes and gold—quite breathtaking. The *DRAPERY VARIANT* water pitcher has a most unusual shape, unlike any other, being short and bulbous, its neck angled into a somewhat frilly effect. Bowls and plates in this pattern have the drapes separated by ribs containing beaded diamonds. Four different sizes of tumblers were illustrated in Markhbeinn's 1936 catalog of Inwald's glass—described as *irisé* (iridized) these graduated sizes were shown (in size order, smallest first) for liqueur, port, wine and water.

    Shapes: pitcher, tumbler, plate, bowl, wine or port glass, shot glass and decanter

    Color: marigold

DRESDEN DRAPE aka FOUR GARLANDS—Inwald

This elegant vase is the only shape that we are aware of in this pattern. It is illustrated in Inwald's 1928 catalog amongst a selection of vases in a variety of different designs. We're not aware of an original pattern name for this vase—the two names shown above were given to it by the collectors who found the first examples (and who were both unaware of each other's "find"). Both names acknowledge the main pattern motif, a draping "garland" of foliage. This splendid vase stands 7 inches high and has an exceptionally wide 7.5 inch flared mouth.

    Shape: vase
    Color: marigold

This elegant *DRESDEN DRAPE* vase stands 7 inches high. It was illustrated in Inwald's 1928 catalog where it had the pattern number 8838. SP $400-$600

GOLDEN DELICIOUS aka FRUIT BONBONNIÈRE—Inwald

Identified in Inwald's catalogs by the number 8588 (introduced circa 1922) this delightful bonbonnière (covered sweet dish) comprises two identical dishes (just over five inches across) each with a deeply serrated saw tooth edge, that interlock perfectly to form a lidded item. Of course, the pieces could also be used as individual dishes—multi-purpose flexibility added to the appeal of merchandise. The catalog suggests they are used for ice cream or desserts, under carafes or as a two-part covered sweet dish. They are shown both individually and fitted together as the two part dish, in the Inwald catalogs. Other covered bonbonnières are shown in the catalogs as iridized—they have the same shape and similar exterior moulded patterns, but the central design varies (one is shown with a grape design while another has a whirling star motif).

The iridescence is typical Inwald—high quality marigold, shimmering with color—the overall decorative effect is further enhanced by frosting (acid etching) of the fruit pattern, which provides a magnificent contrast. An interesting twist is that this pattern appears to have been copied in the 1940s by Federal Glass in the USA (it is their *PIONEER* design). The fruits on *PIONEER* are, however, very different and are not frosted.

    Shape: covered bonbonnière
    Color: marigold and frosted

INWALD STARS—Inwald

An elegant water pitcher in this pattern was illustrated in the 1928 catalog of Inwald's glass—it has pattern number 7978 which dates its introduction to 1922. The pattern is a simple geometric featuring star shapes and blocks. Currently the pitcher is the only example of this pattern is known in Carnival, however a very wide range of shapes was also depicted in the catalog.

    Shape: water pitcher
    Color: marigold

The interplay of light and superb iridescence on Inwald's *GOLDEN DELICIOUS* covered bonbonnière dish is breathtaking. NP

Magnificent iridescence, typical of Inwald, on this *INWALD STARS* water pitcher. NP. *Photo courtesy Tammy Murphy.*

This illustration is from a 1928 Markhbeinn catalog of Inwald's glass. It shows the *INWALD STARS* pitcher and tumbler—note only the pitcher is currently known in Carnival.

JACOBEAN aka *JACOBEAN RANGER* originally also *LORD* or *MILORD*—Inwald

A familiar block pattern that usually exhibits top notch iridescence, *JACOBEAN* (originally known by Inwald as *LORD*) was designed by Rudolf Schrötter; the first item (a 8.6 inch dish) being introduced in 1921. The range of shapes designed by Schrötter was astonishing, though only a handful of the 300 or more different shapes were made in Carnival. The *JACOBEAN* pattern has a fascinating history that reflects trade and politics in Europe during the 1920s and 1930s. It had one of the biggest and most impressive advertising campaigns ever devoted to glass. It was also arguably the most widely distributed and sold pressed glass pattern of its time. In the UK, an agent called Clayton Mayers marketed the *JACOBEAN* range heavily. The British trade journals ran ads and special promotional supplements were included with some issues of the Pottery Gazette. *JACOBEAN* glassware was also offered in exchange for cigarette coupons by the International Tobacco Company in London. By 1925 it was reported that *JACOBEAN* glassware had spread all over Britain "like wild fire". In 1931 a cinema film was even produced to sell the glass: called "A visit to Miss Madeleine Carroll's Flat" it was intended to show "the beauty and utility of Jacobean Glassware in a modern home."

In 1932 a change took place as tariffs on imported glass began to take their toll in Britain. Clayton Mayers announced that some (not all) of the *JACOBEAN* tumblers were to be made in Britain. Until that point, all the *JACOBEAN* items had been manufactured in Czechoslovakia. Within a few years, several more items in the range were also made in Britain by various firms that probably included Davidsons on Tyneside (but note that these were **not** iridized).

It wasn't only the UK that imported Inwald's *JACOBEAN*, in France the range was known as *MILORD* and was marketed by the Parisian wholesaler, Markhbeinn, with a huge range of shapes on offer. In Argentina, *JACOBEAN* vases were marketed by the glass firm Cristalerias Papini under the pattern name "Lirio." In the USA, the distributor F. Pavel & Co., of New York, offered an assortment of Inwald's *JACOBEAN* glass.

It is most likely that all *JACOBEAN* Carnival was made in Czechoslovakia prior to 1932. The iridized tumblers (in all four sizes) may have the registered design number 702446 moulded into the glass. This was registered in the United Kingdom by Clayton Mayers in 1923—at that time there was a certain *cachet* in having a British registration number on the glass—no doubt Josef Inwald, intent on marketing their glassware widely in the United Kingdom, believed that it would help them.

Shapes: tumblers in four sizes, ranging upwards from a diminutive tot with a tiny 1 inch base that stands just over 2 inches high; water pitcher, decanter and tumble-up. A full dressing table set including powder jars, perfume, atomiser and cologne bottles in various sizes, a large tray, small pintray and a ring tree. Cylinder vase and a variation with a "spittoon" shaped neck. Possibly many more items were iridized and have yet to be discovered by collectors

Color: marigold is the only reported color so far

A selection of *JACOBEAN* items in marigold—all are dressing table or boudoir items. From left, tumble-up ($150-$250), tall cologne ($100-$250), ring holder ($50-$100), two sizes of perfumes ($75-$150), trinket tray ($40-$100), covered powder jar ($100-$250), covered pomade jar ($100-$150). *Photo courtesy David Doty*.

LAURIER NELLY—Inwald

A range of shapes in this pattern is depicted in the Markhbeinn catalogs of Inwald's glass, however only a few scarce examples of it are currently known in Carnival, one of which is a splendid, statuesque vase in pumpkin marigold, with a polished, mirror-shiny base (described as a *fond polis*). The interpretation of the design (called *NELLY* or *LAURIER NELLY*) on the vase features eight, intaglio, stylized laurel or sweet bay leaf motifs which encircle the item over eight panels. A series of elegant horizontal "steps" encloses the leaf band while at the top of the vase eight gentle scallops surmount the vertical panels.

Shape: vase (standing 7.5 inches high), water pitcher and oval jardinière
Color: marigold

NOLA aka *PANELED TWIGS* originally *POMPÉI*—Inwald.

The design is a paneled, intaglio zig zag effect—simple yet very effective and almost always found with a breathtaking iridescence. The British *Pottery Gazette* ran an ad in 1929 for "International Glassware" which featured the *NOLA* tumbler with its distinctively shaped diamond base. An impressive vase was first reported in 2006: it stands 10 inches high and measures 5 inches across its mouth. The vase was illustrated in Inwald's 1928 catalogue in two sizes—the one photographed here is the larger of the two. It is of interest to note that the same vase shape and form was also used by Inwald without the distinctive zig-zag pattern.

Shapes: water set (pitcher and tumblers have the diamond shaped base). Full dressing table set including colognes, perfume bottle, ring tree, tray, powder boxes, a tumble-up and a rare vase. Note that the tumbler in the tumble-up has a round base

Color: marigold

The intense and deep, pumpkin marigold iridescence on this *LAURIER NELLY* vase by Inwald may well be the effect that was described in the maker's catalog as "Ambre Irisé". SP $350-$500

PINWHEEL originally *PICADILLY*—Inwald.

Not only is this a complex design (featuring stars and similar intaglio motifs) it is also a pattern with a complex history, as it was produced in Carnival by three different makers in three different countries: Inwald in Czechoslovakia, Sowerby in England and Hortensja in Poland. There are various distinguishing features that assist in determining the maker. This pattern was called "Picadilly" when it was shown in a full pattern suite in the wholesaler Markhbeinn's catalog in 1927, however only few items in the pattern were shown in their later catalogs.

The cylinder vase was made by Inwald, Sowerby and Hortensja—so is it possible to determine which maker made which vase? Color is the first indicator and marigold is the only common color (Sowerby made their *PINWHEEL* vases in amethyst and rare blue as well as marigold). Size gives us some common ground too, as the 6, 8 and 10 inch vases appear to have been made by all three companies. The item most likely to puzzle, however, is the 8 inch marigold cylinder vase. We suggest that there are two ways to assist identification: first, look at the large diamond motifs above and below the central star. With the large diamond are found smaller diamonds, each of which should be bisected—if there are indented (inward) small triangles within these bisected diamonds, then the vase is probably from Inwald or Sowerby. If there are no indents, then

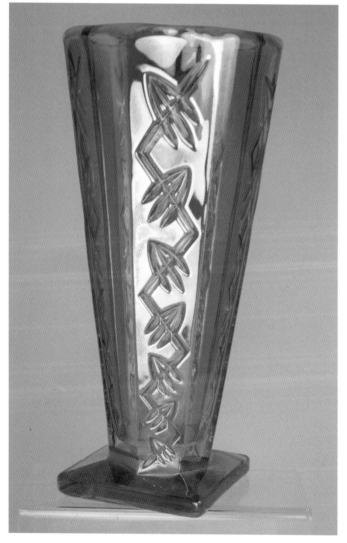

The iridescence on this rare *NOLA* vase from Inwald is so hard to capture—pink, green and gold shimmer on its surface. SP $600-$1000

This extract from Markhbeinn's 1927 catalog shows the Inwald *INTAGLIO STARS* tumbler, which is actually part of their *PICADILLY* (aka *PINWHEEL*) pattern range. *Courtesy Siegmar Geiselberger and Dieter Neumann.*

it is probably a Hortensja vase. To further distinguish between Inwald and Sowerby, check the lower part of the vase—if there are scallops/swags, then it's probably Sowerby. Finally, there appears to be a file pattern on the diamond shapes on the Inwald vase, but we cannot confirm this with certainty. You can read more about all these distinguishing features in much greater detail by going to our website http://www.carnival-glass.net and going to the European Index > PINWHEEL.

There is also a small PINWHEEL vase that stands just under 5 inches high and has a flat ground base with a recessed intaglio star. It was previously thought to be by Inwald however, through careful comparison of Inwald and Hortensja catalog illustrations we feel that the little vase is almost certainly a Hortensja item. The tumbler in Inwald's PINWHEEL pattern has been given a different name by collectors in the past—it is known as INTAGLIO STARS. It was matched with a wine carafe (there is no water pitcher in this pattern) and was described as gobelet á vin.

Shapes: vase (8 inch), tumbler (INTAGLIO STARS) and bowls. Possibly other items in this pattern were iridized

Color: marigold

PRAGUE—Inwald

No name was given to this vase by Inwald and thus it has been named for the city in which the first example was reported. The vase, featuring a simple linear cross pattern, was illustrated in catalogs of Inwald's glass in the 1920s. Only a handful of examples are currently known. The catalog illustration of the vase shows a slightly bulbous form with two different top shapings—flared and incurved. However a further shape is known whereby the vase sides are not bulbous, but are straight with a very slight outward curve at the top.

Shape: vase
Color: marigold

This 1933 catalog illustration from the wholesaler, Markhbeinn, shows the PRAGUE vase from Inwald, with the pattern number 9066. Although the height given is shown as 200 mm (about 8 inches) the known examples of this vase are actually closer to 7 inches high. *Courtesy Siegmar Geiselberger and Dieter Neumann.*

PROVENCE aka BARS AND CROSS BOX originally RIVOLI—Inwald

This stunning pattern is known in the form of a single water pitcher that was discovered in a street market in the south of France (hence the name PROVENCE, given by the authors) and a single, matching tumbler. The iridescence on these marigold items is quite incredible, with pinks, greens and blues flashing off the glass surface. The pattern is simple yet elegant; a combination of grooves and crosses (thus the alternative name BARS AND CROSS BOX). Confirmed as Inwald manufacture by catalog identification, where it was given the original name RIVOLI. In Markhbeinn's 1936 catalog of Inwald's glass four different sizes of tumbler were illustrated, described as irisé (iridized). They were noted to be (in size order, smallest first) for liqueur, Madeira, wine and water.

Shapes: water pitcher and tumbler
Color: marigold

This marigold PROVENCE water pitcher (found in Provence, France, in 1987 and named by the authors) has breathtaking iridescence and is currently the only example reported. Made by Josef Inwald and originally named RIVOLI. NP

Josef Rindskopf's Sons A.G.

Acknowledgment

In 2001, in our book "A Century of Carnival Glass" (Schiffer) we revealed a previously unknown Carnival Glass maker—Josef Rindskopf's Sons. Rindskopf was not unknown as a glass maker, in fact they were renowned for the production of high quality art glass in the late 1800s and early 1900s, however, our study of the Rindskopf catalogs from the 1920s and 1930s showed that they also made a large amount of pressed Carnival Glass.

In 2004, we were contacted by Professor F. F. Ridley, the great grandson of Josef Rindskopf. His memories and amazing family archive of unique photographs form an astonishing historical record, not only of a great glassmaking heritage, but also in the context of the history of pressed glass manufacture. They show the factory floor and the glass making machinery as well as the buildings, the workers and their living conditions at Rindskopf's Kosten glass works. We are privileged to show some of these photographs here and we are deeply grateful to Professor Ridley for his constant help. Sincere thanks too, to Howard Seufer, for technical information that helped identify the processes shown in the photos.

History of Rindskopf's Sons A.G.

Josef Rindskopf (later Riethof) was born in 1829. He married an American, Fanny Phillips, and in 1876 became co-owner, with several of his brothers, of a glass works called Brüder Rindskopf (Rindskopf Brothers) in the spa town of Teplice. A year after his death, in 1891, four of his sons (Sidney, Albert, Edwin and Sherman—note their American/English names) established a new company called Josef Rindskopf's Söhne A.G. (Josef Rindskopf's Sons) at Kosten. Soon after, factories at Dux and Tischau (all near Teplice) were added and were principally used for the production of mainly ornamental art glass.

It was a massive glass empire. The factory at Kosten was called Josefhütte, the one at Tischau was Barbarahütte while Fannyhütte was the factory at Dux. The glass houses (hüttes) were named after members of the family, for example, Fannyhütte was named for Fanny Phillips, the wife of Josef Rindskopf and Barbara was Josef's mother. In 1903, the factory at Kosten was faced with re-building following a serious fire—the constant scourge of glass works. The opportunity was taken to construct a new factory, fully equipped with state-of-the-art machinery for efficient mass production of huge quantities of glassware. The new factory had modern installations for the production of glass articles, its own water systems, high pressure ventilators, modern compressors and full facilities for semi-automatic glass production. Furthermore, there was in-house production of all their own iron moulds. This would have been where the Carnival Glass items were pressed and iridized, ready for export, alongside clear flint glass items. Some time around 1930, perhaps because of the financial problems that surely must have been associated with the large size of the undertaking then (or possibly because the surviving founding brothers had reached retirement age) the Rindskopf firm and its factories were taken into the Inwald company.

Rindskopf's Carnival Glass is found primarily in marigold, with occasional items being found on yellow or amber base glass. The quality of both glass and iridescence varies tremendously, perhaps reflecting the fortunes of the company. Their range of "King Tut" style items (see CLASSIC ARTS and EGYPTIAN QUEEN below) are unusual in that they feature faux verdigris decoration.

Catalogs of Rindskopf's pressed glass are known from 1915, 1920, 1927 and 1936. The 1915 one has allowed us to give some original names to Rindskopf patterns, for example DIAMOND OVALS (a very comprehensive suite of shapes) was called ORIENT and indeed it is possible that Carnival was first made by Rindskopf around that time.

Part of the Rindskopf glass factory buildings at Kosten. Note the railway line in the bottom left of the photo—no doubt used for transporting the coal that can be seen on the right of the picture. The workers are both male and female. *Courtesy Professor F.F. Ridley.*

This is the factory floor at the Rindskopf glass factory in Kosten, where Carnival was made. Note how the workers (mainly men and boys but there are a few women and girls too) all turn to look at the camera. In view are the furnaces, punty rods and other typical glass making equipment. Note also the many pipes in the photo—these would be used for "wind", i.e. cooling air delivered by hanging vertical down-pipes to an operation—such as is seen now in current glass factories. *Courtesy Professor F.F. Ridley and extra information courtesy Howard Seufer.*

A section of the mould shop at Rindskopf's Kosten factory. It appears that the men in this photograph are engaged in a polishing operation to keep a smooth surface in the moulds, (this would follow on from cleaning the moulds). *Courtesy Professor F.F. Ridley and extra information courtesy Howard Seufer.*

The mould shop at Kosten—this looks like a benchhand area where the actual patterns were chipped into the mould. A small mould-maker sized hammer can be seen in one man's fist. These men are seated on three-legged stools instead of the upturned crates and boxes that were in use as seating in some other parts of the factory. They are also all wearing artisans' overalls. A more elite section of the factory, perhaps? *Courtesy Professor F.F. Ridley and extra information courtesy Howard Seufer.*

The workers at Kosten were provided with fairly Spartan dining facilities, but here we have a glimpse through into the smartest dining room which would have been provided for the management at the glass factory. Here there are flowers on the tables and fabric tablecloths. Note the vases on the tables which are almost certainly from the factory. They bear a resemblance to the cylinder shaped CLASSIC ARTS vases. On the right you can see glass mugs and stemware, as well as several bowls. On the left is a poster advertising various musical and theatrical events in the area. *Courtesy Professor F.F. Ridley.*

Another fascinating photo showing life at the Rindskopf glass works. Here there are tidy bunk beds separated by wooden wardrobes. No doubt these facilities would have been provided for the apprentices—quite possibly many of them would have come from further afield to learn the trade at this major glassworks. *Courtesy Professor F.F. Ridley.*

CLASSIC ARTS and EGYPTIAN QUEEN—Rindskopf

The *CLASSIC ARTS* and *EGYPTIAN QUEEN* items are "sister" patterns, distinguished from all other Carnival Glass in that they have a kind of green (verdigris effect) staining as part of the decoration. Basically marigold items, they feature a decorated band of dancing figures that is picked out in the green effect. This gives an antique look and was almost certainly an attempt to evoke the 1920s Art Déco "King Tut" craze. (In 1922, the tomb of the Egyptian king Tutankhamen had been discovered). Other items from Czech manufacturers such as Moser, Walther and Harrach featured similar decorated bands of dancing figures, although none of these were iridized. See the section on Riihimaki in the Chapter on Scandinavia (below) for further information on Moser and on Riihimaki's *AMAZON WOMEN* vase, which has a similar pattern band.

CLASSIC ARTS

The *CLASSIC ARTS* pieces have a pattern band that features Roman type figures, playing instruments and dancing. Several shapes are depicted in this pattern: a wide vase 7.5 inches high (pattern #1658); a finger bowl or open sugar bowl that is often incorrectly described as a rose bowl (pattern #1642) and a covered sugar or marmalade bowl that is often incorrectly described as a covered powder jar (pattern #1642 for the bowl and #1704 for the lid).

Shapes: large vase, open sugar bowl (or finger bowl) and covered sugar bowl

Color: marigold with green stain band

EGYPTIAN QUEEN

The *EGYPTIAN QUEEN* items are "sister" pieces to *CLASSIC ARTS* but are distinguished by their green, pattern band with distinctly Egyptian looking figures playing harps and other instruments. It has long been accepted that the smaller of the two vases in this pattern (#1641) may have been a lemonade glass, but study of the Rindskopf catalog indicates that it was, in fact, simply a small version of the vase (the taller example has the pattern #1659).

Shape: vase in two sizes (6 and 7.5 inches high)

Color: marigold with green stain band

The *EGYPTIAN QUEEN* vase is on the left and the *CLASSIC ARTS* vase is on the right—the patterns are often confused. Values are similar for either piece. In 1998, auction prices touched $1000 for the *CLASSIC ARTS* vase, but have settled to around $200-$500 in recent years.

DIAMOND OVALS originally ORIENT—Rindskopf

DIAMOND OVALS is Czech and was made by Josef Rindskopf in a wide range of shapes and sizes. The main pattern motif is a diamond filled oval shape and alternate fans. It was undoubtedly a very popular pattern, as a comprehensive range of shapes was illustrated in Rindskopf's catalogs. The first appearance we can confirm of this pattern was in 1915, suggesting that Carnival Glass may well have been made by Rindskopf at that time.

Shapes: creamer, stemmed sugar, butter dish, large and small bowls, tumble-up, stemmed cake plate or salver in various sizes, rare candlesticks, and perfume bottle

Color: marigold

An impressive footed cake stand from Rindskopf in the *DIAMOND OVALS* (aka *ORIENT*) design. This item stands 5 inches high and measures 10 inches across. SP $75-$150

FINE FLOWERS BORDER—Rindskopf

A cylinder vase featuring a repeated pattern of crosses, finished off at top and bottom with a border of stylized flowers. This vase was given the pattern number 1741 in Rindskopf's 1920 catalog.

Shape: vase

Color: marigold

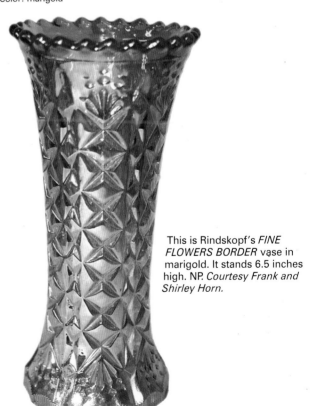

This is Rindskopf's *FINE FLOWERS BORDER* vase in marigold. It stands 6.5 inches high. NP. *Courtesy Frank and Shirley Horn.*

MARIANNA—Rindskopf

The pattern on *MARIANNA* is a combination of notched bands and a simple fan shaped spray on a panelled background. Known in an 8 inch high, pedestal footed vase, it has the press moulded words on the base MADE IN CZECHOSLOVAKIA, which indicates it was made for export. The vase is illustrated in the Rindskopf catalog 11 (pattern #1867). The pattern on the *MARIANNA* vase is very similar to the design on the *MARTHA* bowl, suggesting that *MARTHA* might be a Rindskopf product.

    Shape: vase
    Color: marigold

A most attractive marigold item from Rindskopf, this vase is known to collectors as the *MARIANNA* Vase. SP $150-$250

PORTHOLES—Rindskopf

Illustrated in Rindskopf's 1934 catalog (pattern number 8236), this is a solid looking and rather chunky pitcher that stands just over 6 inches high and is 6 inches wide. The design features alternate panels of ovals and incised ribs which are repeated four times around this oval shaped pitcher. A tumbler in this pattern is shown in Rindskopf's catalogs but we are not yet aware of one being found in Carnival.

    Shape: pitcher
    Color: marigold

Appropriately named, the marigold *PORTHOLES* pitcher, made by Rindskopf, features large, flattened circles. NP. *Courtesy Carol and Derek Sumpter.*

PROTRUSIONS—Rindskopf

Shown in Rindskopf's catalog 11 with the pattern number 8279, this tumbler stands 3 inches high and features a pattern of divided columns and blocks in three horizontal bands. The example of this item we have studied has the word TCHECOSLOVAQUIE etched on the ground base (which also features a 12 petalled design).

    Shape: tumbler
    Color: marigold

A cameo interpretation of a simple geometric pattern can be seen on Rindskopf's *PROTRUSIONS* marigold tumbler. NP. *Courtesy Carol and Derek Sumpter.*

ROUND THE BLOCK—Rindskopf

Both pitcher and tumbler are known in this simple yet effective circle and panel design. The base of the tumbler has a recessed star and is highly polished and ground, more in the style of Inwald than Rindskopf. The pattern is shown in Rindskopf's catalog 11.

    Shapes: pitcher and tumbler
    Color: marigold

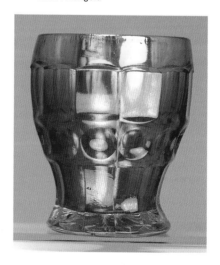

Named for both the round and block shapes that encircle this tumbler, Rindskopf's *ROUND THE BLOCK* pattern is known in both tumbler and pitcher forms. SP $50-$100

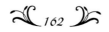

Libochovice
aka Libochwitzer Glashuette C.S.
aka Libochovické Sklárny

The Libochovice glass works was founded in 1912 by Josef Feigl and Vladislav Móravek. The company's main output was container glass, although utility glass and decorative glass was also made on a small scale (they had special decorating workshops). In the 1920s and early 1930s, Libochovice produced small amounts of very high quality, decorative items in an interesting range of colors that included amethyst, smoke, green and a color described as "absinthe" (which was almost certainly vaseline glass). The authors have now discovered that, around that time, Libochovice also made a small amount of top notch iridized Carnival. A Libochovice catalog has been found by Sklo Union researcher, Marcus Newhall, which clearly shows some known Carnival items and furthermore helps to provide small circumstantial evidence for attributing others to this important glass works, for example, the large Deco vases like the *SEAGULLS*. These items are included below, but it is clearly noted where the evidence is circumstantial rather than fully attributed and proven.

Marcus Newhall has also uncovered the fact that moulds for the decorative glass at Libochovice were made by Herman Kiko at Brno, Czechoslovakia. Kiko already had a main factory in Vienna producing presses and tools for the glass industry but in 1924 he set up a branch in Brno that specialised in making high quality, hand-tooled moulds, concentrating on pattern and form. They made moulds for Libochovice between 1920 and 1940, using designs by the academic glass sculptor, Karel Zentner, who had been trained at the Prague Academy of Arts. Kiko's mould factory was one of only two in Czechoslovakia at that time (the other was Ullrich and Christl at Mstišov u Teplic that reportedly made moulds for Inwald); other major pressed glass makers such as Rindskopf had their own mould making shops. In 1993, Kiko became Brnoform and still produces moulds and tools for the glass industry.

Libochovice was substantially reorganised after 1945 and technological advancement was subsequently put in place. Some glass from Barolac (linked with Inwald) designs were produced from the 1950s on, possibly using old moulds or freshly cut ones. Recent changes have seen the fortunes of the glass works fluctuate, but rejuvenation is likely.

SUBLIME DECO CANDLESTICK—Libochovice

Possibly one of the most stunningly beautiful Carnival candlesticks, this single candleholder was made by Libochovice, in Czechoslovakia, in the early 1930s. It is depicted on a page in a Libochovice catalog (courtesy Marcus Newhall and Zdenk Hrabák, Liberec) among a selection of twenty other candlesticks, including the double stick version of this item. The single *SUBLIME DECO* (named by the authors) had the Libochovice pattern number 1224. The double candlestick had the pattern number 1686.

The iridescence on these candlesticks is magnificent; turn them one way and they are loaded with aqua, gold and shimmering turquoise—turn another way and a myriad of darker blues, purples and raspberry-pinks cascade over the glass. The candlesticks are partly frosted and the iridescence was applied to both types of surface, thus providing a spectacular and breathtaking contrast. The frosted / iridized surfaces on the single candlestick are those that have the curving scrolls. The iridized only surfaces are at the top, the bottom and on the central diamond section. The single candlestick stands 7 inches high and moulded on the base is the word TCHECOSLOVAQUIE.

Shapes: single and double candlesticks
Color: pastel (possibly using titanium dioxide) and frosted

Probable Libochovice items

A most unusual moulded neck structure can clearly be seen on several vases in the Libochovice catalog. There is a most distinctive mould seam that runs horizontally around the neck, and this characteristic neck structure is found on a number of Carnival vases. This evidence, coupled with Art Déco style (that we know was typical of Libochovice) and the unusual colours of these vases strongly suggests that they were made by Libochovice.

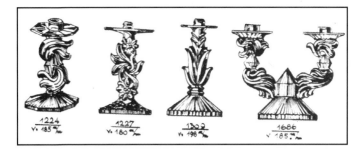

This catalog illustration from Libochovice shows two items known in Carnival. On the far left is #1224, a single candlestick and on the far right is #1686, a double candlestick. Named by collectors *SUBLIME DECO*, these items are known with magnificent pastel iridescence. *Courtesy Marcus Newhall and Zdenk Hrabák.*

From Libochovice in Czechoslovakia, this exceptionally rare *SUBLIME DECO* candlestick has a scintillating—indeed breathtaking—iridescence. NP

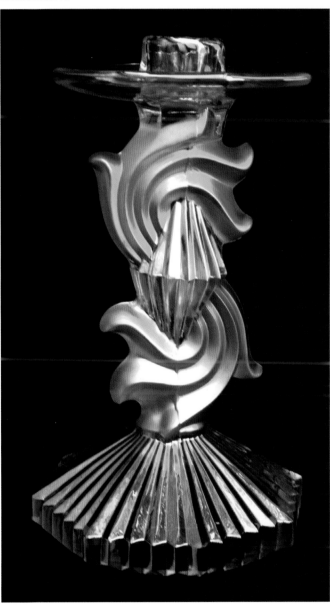

GIANT LILY vase—Probably Libochovice

Standing 9 inches high and with a girth of 27 inches, this bulbous, blow-moulded vase has a characteristic, moulded neck structure in common with the vases described below (*INCA, PEBBLE & FAN* and *SEAGULLS*). The moulded pattern on the *GIANT LILY* is in high relief and depicts a stylized lily and a five budded spray, repeated three times around the vase. The style is pure Art Déco; boldly executed and with excellent mouldwork. The lily buds are highly embossed, projecting out from the sides of the vase while below them are curved wedge shapes in deep relief. At least two known examples of this vase have the acid etched mark CZECHOSLOVAKIA, while on the shoulder of the marigold example is a golden paper label featuring a crown inside a laurel wreath, stating TRADE MARK "CORONET". This was the trademark of a major U. S. importer called George Borgfeldt and Co. who was located at Irving Pl. & E. 16th in New York City. It is shown in White-Orr's 1930 Classified Business Directory, New York City section, under the heading *China, Glass and Earthenware, Importers and Wholesale Dealers*. Our understanding is that Borgfeldt imported goods from Czechoslovakia to the USA.

  Shape: vase
  Colors: marigold and black amethyst

This bulbous, marigold *GIANT LILY* vase has a paper label and an etched stamp that show it was made in Czechoslovakia. It stands nine inches high. SP $800-$2000

INCA vase— Probably Libochovice

This breathtaking vase stands almost 12 inches high and measures nearly 32 inches around the fullest part of its circumference. It has a typical Art Déco style with broad sweeps of line and geometric 'wrap-around' motifs. It's yet another impressive and striking item of glass that shares the distinctive neck structure of the other massive bulbous vases listed here. All examples are considered very scarce indeed.

  Shape: vase
  Colors: marigold, black amethyst and cobalt blue (only one example of the latter confirmed). Vaseline ("absinthe") is known although not iridized—but it is always possible that an iridized example will be discovered

Measuring 32 inches around its circumference and standing 12 inches high, this is the biggest of the blow moulded Art Deco style vases from Czechoslovakia. The *INCA* vase is a rare find indeed, and only one of these is currently known in cobalt blue—as shown here. SP $1000-$3000

PEBBLE AND FAN vase— Probably Libochovice

Similar in height to the *INCA* and *SEAGULLS* vases, though not as massive in girth, *PEBBLE AND FAN* measures 23 inches around its widest part. The style is again pure Art Déco, featuring broad sweeps of 'wrap around' pattern, faceted angles and curves. The "pebble" in the pattern name refers to the "hammered", textured effect that fills the large oval shapes. The "fan" refers to the broad, fan-like sweeps that divide the ovals. *PEBBLE AND FAN* has the same distinctive neck structure as the other large vases mentioned here: it is also blow moulded, as the others are, and the glass is thick.

  Shape: vase
  Colors: marigold, blue, amber and vaseline ("absinthe")

Typical Art Deco styling on these marigold (left) and blue (right) *PEBBLE AND FAN* vases. SP $300-$1000 for either

SEAGULLS vase— Probably Libochovice

This vase stands almost 11 inches high and is impressively bulbous! It measures 30 inches at the widest point on its girth. The magnificent Art Déco moulded design features seagulls, foaming waves and clouds—it is exuberant, bold and perfectly fits the sculptural form of the blow-moulded vase. It is possible that this (and the other vases above) was the work of the glass sculptor, Karel Zentner, for Libochovice. The *SEAGULLS* vase is blow moulded, the glass itself is thick and there is the same distinctive mould seam running horizontally around the neck. This neck construction is unusual and is a characteristic of this vase and the others mentioned here.

Shape: vase

Colors: marigold, black amethyst, vaseline ("absinthe"), light blue and UV reactive delicate aqua (produced by combining chromium and uranium in the glass batch)

The base color of this impressive *SEAGULLS* vase is a delicate aqua that glows under U.V (black) light. SP $1500-$1750

LOURDES— Possibly Libochovice

This is a small, Art Déco style, blow moulded vase featuring "Melon Rib" or "doughnut" rings. The single example currently reported and studied has the word TCHECO acid-etched on its base, indicating that it was made prior to World War Two in Czechoslovakia and was for export to France. Inside the example examined by the authors was an old, yellowed card, with a hand-written note indicating that the item had been purchased in Lourdes (France) in 1938, as a souvenir. This is a small vase and although it does not have the characteristic neck structure of the others mentioned here (its size would almost certainly preclude it), its color, style and marking suggest Libochovice as a possible manufacturer.

Shape: vase

Color: black amethyst

This exquisite *LOURDES* vase has a "Melon Rib" style of pattern. The base glass is a rich, black amethyst. It stands just 5 inches high and has the word TCHECO (indicating it was intended for the French market) acid-etched on its base. NP

Unknown Maker
Possibly Josef Schreiber & Neffen A.G. at Lednické Rovne

In 2007 a previously unreported catalog showing familiar Carnival Glass patterns was found in the archives of Rona Crystal in the northwestern Slovakian town of Lednické Rovne. This discovery (by Siegmar Geiselberger) was a revelation with a sting in its tail as the title page was missing and although many previously unknown shapes and patterns can be identified, the maker was not named on the catalog. We can, however, be almost completely certain that the mystery maker was in Czechoslovakia, as some of the items that we can now identify from this catalog are known from either contemporary advertising that states the items were from Czechoslovakia, or have a moulded CZECHOSLOVAKIA trademark.

Is it possible that the catalog belonged to any of the previously known Czech makers—Inwald, Rindskopf or Libochovice? Possible but extremely unlikely. There are patterns in the unknown catalog that slightly resemble items from both Inwald and Rindskopf, but there are very significant differences and the actual characteristics of the glass don't feel right either. Furthermore, the catalog itself doesn't resemble the house style of either Inwald or Rindskopf. So who are the likely suspects? There are two strong contenders: Josef Schreiber & Neffen (Nephews) A.G. at Lednické Rovne and S. Reich (see "Other Czechoslovakian Makers" below). A possible third contender is Václav Hrdina at the former Carl Stölzle works, though there is no firm evidence yet for Hrdina.

Josef Schreiber & Neffen A.G. is our strongest candidate for a number of reasons. First, Rona Crystal (where the catalog was found in the archives) was a Schreiber factory and indeed other Schreiber catalogs were sourced there too, along with a catalog from the Polish glassmaker, Zabkowice, who is known to have made Carnival. (Zabkowice was owned at one time by Schreiber himself—you can read much more about Zabkowice in the chapter on Poland below). Interestingly, there are a few items in the Zabkowice catalog that bear a similarity to those in the Unknown Maker's catalog, which further strengthens our belief and, more significantly, there appear to be several close pattern matches between the Schreiber and Unknown Maker catalogs too. One specific "find" is very relevant—a Schreiber pattern called *HERMA*, which is identical to the pattern of the *BRYONY STAR* vase found in the Unknown Maker's catalog. Moreover, there is further evidence for Schreiber's production of Carnival. An oval, handled platter with an intaglio fruit design on its base is known in marigold that is almost certainly a Schreiber piece (details courtesy John Hodgson). The intaglio design on its base is virtually identical to others seen in the Schreiber 1927 catalog, while its shape and handles are exactly like that seen on oval platters illustrated in the same Schreiber catalog.

Schreiber had a major glass empire, with factories in Czechoslovakia, Moravia, Hungary, Poland, Russia and Germany. They had warehouses in Vienna, Prague and Budapest and agents in Berlin, Leipzig, London, Paris, Trieste, Milan, Warsaw, Kiev, Odessa, Alexandria, Tbilisi, and Melbourne. Furthermore, iridescence was nothing new to Schreiber's—they had produced iridized art glass in the late 1800s—so it seems logical that they would try their hand at pressed Carnival Glass around the same time that the other major players in the Czech arena were doing so too.

Further strong circumstantial evidence is provided by the fact that a major glass craftsman and designer, Karel Hološko, worked for Josef Schreiber & Neffen A.G. at Lednické Rovne between 1930 and 1935. Subsequently Hološko worked at Cristallerias Rigolleau from 1935 to 1947, ultimately returning to Czechoslovakia to design for the Lednické Rovne factory in 1947. We know that Cristallerias Rigolleau made some splendid Carnival Glass and this link with them lends further weight to our theory that Josef Schreiber & Neffen A.G is the Unknown Maker. (Thanks to Marcus Newhall for this important information on Karel Hološko —source: "Modern Bohemian Glass": edited by J. Raban, Artia, Prague—1963). See the chapter on South America below for more information on Cristallerias Rigolleau.

BALMORAL aka *HEAVY VINE* aka *LADY*—Unknown Czech Maker

This is a plain panelled pattern featuring an encircling band that has been loosely interpreted as a vine. *BALMORAL* was illustrated in the British *Pottery Gazette* in July 1930, with the words "Made in Czechoslovakia." Over seventy different shapes were offered in crystal, a number of which are currently known in Carnival. The ad was placed in the *Pottery Gazette* by the National Glass Company of London—a 1928 British Registered Design number (RD 737581) was quoted in the ad. The National Glass Co. was acting on behalf of the Czech manufacturer and would have registered the design for them. Some of the known items have superb marigold iridescence while others are very pale. It is possible that this pattern was aimed as a challenge to Inwald's *LAURIER NELLY*, which is somewhat similar.

A very wide range of shapes in *BALMORAL* is shown in the Unknown Maker's catalog (where the pattern is called *LADY*) including many boudoir and table set items as well as dishes, compotes, salvers and so on.

Shapes: water pitcher, tumbler, tumble-up, large water bottle, butter dish, cordial and stemmed wine in a variety of sizes, plus a very full range of boudoir items, including powder jar, perfume, cologne, ring tree, tray etc.

Color: marigold

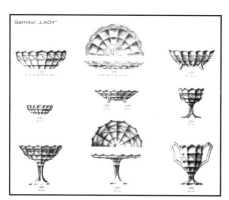

This extract from a catalog that carries no maker's name shows a range called *LADY*, which is known to Carnival collectors as *HEAVY VINE* or *BALMORAL*. *Courtesy Siegmar Geiselberger.*

The British Pottery Gazette and Glass Trade Review advertised the "Balmoral" Tableware range in this 1930 ad. According to the ad it had the Registered Design Number 737581. This pattern is known in Carnival Glass as *HEAVY VINE* and is clearly shown in the Unknown Maker's catalog. Note that the ad text states that this range was "Made in Czechoslovakia".

BAND OF OVALS—Unknown Czech Maker

Illustrated in the Unknown Maker's catalog, where it was given the catalog number 1462, this item is known only in a pedestal footed vase form. Two sizes were indicated in the catalog (approx 6 inches and 8 inches high) though only the larger of them is currently known in Carnival. It is very likely that the smaller size was also made in marigold too.

Shape: vase
Color: marigold

Standing 8 inches high on a pedestal base, the *BAND OF OVALS* vase has a simple, yet effective, design. SP $80-$150. *Courtesy Carol and Derek Sumpter.*

BRYONY STAR—Unknown Czech Maker (very strong evidence for Schreiber)

Although the main pattern elements of this pedestal footed vase are circles and elongated prisms, the name reflects both the pointed protrusions that form a star at the top of the pedestal base and also the star on the vase foot. Only one size of vase is known in Carnival—slightly over 8 inches (as depicted in the catalog at 210 mm).

In the catalogs of Josef Schreiber & Neffen a pattern suite called *HERMA* is illustrated. The design—a very distinctive blend of encircling "bullseye" motifs and angular projections—is absolutely identical to that found on the *BRYONY STAR* vase. We believe this further adds very strong evidence to show that Schreiber was the maker of these items.

Shape: vase
Color: marigold

The *BRYONY STAR* vase is named for the protruding star shape just above the pedestal base, which is then repeated on the top of the base itself. Known only in marigold, SP $70-$150

DELLA—Unknown Czech Maker

This is a diamond point design with a stylized leaf border and it had the pattern number 3504 in the Unknown Maker's catalog. Three sizes of jardinière are noted, measuring 5, 7 and approximately 9 inches in length.

Shape: jardinière

Color: marigold

DIAMOND CUT aka *EDITH*—Unknown Czech Maker

This pattern appears to have been made by at least four different manufacturers—two in Czechoslovakia (Inwald and the Unknown Maker), Crown Crystal in Australia and Hortensja in Poland. You can read more about the other makers' examples in the relevant chapters.

The Unknown Maker's catalog shows seven shapes in a pattern suite called *EDITH*, two of which are stemmed compotes. A curved in rose bowl shape is shown in three sizes (4 inches, slightly less than 9 inches and almost 10 inches) although we cannot be certain if this company made it in Carnival. This shape was also made by both Hortensja and Crown Crystal.

Shape: uncertain, but possibly rose bowl

Color: uncertain if this was made in Carnival, but if so, then it would be marigold

DOUBLE TULIP—Unknown Czech Maker

The style of the vase is typical of Czechoslovakian production: solid, heavy glass with a bold, classical, moulded intaglio design. On the *DOUBLE TULIP*, the main motif is a stylized floral motif (the tulip) that appears as a mirror image—hence the word "double" in the pattern name given by collectors. The base of the vase is ground and it has a deeply-cut many rayed star. The top edge may be cupped in or waisted and flared. A jardinière in two sizes (8 and 10 inches) was depicted in the Unknown Maker's catalog.

Shape: vase in at least two sizes: heights of approx. 6 and 10 inches (165 mm. and 265 mm). A mid size was listed in the catalog, approx. 9 inches (220 mm).

Color: marigold

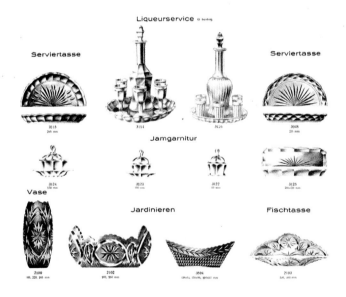

This extract from the catalog that carries no maker's name shows a variety of interesting items: liqueur sets, jam (jelly) dishes, a vase, jardinières and even a dish for fish. The vase bottom left that has the number 2100 is known in Carnival as *DOUBLE TULIP*. The jardinière 3504 in the middle of the bottom row is known in Carnival as *DELLA*. It is quite likely that any of the other items on this page might be found in Carnival. *Courtesy Siegmar Geiselberger.*

FORTY NINER aka *ROYAL DIAMONDS* aka *LONDON*—Unknown Czech Maker

There is some confusion between the *FORTY NINER* and *ROYAL DIAMONDS*—are they one and the same pattern, differing as alterations in shape and function change the design? Very possibly! This pattern was shown in a range of shapes for both table and boudoir use, in the Unknown Maker's catalog (where it was called *LONDON*). The pattern name describes the design—a series of slightly concave large diamonds covers the entire surface of the pieces. A variant was made by Rindskopf in the tumbler shape.

Shapes: pitcher and tumbler, covered sugar, stemmed wine glass, decanter, tray and shot glasses (cordials) and tray. Dressing table items including powder jar, perfume and ring tree.

Color: marigold

A covered sugar with a light marigold iridescence in the *FORTY NINER* or *ROYAL DIAMONDS* pattern. SP $60-$100

FRED—Unknown Czech Maker

Shown in the Unknown Maker's catalog, where it was given the unusual pattern name *FRED*, this is a plain panelled design that was clearly intended to be functional. The footed base and top edges of shapes in this pattern have a distinctive, thick, scalloped edge.

Shape: small bowl and covered sugar

Color: marigold

A distinctive scalloped edge can be seen on both top and bottom edges of this marigold *FRED* covered sugar from the Unknown Maker. NP

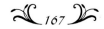

REGAL TULIP—Unknown Czech Maker

This pedestal footed vase is pinched in near the top and has a flared mouth opening. The design (in common with several other vases shown in the Unknown Maker's catalog) has six vertical panels and an encircling horizontal pattern band. On this vase, as the name implies, the motifs are stylised tulip heads, lying sideways rather than upright. Only one size is depicted in the catalog—8.5 inches high (215 mm).

    Shape: vase
    Color: marigold

A band of stylized petal shapes encircle this pedestal footed vase—hence the "tulip" in the pattern name *REGAL TULIP*. Known only in marigold, SP $70-$150

This version of the marigold *RING OF STARS* vase is the unfrosted one. SP $70-$150

RING OF STARS—Unknown Czech Maker

Currently known only in the vase shape with a pedestal base, *RING OF STARS* features a six sided panelled design, encircled near the top by a band of six intaglio star motifs. The vase is known with both frosted band (described in the catalog as *mattband*) and plain or smooth (*glatt*) iridized background. It stands almost 9 inches (220mm.) high.

    Shape: vase
    Color: marigold and frosted

VINING LEAF—Unknown Czech Maker

VINING LEAF has an encircling (sometimes frosted) band with a sinuous scroll-like pattern on a plain panelled background. It is known in several shapes, only one of which (the footed vase) was shown in the Unknown Maker's catalog. The pedestal footed vase was made in two sizes, 6 and 9 inches.

    Shapes: pedestal footed vase, large, pedestal footed bowl (sometimes called a spittoon), large vase
    Color: marigold and frosted

Other Czechoslovakian Makers

S. Reich

Only one item can currently be identified as a Reich pattern, indeed at the moment we are not aware of any other patterns made by Reich in Carnival. It's just possible that another manufacturer used (or copied) the mould. We will continue to research this.

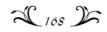

PLANTAGENET—Reich

This pattern was shown in the 1926 catalog of the agent, Markhbeinn, where it was called *PLANTAGENET*. Most of the glass offered in the Markhbeinn catalogs is from Josef Inwald, but when we saw this pitcher it didn't strike us as having the characteristics of Inwald's iridescence. It was lighter in colour and the iridescence neither deep nor powerful enough. The big surprise came when we saw several pages from the catalogs of S. Reich dated 1925 and 1934—here was the same pattern! The item numbers in both the Reich and the Markhbeinn catalogs matched up exactly, so that confirmed Reich as the maker of the pattern range. Reich called it *SPIEGELDESSIN* (Mirror design).

Information from New Zealand collector, Tony Hodgson, allows us to date the introduction of this pattern. Tony has three items of clear glass in the *PLANTAGENET* pattern which have the moulded mark—Reg No 700547 (registered by S. Reich and Company on 17th September, 1923).

    Shape: pitcher
    Color: marigold

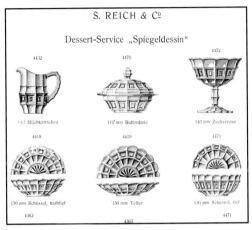

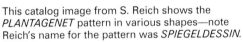

The *PLANTAGENET* water pitcher was named thus by Markhbeinn, and was illustrated in the wholesaler's catalog with the item number 4646.

This catalog image from S. Reich shows the *PLANTAGENET* pattern in various shapes—note Reich's name for the pattern was *SPIEGELDESSIN*.

Kralik

A mould blown marigold water set was found in 2006 with a paper label featuring a lion and urn and the letters WI KRA SO Bohemia. Our study of the label pointed us to Kralik—the famous Czech Art Glass manufacturer. The lion holding an urn features on the trademark of Eleonorahutte (aka Eleonora Glass works) and the letters WI KRA SO stand for the name of the factory: Wilhelm Kralik Sohne— Wilhelm Kralik Sons.

Kralik's glass empire was founded at Eleonorahutte in 1833 by Johann Meyr, passing first to his nephews (Wilhelm Kralik and Josef Taschek) and then to one of their sons, who changed the name to Wilhelm Kralik Sons. They produced high quality art glass, later adding household glass to their repertoire and exporting throughout Europe and the Americas. In 1946 the company was nationalised and merged with Cesky Kristal, which became part of Cristalex. In 1995 the glass works at Eleonora was closed down. We are currently only aware of one moulded pattern in Carnival from Kralik, but it is possible that more may be discovered in time.

THISTLEWOOD RIB—Kralik

Found by Della Breukelaar who kindly named the pattern after the authors (who had provided help with identification) this is a mould blown water set comprising a cannonball shaped pitcher with an applied handle plus six glasses. The bulbous shape of the pitcher—its neck being narrower than its body—prohibited the use of a plunger and thus the glass was blown into the mould (not pressed). The pattern on the water set is a simple but effective vertical ribbed design that enhances the marigold iridescence to full effect.

    Shapes: water pitcher and tumblers
    Color: marigold

This blow moulded, marigold water set bears a Kralik label and was named *THISTLEWOOD RIB* by the then owner, Della Breukelaar. NP. *Photo courtesy Della Breukelaar.*

Other Carnival Glass Items from Czechoslovakia

Buttons, Beads and Bags

The Czech costume jewelry (bijouterie) industry was—indeed still is—concentrated in and around the area of Jablonec nad Nisou (Gablonz) and Zelezny Brod (aka Eisenbrod). The area produced vast amounts of beads, hatpins and buttons, many of them in iridized glass, around the latter part of the 1800s and the early 1900s. Production of beads, buttons and hatpins, was carried out in a series of stages, with one workshop producing the glass and yet another crafting and finishing the jewelry. It was essentially a cottage industry with a complex, supporting infrastructure. Iridescent black beads were very popular in the late 1800s and early 1900s. Such beads were used not only for necklaces and other adornments, but also for making pretty bags and for embroidering on clothing. A huge amount was exported. The industry suffered during the war years and the ensuing political regime. Development resumed in the 1960s and 1970s and is thriving again today, indeed some of the buttons being made today are from old Classic moulds as well as new moulds! In 1991, the Association of Costume Jewelry Manufacturers (SVB) was founded to promote and protect the industry. There is a museum in Jablonec nad Nisou devoted to Glass and Costume Jewelry. You can read more about this in our book "A Century of Carnival Glass".

Enameled Lampshades

A variety of marigold lampshades decorated with typical central European scenes are known. Castles, churches, houses, rivers, flowers, snow capped mountains and trees (glass frit was used to give the impression of snow on mountains, roofs and trees) are all featured. The architectural style depicted is very typical of middle Europe. We know the origin to be Czechoslovakia owing to the presence of an old label fragment that reads "Made in Czechoslovakia" on one lampshade, though it is entirely possible that other countries such as Germany may also have produced similar items. The catalogs of Karl Palda (Novy Bor aka Haida) from the 1930s illustrate a wide range of lampshades with shapes, scenes and paintwork that is very similar to the enameled Carnival lampshades. Another Bohemian manufacturer, Ruckl, also produced similar enameled shades around the same time. We urge caution, however, as the evidence is purely circumstantial at present.

This enamelled marigold lampshade has the remnants of a paper label saying "Made in Czechoslovakia" $70-$100

Eda Glasbruk—Sweden

A glass works was established in the little town of Eda Glasbruk in 1830 with window glass and bottles being its first products. Press moulded glass began to be made at Eda in 1920. Around five years later, Carnival Glass production began—it was to continue at Eda Glasbruk for barely four more years, ceasing around 1929 or perhaps 1930. A catalog called *Fargglas fran Eda Glasbruk* (Colored Glass from Eda Glass Works) believed to have been produced in 1925, illustrates the range of glass that was being iridized at that time. Eda's Carnival Glass was made mainly in marigold and blue, while scarcer shades of pearl, purple, amethyst and pink were also produced. Top notch iridescence and high quality workmanship were characteristic of this factory's output.

In 1927, a new management team, husband and wife Gerda and Edvard Stromberg took over. Gerda was a designer and her preference for pale browns and yellows in the then fashionable minimalist shapes and patterns meant that the rich designs and colors of Eda's wonderful Carnival production soon ceased. Fortunately for today's collectors, Eda Glasbruk left a legacy of superlatively beautiful (albeit scarce) items in their magnificent *lysterglas*.

A complication with some of the patterns made by Eda is that they were also produced by Riihimaki and Brockwitz. Fortunately, sorting out the overlaps and look-alikes isn't too hard, as often the different factories made different shapes and colors.

ROSE GARDEN was made in the oval vase shape and possibly (but not certainly) in bowl form, by Eda. *ROSE GARDEN* was made in many varied shapes including vases, plates, bowls and table items, by the German maker, Brockwitz

SVEA was made by both Eda and Riihimaki (and possibly Karhula) plus a few examples from Elme, but color helps to separate the makers. Marigold and blue could be from either maker, but pearl, true pink (with pastel pink iridescence) or purple was made by Eda while amber or Rio-pink (pink base glass with marigold iridescence) was from Riihimaki. Elme pieces often have a paper label and exhibit a taffy-like, shiny pale iridescence

EUROPEAN FOUR FLOWERS aka *OHLSON* was made by both Eda and Riihimaki, but the colors can help to differentiate, as detailed above

SUNK DAISY aka *AMERIKA* was made in Carnival by both Eda and Riihimak: the colors detailed above help to differentiate. Cambridge made it, but not in Carnival. Marinha Grande's (Portugal) 1901 cqtalog also shows this pattern.

CURVED STAR aka *LASSE* and *DAGNY* from Eda is distinct and different from the versions made by any other factory (see patterns below)

SUNFLOWER AND DIAMOND aka *SOLROS* from Eda is distinct and different from the version made by Brockwitz. 20 petals on the Eda daisies on their 7 inch vase (only size). Color too helps, if it is purple or pearl, then it is from Eda.

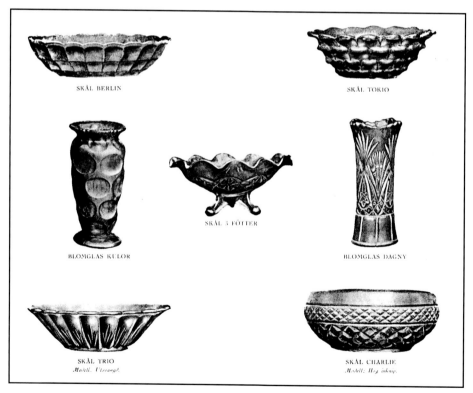

An extract from the Color Catalog (*Fargglas*) of Eda Glasbruk in 1929, this illustration shows—top row, left to right: a bowl in the *BERLIN* pattern, which was quite possibly Eda's copy of Inwald's popular *JACOBEAN* design and a *TOKIO* bowl. Middle row, left to right: a *KULOR* vase, a *TREFOTTER* bowl and a *DAGNY* vase. Bottom row, left to right: a flared-out *TRIO* bowl and a cupped-in *CHARLIE* bowl

CURVED STAR aka *LASSE* and *DAGNY*—Eda Glasbruk

Eda made their own version of the well known *CURVED STAR* pattern, but it's easy to differentiate it from the much more frequently found Brockwitz pieces. The pattern is a complex geometric design featuring a variety of star, fan and file motifs. On Eda's examples, the familiar pattern motifs are present but with a difference. Look at the claw shapes—there is **no file** pattern on the claws on the Eda version. In reality there are not many examples of Eda's *CURVED STAR* to be found, if you come across an example of this pattern the chances are it will be a Brockwitz piece.

Another difference comes with color, for if the item should be purple then it is an Eda example. Shape presents a further distinction, as Eda made a *CURVED STAR* vase in a wholly different shape to the familiar cylinder vase. This is their *DAGNY* vase, which is distinctive in that it has a plain panelled section on the lower two inches of the vase, the fan motifs are more pronounced on the pattern and the file claws are almost absent.

Shapes: bowl and vase. The *DAGNY* vase is 8 inches high; a smaller 5–6 inch size may exist but we cannot confirm

Colors: marigold, blue and purple for bowls; marigold and blue for *DAGNY* vase

CURVED STAR with a difference—the base glass is purple, indicating the maker to be the Swedish glass manufacturer Eda Glasbruk. To find a piece in purple is rare indeed. This small oval dish is the only one the authors are aware of in this color. NP

This is Eda Glasbruk's version of the Brockwitz *CURVED STAR* pattern—they named the vase *DAGNY*. Shown here as two vases, marigold (left) and blue. It's hard to establish clear values are these are very scarce vases. SP $200-$700

DIAMANT—Eda Glasbruk

DIAMANT is similar to the well known "American" (ice cube) design by Fostoria and Jobling, but this specific lidded sweet jar shape (covered bonbon or bonbonniére) in Carnival is specific to Eda. The lid fits the base along a jagged line of interlocking triangles—cleverly done and neatly moulded. The blueprints (shown as No. 1802) for this splendid item were found at Eda Glasbruk.

Shape: covered bonbon
Color: marigold and blue (one of each currently reported)

Reminiscent of Fostoria's "American" pattern, this is Eda's *DIAMANT* covered bonbon dish in marigold. Both top and bottom have a jagged sawtooth edge which perfectly fit each other. Only one other example is reported and it is impossible to gauge a value. NP

FLORAL SUNBURST aka *TUSENSKONA* aka *DAISY SPRAY*—Eda Glasbruk

The Swedish name *TUSENSKONA* literally means "a thousand beauties"—the pattern is fittingly named, for it is an exquisitely lovely design featuring a stylized, yet flowing, intaglio floral interpretation. The *FLORAL SUNBURST* vase has been found with at least four different hand finished shapes to the mouth: a simple flare, a spittoon shape, incurved like a rose bowl and tricorner shaped.

Shapes: vase in two sizes: a smaller 6-7 inch and a large 8 inch; round bowls and oval jardinières in various sizes

Colors: marigold, blue, pearl, purple and pink

KULOR—Eda Glasbruk

A simple yet incredibly striking design consisting of large, indented circles or ball shapes that reflect iridescence very well indeed. The pattern is known only in the form of a pedestal footed vase with a flared top. Like virtually all European Carnival vases, it is not swung, but left as moulded. This item is shown in the Eda catalog, pattern number 2471-73.

Shape: vase in three sizes, 6 and 8 inches plus a rare "Giant" 10 inch version

Colors: marigold, blue, pearl and purple (only marigold and blue currently known in the 10 inch size)

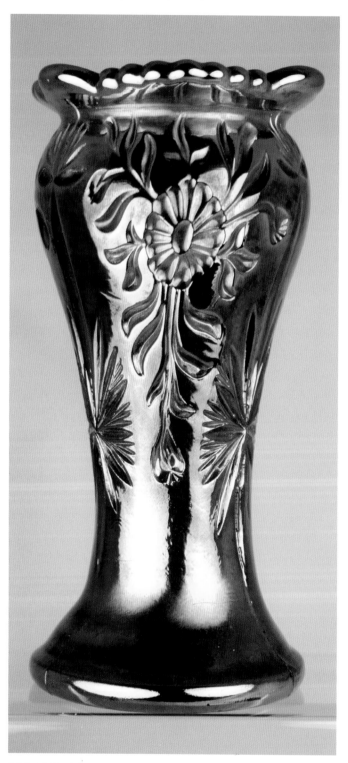

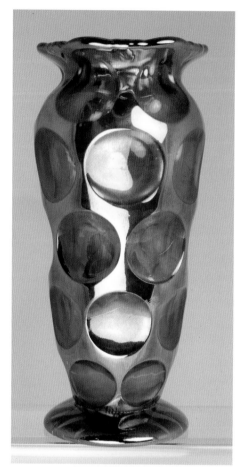

Eda Glasbruk's *KULOR* design is only known in the vase shape. Here is an 8 inch high blue version. $400-$900.

LAGERKRANS—Eda Glasbruk

Known currently only in marigold and blue, *LAGERKRANS* (meaning laurel wreath) was the Swedish name given to this scarce, covered candy jar (bonbonniére) from Eda Glasbruks. The swagged garlands (which actually resemble flower heads rather than laurel leaves) are repeated on the jar, the lid and again on the finial.

Shape: covered bonbon

Colors: marigold and blue

Eda's *FLORAL SUNBURST* vase is known with several different top shapes—this 7 inch example is the spittoon shaped version in blue, which is probably the hardest shape to find. SP $700-$1900

The floral design loops around the lid of this pretty *LAGERKRANS* covered bonbon from Eda Glasbruk. In marigold, as shown here, SP $200-$500

REKORD aka **DIAMOND WEDGES**—Eda Glasbruk

Alternate plain and diamond cut panels are the main pattern motif. It was depicted in Eda's range in 1929 where it was named *REKORD*. On the bowl shape the pattern is not especially exciting, but on the vase shape it really comes alive. The contrast between the smooth and textured panels allows for the drama of the iridescence to be fully appreciated.

Shapes: bowl and vase

Color: blue (though we are not aware of marigold examples, it is likely that they exist)

REX—Eda Glasbruk

REX, illustrated and named in the 1929 Eda catalog, is a variation on the "plain block" theme. The top-notch iridescence that is usually found on Eda's Carnival and the stately shape of the vase, combine to make a most attractive item.

Shape: vase, with a variety of neck shaping including spittoon top and flared. Known in at least three sizes—3.5 inches, 5 inches and 8 inches.

Colors: marigold, blue, pearl and purple

This purple *REX* vase from Eda Glasbruk stands just 5 inches high and is one of just a few currently reported. NP

REKORD is an Eda block design that showcases the iridescence by contrasting smooth and textured surfaces. Shown here on an 8 inch high, blue cylinder vase. SP $450-$800

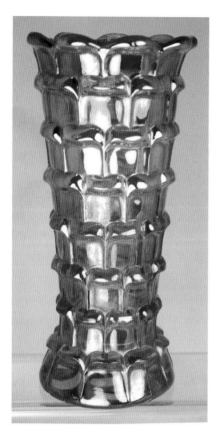

The *TOKIO* vase has an effect not unlike a waterfall—quite lovely. This marigold vase was made by Eda Glasbruk. $300-$450

TOKIO—Eda Glasbruk

A bowl and vase in the *TOKIO* pattern were named and illustrated in Carnival in the 1925 Eda catalog. The main pattern motif is of overlapping squares in a waterfall effect, but the most intriguing aspect to *TOKIO* is the motif on the base, where an anti-clockwise (left facing) swastika fills the marie. The swastika has a wide symbolism which could, in this instance, be either Norse (it symbolises the Hammer of Thor) or that of China (where the swastika is believed to bestow great happiness and longevity).

Shapes: large and medium sized bowls and vase
Colors: marigold, blue and pearl

Elme Glasbruk—Sweden

The Elme glass works at Almhult was located in the very heart of the country's "kingdom of glass"—Smaland. There was, of course, much competition between the glass factories, and a small number of patterns known in Carnival were shown in the Elme catalog in the late 1920s. A number of Carnival pieces with a pale lilac, pale blue, light amber or pink base glass and a very distinctive iridescence like light golden taffy have been found bearing paper Elme labels. Various bowls and small plates were made by Elme, but overall their Carnival output was undoubtedly limited.

SOPHIA aka *RANKA*—Elme

Illustrated in the Elme catalog, *SOPHIA* is a pedestal footed vase with a square base with a simple fan like pattern. The coloring and iridescence of those that we have seen are typical of Elme.

Shape: vase
Color: pale amber-pink

Elme made this *SOPHIA* vase using a distinctive taffy-like iridescence on a pale amethyst base glass. On the pedestal vase is a remnant of the Elme paper label. SP $150-$350

Riihimaki—Finland

The town of Riihimaki lies about forty miles north of the Finnish capital, Helsinki and a glass works, also known as Riihimaki, was established in the town around 1910. In 1927, Riihimaki took over the Kauklahti glass works—the authors' study of that factory's catalogs indicates that many patterns known in Carnival were originally made by them. Our theory is that Kauklahti were possibly the impetus behind the introduction of Carnival in Finland. Several of the patterns, for example *TIGER LILY* and *GRAPE MEDALLION* seen in the Kauklahti catalogs were clearly inspired by USA Carnival designs. Thus, when Kauklahti were taken over by Riihimaki in 1927, their patterns and possibly their development ideas were absorbed by Riihimaki. It is known that Riihimaki were producing Carnival in 1929 (as the *TURKU ASHTRAY* known in marigold, has the date moulded into the design). It seems likely to assume therefore, that Carnival production began shortly after the Kauklahti acquisition. Known colors in Riihimaki Carnival are marigold, blue, dark amber, light pink (with marigold iridescence) and several rare shades—green and amethyst plus two possibly experimental colors—iridized milk glass and iridized slag (malachite). The iridescence on Riihimaki's Carnival is usually excellent and multi-coloured. Most of the patterns are (in common with a lot of European and Nordic Carnival) intaglio or "near-cut".

In 1939 a catalog was issued by Riihimaki that illustrates the splendid range of glass they produced. Unfortunately, it's not possible to be certain from the catalog which items were made in Carnival Glass, but Kaisa Koivisto, the curator of the Riihimaki Museum, informed us it was possible that many of the items depicted were iridized. She also confirmed that Riihimaki bought in moulds from other manufacturers. Indeed, there are several patterns in their catalog that are also in the Eda catalogs and the Brockwitz catalogs! The *SUNK DAISY* items have already been mentioned above with regard to Eda. They also appear in the Riihimaki catalogs and were very probably iridized by both manufacturers. It isn't possible to say for certain which factory made which items in *SUNK DAISY* if the item is marigold or blue. A small amount of Carnival was also made by Riihimaki at a later date, mainly in plain shapes.

Many examples of Riihimaki's splendid Carnival have been found by the authors during their research visits to the Nordic countries and you can read about some of them below. However, one pattern—*DRAPERY VARIANT*—previously believed to be by Riihimaki is now known to have been made by Josef Inwald in Czechoslovakia.

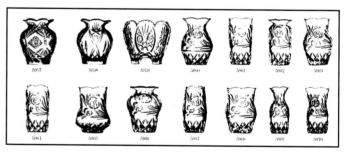

An extract from the 1927 Riihimaki-Kauklahti catalog showing an astonishing **eleven** different shapes in the *WESTERN THISTLE* (aka *KUUKA*) vase. Three other patterns are also shown in vase form: top row, from the left—*TENNESSEE STAR* vase, *JUPITER* vase, *SUNK DAISY* (aka *AMERIKA*) rose bowl. All the other vases shown are *WESTERN THISTLE*.

AMAZON WOMEN VASE—Riihimaki

Just one example of this vase is known—it has amber-pink base glass and rich, deep marigold iridescence and stands 8 inches high with a 5 inch mouth. It was illustrated in Riihimaki's 1939 catalog, but could well have been made in the decade leading up to that date. The main feature of the vase is a fabulous 2 inch wide, richly iridized, pattern band. The figures seen on it are highly detailed, lightly clad warrior women, holding spears and shields or wielding bows and arrows. Between each female figure is a sinuous band of stylized leaves. There are four different figures repeated around the splendid vase.

A study of Bohemian glass from around 1920-1925 indicates that the inspiration for this example of Riihimaki's Carnival was surely Moser's "Fipop" Amazon pattern range which featured their trademarked "Oro-plastique" decor. This technique was developed by Leo Moser and was an acid etched band colored in olive green and dark red-brown, with a gold band above and below. Moser's items were made at their Karlovy Vary glass works in Czechoslovakia. Bowls, vases and other items were

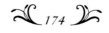

made by Moser featuring an acid-etched band of Amazon warriors (of course, none of these were in Carnival). Riihimaki clearly used the design as inspiration for their press moulded rendition. Similarly, the *CLASSIC ARTS* and *EGYPTIAN QUEEN* items from Rindskopf in Czechoslovakia also appear to have been inspired by Moser's "Oroplastique" technique.

Riihimaki's 1939 catalog also shows a bowl in this pattern, but none have yet been reported.

Shape: vase
Color: amber-pink

A closer look at the pattern band on the *AMAZON WOMEN* vase.

Riihimaki's *AMAZON WOMEN* vase has a detailed pattern band featuring warrior women. An impressive looking vase, it is currently the only Carnival example known and has an amber-pink base glass. NP

DOUBLE STARFLOWER—Riihimaki

Illustrated in Riihimaki's 1939 catalog in the form of a handled sugar and creamer (with the pattern numbers 5645 and 5646 respectively) this stylized floral pattern is a cameo design. The shape of the handles on the items is in the "Chippendale" style. The *DOUBLE STARFLOWER* pattern is also found on the exterior of Riihimaki's *GRAPE MEDALLION* plates and bowls. For more information on *GRAPE MEDALLION* and *RIIHIMAKI GRAPE* (two more cameo designs from Riihimaki that are stylistically reminiscent of Classic USA Carnival Glass) see "The Art of Carnival Glass" by the authors.

Shapes: sugar, creamer and exterior on plates and bowls
Colors: marigold and blue

A stylized, cameo, floral design on a stippled background encircles this marigold *DOUBLE STARFLOWER* sugar and creamer from Riihimaki. The shape of the handles is reminiscent of *Chippendale* items. The bases of both items on this rare set are ground flat. NP

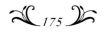

FIR CONES—Riihimaki

Twelve, smooth, angular panels make up the top and bottom sections of this pattern, while in the middle is an intricately detailed pattern band featuring fir cones. *FIR CONES* is illustrated in the Riihimaki-Kauklahti 1927 catalog in a variety of somewhat unusual tableware shapes, including a handled serving basket and two shapes of water pitcher. Two different shapes of tumbler were also shown: straight sided and bulbous barrel shaped. The pattern was not named in the catalog and it is not possible to know if all the pieces were made in Carnival.

Shapes: water pitcher and tumbler, rare cuspidor / sugar bowl and rare creamer

Colors: marigold, blue, light pink (with marigold iridescence) and amber

HOBNAIL BANDED—Riihimaki

This is a seldom seen tumbler, and is the only shape shown in this pattern in the Riihimaki 1939 catalog. Its pattern is a series of tiny hobnails (like reflective pools of iridescence) in twelve horizontal bands with a 16 point star on its base. A pitcher is depicted in the Riihimaki catalog but it is not yet reported in Carnival, as far as we are aware.

Shape: tumbler

Colors: marigold and blue

On the left, a *FIR CONES* tumbler from Riihimaki in blue. On the right, a most unusual *FIR CONES* cuspidor shaped sugar in amber. SP for a blue tumbler $350-$500. NP for the rare cuspidor.

A trio of unusual tumblers from Riihimaki. On the left is a seldom seen, blue *HOBNAIL BANDED* tumbler by Riihimaki which reflects iridescence beautifully. SP $400-$600. In the center is the larger version of *LAUREL BAND*, a hard to find, straight sided tumbler in blue from Riihimaki. SP $200-$400 On the right is a rare *STARBURST* tumbler. Why is it rare? Because it is in green—a most unusual color for Riihimaki. SP $400-$600

HUNTER—Riihimaki

This design style, employing a figural frieze against a plain panelled background, was used by Riihimaki on two other patterns: *AMAZON WOMEN* (see above) and the *HARE AND HOUNDS* (see "The Art of Carnival Glass" by the authors). On the *HUNTER*, a figure is depicted, levelling his rifle at a running stag (with full antlers) and two smaller deer (fortunately none appear caught!) In the background are fir trees and in the foreground we can see clumps of grass. The pattern is repeated four times around the bowl. The entire scene is cameo (raised up from the surface of the glass). It is known on a scalloped edge, master bowl, measuring 8 inches across and stands 3 inches high. The base of the bowl is ground and features a large star.

Shape: bowl

Color: amber

The pattern band on this amber *HUNTER* bowl from Riihimaki features a hunter in the act of shooting at deer. The background of conifer woods evokes a typical Finnish landscape. SP $300-$600

JUPITER—Riihimaki

A tumbler in this pattern has been known for some time, but it went by the simplistic name *RIIHIMAKI Tumbler*, on account of the moulded factory name on its base. However, we are now aware of a range of items in this geometric design and we also know the original factory name for the pattern was *JUPITER*. A range of *JUPITER* shapes was depicted in the Riihimaki-Kauklahti 1927 catalog and many of them have now been reported in Carnival. The design is in essence, just interlocking crosses, but add great color and magnificent iridescence (as most examples of this pattern seem to have) and the effect is totally mesmerising.

Shapes: vases with a variety of top shaping, miniature vase (rare); creamer, handled sugar, jardinière, tumbler, ashtray and tray

Colors: marigold, blue, light pink (with marigold iridescence) and amber

LAUREL BAND—Riihimaki

This simple ribbed design, enhanced by an encircling laurel band, is made special by the use of almost "hidden" pattern features. On the lidded bonbon (candy jar) there's a double surprise. Lift the lid and an exquisite laurel garland is revealed—a flower at its very center—then "double-take" as you turn the item over to look at the base and another laurel garland is revealed.

The tumbler in this pattern is straight sided and is illustrated in two sizes in the 1939 Riihimaki catalog. Its pattern comprises 24 vertical ribs and an encircling band of laurel. An intricate circular design (matching the one on the lid of the Laurel Band covered bonbon) is featured on the base of the tumbler.

Shapes: covered bonbon, tumbler and pitcher
Color: blue

Three splendid vases from Riihimaki with fabulous iridescence and distinctive hand shaping. On the left is the *TENNESSEE STAR* vase in blue in an unusual bulbous shape with a pinched in top. In the center is the *JUPITER* vase in amber while on the right is a blue *WESTERN THISTLE* vase in an unusual form. All are hard to find, SP for any one of the three $400-$800

RIP VAN WINKLE CANDLE HOLDER—Riihimaki

This item was shown in Riihimaki's 1939 catalog with the catalog number 6730, but no pattern name. It's not easy to remember a number, so we have given this little chamberstick (it is just 3 inches high) a long name, to make up for its lack of height. It's essentially functional—the little handle allows easy and safe carriage of a lighted candle.

Shape: chamberstick
Color: marigold

A delightful object used to light one's way to bed before electricity was common-place—this marigold *RIP VAN WINKLE* candleholder was made by Riihimaki and is currently the only example reported. NP

A closer view of the pattern band on the *HUNTER* bowl (at left) shows how intricately detailed the design is.

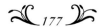

STARBURST and DOUBLE STARBURST originally KERO—Riihimaki

This pattern can be distinguished by its alternate whirling buzz stars and eight pointed stars within oval medallions—between the ovals are geometric motifs. The pattern changes slightly to accommodate the shapes on which it appears, a wide range of which was illustrated in the 1927 Riihimaki-Kauklahti catalog, where this pattern was named KERO. Vases in many forms, including massive cylinder ones that are double the height of the regular ones (and thus feature the pattern motifs twice, one above the other) as well as a variety of tableware items, were depicted. Collectors called the pattern STARBURST before they knew the original manufacturer name. The massive cylinder vase is known as DOUBLE STARBURST.

Two small bowls in rare (possibly experimental) colors have been found: one is in iridized milk glass, the other is iridized slag glass (malachite). Discovered in Finland, these may be the only examples of such colors made by a manufacturer outside the USA. The iridescence on the slag bowl is a rich butterscotch loaded with pinks and golds. The base color is an astonishing mixture of opaque white and grey-brown swirls. Another rare color found in the STARBURST pattern is green, which has thus far only been found in the tumbler shape.

    Shapes: vases in several shapes and sizes including pedestal footed; bowl, plate, oval dish, creamer, sugar, butter-dish, rose bowl, nut bowl, cuspidor and tumbler

    Colors: marigold, blue, amber, green (currently tumbler only), iridized milk glass and iridized slag glass (malachite)

TENNESSEE STAR—Riihimaki

The pattern is an intricate geometric featuring hobstars and intersecting arches. It would appear that Riihimaki made only vases in this pattern, in fact there were eight different vase shapes shown in both the 1927 Riihimaki-Kauklahti catalog and the Riihimaki 1939 catalog. The appearance of the pattern alters markedly according to the shape of the vase. This can cause the collector to suspect that different shapes may be different patterns—not so!

This pattern was also made by August Walther and Sons, who called it TAURUS. The colors and shapes of the Carnival items currently known conform to Riihimaki, however, it is not possible to rule out the fact that examples of the cylinder vase in marigold may be Walther's. The standard cylinder vase made by Riihimaki stands between 7.5 and 8 inches high (bulbous and other shapes will be somewhat less due to the hand shaping). The heights of the Walther cylinder vases are 6.5, 8.5 and 10.5 inches—however we cannot confirm them in Carnival from Walther.

    Shape: vase (in eight different forms)

    Colors: marigold, blue, amber and rare amethyst

WESTERN THISTLE originally KUKKA—Riihimaki.

Originally called KUKKA in the 1927 Riihimaki-Kauklahti catalog, this pattern is a successful blend of stylized floral and geometric elements (featuring flower head, leaf spray and a distinctive diamond pattern) that adapts well to use on a wide variety of shapes—including eleven different variations of the same basic vase form. Tumblers are known in three different shapes—straight sided, flared with a distinct curve at the top and barrel shaped. The base has an 8 point hobstar.

    Shapes: bowl, plate, vases (note different shapes), tumbler, water pitcher, sugar, creamer and rare cuspidor

    Colors: blue, marigold, amber, pink base glass with marigold iridescence and rare green (currently tumbler only)

Karhula and Jittala—Finland

The glass works at Iittala was founded in 1881, the glass works at Karhula was founded 18 years later in 1899. A decade and a half later, in 1915, the two companies merged to forge a company that was to produce much award-winning glassware. In 1987 they merged with Nuutajarvi. We believe that they began producing Carnival Glass during the 1920s.

Our recent research has shown that the DIAMOND OVALS pattern that we once thought was made by Karhula was in fact made by Rindskopf in Czechoslovakia. See "A Century of Carnival Glass" by the authors for further information.

BALTIC WHIRL—Karhula

This geometric design has similarities with Riihimaki's STARBURST AND CROWN but it lacks the fanned "crown" motif and instead has just the three, framed whirling star motifs. Its base is totally plain. This tumbler was illustrated in the Karhula catalogs in the early 1930s and is very seldom seen.

    Shape: tumbler

    Color: blue

BORDERED PENDANT—Karhula

Illustrated in an early Karhula catalog from 1922, this pattern is currently only known in Carnival in the water set. The simple yet elegant cameo design features a border filled with small diamond shapes from which are suspended eight stylized stars. On the base of tumblers we have studied is the moulded word KARHULA.

    Shapes: tumbler and water pitcher

    Colors: marigold and blue

BRITT—Karhula

A distinctive geometric design based on four, interlocking, pierced medallions characterizes this pattern from Karhula. Both tumbler and water pitcher were depicted in the company's catalogs in the early 1930s. Like most Carnival items from Karhula and Iittala, it is very seldom found and should be considered scarce.

    Shapes: tumbler and water pitcher

    Colors: blue and marigold

QUILTED PANELS—Karhula

Twelve panels (alternate ones have a diamond lattice design—the "quilted" effect in the pattern name) encircle this tumbler, which is the only known shape in the pattern. Above the panels is an inch wide band decorated with curlicues and leaf motifs. On the base of the tumbler we have studied is the moulded word KARHULA, so there's no doubt about the maker of this piece! In fact this seldom seen item was depicted in the 1922 Karhula catalog.

    Shape: tumbler

    Colors: marigold and blue

QUILTED FANS—Iittala

An open candy dish in a geometric design composed of fan shapes and diamond file. This piece was observed by Bob Smith at the Finnish Glass Museum. He noted that it had the letters IITTALA moulded into it. The item is depicted in the 1922 Karhula-Iittala catalog and has the catalog number 4080.

    Shape: candy dish.

    Color: blue is the only color reported

Two seldom seen tumblers from Karhula: on the left is QUILTED PANELS in blue, while on the right is BORDERED PENDANT in marigold. SP for either one $250-$500

Two tumblers from Karhula—on the left BALTIC WHIRL and on the right, the scarce and distinctive BRITT tumbler in marigold. There are three whirling star motifs around the BALTIC WHIRL tumbler from Karhula. This example is in blue—the only color currently reported in this pattern. SP $250-$400. Marigold BRITT, SP $300-$450

Sowerby

In 1852 Sowerby's Ellison Glass works opened in Gateshead-on-Tyne in the north east of England—by 1865 it had become one of the largest pressed glass works in the country. In the early 1920s, under General Manager Adam Dodds Snr., they brought in new machinery, including a new 12 pot *Stein Atkinson* gas fired furnace that allowed the glass to be worked at much higher temperatures. Sowerby's were lucky to have the skills of the innovative chemist, Percival Marson, who had experimented with iridescence on glass in the Stourbridge glassmaking region several years earlier. No doubt in response to the success of American Classic Carnival in the UK, Sowerby's decided to make their own and in October, 1926 they took a full page ad in the Pottery Gazette that proclaimed: "Sowerby's Ellison Glass works beg to announce the Opening on October 1st, of their New London Showroom".... and on offer was "Iridescent" Glass.

Sunglow was the name for Sowerby's version of marigold and *Rainbo* was the term they used for amethyst and blue. Amethyst Carnival from Sowerby is less frequently found than marigold, but even more scarce is blue. Sowerby's blue varies from a rich cobalt shade to a greeny aqua. Black amethyst, a very dense almost opaque color, can sometimes be found, as can rare examples of vaseline. Sowerby's trademark, introduced in 1876, was the famous peacock's head. It was used until 1930, but not on every piece of glass they produced. However, it is very occasionally found moulded into Sowerby's Carnival. Rarely found is the paper label bearing the Sowerby trademark.

The Carnival output from Sowerby can be broadly divided into two main groups. The first group is that made by utilizing revived old moulds that had been originally used in the 1800s and were then re-used for making Carnival in the 1920s. A unique and fascinating combination of iridescence and Arts and Crafts style is found on these splendid, and quite scarce, items. Some other old moulds, dating from around 1912, were also used for Carnival. The second group comprises new moulds that were made in the 1920s and early 1930s and put to use for Carnival production. Some of these newer items were made in plentiful quantities and are fairly easy to find today. Others, however, are very scarce indeed.

A number of items that were quite possibly made in England are often seen "casually" attributed to Sowerby. These include *THISTLE AND THORN* and *SPLIT DIAMOND*. It should be noted the authors have yet not been able to establish any catalog or other evidence to show that Sowerby made either of these patterns (see section on the Wear Glass Works below for further information on *THISTLE AND THORN*).

As noted above, Sowerby's introduced their Carnival in the mid 1920s and produced it probably up to the start of World War Two. However, they also had a short later production of Carnival in the early 1950s that was predominantly in two patterns: the *Chic COVERED HEN* butter and the #2266 aka *CHUNKY* or *ENGLISH HOB AND BUTTON*. Sowerby's finally closed in 1973.

DAISY BLOCK ROWBOAT— Sowerby

The mould for this item was originally made in 1886. Four sizes of these boats were made at that time in crystal glass. A single stand was also designed to fit all the boats except for the smallest one. When the mould was revived in the 1920s, however, only the 12 inch boat was made in Carnival. No Carnival stand has yet been found. The interior of these boats usually has a ribbed design though rare examples are reported with a plain interior and the peacock head trademark plus a moulded Registered Design (RD) #42947. The piece was probably intended as a table decoration, to be used for flowers or candies.

Shape: boat novelty
Colors: marigold, amethyst and rare aqua shades

Three Sowerby *DAISY BLOCK ROWBOATS*—all are the same length (12 inches). From the top the colors are: aqua (SP $250-$350), amethyst (SP $200-$250) and marigold ($100-$150).

DERBY aka *PINWHEEL*—Sowerby

This intaglio geometric pattern is found in a variety of shapes. What is particularly interesting about it is that an almost identical pattern was produced by both Josef Inwald of Czechoslovakia and Hortensja of Poland, although the range of shapes is not identical and there are other differences, such as ground bases on the Inwald and Hortensja pieces. The item found most often (though it should be stressed that this is actually rather a scarce piece) is the vase, which Sowerby produced in three heights: 6.5, 8 and 10.5 inches. The Sowerby *PINWHEEL* rosebowl has been seen in the rare color of black amethyst. An unusual shape, the Sowerby rosebowl is not the typical cupped-in form, but is actually flared. See the entries on *PINWHEEL* in the chapters on Inwald and Hortensja for more information.

Shapes: vase (3 sizes), cookie jar (biscuit barrel), bowls in various sizes and rare rosebowl

Colors: marigold, amethyst, rare black amethyst and rare examples of the blue vase

Three Sowerby 8 inch *PINWHEEL* aka *DERBY* vases. From left to right the colors are marigold ($200-$350), rare blue (NP) and amethyst ($300-$450). *Blue vase courtesy of Val and Bob Appleton.*

DIVING DOLPHINS—Sowerby

This was made from one of Sowerby's old moulds that dates back to 1882. The bowls stand on three feet, each styled to form the shape of a dolphin's head while their bodies curve sinuously up and onto the main part of the bowl. Around the sides of the bowl are stylized flowers and leaves, the combination of elements forming a most attractive, overall design. In the 1920s, when Sowerby began to make iridized glass, *DIVING DOLPHINS* was one of the moulds that they revived, but one change was made. The interior of the original bowls had no pattern, but Sowerby updated the old mould by adding their own plagiarised version of Imperial's *SCROLL EMBOSSED* pattern. Sowerby also subsequently utilized *SCROLL EMBOSSED* on several other small Carnival items too.

Shapes: ruffled or smoothly flared bowls, as well as rare square, hexagonal, tricorn and cupped in rosebowls, all shaped from the same mould

Colors: marigold, amethyst, amber and aqua

The amethyst rose bowl in Sowerby's *DIVING DOLPHINS* is a scarce shape and color. SP $250-$550.

Sowerby's splendid *DIVING DOLPHINS* marigold bowl is shown here in a most unusual shape—a hexagonal form. SP $250-$550

ELLISON FLOWER BLOCK—Sowerby

This moulded flower holder was registered in 1924 and has the RD 706202 moulded on its base. Illustrated in Sowerby's catalogs during the 1920s, it was named "Number 2" *ELLISON FLOWER BLOCK* and was made in four sizes (two are confirmed in Carnival). The name Ellison in the pattern name refers, of course, to the Sowerby factory, which was called the Sowerby Ellison Glass Works. Ellison was a well known Gateshead landowner and benefactor and he had previously owned the land where the Sowerby factory was located.

    Shape: flower holder
    Color: marigold

The illustration shows two *ELLISON FLOWER BLOCKS* in marigold. The smaller of the two has six holes around a center hole and measures 2.5 inches high by 4 inches diameter. The larger one shown has four holes in the center and eight holes around the edge, it measures 2.75 inches high and is 4.5 inches in diameter. SP $50-$100. *Information courtesy Carol Sumpter.*

ROYAL SWANS—Sowerby

ROYAL SWANS is a particularly lovely item—its centre section is an oval, boat shaped container, either side of which is a swan with outstretched wings. A waterlily and cattail pattern covers the side of the boat shape. This rare item was first shown in Sowerby's 1882 catalog. Westmoreland's "Swan" sugar and creamer set were very possibly modelled on this Sowerby original. *ROYAL SWANS* is a novelty item, to be used as a posy vase, salt dip or spill holder. It stands 5 inches long and is 3 inches high. Known in various Sowerby non iridized colors from the 1880s, it was re-used in the 1920s for Carnival production.

    Shape: extremely rare posy vase
    Colors: marigold and amethyst

GOODNIGHT—Sowerby

This delightful little item is actually a chamberstick, designed to be carried up to one's bedchamber by means of the little handle. This unusual, plain panelled item was in production during the late 1920s and early 1930s. The original Sowerby name for the item was *GOODNIGHT* and it had the pattern #2434.

    Shape: candlestick
    Color: black

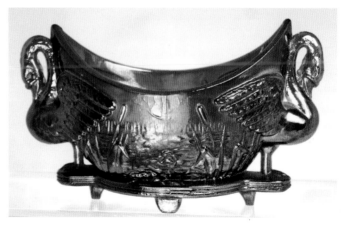

Sowerby made this exceptionally rare amethyst *ROYAL SWANS* posy vase using an old mould from the 1880s. SP $1500-$2500

A rare item—the *GOODNIGHT* chamberstick made by Sowerby is shown here in black amethyst. NP

SOWERBY DRAPE aka *(LADY) CYNTHIA*—Sowerby

In 1929 the British *Pottery Gazette* ran an ad for Sowerby stating that they would be showing their glassware at "The Industries Fair" in London. In the center of the ad was the splendid *SOWERBY DRAPE* vase and it was a new design for Sowerby, not a revival of one of their old Victorian moulds. This magnificent item stands almost 10 inches high and in Carnival, it is found only in a dense black amethyst. So dark is the color that it is exceptionally difficult to see any purple coloration at all, even when held to a very intense light source. The paneled pattern itself is essentially very simple, the vase stands on a pedestal and the top may be either cupped in or flared out. But what distinguishes this vase is its astounding, electric iridescence. The few scarce examples that we have seen have all had this incredible effect. The combination of dense, black amethyst base glass and electric iridescence makes this one of Sowerby's most impressive pieces of Carnival Glass.

Shape: vase
Color: black amethyst

A pair of *SOWERBY DRAPE* black, amethyst vases with splendid iridescence, standing 10 inches high. Note the different top shapings.
$700-$1000

WICKERWORK—Sowerby

WICKERWORK is an intricate, open edged design that dates back to the 1880s. Comprising a plate or low bowl and separate stand, it is often possible to find the Sowerby peacock's head trademark on the three-legged base. Oddly, the stand usually has two peacocks' heads on it while the top usually has none. Early non-Carnival versions of the plate and stand were often stuck together, the iridized versions, however, were separate. The 1927 Sowerby catalog indicates that the top half was available as either a cupped up bowl shape or a flat plate. The three-legged base was available as a matching stand and was actually sold separately as well, as a pin tray. Indeed, the stand fits several other Sowerby items, including some *PINEAPPLE* bowls, and was a useful multi-purpose item.

This item was also made by Eda Glasbruk in Sweden. Examples are known in milk glass (trademarked Eda) and a stand has been seen in marigold bearing the moulded Eda Glasbruk trademark.

Shapes: flat plate, bowl and three-footed stand
Colors: both plate and stand are known in marigold and very rare amethyst

This is the first complete Sowerby *WICKERWORK* stand and top known in amethyst. (In 2008 another amethyst stand without the top appeared on UK eBay making just two amethyst stands known). NP. *Courtesy of Dave Richards.*

The discovery in early 2008 of an unusual item of Carnival (see *LEAF AND GRAPE* below for full details) marked with a British glass Registration diamond-shaped lozenge, was startling. The moulded lozenge showed that the design for the item had been registered on the 29th of July, 1876 by Henry Greener of Sunderland. The registration was for the style of the pierced edging (rather than the pattern on the item). This information indicated that Carnival Glass had been made at the Wear Glass Works, by Greener and Co. and/or Jobling and Co. Despite the 1876 date reference on the Registration lozenge, it is most unlikely that the item was made in Carnival at that time. It would be more plausible to suggest that the original Greener mould was re-used at a later date to produce Carnival (like Sowerby did).

The Wear Glass Works was in the north east of England—it was close to, contemporary with, and undoubtedly a competitor of its near neighbour, Sowerby. The glass works had been started by James Angus and Henry Greener in 1858. Despite a good start, times became difficult: in 1870 Angus died and by 1877 Greener owed his banker over £9000. A few years later Greener also died. The Wear Glass Works was in trouble and deeply in debt to James Augustus Jobling, a Newcastle businessman, who had supplied Greener and Co. with their glass-making chemicals. In 1885 Jobling took over the Wear Glass Works as a bad debt (he kept the Greener and Co. name, only changing it to James A. Jobling and Co. in 1921). Despite all its money troubles when Jobling took over, the Wear Glass Works was still an active business, manufacturing over 600 different shapes of domestic pressed-ware. (For further information on Jobling see the Glass-Study.com)

The company continued on (though economic conditions became harder for all the glass works in the area) producing a wide variety of pressed "flint glass" that ranged from "fancy" and ornamental glassware through domestic and utilitarian goods (supplying Woolworth's and Marks & Spencer) to industrial articles. Baker and Crowe (in *A Collector's Guide to Jobling 1930s Decorative Glass*: Tyne & Wear County Council Museum, 1985) observe that the company had developed some of their glassware "in an attempt to challenge the market primacy of a Czechoslovakian pressed glass called 'Jacobean' ". This is especially interesting, as it shows that the Wear Glass Works saw itself as being in direct competition with Josef Inwald (who of course made much Carnival Glass).

In the early 1920s, James A. Jobling and Co. (as the company was then called) acquired the right to manufacture Pyrex glassware, which quickly transformed the Wear Glass Works from a small concern to an internationally known one. Flint glass continued to be made as well, though its profitability declined. In the early 1930s Jobling introduced its Art Glassware range, in direct competition with Lalique. Despite its beauty, its high production costs meant that it was not the money-spinner Jobling had hoped it would be and it was discontinued as WW2 dawned. From there on it was all about Pyrex, as the oven-to-table ware continued to grow in popularity. However, in 1973, Jobling's licence expired and Corning took over control of the company, renaming it Corning Limited.

Until the appearance of the *LEAF AND GRAPE* low bowl (or tray) it was not thought that Greener/Jobling had made any Carnival Glass. However, catalogs showing their glass are not easily found, with the exception of the later Art Glassware range and of course, Pyrex. Further evidence of likely Carnival production at the Wear Glass Works is provided by a very significant fact reported by Jobling researchers, Baker and Crowe, who state (in *A Collector's Guide to Jobling 1930s Decorative Glass*) that a stannous chloride wash was used to give a decorative effect on the glass. Stannous chloride is, of course, used by glass makers to produced iridescence on glass—Carnival Glass! Let's consider this fascinating example of Greener / Jobling Carnival and then discuss the possibility of further examples of Carnival Glass from the Wear Glass Works.

LEAF AND GRAPE—Greener / Jobling

A striking piece of glass, this oval dish has a moulded pattern of vine leaves and grapes in the central section with a very distinctive pierced "open edge" style border. This rare item was reported by John and Loretta Nielsen, who tell us that the leaves are stippled and the grapes stand up from the surface (indeed are reminiscent of Imperial's *HEAVY GRAPE*) and are very realistic. The iridescence is a brilliant purple with pink and gold tones, which enhances the realism of the fruit. It measures 11 inches by 8 inches and the base (marie) is ground flat.

The dish bears a moulded diamond Registration lozenge with the characters 29, V, I, 6, thus indicating it was registered on the 29th of July, 1876 by Henry Greener in Sunderland, England. The registration was for the style of the pierced edging rather than the pattern on the item. The edge is very similar to Sowerby's *WICKERWORK* which was first introduced (not in Carnival) in the 1880s (see above).

It is most unlikely that the *LEAF AND GRAPE* was made in Carnival in or near 1876—the date was simply when the pattern was first registered. The period of iridised production is more likely to have been in the early 1920s, possibly a little earlier, but certainly before the 1930s when Jobling's Art Glassware came into being. Note that Sowerby brought their old *WICKERWORK* moulds out of store and re-used them for Carnival production in the early 1920s. It is highly probable that Greener / Jobling did exactly the same thing—but which company re-introduced it first and which company followed, are not questions that can currently be answered.

Shapes: low bowl or tray
Colors: purple

The *LEAF AND GRAPE* low bowl with its splendid pierced edge and magnificent iridescence. This piece carries a registration mark showing that it was a product of Greener / Jobling at the Wear Glass Works in Sunderland. NP. *Courtesy of John and Loretta Nielsen.*

Was any other Carnival Glass made at the Wear Glass Works?

Tantalizingly, there are a number of Carnival patterns believed to have been made in England (on account of their characteristics and sourcing) for which no specific maker has yet been attributed. Much of the circumstantial evidence for some of those items points directly to Greener / Jobling at the Wear Glass Works. The *MYSTERY GRAPE*, the *FOUR FLOWERS VARIANT* and the *THISTLE AND THORN* items all have characteristics that suggest Greener / Jobling could have been the maker.

The *MYSTERY GRAPE*, the *FOUR FLOWERS VARIANT* both came from the same maker—they have the same exterior *THUMBPRINT* design, the same appearance (color and iridescence), identical ground base and were both made from a one piece mould. In the past we have suggested that these items are of English manufacture (based on location of finds and other factors) and in *A Century of Carnival Glass* we speculated they might even have been made by Sowerby. However, now that we have firm evidence for the production of Carnival at Greener / Jobling's Wear Glass Works, the possibility that the *MYSTERY GRAPE* and the *FOUR FLOWERS VARIANT* could have been made there is very real. Consider the evidence:

The naturalistic grape and leaf design on the *MYSTERY GRAPE* is very similar to that on the *LEAF AND GRAPE.*

The deep purple color of the *LEAF AND GRAPE* is very similar to the deep purples seen on many of the *FOUR FLOWERS VARIANT* pieces.

The vivid iridescence on the *LEAF AND GRAPE* is very similar to that on the *MYSTERY GRAPE* and the *FOUR FLOWERS VARIANT* pieces.

All have a "stuck-up" base that has been ground

The *MYSTERY GRAPE* examples we have studied all have a strange mark and a series of little bumps in the very center, as if something has been removed from the mould. In the past we speculated that it could have been a peacock head mark (Sowerby) that had been removed, although why Sowerby would have done that to their own glass is not immediately apparent. Our current suggestion is that maybe the removed mark was actually a Greener lion trademark from an old Greener mould—the features which are discernible correspond to the shape of the Greener lion moulded mark. The dimensions and proportions are correct. Furthermore, it could have been removed if the Carnival production using the old mould had been after 1921 when the company name was changed to James A. Jobling (who did not use the Greener lion trademark).

The colors of the *MYSTERY GRAPE* and the *FOUR FLOWERS VARIANT* pieces are similar colors to those made at the Wear Glass Works by Greener / Jobling. In particular, examples with a milky opalescent edge are known—this is entirely in keeping with Greener / Jobling production.

The *THISTLE AND THORN* pattern is very similar a known Greener design.

Thus, we are suggesting that the *FOUR FLOWERS VARIANT* and the *MYSTERY GRAPE* pieces could indeed have been produced at the Wear Glass Works in Sunderland by Greener / Jobling. We know that Woolworths were supplied by them, and a special run for a customer is a possibility. Furthermore, the lack of catalog evidence for these two patterns (and similarly for the *THISTLE AND THORN* pieces) ties in with Greener / Jobling, as there are very few of their catalogs currently available (unlike Sowerby, for which many catalogs are now sourced). Another item that now seems likely to be a Greener / Jobling piece is the *TINY DAISY* (see *A Century of Carnival Glass*). Further research will confirm or disprove our suggestions.

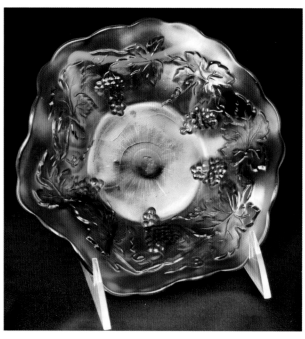

The scarce *MYSTERY GRAPE* bowl measures just 6 inches across. So far it is known only in green, as here. SP $150-$250

Other English Makers

Canning Town Glass Works Limited

Small amounts of Carnival Glass were made by other manufacturers in England. One of them, Canning Town Glass Works Limited, was located on the Isle of Sheppey near London, though its head office was in the city itself. The *THISTLE* vase is a chunky, press moulded vase in the shape of a thistle flower, and stands about 6 inches high. It's fairly easily found in the United Kingdom in marigold, though scarce smoky grey-blue Carnival versions are also known. It's possible that a similar shaped vase known as *ROYAL PINEAPPLE* (also known in marigold and scarce smoky grey-blue) was made by this company. Canning Town Glass Works was incorporated into the Bells Whisky Group, making bottles and subsequently became part of United Glass.

Thomas Webb and Sons

Thomas Webb and Sons of Stourbridge (Harry Northwood's birthplace) are well known for their free-blown, deep green "Bronze" glass (first made in 1878) that was iridized in shades of purple. They also produced an iridized golden effect glass called "Iris." Queen Victoria herself bought some of Webb's iridized "Bronze" glass. Other iridized items were almost certainly produced by Webb, and we believe that the *TORNADO VARIANT* vases were made in Stourbridge by them, probably in the early 1900s.

Stevens and Williams

This famous Stourbridge glass firm was linked with Northwood Glass in the USA by the fact that Harry Northwood's father, the great glass artist John Northwood I, and Harry's brother John II, were both Artistic Directors at the company (consecutively). Stevens and Williams are known to have produced free-blown lilies and trumpets for epergnes as well as a variety of salt cellars that are typically iridized (in marigold) only at the top. They are often found on a variety of metal mountings.

Molineux, Webb and Co. Ltd.

The Manchester firm, Molineux Webb was a distinguished glass manufacturer, dating back to 1827. Its latter years are not well documented at all, with some sources saying it closed in 1936 while others report that it ceased trading in 1927. However, information from Professor Ridley (a descendant of the Josef Rindskopf family) provides interesting insights. Joseph Riethof—a member of the Czech Rindskopf glass family—went to England in 1932 on a dual purpose: to represent Rindskopf Glass at their showroom in London and also to organise the revival of Molineaux Webb in Manchester. It is very possible that some Carnival was made during the two years that Reithof was at the works. An item is known in marigold, in a pattern that was shown in the Rindskopf catalog from the 1920s, but it has BRITISH MAKE moulded on the base. We do not have proof, but it is very possible, that it was made at the Molineaux Webb factory when Reithof was there. Another item, an amber posy vase called *MANCHESTER* by collectors, is shown in Molineaux Webb ads in 1925. It is also known in Carnival, and perhaps was also produced during Reithof's time at the factory.

Jackson Brothers Ltd.

Jackson Brothers of Knottingley, trademarked their post war glass production with a distinctive, entwined, moulded JBK—bottles and jars were their main lines. Lightly iridized lidded jars in pale smoke, lilac and marigold (intended for cosmetics) are known with this trademark. In 1962, Jackson Brothers took over the Bagley Glass Company (aka the Crystal Glass Company) and were themselves absorbed by the Austrian glass company, Stolze Oberglas, in the 1990s. Oberglas are also known to have made iridized items, such as the *FOUR PANELLED TREETRUNK* vase.

Matthew Turnbull

It is possible, but currently not verified by catalog or similar proof, that Matthew Turnbull made some Carnival Glass. Evidence hinges around a vase known as *TOWERS*, which was made in plain glass by the Davidson Glass factory from 1961. According to Davidson experts, Chris and Val Stewart, the mould was marked M.T.1. possibly indicating that it was previously a Matthew Turnbull item (Davidson had various other close links with Turnbull). It seems possible that the *TOWERS* vase was previously made in Carnival by Turnbull. Other currently un-attributed Carnival may also have been made by Turnbull, but there is currently no firm evidence.

The marigold *DERBYSHIRE* vase (aka *BEADED SWAG MEDALLION*) is another un-attributed item that bears close resemblance to a similar vase made by the Manchester firm John Derbyshire. Was the Carnival version also made by Derbyshire, or was this also a Turnbull product? Research continues.

The maker of this *DERBYSHIRE* vase is unknown, although it is believed to be English. This unusual and attractive item stands 5.5 inches high. SP $300-$500

Hortensja

The Hortensja glass works was situated in Piotrków Trybunalski, in the heart of Poland, some 70 miles south west of Warsaw and around 130 miles north of Cracow. One of Poland's oldest cities, dating back to the 1200s, Piotrków (actually part of Russia between 1815 and 1915 before reverting to Poland in 1919) has a history that is dominated in recent times by the worst of the Holocaust. In happier times, glass making, textiles and timber were Piotrków's main industries, and its location at the crossroads of primary communication routes as well as being close to river crossings, gave it an important advantage.

Credit for uncovering Hortensja as a maker of Carnival Glass goes to Malcolm and Hilary Ross, who (while working in Poland) came across a 1936 catalog of the company. Through our study of the catalog found by them we believe that iridised Carnival Glass was made at Hortensja in Poland during the 1930s (and possibly from the late 1920s). A wide range of domestic glass and tableware is shown in the catalog—bowls, vases, lighting, ashtrays, covered jars and much more. We immediately recognised some patterns as mysteries, previously un-attributed to a maker. But we also realised that some items were disturbingly familiar in that they were already attributed to other makers. Possibly some of them were made by more than one manufacturer, but equally, some had been wrongly attributed and Hortensja was indeed the maker.

An exuberant Art Déco style was used on many patterns and shapes shown in the Hortensja 1936 catalog. Contrasting effects and "textured" finishes were often used on the glass. A mixture of vibrant marigold and white frosting can sometimes be found and a marigold and clear combination was also used, especially where the marigold was applied on incised designs as on the *GOLDEN* patterns that have so long been a mystery regarding maker.

BLACKBERRY INTAGLIO—Hortensja

A delicious contrast of rich marigold iridescence and frosted glass appears to be one of Hortensja's signature decorating techniques. The blackberry design on these items is intaglio on the polished base, the pattern being brought out in relief when viewed through the glass. It's a clever technique that can be seen in other combinations (for example, with a golden intaglio design and clear surround, as on the *GOLDEN CARP*, see below). The blackberry motif alters slightly according to the size of the item it appears on—larger pieces have bigger leaves and more blackberries.

Shapes: bowl and plate in several different sizes, ranging from just over 4 inches to around 10 inches—possibly smaller and larger items too
Color: marigold and frosted

DECO STRIPES—Hortensja

A contrasting blend of rich marigold and acid etched frosting form the stripes on this splendid Deco style vase. It features a curved diamond shaped base, winged sides and a deeply fluted zigzagged top; its base is ground and it stands around 10 inches high. A number of other, similar winged Deco vases (for example *DECO LEAF* and *DECO STAR*) share this style and also have similar bases, though *DECO STRIPES* is the only one with alternate acid etching and marigold iridescence.

We speculated in the past that the maker might have been Rindskopf, then a sighting in a STS (Steklarna, Jugoslavia) catalog made us think again. The problem with that was that STS are not known to have made Carnival, and no other items known in iridized form are in the STS catalogues. A similar vase also appears in Rosice catalogs (courtesy Marcus Newhall), but Rosice are not known to have made Carnival. So the mystery remained—who made this fabulous vase and its "sister" patterns? The puzzle was solved by the appearance of the *DECO STRIPES* vase (pattern number 430) in the Hortensja catalog.

Shape: vase
Color: marigold and frosted

These Art Deco style, frosted and marigold vases from Hortensja are both unusual and distinctive. On the left is *DECO LEAF* and on the right is the *DECO STRIPES*. SP for either $250-$500

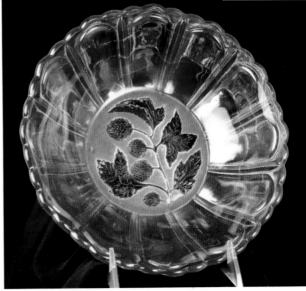

The base of this 9 inch *BLACKBERRY INTAGLIO* bowl from Hortensja features an incised blackberry pattern. The pattern itself is clear while the rest of the base is frosted, producing a most attractive contrast. The sides of the bowl are marigold. SP $100-$175

DIAMOND CUT—Hortensja

Previously, the only accepted attribution for *DIAMOND CUT* has been that it was made by Inwald (in the vase form) and Crown Crystal in Australia (in bowl form). However, the discovery of the Hortensja catalog has changed this. In the Hortensja catalog the cylinder vase is very clearly illustrated and two sizes are shown; 6 and 10 inches. In fact two further sizes were most likely made by Hortensja too—8 and 14 inches. This vase was given the number 346 in the Hortensja catalog. So, it would appear that the cylinder vases were made by both Inwald and Hortensja.

    Shape: vase in several different sizes, ranging from 6 to 14 inches
    Color: marigold

MAZURKA—Hortensja

This pattern features a series of square panels that enclose (alternately) a textured cross and a whirling abstract shape, full of "movement". The only shape currently reported is a lidded bonbon dish that has a polished ground rim on its base. This is an exceptionally scarce item.

    Shape: covered bonbon dish
    Color: marigold

This unusual, marigold *MAZURKA* covered bonbon dish from Hortensja has its pattern on the **exterior** of the body but on the **interior** of the lid. The pattern has perfect register on both shapes. SP $250-$500

The iridescence on this exquisite 6.5 inch high *DIAMOND CUT* vase is outstanding. The cylinder vase was made by both Inwald and Hortensja and is shown in both their catalogs. SP $400-$700

GOLDEN CARP—Hortensja

The *GOLDEN CARP* oval dish is clearly illustrated in the Hortensja catalog along with a number of other similar styled "intaglio base design" items. The carp is intaglio on the base which is fully iridized ("Golden") while the sides of the dish are, by contrast, very plain. There were two sizes made: 5.5 inches and 11 inches (shown as 12 cm and 28 cm in the Hortensja catalog).

    Shape: shallow oval dish in two sizes
    Color: marigold and clear

The form of the carp is intaglio (incised) and iridized on the clear, smoothly polished base. This *GOLDEN CARP* bowl is a Hortensja item. $80-$175

PINWHEEL—Hortensja

This familiar geometric design featuring star and diamond motifs, has previously been attributed to Josef Inwald (Czechoslovakia) and Sowerby (when it is also known as *DERBY*). However, the pattern is clearly illustrated in the Hortensja catalogs, and it appears that some of the items attributed to Inwald in the past were in fact made by Hortensja. Details on how to distinguish between the makers and what shapes were probably made by each of them can be read in the Inwald section above (see the *PINWHEEL* entry).

The small *PINWHEEL* vase that stands just under 5 inches high and has a flat ground base with a recessed intaglio star is almost certainly a Hortensja item. It was previously thought to be by Inwald however, through careful comparison of Inwald and Hortensja catalog illustrations we feel that the little vase which is known in marigold Carnival was made by Hortensja and not Inwald.

Shape: vase in several sizes (6, 8, 10, 12 and 14 inches are all possible—plus the small 5 inch vase)—research continues

Color: marigold

This 5 inch high *PINWHEEL* vase has a complex central star cut into the shiny, mirror ground base. Previously thought to be an Inwald item, its appearance in the Hortensja catalog confirms its Polish origin. $300-$500

RISING COMET—Hortensja

This vase had been a mystery for a long time. We had in the past speculated that it might have been a Rindskopf item but no proof had been forthcoming. Now the mystery is solved—the *RISING COMET* vase is clearly depicted in the Hortensja catalog in three sizes, all of which are known in Carnival. The pattern on the vase resembles stylized shooting stars—hence the name.

    Shape: vase in three sizes; 6, 8 and 10 inches
    Color: marigold

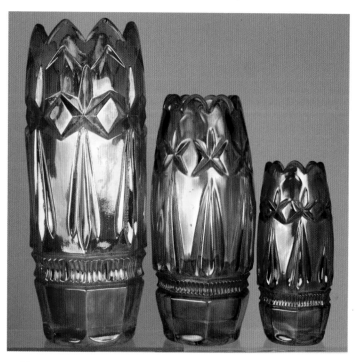

Shown as item #291 in Hortensja's 1936 catalog, the *RISING COMET* vase was made in three sizes as shown here: left to right, 10 inches, 8 inches and 6 inches. $200-$400 for any size.

DAISY AND SCROLL—Uncertain

The *DAISY AND SCROLL* decanter, matching stemmed cordial, shot glass and undertray are all depicted in the Hortensja catalog. This presents something of a conundrum, for the Carnival versions of this pattern are thought to be Argentinean (based on circumstantial evidence). So, were they in fact made in Poland, or was this pattern made by both Hortensja and a South American maker?

The Hortensja illustration of the decanter is almost identical to the actual item: there is a slight difference in the ribbing on the neck, but this could simply be "artistic licence". It's a different story, however, when it comes to the shot glass. The known Carnival Glass examples have a very distinctive angular foot (an unusual shape that is actually a small version of the Riihimaki *GRAND THISTLE* tumbler). The cordial and shot glass illustrated in the Hortensja catalog, are however, completely different. Indeed those two shapes shown there are not currently known in Carnival Glass

DAISY AND SCROLL items are known in marigold and blue (colours used by the Argentinean Carnival makers), whereas so far, we are only aware of Hortensja Carnival Glass in marigold. The source of most of the *DAISY AND SCROLL* pieces has been Argentina, but of course, it is not possible to use this as absolute proof of manufacture. The evidence is not conclusive: if we have to go on "gut feel" we'd say that the *DAISY AND SCROLL* Carnival decanter and shot glass/cordial were most likely made in Argentina, but there is currently no proof and the only catalog illustration of the pattern is in the Hortensja catalog!

    Shapes: decanter and shot glass
    Colors: marigold and blue

A fascinating look back at social habits: this *GOLDEN DAYS* ashtray from Zabkowice features an image of a young lad smoking. SP $200-$400. *Photo courtesy John and Frances Hodgson.*

Zabkowice aka Zombkowice

The Zabkowice glass works was built in Silesia, Poland, by the Czech glass maker, Josef Schreiber Jnr., in 1883 with production beginning in 1884. The location was good as it had cheap, local energy from newly found charcoal and good connections via new railroads. Schreiber owned the factory personally in as much as it was not part of his main company, Josef Schreiber & Neffen (nephews). Around 1892-96, Schreiber sold it and some of the pressed glass subsequently produced there (using old Schreiber moulds) bore a trademark which had a circle and Russian / Cyrillic text plus a date. Schreiber's idea had been to produce and sell glass within the borders of Russia without paying the high Russian customs tariffs (information courtesy Siegmar Geiselberger).

In the 1920s and 1930s Zabkowice produced a range of Carnival Glass pieces, including a number of "Golden" designs (where the motifs are iridized and the surrounding glass is clear). In the years leading up to World War Two they were the biggest and most important glass works in Poland for household glass. They were in operation until around 2005, when the authors corresponded with the factory regarding the production of iridized "Golden" items. Several of these are noted below, others are known, for example *GOLDEN DAYS* ashtray that features a young man smoking.

Both Martin and John Hodgson have been of great help in researching the Zabkowice glass works and we are grateful to them for their help. A fascinating marigold jardinière, owned by Martin and Sue Hodgson, (named *EGYPTIAN LOTUS* by them) bears a paper label with printed lettering reading ZOMBKOWICE (the French form of the Polish Zabkowice). The item is clearly illustrated in the 1930 Zabkowice catalog (courtesy Siegmar Geiselberger). Of great further interest is the fact that the label for Beverley Crystal Poland (which has been found in Australia and New Zealand on *GOLDEN CUPID* and *ROSE AND DRAPE* items) is identical in shape and design appearance to the Zombkowice label. This raises the possibility that these items and, by association, *DIANA THE HUNTRESS*, may also be by Zabkowice.

EUREKA CROSS aka *GOLDEN PANSIES*—Zabkowice
    Illustrated in the 1930 Zabkowice catalog in a variety of sizes, this is an excellent example of a "Golden" design and has long been a mystery regarding maker. There are two variations on the pansy theme. One features a single pansy on the intaglio design, the other features a stylized grouping of four pansies in a "wheel" formation, their stems meeting in the very center, this latter has also been called *EUREKA CROSS*. The base, where the intaglio design is found, is highly polished.
    Shapes: small plates, large and small bowls and a flat dresser tray
    Color: marigold and clear as well as marigold and pink base glass (rare)

GOLDEN POPPIES—Zabkowice
    Another example of a "Golden" design that was illustrated in the 1930 Zabkowice catalog in a variety of sizes. A moulded, V shaped design can be found around the sides of this pattern, while on the polished base is an intaglio "golden" design of poppies.
    Shape: small bowl known, possibly other shapes
    Color: marigold and clear

EUREKA CROSS is also known (perhaps more descriptively) as *GOLDEN PANSIES*. The name stems from the cross-like shape of the floral design (as seen on the Australian Eureka Flag). The stylized pansies are intaglio on the base and are iridized in rich marigold. This circular dish is 4.5 inches across. SP $150-$250

The detail on the stylized poppies shows exceptional mouldwork. The pattern on this 4.5 inch *GOLDEN POPPIES* bowl from Zabkowice is iridized and intaglio on the base. SP $150-$250

GOLDEN ROVER—Zabkowice
    GOLDEN ROVER is an ashtray featuring a richly iridized intaglio dog's head moulded into the base. The entire base is highly polished and is clearly high quality work. We had speculated in the past that the maker might have been Czech (Hoffman) and possibly Hortensja, however, the appearance of the exact item in the Zabkowice 1920 catalog (courtesy Siegmar Geiselberger) has cleared up the mystery.
    Shape: ashtray
    Color: marigold and clear

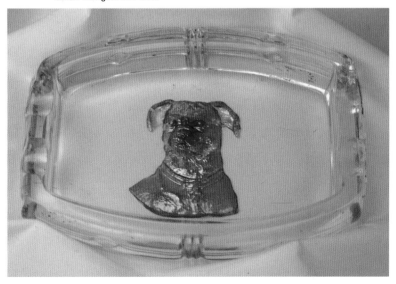

Another "Golden" design from Zabkowice, this time on an ashtray—this is *GOLDEN ROVER*. SP $200-$400

DIANA THE HUNTRESS—Probably Zabkowice

DIANA THE HUNTRESS is found on scarce bowls only and is a truly magnificent example of mouldmaking. The main part of the piece is clear crystal of high quality and polish, with a moulded geometric panelled motif around the sides—the golden design features Diana the huntress, the Roman goddess, accompanied by a stag and equipped with bow and arrow. This design is intaglio on the polished base of the bowl, in relief, and moulded to different depths. Thus, the golden iridescence takes on many shades and nuances of pink and gold when viewed from the top side of the bowl. The effect is breathtaking, the detail of the figure and the drapes of her robe are quite superb.

DIANA has been found along with several small, matching bowls known as *GOLDEN CUPID*. These smaller bowls were part of a full berry set and are fashioned in the same manner as *DIANA THE HUNTRESS*.

They feature winged creatures armed with bows and arrows and are probably not actually "cupids" but are more likely acolytes of the hunting goddess. In Australia, several full sets in cardboard boxes, consisting of the large *DIANA* bowl and six or more small *CUPIDS* have been discovered over the past twenty-some years.

This pattern was illustrated in Oskar Hallberg's catalog in 1914 (Hallberg was a Swedish wholesaler) where some Eda Glasbruks items were shown. However, non-iridized *GOLDEN CUPIDS* have been found bearing Beverley Crystal paper stickers that read "Made in Poland." It seems most likely that these were made in Poland by Zabkowice and the appearance of the pattern in the Hallberg catalog probably denoted a Polish import.

Shapes: master bowl and small berry bowls
Color: marigold and crystal combination

This splendid intaglio design featuring *DIANA THE HUNTRESS* is moulded into the polished base. SP $800-$1000. *Courtesy of Fiona Melville.*

ROSE AND DRAPE—Probably Zabkowice

This pattern is known only in the form of a cylinder vase that features six plain panels bisected by an encircling "draped" band of cameo roses. The top edge of the vase has distinctive three-fluted scallops. The bases of these vases are ground and have a polished finish. Three sizes are known: the tallest is 7.5" high, the mid-size stands 6" high and the smallest is a diminutive 4.5" high. A black (not iridised) example of the *ROSE AND DRAPE* vase bearing a paper label that reads "Beverly Crystal Poland" was found in New Zealand by Tony Hodgson. The label is identical in shape, size and lettering to the Zabkowice (Zombkowice) label.

Shape: cylinder vase
Color: marigold

Three of a kind—this is the *ROSE AND DRAPE* cylinder vase in three sizes: 4.5 inches, 6 inches and 7.5 inches. SP $250-$500

J. Stolle "Nieman"

Huty Szklane (glass works) J. Stolle "Nieman" was established on the banks of the River Nieman in Belarus in 1883. It was created by the merger of Julius Stolle, a Russian factory from Dyatkovo in Bryansk, famous for its lead crystal, and Vilhelm Kraevski glass works. Originally a small factory with one glass melting furnace and just twenty workers, the Nieman glass works grew and began pressing glass in 1894. By 1897 there were over 800 people employed at the works and soon foreign skills were brought in, including Barts, a Czech engineer, and Iohan Khalik (who was an author specializing in glass writing). The company survived difficult times through WW1 by the production of insulators for the Russian army. After the death of Julius Stolle in 1927, his family took over the business, growing it further and bringing many social improvements to the locale (including a school, kindergarten, shops and a local fire brigade). After World War Two, reconstruction of ruined parts of the glass works began and the company built itself back up again to become what is today a large glass concern exporting glass tableware and novelties world wide— OJSC "NEMAN Glassworks"

CATTEAU Vase—J. Stolle "Nieman"

This vase was originally designed by Charles Catteau in Belgium. (Catteau had previously worked for the Belgian ceramics firm Boch; he was awarded a Gold Medal during the International Exhibition of Decorative Arts in Paris in 1925 for his designs). It is a 9 inch high, blow moulded item featuring a stylized petal design on a grand scale. Interestingly, this vase was also made by Scailmont in Belgium, in frosted, non-iridized colors (for example, blue, pink, Vaseline and amber). The Scailmont examples should be marked with the moulded words "Ch. Catteau".

A virtually identical vase is illustrated in the Huty Szklane J. Stolle "Nieman" catalog (1925—1936). Our understanding is that all these vases from Scailmont were marked with "Ch. Catteau" and any without the marking are most likely to have been made by J. Stolle "Nieman". A pair of these vases in marigold were found in France in 2002 (reported and illustrated in the Carnival Glass Society Newsletter 101).

HUTY SZKLANE J. STOLLE · „NIEMEN"

1107.   1108.   1109.

This page from the Huty Szklane J. Stolle "Niemen" catalolg (circa 1926) shows the bulbous, blow-moulded *CATTEAU* vase. It has the pattern number 1109 and is on the right of the trio of vases depicted. *Courtesy Malcolm and Hilary Ross.*

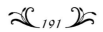

Leerdam Glasfabriek—The Netherlands

Pressed glass making at the Leerdam factory, near Rotterdam, began in the 18th century, primarily for the production of bottles. Later, a whole range of shapes was introduced and by the beginning of the 20th century, the factory was turning out tumblers, table sets, bowls and many drinking vessels, often in matching suites—only a handful of patterns and shapes are known in Carnival, though. Most Carnival items attributed to Leerdam are parts of table sets (creamers, stemmed sugar and butter dishes). In 1953 the company became Royal Leerdam and now concentrates on fine crystal.

BEADED SWIRL aka *REMBRANDT* aka *BEADS AND DIAMONDS*—Leerdam Glasfbriek

This is a detailed geometric design that contrasts plain panels with intricately patterned panels. The overall effect is rich and it reflects the light well.

Shapes: creamer, stemmed sugar, butter dish, stemmed fruit dish and stemmed cake plate

Color: marigold

A dainty little marigold creamer from Leerdam in the *BEADED SWIRL* pattern. $40-$75

DUTCH STAR—Leerdam Glasfbriek

DUTCH STAR is one of Leerdam's older patterns. It was illustrated in their 1900 catalog and was maintained in production for at least thirty more years. A complex geometric design, its many years of use are borne out by the flatness of moulded detail on the finished Carnival items. The little creamer is only 4 inches high while the stemmed sugar stands 5 inches high. The latter is known in just one example which is marigold.

Shapes: creamer, small bowl and a recently discovered stemmed sugar or compote

Colors: marigold and amethyst

MEYDAM aka *GRETA*—Leerdam Glasfbriek

MEYDAM features interlocking tear-drop motifs in a complex geometric design. It must have been a best seller for Leerdam, as it appears in their catalog in several variations of the same basic pattern. Two versions of the table set comprising stemmed sugar, covered butter dish and creamer were produced. The differences are fairly minor, yet distinct enough for Leerdam to illustrate and catalog them separately as 2127/no.1 and 2127/ no.2.

Shapes: creamer, stemmed sugar, butter dish (as mentioned above—in two variations). Leerdam's catalogs illustrate several bowls in this pattern but we are not currently aware of them in Carnival

Color: marigold

Three creamers are shown in this Leerdam catalog extract thought to be dated 1906: on the left is one not currently reported in Carnival, in the center is the *BEADED SWIRL* creamer (#2087) and on the right is the *MEYDAM* aka *GRETA* creamer (#2127).

A seldom seen pattern from Leerdam, this is *DUTCH STAR*. This marigold creamer—SP $45-$80

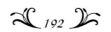

The research that led us to the discovery of Saint Gobain as a Carnival maker is tied in with the story of the *FIRCONES* vase. As the two are inextricably intertwined, we have written the full story below.

FIRCONES vase—Saint Gobain/Coty in France and Saint Gobain in Brazil

This is an impressive bulbous vase, patterned with deeply moulded fircones and foliage. The words "COTY" and "FRANCE" may be found moulded into the base. The research that led to our discovery that Saint Gobain (first in France and subsequently in Brazil) was the likely maker of these vases is interesting.

In 2005, a number of these vases were reported in Brazil. Our enquiry to the finder in that country revealed that he believed the vases were made in Brazil during the 1950s or 1960s. Our line of research then focussed on a link between France, Coty and Brazil—and we were ably aided by glass researcher Marcus Newhall.

Our conclusion was that the *FIRCONES* vase was originally made (possibly during the early 1930s) at the glass works at La Chapelle-Saint-Mesmin, near Orleans in France, owned at the time by the famous perfumier, Francois Coty. In 1930, the "Societe des Parfums, Coty" had acquired the glass-works of La Chapelle to produce their flasks and jars— they then formed the "Societe des Verreries de La Chapelle-Saint-Mesmin". Three furnaces were in operation at the semi-automatic plant and in 1932 a production hall was constructed; but skilled workers proved difficult to find and some problems in manufacture combined with the death of Francois Coty in 1934, saw the factory going into liquidation and it was purchased by Saint-Gobain. Upon that acquisition, the "Societe d'Exploitation Verriere (S.E.V.) Beauce-Bourgogne" was formed, consisting of the La Chapelle-Saint-Mesmin and Genlis (Cote d'Or) glass-works. Further amalgamations continued and the production of perfume bottles was reduced as goblet production increased. The original small pot furnaces (that were able to achieve colors and mixes of composition, relative to the function of the requested item) were replaced by larger capacity basin furnaces.

In more recent years, the Saint Gobain works at La Chapelle-Saint-Mesmin was turned over to the production of Duralex (tempered glass that is break resistant and shatterproof) table ware, with around 500 workers employed at the factory. Today Saint Gobain ranks among the world's top hundred industrial corporations, operating in 46 countries, owning more than 1,200 companies and employing more than 170,000 people throughout the world.

The Saint Gobain Group had begun to acquire businesses in Brazil in 1937. Our belief is that the mould for the original Coty *FIRCONES* vase (that was made in France) was produced at La Chapelle-Saint-Mesmin in France and was later shipped over to the Saint Gobain subsidiary in Brazil sometime during the 1940s or 1950s. You can read more about the subsequent production of the *FIRCONES* vase below, in the chapter on South American Carnival Glass.

Shape: vase
Color: marigold

The *FIRCONES* Vase in marigold is an impressive, blow moulded vase. SP $1000-$1500. *Courtesy Charles and Jeanette Echols.*

Unknown Maker—France

In early 2008, a most unusual, blow-moulded vase was discovered in the Toulouse area of France. Currently it is not possible to assign the vase to a maker on the available evidence. It is, however, very clear that the maker was French—for moulded on the bottom of the vase are the words MADE IN FRANCE. To date, this is the only reported example of this vase.

DÉCORATIF vase—Unknown French Maker

This blow-moulded, bulbous vase stands just 7.5 inches high, yet measures a huge 26 inches around its girth. The design style is pure Art Déco; typical stepped forms and sweeping curves encircle the vase and focus attention on the sculptural geometric motifs at the most bulbous section of the item. It is a magnificent work of art. (The Art Déco movement arose from the work of a group of French artists who organized the 1925 *Exposition Internationale des Arts Décoratifs et Industriels Modernes*— International Exposition of Modern Industrial and Decorative Art).

The vase has a smooth, wonderful stretchy-iridized base, where the moulded words MADE IN FRANCE can be seen, indicating that it was intended for export. The iridescence, although patchy in places, is incredibly dramatic, with vivid highlights of turquoise, lime and purple. Viewed from the exterior, the base glass appears very dark, almost black, but a breathtaking surprise appears when the base glass is viewed from the inside. The vase is ruby-amberina! The bottom section of the vase and one entire side is deep ruby red while the other side of the vase shades to lighter, yellowish amberina. Of course, this vase is blown and not pressed. The glass batch would most likely have had a small amount of gold in solution dispersed within a transparent amber-glass batch. Subsequent cooling and re-heating would have "struck" a red color, causing the shading from amber to ruby red over the vase. Research continues on what company might have made this splendid *DÉCORATIF* Vase. Names in the frame are Coty/St. Gobain, Bayel-Fains, Cristallerie de Choisy-le-Roi, Hunebelle or even Verlys.

Shape: vase
Color: ruby-amberina

The style of this splendid ruby-amberina vase is pure Art Déco, hence its name—*DÉCORATIF* Vase. NP

On the richly iridized bottom of the *DÉCORATIF* Vase the moulded words MADE IN FRANCE can be seen clearly.

Crown Crystal Glass Company Limited (originally Crystal Glass Ltd.)

Carnival Glass was produced in Australia by Crystal Glass Ltd. (later known as Crown Crystal Glass Company Ltd.) who were located in Sydney, New South Wales, Australia. Their Carnival Glass is typified by delightful designs featuring Australian flora and fauna such as the kookaburra, kingfisher and kangaroo as well as fabulous waratah blooms and dainty Christmas bell flowers. The shapes generally found are bowls (master bowls, small bowls called nappies and rather scarce, large "float" bowls) and compotes. The edges of the bowls may have various types of ruffling or fluting. Water sets (in the *BANDED DIAMONDS* pattern), *GUM TIPS* and *LILY* vases and breakfast or table sets (sugars and creamers) are less frequently found.

Australian Carnival is primarily found in either marigold or "dark" (which is a superb, dense black amethyst), both usually having excellent iridescence. Rare examples of aqua base glass with marigold iridescence are found and rare, pale pink base glass is reported. In a Crown Crystal catalog dated 1929, the Carnival items are divided into two categories: Iridescent and De Lustre—quite possibly equating with marigold and "dark". It is thought that iridizing probably began at Crown Crystal in 1919 (although the first designs were not registered until 1923) and continued until the early 1930s.

This is Crown Crystal's *BUTTERFLY BUSH* un-ruffled compote in dark. It differs from the *BUTTERFLY BUSH AND CHRISTMAS BELLS* in that its central motif is simply a butterfly, instead of the bellflower motif. It is 4.5 inches high and just under 7 inches across. $175-$250

BUTTERFLY BUSH AND CHRISTMAS BELLS—Crown Crystal

This is a delightful pattern featuring a spray of Christmas bell flowers (native to New South Wales) as a central motif. Five symmetrically placed stylized flower sprigs and butterflies surround the Christmas bells.

Several other compotes feature patterns that are based on the concept of the central motif and five symmetrically placed flower sprigs and butterflies. Though there are slight differences in the five surrounding butterfly bush motifs, it is really only the central motif that changes. The Christmas bells are replaced by a butterfly in *BUTTERFLY BUSH*, by a waratah flower in *BUTTERFLY BUSH AND WARATAH* and by a flannel flower in the aptly named *BUTTERFLY BUSH AND FLANNEL FLOWER*.

Shape: stemmed compote
Colors: marigold, black amethyst and aqua

The *BUTTERFLY BUSH AND CHRISTMAS BELLS* ruffled compote in dark from Crown Crystal. It stands 4 inches high and measures 7.5 inches across. $350-$450

EMU—Crown Crystal

The emu is a native bird of Eastern Australia, mainly frequenting grasslands and open woodland in pairs or flocks. On the Carnival items, the emu is spotlighted in the centre of the pattern, surrounded by wattle flower sprigs and butterflies. The pattern can be found in a splendid master berry bowl as well as an individual berry bowl. The floral sprays and indeed the emu itself, as you would expect, are bigger and more detailed on the larger bowls. On the reverse of the master berry bowls there is a back pattern called *FERN & WATTLE*. The emu is also featured on a rare and desirable compote, this time without the floral sprays, but instead pictured in a bushland setting with trees and grassland. There are variations to the edge shaping of this piece. The *EMU* design was registered on November 4, 1924 as No. 40360. The number is not incorporated in the pattern in the way that it is with various other Australian items, such as the *SWAN* or the *KANGAROO* (see below).

Shapes: 9 inch master berry bowls and 5 inch nappies (individual berry bowls). Various edge finishes are found on these bowls. A rare compote is also found, again with various edge shapings

Colors: marigold, black amethyst, aqua with marigold iridescence and pale Rosalin pink

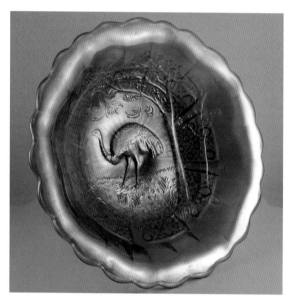

Crown Crystal's EMU compote is a rare item. It is seen here on a most unusual, pale pink base glass with a rich marigold iridescence. It stands around 6 inches high and is just over 10 inches across. NP
Photo courtesy of Neil and Wilma Berry.

The exterior design on the EMU compote is *HOBNAIL AND CANE*.
Photo courtesy of Neil and Wilma Berry.

KANGAROO—Crown Crystal

The kangaroo is arguably one of the most easily recognized and familiar of all the Australian creatures. This pattern features a kangaroo amidst oddly stylized trees and there are actually two versions of the design (registered on January 15, 1924) to be found on the large master berry bowls. One version (the "Small Roo") has a smaller kangaroo and a loose branch above the RD number—the other version has a larger kangaroo and no branch. All pieces found in this distinctive design have the moulded RD 4696 on the face of the pattern underneath the kangaroo. The master berry bowls usually have the *FERN AND WATTLE* exterior pattern while the small bowls have no exterior design.

In 2006 and 2007 some fake *KANGAROOS* appeared on Australian eBay. They are the "Small Roo" or "Doe" version with a branch below the kangaroo. Like the original Crown Crystal bowls, these imitations also have the registered design number 4696 moulded into the pattern, though this sometimes looks like RO instead of RD. The fake also has what appears to be a *FERN AND WATTLE* exterior pattern. Examples have been seen in marigold, amber, pink and light blue or crystal with pastel iridescence. Comparative study of the original and recently seen Kangaroo patterns, however, shows very clearly that this new bowl is not like the original design, as there are many differences. Possibly the most striking characteristic of the fake *KANGAROO* is the stripey and bold appearance of the grass. On the Crown Crystal original, the grass is in clumps and understated while on the fake it is everywhere, in long stripey lines.

Another difference is one that can also be noted and recognised easily. On the original item there is a quite a big gap between the R of the RD number, and the base of the tree. On the imitation version on the left, however, the R of the RD number almost touches the tree base. This is a very clear characteristic of this new bowl. Also on the imitation new bowl, the RD looks more like RO. There are many other differences in proportion too. The leaves are very close to the kangaroo's face on the fake version but are much further away on the original (in fact on some old bowls the leaves to the left of the kangaroo's face are very indistinct and hard to see). Yet another clear difference is the base of the tree seen at the left of the kangaroo. On the original, the roots at the base of the tree go off to the left, over the circle of the base (marie). But on the new one, the base of the tree goes straight down on its left hand side, and does not go over the circle of the marie.

Shapes: 9 inch master berry bowls and 5 inch nappies (individual berry bowls). Various edge finishes are found on these bowls

Colors: marigold, black amethyst and aqua with marigold iridescence

Crown Crystal's *KANGAROO* bowl in dark. This is the version with the larger kangaroo and no loose branch above the RD number. $300-$600

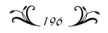

KINGFISHER—Crown Crystal

The design features a little bird perched upon a branch. It was registered in 1923 and the design number—RD 4184—is moulded onto both the 9 inch master and the 5 inch berry bowls. There are two versions of both the master and the berry: one has sprays of wattle leaves encircling the bird, the other has wattle leaves with the addition of blossoms. None have exterior patterns. The pieces were made from a one piece mould by the "stuck-up" method and consequently have ground bases.

In 2006, there were various reports of several versions of fake small 5 inch nappies in the KINGFISHER design. Currently only the nappy has been faked and they are rather easy to spot. At least four faked versions have been observed, none of which were produced from an original mould.

On one of the early fakes the location of the crossover of the encircling twigs was in the wrong place entirely (at the top instead of the bottom of the piece). In another version of the fake a letter P was used instead of the underlined D in the moulded RD number. The Crown Crystal original KINGFISHERS have no mould seams (they were made from a one piece mould) and the original has a ground base which measures just over 2.25 inches. Some of the fakes have a much wider base than that which may carry traces of iridescence. There are many other little differences, including color (some have been seen in a pearly white Carnival effect) and overall the fakes are easily spotted and are nothing like the quality of the original versions.

Shapes: 9 inch master berry bowls and 5 inch nappies (individual berry bowls)

Colors: marigold and black amethyst

The KINGFISHER bowl from Crown Crystal seen here in dark. This version has wattle sprays around the bird but no blossoms. $250-$400

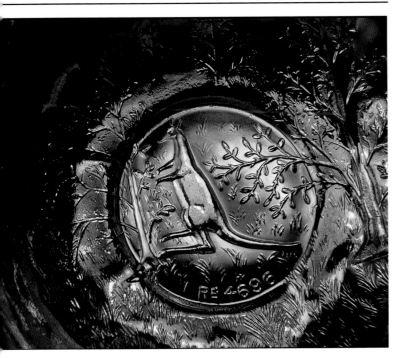

Close-up of the KANGAROO bowl.

KOOKABURRA—Crown Crystal

The *KOOKABURRA* design on glass was registered by Crown Crystal in 1924 and has the number 4184. The actual interpretation of the pattern varies according to the different sizes of bowl but the basic design concept remains constant—the delightful kookaburra in the center, perched on a branch and surrounded by floral motifs. The small bowls usually (not always) bear the registration number RD 4184. The flowers shown on the master berry bowl are the waratah (to the left and right of the bird), a single flannel flower below and a wattle sprig above (tied with a bow). A butterfly hovers at the top.

There are two versions of the nappy. One is a smaller interpretation of the master berry bowl, complete with flanking waratahs, wattle garlands and butterflies (top and bottom). The other version differs in that the background is stippled and the flower sprays are limited to encircling wattle sprigs that are quite sparse in appearance. The float bowl is different again—on this shape the central bird is surrounded by five individual waratah heads.

Shapes: 10.5 inch float bowl with bullet edge, 9 inch master berry bowls and 5 inch individual berry bowls

Colors: marigold and black amethyst

A splendid large item, this is Crown Crystal's *KOOKABURRA* float bowl in marigold with a "bullet edge". SP $1000-$1500.

SWAN—Crown Crystal

The swan sits serenely on the gently rippling water right in the very center of this beautiful pattern. It's a pleasing design that is beautifully composed. Sprays of Christmas bells (native flowers) frame the central motif. At the bottom of the design the registered design number RD 4697 is moulded into the pattern. The individual berry bowls in this pattern have slight variations in their design, also, some have the registered design numbers and some do not. The exterior pattern *FERN AND WATTLE* may also be found on the outside of some of the larger bowls.

Shapes: 9 inch master berry bowls and 5 inch nappies (individual berry bowls). Various edge finishes are found on these bowls

Colors: marigold and black amethyst

Crown Crystal's beautiful *SWAN* bowl in dark. SP $200-$400.

Cristalerias Rigolleau S.A—Argentina

Located in Berazategui, Buenos Aires, Cristalerias Rigolleau was founded around the turn of the century by a Frenchman, Leon Rigolleau. In common with many of the other Carnival producers from South and Central America, Cristalerias Rigolleau was originally a glass bottle and container manufacturer. Typical of Rigolleau's Carnival Glass are advertising and novelty pieces, possibly made for commercial customers as promotional lines and featuring the name of the product or the customer. It is possible that links between the Czech and South American glass industries were fostered by an important Czech glassmaker and designer, called Karel (Carlos) Hološko. He had worked for Josef Schreiber & Neffen A.G. at Lednické Rovne between 1930 and 1935, then he worked at Cristallerias Rigolleau from 1935 to 1947, during which time he was concurrently teaching for Escuella de bellas Artes, (School of Fine Arts) in Buenos Aires 1939-1942. Hološko then returned to Czechoslovakia to design for the Lednické Rovne factory in 1947. (Thanks to Marcus Newhall for this important information—source: "Modern Bohemian Glass": edited by J. Raban, Artia, Prague—1963). See the chapter on Czechoslovakia above for more information on Schreiber & Neffen.

BEETLE ASHTRAY—Cristalerias Rigolleau
This is a round ashtray with eight beetle shapes arranged in a ring around the center. The words "Cristalerias Rigolleau. Buenos Aires" surround the very center, where "Sociedad Anonima Usinas En Berazategui F.C.S." is written (note: the lettering translates to mean "Limited Liability Company of Berazategui", the location of Rigolleau's factory). All the words are moulded in the design. Research and correspondence by Wily Adis with Cristalerias Rigolleau gave rise to the following note from Carlos Righetti, the General Manager of the factory in the late 1960s. "This company did in fact make this piece of glass strictly as a souvenir piece that was given to special customers."
 Shape: ashtray.
 Colors: marigold, blue and amber.

Distinctive, scarce and unusual, this is the *BEETLE ASHTRAY* from Cristalerias Rigolleau. The example illustrated is in amber. SP $800-$1250. *Photo courtesy of David Doty.*

Cristalerias Papini (also called Cristalux S.A.)—Argentina

Founded in 1896 and located in Buenos Aires, Cristalerias Papini's trademark was Cristalux; they often used the logo INDUSTRIA ARGENTINA, meaning Made in Argentina, which can sometimes be found moulded into their glass. Cristalerias Papini imported glass from Europe, indeed, in the introduction to their 1934 catalog, Papini explained to their customers that as the price of imported glassware was increasing, they were therefore starting to increase the range of home-made goods. However, a good number of European articles remained, including items from Inwald in Czechoslovakia. Cristalerias Papini also made some of their own Carnival Glass.

At its peak, the Cristalux factory employed 1500 workers producing mainly domestic glassware, barware, bottles and containers, but sadly the company went bankrupt in 2000. Against all the odds, a workers' co-operative was established on the old Cristalux site in Buenos Aires and today, Cooperativa Cristal Avellanada produce plates and tumblers—their clients include Wal-Mart and Makro.

INDUSTRIA ARGENTINA STAR—Cristalerias Papini.
A complex intaglio star is repeated around the exterior of items in this pattern. A most distinctive feature of items in this design is the wording moulded on the glass which reads "INDUSTRIA ARGENTINA". On the bowls and plates it is on the marie or base, while on the vases it can be found on the side, underneath one of the large star motifs.
 Shapes: small and large bowl, small plate, chop plate, vase
 Color: marigold

INDUSTRIA ARGENTINA "GOOD YEAR" —Cristalerias Papini
This must be one of the most unusual ashtrays ever reported. The central section is a marigold disk with the wording "INDUSTRIA ARGENTINA" encircling the words "GOOD YEAR." Around the outside of the central disk is a miniature "Good Year" automobile tire. The date 1928 is inscribed on the tire.
 Shape: ashtray shaped like a tire
 Color: marigold

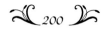

BAND OF ROSES aka *ROSAS*—Cristalerias Piccardo

The name is very apt and descriptive—this is a paneled design with a simple band of roses running horizontally around. In the 1933-4 catalog, a whole range of items, including water pitcher and handled mug, were shown, though it isn't certain whether all were iridized. A decanter with stopper was listed as "irisado" (iridized) in two different sizes: a larger one for port and a smaller one for liqueurs. A water pitcher was also depicted in the catalog as "irisado." The stemmed goblet in this pattern is known with the moulded words "INDUSTRIA ARGENTINA PICCARDO" on its base. This pattern is very similar to a Brockwitz design called *ROSE BAND* (*ARIADNE*) but it should not be confused with the *AZTEC ROSE* scalloped edge bonbon that was made in the USA by Jeanette in the 1960s.

Shapes: tumbler, goblet, water pitcher, decanter and stemmed compote
Color: marigold

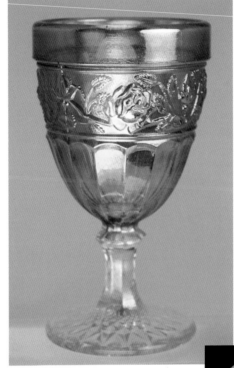

Standing 5.5.inches high, this marigold *BAND OF ROSES* goblet from Cristalerias Piccardo has a cameo pattern band featuring full-blown roses and leaves. SP $100-$200

The factory logo of Cristalerias Papini—INDUSTRIA ARGENTINA—is moulded on the front of this vase. *INDUSTRIA ARGENTINA STAR* vase in marigold. SP $150-$350

A close-up shows the lettering on the *INDUSTRIA ARGENTINA STAR* vase.

Cristalerias Piccardo

Cristalerias Piccardo was also located in Buenos Aires. Some amazing Carnival items are depicted within the pages of their 1934 catalog. Piccardo clearly traded with Inwald in Czechoslovakia, as the very distinctive *DRAPERY VARIANT* water pitcher made by Inwald is illustrated, called (tellingly) *CHECO*. Cristalerias Piccardo also sometimes used the moulded logo INDUSTRIA ARGENTINA PICCARDO.

GRACEFUL aka *FANTASIA*—Cristalerias Piccardo

A full set of *GRACEFUL* items, water pitcher and six tumblers on a glass tray, is depicted in the Piccardo catalog. Single tumblers were also offered. The pattern is a curling scroll design that repeats around the tumbler. The shape of the tumbler is different from most Classic Carnival examples, being somewhat belled out at the bottom. A twelve point star is pressed into the base.

Shape: tumbler and pitcher
Colors: blue and amber—marigold is possible

FANTASIA

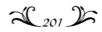

The base of the *BAND OF ROSES* goblet has a magnificently detailed hobstar surrounded by the moulded words: INDUSTRIA ARGENTINA PICCARDO. No doubt who made this!

Although this tumbler is known to Carnival collectors as *GRACEFUL*, it was originally called *FANTASIA* by Cristalerias Piccardo in their 1934 catalog.

IMPERIAL—Cristalerias Piccardo

The design is geometric and the catalog illustration gives the impression that it is all intaglio (cut in)—oddly that is not the case as the design is actually cameo. Consequently it doesn't have the clear cut edges and feel of a "near-cut" design. Instead, the pattern has a softness to it, the hobstars and file effect blur into one another. The name *IMPERIAL* is that given this pattern by Cristalerias Piccardo. It's an interesting choice, suggesting that they were imitating the geometric style of the Imperial Glass Company. The stemmed goblet is very reminiscent of Imperial's *OCTAGON* pattern.

    Shapes: pitcher (in two different styles) and stemmed goblet
    Color: marigold

Cristalerias Piccardo's *IMPERIAL* water pitcher in marigold.
SP $100-$375

Links between United States Glass Company and South America.

There were established and proven links between the United States Glass Company and South America. In 1915 U. S. Glass produced a catalog specifically aimed at the export market of Mexico and South America. The *OMNIBUS* pattern was featured in that particular document. Another U. S. Glass catalog in 1919 was aimed at a more general export market. Both catalogs were written in English and Spanish. Many interesting Carnival items that appeared in the U. S. Glass Company's catalogs have been found in Argentina and other South American countries. Carnival Glass examples of *THE STATES, OMNIBUS, REGAL* and *RISING SUN* have all been found in Argentina, sometimes in shapes and colors not thought to have been used by the U. S. Glass Company. *OMNIBUS*, for example, has been found in the form of a green pitcher and tumbler—the top of the pitcher is flattened and there are subtle pattern differences—it was almost certainly made in Argentina. So, were moulds sold by the U. S. Glass Company to glass manufacturers in South America who then slightly altered them and subsequently put them into iridized production? The answer is not yet proven beyond all doubt, but this certainly does appear to have been the case.

Furthermore, the Indiana Glass Company of Dunkirk, Indiana, is known to have bought moulds from the U. S. Glass Company. They also sold moulds to Argentina. An Indiana Glass pattern, *LUCILE,* has been found in the form of iridized water sets in Argentina. There is no documentary evidence to show that Indiana Glass made *LUCILE* in Carnival. So was it made in Argentina? It's very possible.

Cristales Mexicanos S.A. (now part of Grupo Vitro)—Mexico

The Mexican Glass group, Vitro S.A., was founded back in 1909. Its main product in those early days was beer bottles. Mexico's growing beer industry demanded growing numbers of bottles and by satisfying that demand in the home market, Mexico was able to cut down its imports of glassware. The original glass works there was known as Vidriera Monterrey S.A. The company grew and expanded, at all times being aware of the need to keep up with the latest technology. In 1957, the glassmaker Cristales Mexicanos S.A., who were also located in Monterrey, was purchased too. Cristales Mexicanos were known as producers of dinnerware and household glass. The trademark M inside a larger C, as found on several items of Carnival Glass, was their logo. Iridized glass was produced by Cristales Mexicanos, most likely before its incorporation into the Vitro S.A. group. Any items marked with the CM trademark date from before the 1957 amalgamation.

The *Catalogo General de Cristales Mexicanos S.A.* (dating from just before 1957) shows many bottles (some of them in novelty form) and similar containers in a whole range of shapes and sizes. A number of iridized bottles and jars are known and it is very likely that some of these were made by Cristales Mexicanos

OKLAHOMA—Cristales Mexicanos S.A.

The *OKLAHOMA* tumbler, is a scarce and sought after item. The pattern is geometric, large diamond shapes set amongst smaller diamonds. It is unusual in that the top of the tumbler bells in, making the top diameter narrower than that of the collar base. In the center of the rayed star on the base is the CM trademark. Lois Langdon, a Carnival collector, took several vacations with her husband, in Guadalajara, which lies about three hundred miles from Mexico City (and about five hundred from Monterrey). At a flea market in Guadalajara, some years ago, they found a box that contained six *OKLAHOMA* tumblers and four *RANGER* tumblers. On the box there was a large printed label that read "Cristales de Mexico—Monterrey." This pattern is very similar to an Imperial design #281 as seen in the Imperial 1909 catalog. The shape of the tumbler is very different, however, as the Imperial version has straight sides and a ground base. It would seem that the Mexican version could well be a copy of the Imperial design.

    Shapes: tumbler and carafe (decanter)
    Color: marigold

RANGER—Cristales Mexicanos S.A.

A familiar blocked design, so like many others, yet distinct in that this one has a star base with the CM trademark in the center.

    Shapes: pitcher and tumbler
    Color: marigold

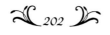

P. and J. Hartinger S.A.—Peru

The company was founded by Senor Pio Hartinger Machalek in 1939. Their trademark has the appearance of a four-leaved clover, but in fact is four stylized hearts (Hartinger) with a central circle that contains the letter *H*. The company ceased to trade in the mid 1990s when the owner, Mr. Hartinger, died and all the company assets were disposed of.

INCA BOTTLES—P. and J. Hartinger S.A.

There are several variations of these splendidly quixotic novelties. Research by Clint Arsenault has shown that some of these bottles were actually sold in a specially designed, plastic carrying case. The case has a moulded insert that fits the bottles precisely for their safety in transit. Labels and moulded text found on the bottles and the case indicate that they were made for Santa Josefa Vina, probably a wine or liqueur producer. The original content of the bottles was known as "pisco" which appears to be a grape distillate (like brandy) that notches up a rather high alcohol content of 43.9 percent. The label on the front of the case states that the contents are *3 PARRAS*—which translates to mean three guys or fellows, in other words, the three *INCA BOTTLES* that were contained within the carrying case.

Four different versions of the *INCA BOTTLES* are currently recorded. Each has in common a grotesque appearance: three feature just a face; the other is shaped like a squat figure with a disproportionately large face and neck. Small wine glasses have also been found with one example of this bottle. *INCA BOTTLES* are scarce and unusual items in collecting circles. According to the text on the bottle labels, they were distributed to Bogota, Colombia and Buenos Aires, Argentina.

Shape: bottle
Colors: marigold, amethyst and blue

This is the scarce, marigold *OKLAHOMA* tumbler with a CM trademark on the base, representing Cristalerias Mexicano, Mexico. SP $200-$400

Saint Gobain—Brazil

The French company, Saint Gobain, has had a presence in Brazil since 1937 when it bought Companhia Metalurgica Barbará and Brasilit S. A. Gradually over the years, it acquired more companies and grew enormously—in fact Brazil has the widest range of activities possible among the countries in which the group operates. In Brazil, Duralex is one of the lines produced at the Saint Gobain plant (in Santa Marina).

Our belief is that the mould for the original Coty *FIRCONES* vase that was almost certainly produced at La Chapelle-Saint-Mesmin in France was shipped over to the Saint Gobain subsidiary in Brazil sometime during the 1940s or 1950s. It's possible that the use of iridescence in other South American glass works had inspired the Brazilian factory to try their hand at Carnival Glass too. And what better piece to use than one that had been made in Carnival before? We know that a few other items in Carnival were also produced at the Brazil factory, including some vases with necks very similar to the *FIRCONES* vase. And we are informed that production for these was also sometime during either the 1950s or 1960s.

FIRCONES and *FROSTED FIRCONES* vase—Saint Gobain, Brazil

The *FIRCONES* vase is a massive and impressive item. Blow moulded and iridised, the pattern is in deep relief and features pine cones and needles, as well as a stylised Art Déco geometric panel up the sides. The Brazilian version of the vase is equally as impressive as the French version, and examples usually have a much longer neck than the original French one. In 2008, collectors Karen and Allan Rath reported a frosted marigold example of the Brazilian Fircones, sourced via Ria de Janeiro. The raised parts of the moulded design (the fircones, needles and geometric side panels) plus several encircling decorative accents around the neck of the vase are marigold, while the background is frosted white. The neck of the *FROSTED FIRCONES* is shorter than the regular Brazilian example, though still slightly longer than the French version. See the section on France in Chapter Seven for more details on the *FIRCONES* vase.

Shape: vase
Color: marigold, marigold/frosted and pale blue with marigold iridescence

Two vases from Brazil: on the left is the marigold *FIRCONES* while on the right can be seen the *FROSTED FIRCONES* vase. NP. *Photo courtesy of Karen and Allan Rath.*

Jain Glass Works (Private) Limited—India

The industrial town of Firozabad is the main location for the manufacture of glass in India. The Jain Glass Works (P) Ltd. was founded by the late Shri Chhadamilal Jain in 1928. It was one of the first companies to bring the (then) latest technology in glass manufacturing and decoration into India. As seen on their factory letterhead, the company's logo is a *sathya* (swastika) which in India, is an auspicious, traditional and sacred symbol. (This emblem is a very old, auspicious good luck symbol, almost certainly first used in India in the first and second centuries. In Sanskrit it is *Svasti*, meaning fortune or happiness).

Carnival Glass was first made at the Jain factory in 1935. Vases and drinking glasses were the main items that Jain produced in iridized glass. Pitchers (sometimes with a frosted design) and tumble-ups are also known. The designs and styles are quite wonderful and exotic, reflecting the rich culture and history of the Indian sub-continent. Drinking glasses and vases were the main items that Jain produced in iridized glass, predominantly in marigold (sometimes with frosted sections) and a light blue that the authors have termed Jain Blue. The founder's son,

the late Bimal Kumar Jain, added his own style of manufacturing the glass and called it "Lustre Glass." The company name JAIN can sometimes be found moulded or acid etched into the glass. The company's swastika logo is also seen on some items of Jain Carnival, most notably on the ELEPHANT VASE. The Jain Glass Works closed down in 1986, however there is a New Jain Enterprises (glass works) in Firozabad, but we cannot confirm any link.

DIAMOND AND GRAPES—Jain Glass Works (P) Ltd
Known only in a juice size tumbler standing 4 inches high, this is a well moulded item with a repeated diamond motif that encloses pendulous bunches of grapes and four-petalled flowers.
Shape: straight sided tumbler (4 inches)
Color: marigold

FISH VASE and FROSTED FISH VASE plus Variations—Jain Glass Works (P) Ltd. and possibly others
The FISH VASE is a weird and quite wonderful piece of glass. The fish twists around the vase, its head being at the base and its tail coiling, first left then right, around and upward. There is great detail in the mould work, the scales on the fish's body being very distinct. Why a fish? In Hindu legend, the god Vishnu reincarnates into a horned, golden scaled fish called Matsya. The golden fish then saved all mankind from destruction during a terrible flood. The image on the vase may well represent this legend. The vase is frequently found bearing the moulded letters JAIN to the left of the fish's mouth. JAIN is also found acid etched onto the underside of the base of the vase. The FROSTED FISH VASE is the same as the regular FISH but it has marigold iridescence on the fish shape only and white acid etching on the body of the vase. Standing at around 9 to 10 inches, these are the tallest of the Indian vases.

There are several further variations to the basic FISH, though the oddest is a vase called the SERPENT vase (this is, in fact, a re-modelled FISH vase and not a snake). On this vase, the fish/serpent usually winds the other way around the vase. It does not have the JAIN trademark and it is not yet confirmed whether the SERPENT is a product of the Jain works. An important characteristic that will help to distinguish between examples of the FISH vase and the SERPENT is that the FISH has two eyes and the SERPENT has only one eye in the center of its head.

The FISH VARIANT is another "spin" on the regular FISH—it is exactly the same as the FISH vase in mould detail, it doesn't have all the re-modelling of the SERPENT, but it winds the opposite way to the regular FISH (that is, the same way as the SERPENT).

There are also variations of the FROSTED FISH VASE. These are from a different mould to the original FROSTED FISH and have a slightly different base as well as differences in the overall mouldwork. One variation is frosted in light blue with parts of the fish picked out in marigold. Another is similar in frosting and marigold application, but the design band around the top of the vase is totally different and features a stylized foliage pattern in marigold.
Shape: vase
Colors: known in marigold and various acid etched versions (FROSTED FISH VASE) including light blue frosted with marigold

This pretty, marigold DIAMOND AND GRAPES juice glass is just 4 inches high with a base measurement slightly over 1.5 inches. On the base are the moulded number 3 and the word JAIN.
SP $50-$100

Three Indian vases, from the left: Jain *FROSTED FISH* vase with acid etching ($200-$400), the *SERPENT* vase (note its single eye—SP $100-$200) and the Jain *FISH* vase without the acid treatment (SP $90-$150).

GRAPEVINE AND SPIKES aka *GRAPE AND PALISADE*—Jain Glass Works (P) Ltd

Grapes and vine leaves curve around the top part of this tumbler while a vertical ribbed pattern is the feature around the lower section (the "spikes" in the pattern name). JAIN is found moulded on the bottom of the tumbler.

Shape: straight sided tumbler (4.5 inches and 5.5 inches)
Color: marigold

The *GRAPEVINE SPIKES* tumbler from Jain in rich marigold. $50-$80

The JAIN mark on the base of the *GRAPEVINE SPIKES* tumbler.

HAND VASE—Jain Glass Works (P) Ltd and others

The *HAND VASE* is captivating and fascinating. It features a human hand, complete with details such as rings and round wristwatch, holding a flared cone shape that is the body of the vase

—indeed the entire form of the vase is also the pattern. In Hindu iconography, the lifted hand protects both the conscious and unconscious order of the creation. Many Hindu gods are multi limbed and have several hands that are frequently placed in divine gestures (*mudras*) very similar to the *HAND VASE*. The vases come in left and right hand versions both with wristwatch and ring. There are two main sizes, 8 to 9 inches high and around 5 to 6 inches high. The moulded JAIN trademark may or may not be present and we are aware that other glass works in Firozabad also produced examples of the *HAND*—an example is known with the moulded letters KP (see below). The neck of the vase is usually crimped and has a beaded band near the top. There is a distinctive, thick circular base. Research by Angela Thistlewood has found three broad categories of *HAND VASE:* those with encircling bead motifs, those with encircling bead and arch motifs and those with flower motifs. Within these three broad categories can be found a wide variety of height, watch detail and variations in neck/mouth shaping

Shape: vase
Colors: marigold and Jain blue

Two *HAND* vases, probably made by Jain, although other makers also appear to have produced their own versions of the *HAND*. A right-hand version on the right of the photo and a left-hand version with flower design on the left. $50-$150

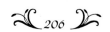

ORDER OF THE CROWN OF INDIA aka *CORONATION*—Probably Jain

This seldom seen and clearly mis-understood little vase is actually an Indian (not an English) item. The moulded crown on the side of the vase is a perfect replica in fine detail of the Crown of India. Above the crown are ribbon swags, which may indicate that the pattern actually represents the Order of the Crown of India—an honor bestowed on Royal ladies, and ladies connected with the Government of India, and worn suspended from a ribbon. The honor was instituted in 1878 and discontinued in 1947, so it is very possible the vase was made prior to 1947, most likely by Jain (who it is believed were making Carnival from around 1935).

Shape: vase
Color: marigold

This delightful little vase, just 5 inches high, features a perfect representation of the *ORDER OF THE CROWN OF INDIA*, hence its name. Maker most likely Jain. SP $200-$400

Four items probably from the West Glassworks in India. From the left: *DIAMANTE STARS* vase, *SHALIMAR* tumbler, *MONSOON* tumbler, *DIAMANTE RAIN* vase. The style of all four is very similar. $80-$150 for either vase or tumbler.

Other Indian Carnival Glass Works

Firozabad is located just to the east of Agra (where the Taj Mahal can be found) and is home to around half million people. Considered to be the glass capital of India, Firozabad has around four hundred glass works, several of which made Carnival Glass. The area accounts for around 70% of India's glass production in the small scale sector. Two other towns that host glass works that made Carnival are Sikohabad (which is quite close to Firozabad) and Sasni (which is about fifty or so miles away). Below we list some of the glass works that we believe made Carnival; it is very likely that other glass works may also have produced some. Jain's Carnival (see above) was made from around the mid 1930s and it seems very likely that other producers, such as Khandelwal and Paliwal, were also making iridized items (mainly tumblers) in that era. However, some other glass works such as West, were most likely making their Carnival in the 1960s and 1970s or even later. Later production is quite possibly characterized by simpler, chunkier patterns often on thick glass.

Advance Glass Works—India

Located in Firozabad and established in 1963, the owner, Shri Balkrishan Gupta, past owner of the company, was president of the All India Glass Manufacturers' Federation in 1983-4. Advance used a paper label ("Advance, Firozabad") that has been found on some items, including *SHALIMAR*. They made water sets and almost certainly a range of vases too, based on similar pattern characteristics and overall appearance. For example, the water sets in patterns *MONSOON* and *SHAZAM* are very much like *SHALIMAR*, while the group of vases *DIAMANTES*, *DIAMANTE STARS*, *DIAMANTE STARS VARIANT* and *DIAMANTE RAIN* are very evocative of the design on *SHALIMAR* and are very possibly also products of Advance Glass Works. (See "The Art of Carnival Glass" for further information). The *PANAJI PEACOCK EYE* vase is another that has the same characteristics and could also be by Advance. Light blue items are known as well as marigold, possibly colored by impurities in the glass batch—the vases in particular have been recorded in this shading.

SHALIMAR—Advance Glass Works

A chunky pattern on thick glass, *SHALIMAR* is a simplified geometric design comprising large and small star and diamond motifs. The base is iridized and has a star design—the top edge is clear of iridescence and can even be slightly frosty in appearance. The tumbler shows four clear mould lines and the rim is ground smooth. The solid looking pitcher has a clear D shaped handle. Quality on these items (and this is true of much Indian Carnival) varies tremendously. Some examples can be absolutely stunning, with fabulous rich iridescence, while others may have bubbles and lumps in the glass and a weak, wishy-washy color.

Shapes: water pitcher and tumbler
Colors: marigold (possibly some items in weak blue)

AVM Glass Industries—India

Another glass works that was located in Firozabad, however they closed in the 1980s. Water sets and vases (allegedly including examples of some *HAND VASES*) have been found bearing the moulded trademark AVM.

CALCUTTA DIAMONDS—AVM Glass Industries

This pattern features a repeated diamond pattern in relief (the center of the diamonds is depressed) with a flower motif on the base. In the middle of the flower is the moulded logo AVM. As with the example reported above from Advance, the tumbler shows four clear mould lines and the rim is ground smooth—there is also a clear band around top of both tumbler and pitcher

    Shapes: water pitcher and tumbler

    Color: marigold

The moulded logo AVM on the base of this *CALCUTTA DIAMONDS* marigold tumbler indicates the maker. $50-$80

B. M. Glass Works—India

Little is known about this factory other than it was located in Firozabad. Tumblers have been found trademarked B.M.

C.B.—India

C.B. were located in Etmadpur, in the district of Agra, not far from Firozabad. The letters C.B. have been found as a moulded mark on some tumblers, on the *ELEPHANT VASE* and, most interestingly, on the C.B. vase. A paper label has also been found on a *FISH VARIANT* vase with the latters C. B. Etmadpur.

Khandelwal Glass Works—India

The Khandelwal Glass Works is located at Sasni, near the town of Aligarh, in Uttar Pradesh. The company used the moulded logo SASNI on some of their tumblers. Khandelwal was founded in 1932 and belongs to the family of the Late Shri Prakash Chandra Jain, who was past president of the All India Glass Manufacturers' Federation in 1959-60. The *VINEYARD HARVEST* tumbler was made by this glass works and bears a SASNI moulded trademark. Bob Smith also reports a variation of the *STARS OVER INDIA VARIANT* tumbler with a moulded SASNI trademark (see also entry on Paliwal below). For clarity it is possibly best to refer to this as the *STARS OVER INDIA SASNI VARIANT*

K.P. Glass Industries—India

Another glass works that was located in Firozabad, but we are currently unable to find further information. Carnival jars and a version of the *HAND VASE* have been found with the moulded trademark KP.

Paliwal Glass Works—India

Paliwal is located in Shikohabad in Uttar Pradesh, just under twenty miles from Firozabad. The company was established in 1922 and thus was the oldest of the Carnival producers in India. The first actual glass factory in India was the Paisa Fund Glass Works which was established in 1908, although glass was made in Firozabad from as early as the eighteenth century as a cottage industry. The owner of Paliwal—Shri R.K.Paliwal—was president of the All India Glass Manufacturers' Federation in 1997-9. The company marked their Carnival with at least two different versions of the moulded words PALIWAL and also the letters PGW.

Two rare, older tumblers from Paliwal. On the left is the *GANGES GARDEN* in rich marigold, standing just under 5 inches high, while on the right is the *STARS OVER INDIA PALIWAL VARIANT* tumbler, standing 5.5 inches high. The moulded word Paliwal is in script writing (upper and lower case) on the base of the *GANGES GARDEN* while the *STARS OVER INDIA PALIWAL VARIANT* has the same word moulded in block letters. SP for either $80-$175

GANGES GARDEN—Paliwal Glass Works

A delicate and exquisite design of ferns and floral fronds adorn this thin walled tumbler. Around the top is a curving repeat of stylized lotus blossoms and fern fronds. Hatched lines encircle the top while concentric circles encompass the base.

    Shape: tumbler

    Color: marigold

STARS OVER INDIA PALIWAL VARIANT—Paliwal Glass Works

The *STARS OVER INDIA* tumbler is straight sided and has a full moon and star motif in a band around the top. The rest of the tumbler has a stepped design and on the base there is a very unusual motif—alternate tear drop and rounded triangles (eight in all). There is no makers mark (and thus the maker is not certain). The *STARS OVER INDIA PALIWAL VARIANT* is taller and has an extra encircling design at the top—a floral band and concentric circles. These tumblers are made of thin walled and rather delicate glass on which the designs are intricately moulded. Bob Smith reports a further variation of the *STARS OVER INDIA VARIANT* which has some slight pattern differences and, significantly, the moulded word SASNI on the base (see Khandelwal Glass Works above). Clearly this pattern was made by more than one Indian maker.

    Shape: tumbler

    Color: marigold

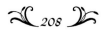

West Glass Works—India

Another Firozabad glass works that produced water sets, some have been found with WEST moulded on their base. Production at West commenced in May, 1971, so their Carnival is fairly recent. Known water pitchers from West also have a D shaped handle similar to that made by Advance. The *PANELLED DIAMOND* water set was made by West (their logo is on its base). This is a fairly plain design featuring vertical panels of diamonds and plain ribs. The band around the top of the items is clear and not iridized

Possible Indian Carnival Works

Agarwal Glass Industries Ltd. *aka BK Glass Ltd—India*

A large concern that was established in Firozabad in 1990. They produce glass tumblers but the authors cannot find any evidence that they made Carnival.

Om Glass Works Pvt. Ltd. *aka Pankaj Ltd—India*

A Firozabad glass works that was established in 1947. They produce tumblers (amongst other items) but no evidence has yet been seen by the authors to prove Carnival production.

Sun Glass Works Pvt. Ltd—India

Production commenced at the Sun Glass Works in Firozabad in 1971. They make tumblers, jars and bangles, so again it is possible that they produced some Carnival.

Note: many photos, drawings and extra information on further Indian tumblers and vases can be seen in "A Century of Carnival Glass" and "The Art of Carnival Glass" by the authors.

Carnival from China—no named factories known

A number of tumblers are reported that share a prominent feature, a common trademark—a small triangle (about an eighth of an inch long) on the base of each tumbler, which very possibly links them to one factory. Their bases are uniridized and all are marigold. Tumbler collector, Bob Smith, suggests that the pattern of numbers on some of the tumblers might indicate limited editions. Only a limited number of examples in six different Chinese patterns are currently known but no pitcher has yet been found to go with any of these tumblers.

All these items would appear to be bar-ware and thus made for places like hotels, restaurants or bars. The numbers on the base point to a special order made particularly for such places. The fact that they have been found in ones and twos, and in places as far apart as the USA and Australia, suggests that it might be a case of tourists bringing back souvenirs! In Bob Smith's opinion "There's no doubt that they were made in China, and further were made in Shanghai in particular—else why would *Shanghai China* be moulded into the base? If it was a souvenir it would be on the face of the glass, not hidden on the bottom. Being made in Shanghai presents a problem however, in terms of further research. The Communist government changed all the names of the glass factories from proper names into mundane names such as Glass Factory #3 and Glass Factory #12, etc. That is how all factories were described in the 1980s Chinese Business Directory—about a dozen glass factories in the Directory were located in Shanghai."

ORIENTAL MYSTERY—Chinese origin

A fascinating marigold compote was found in Australia in 2007 by Lesley Smith. At first sight it appeared to be an English (non-Carnival) pattern known as "Blackberry Prunt" aka #269, made by the well known firm, Davidson—except that Davidson are not known to have made Carnival Glass! The comport stands 3.5 inches high and measures 6 inches in diameter and is a most attractive item. Further study, however, revealed that the pattern (now named *ORIENTAL MYSTERY*) was not quite like the Davidson interpretation (there are seven points on all the prunts on the Davidson pieces but the *ORIENTAL MYSTERY* comport has six points on all the prunts). Then came the revelation that "Old Chinese" characters were moulded into the glass on the base. These characters read from right to left and are written in an old style of writing that is now defunct (it was used up to 1949) and thus there is a feeling that the comport may well date from the 1940s or possibly slightly earlier. The writing appears to give the name of a factory and the factory's founder, but it is not currently possible to be more precise.

Shape: comport
Color: marigold

Thin walled marigold vases have been found with a label stating: GOLDFISH Made in China. These items usually have an etched design on them and are somewhat similar to the thin glass, lidded jars that are seen with etched fern and floral designs. The authors believe that these were made for the gift market in circa the 1970s and 1980s.

Finally, it's worth noting that a very recent (2007) production of Carnival has taken place in China for Colourful Dragon Imports in Australia. These are blue, purple and white large, crimped bowls that feature a koala or a platypus. The exterior of these bowls features a reproduction of the Classic Australian *FERN AND WATTLE* design. The interior uses a facsimile of the encircling waratah and flannel flower design that is found on the old Crown Crystal *KOOKABURRA* bowls. On the base of the bowls is the word SUMMERLAND. The bowls have a paper sticker stating Made in China. Five hundred of each color and pattern has been made—a total of three thousand items.

A fascinating blend of mystery and intrigue, this is the *ORIENTAL MYSTERY* comport. The item is displayed on its side to show the prunt detail on the underneath. The top is un-patterned and richly iridized. NP

Close-up showing the moulded Chinese characters on the *ORIENTAL MYSTERY* comport. There are three lines of "writing" - the top line has two symbols, the middle has three and the bottom has two—in all seven symbols are moulded on the glass, quite small and very hard to read.

Carnival Colors Defined

Shades of Marigold (Lightest First)

Marigold is probably the color most people associate with Carnival. Indeed, new collectors can be forgiven for thinking that Carnival only comes in marigold! It surprises many to learn the myriad of shades available. It's a golden, glowing color that was almost certainly the first color produced in Carnival Glass, though it wasn't called "marigold" at the time. Instead, it was tagged with names such as "Golden Iris" and "Rubigold." It is certainly the most easily found of all the Carnival colors. No doubt it was a popular shade when it was first introduced—its bright, gold coloration standing out against the dark, drab house interiors of the time. Marigold is different from most of the other Carnival colors in that its base glass is clear, not colored. Clear glass was known as crystal in the United States and flint glass in the United Kingdom. It was the application of a metallic spray that gave the clear glass a distinctive orange-marigold coloring. The range of shades in marigold is great, although they don't all have specific names.

So when was the name marigold first used...and why? In Minnie Watson Kamm's books dating back to the 1950s there are various references to iridized, press moulded glass. In her fourth book[1] there is a reference to a pattern she calls "Marigold Windmill"—this was what collectors now know as Imperial Glass Company's *WINDMILL* design. In describing the glass she is referring to, Kamm explains that it was an imitation or approximation of Tiffany and Aurene Glass, though in a much less expensive form. She then adds "it was called 'Marigold Glass' at the Imperial plant from its bright, coppery color but it now goes by such names as 'Carnival Glass,' 'Bronzy Glass,' 'Lustre Glass,' and other less complimentary names." It seems quite possible then that the first use of "marigold" was by the workers at the Imperial Glass factory.

Pastel marigold is a very pale shade that usually has a delicate, multi-colored iridescence, shot with pinks, golds, and greens. It is sometimes referred to as a "Tiffany like" iridescence and is most attractive.

Clambroth generally refers to a pale "ginger ale" tint and is most often seen on Imperial Carnival. Some collectors report the clambroth effect on clear base glass too.

Light or pale marigold is an insipid shade that might be called "wishy-washy!"

Peach opalescent is found in varying shades of marigold, although there is only one name for the color. Basically, it is marigold glass with an opalescent edge—but as the marigold can go from very light and delicate up to strong and very intense, there is quite a range that technically can be called peach opal. Also, the opalescent effect can be pale and delicate (Fenton's peach opal usually is like this) right through to deep and solid opal effects (usually from Dugan/Diamond, who produced the bulk of the peach opal Carnival).

Marigold is a balanced mid-shade between red and yellow—a true orange.

Pumpkin is a gorgeous deep and rich shade, golden and glowing and full of multicolored highlights usually showing much red in the iridescence.

Shades of Purple (Lightest First)

Purple and amethyst were used by most of the Carnival Glass manufacturers. The color ranges from a fragile whisper of lavender right up to a deep, dense color that verges on black. The iridescent effects vary greatly on the purple colors. Amethyst, for example, is a light shade of pinky purple, yet the iridescence on most examples gives quite a deep bronze effect that makes the item look much darker. Some purple Carnival can have an amazing "electric" iridescence that makes the item look blue. It almost vibrates with color.

Sun colored lavender is a scarce effect caused by allowing clear glass to be exposed to strong sunlight over a long period of time. It is the merest whisper of lavender, a delicate hint of color. Some base glass may have the same delicate color effect through manganese impurities in a crystal batch.

Lavender is a delicate, pale shade of purple. This is quite a scarce shade and when it's combined with a light iridescence that enhances the pale base color, it can be extremely beautiful and subtle.

Amethyst is a mid-shade, with definite pink tones. The heavy bronze iridescence often found on much amethyst glass tends to mask the base color.

Amethyst opalescent is rarely found. It is basically amethyst glass with a light, opal edge. Owing to its scarcity, it's unlikely it was a production line color.

Purple is a balanced mid-shade, between red and blue.

Violet is deeper than purple with more blue tones.

Fiery amethyst may also be called oxblood or overshot/overbalanced amethyst. It looks ruby red in some lights, but is, in fact, a deep, rich red/purple. There are some excellent examples of this shade by Dugan/Diamond.

Black amethyst is a dark (almost black) purple. It is hard to see the base color on this shade unless viewed against a very bright light. Australian collectors call black amethyst Carnival from Crown Crystal "dark." Dugan/Diamond, Fenton, and Sowerby made scarce black amethyst examples.

Black is an exceptionally rare base color derived from using such a dense shade of purple that it is impervious to light, thus creating the impression that black has actually been used to color the glass. Sowerby in the United Kingdom made some very scarce examples of black Carnival. Iron and coal (slag) were added to their glass batch to achieve this color

Shades of Blue (Lightest First)

There is an extremely wide range of shades that fall into the definition of blue; many of them are very scarce indeed. The iridescent effects on these shades are similarly varied and wide ranging. Acid frosting, stretch effects, and opalescent edges—all are represented here.

Ice blue is the palest of the blue shades with a frosty, acid treated iridescence and was mainly from the Northwood factory. The overall appearance of this color is a pale whisper of blue. The iridescence does not mask the base color at all, but is a pastel effect that enhances the overall lightness.

Ice blue opalescent is a light, opal edge on ice blue. This is extremely rare.

Powder blue is a very light blue shade, but not frosty. The dark, bronze iridescence usually used on powder blue makes the piece appear much darker. A lighter marigold iridescence may also be seen on powder blue.

Persian blue is a semi-translucent, light blue glass. It usually has a marigold iridescence that ranges from a gentle golden effect to a much deeper coloration. Strictly speaking, Persian blue is iridized blue moonstone, and is semi-opaque. Moonstone (a Fenton shade) is a translucent white glass. It's interesting to note that most of the Persian blue Carnival items have been found in England.

Celeste is a scarce color which usually has a frosty iridescence, often with the stretch onion-skin effect that usually has a rough-feeling texture. It's light blue in color, but more intense and brilliant than ice blue. Virtually all examples of celeste are from Fenton or Dugan/Diamond. Like Persian blue, many examples have been found in England.

Sapphire is a Northwood shade, sometimes likened to a sky blue. It is deeper than ice blue and celeste, though it is closer to the latter. The iridescent effect is different, however, as sapphire does not have the characteristic stretch glass type of frostiness that much celeste has.

Iridized blue milk glass is a dense, solid, blue milk glass base with a clear iridescent effect. Typical examples (though scarce) are from Westmoreland. Milk glass is a dense, opaque white glass.

Aqua is a light, fresh shade that is a balanced mix of blue and green.

Aqua opalescent is a whitish opal edge on an aqua base. This is a typical Northwood color, with exceptionally rare examples from Fenton. It's also a very desirable color—some of the rarest Carnival items are found in this shade. For example, only one *GRAPE & CABLE* punch set is currently known in aqua opal (found in 1996). Different types of iridescence will give very different final effects on aqua opal. The rich, golden orange iridescent effect is called butterscotch, while the lighter, multicolored effect that allows more of the base aqua color to show through is termed pastel iridescence.

Renninger blue is a turquoise mid-shade combining blue and green with a hint of gray. It is mainly from Northwood.

Teal is a green-blue mid-shade, but with more green tones than Renninger blue. This color is often associated with the Westmoreland company.

Blue is a mid-shade, not quite as intense a color as cobalt.

Blue opalescent is seen as a light, opal edge to blue. Examples from Westmoreland are on a lighter base glass with more opalescence than the rare cobalt blue opals from Fenton (see below).

Cobalt blue is a vibrant, royal blue color, mainly from the Northwood and Fenton works. It is a beautiful rich shade that is popular amongst collectors.

Cobalt blue opalescent is not easily found; indeed, there are very few examples of it. In the International Carnival Glass Association's Color spread dated September 1986, Don Moore noted that Frank M. Fenton (Frank L. Fenton's son) "feels this unusual coloring resulted from either a chemical imbalance of some kind or an accident." Cobalt blue opalescent is a Fenton color.

Blue slag is a solid, opaque color with a marbled effect. Also called Sorbini, this is a very rare color.

Shades of Green (Lightest First)

Ice green is the palest of the green shades with a light, frosty iridescence. Frequently, the frostiness of the acid effect on ice green is not very pronounced—but there should be some obscuring of the surface of the glass to be a true ice green. Ice green is usually from Northwood, with a little from the Dugan/Diamond factory.

Ice green opalescent is another extremely unusual and seldom seen variation. This is a light opalescent edge on ice green.

Florentine green is only very slightly deeper than ice green. It is Fenton's version of ice green and can be found on some enameled Carnival. Not quite so frosty as ice green, Florentine green often gives a glow under ultra-violet (UV) light, though not as intense as the glow given by vaseline glass.

Lime green is just a shade deeper than ice green, but with no frosty effect. It may have a slight yellow tint to it.

Lime green opalescent is seen as a light, opal edge on lime green: not often seen.

Vaseline is a base shade that varies from a light yellow base color with a hint of green through a more predominantly, greenish yellow shade. Vaseline Carnival usually has an orange, marigold iridescence, but not always—it can have a clear iridescent effect that allows the vaseline base color to show through very clearly. Check out marigold pieces for this scarce base color. Holding a UV (black light) to vaseline glass produces a see-through, vivid yellowish green, fluorescent glow. Vaseline glass contains about 2% uranium oxide, the electrons of which react strongly to (in fact they are "excited" by) ultra-violet light. Vaseline glass is also known as uranium glass; uranium was used as a coloring agent in glass by Josef Riedel in Bohemia in 1830. The radiation given off by the glass will produce a reading on a Geiger counter, but is not harmful. Indeed, it is comparable to that given off by a TV set or microwave oven.

Vaseline opalescent is a light opalescent edge on vaseline that is very seldom seen. It is usually Fenton.

Helios is a light fresh green base shade with a distinctive gold/silver iridescence. It was a signature color of the Imperial factory.

Moss green is a yellow-green shade, but darker than lime and vaseline.

Emerald is a brilliant mid-shade, a true vivid and vibrant green that is highly prized. Emerald Carnival has a dazzling iridescence that is shot with mainly petrol blue/green effects and other highlights—it can be likened to the "electric" effect on electric blue (see Part One, Chapter Two).

Green is a standard shade of green, not as vibrant as emerald.

Nile green is an exceptionally rare shade of opaque yellow-green. Not a particularly attractive shade, but interesting nonetheless, it was possibly an experimental shade and is credited to Jacob Rosenthal who worked for Fenton.

Olive has some yellow tones, it is a kind of russet.

Shades of Red

Red is one of the most desirable of Carnival base colors. It was only introduced during the later years of Carnival production—the 1920s. Se-

lenium was the coloring agent used: it was notoriously difficult to stabilize or "strike," temperature being the critical factor. Red and its variations were primarily Fenton colors, though the Imperial Company also made a small amount. Iridescent effects on red vary. The most desirable is probably where the iridescence is pastel and doesn't mask the red coloration of the glass. It looks unmistakably red. The other main iridescent effect seen on red is a heavy, dark blue/green effect that tends to mask the base color somewhat.

Amberina. Pure cherry red is a difficult color to make and frequently yellow shading occurs where the heat has not been great enough on that portion of the item being made. The shading into yellow is called amberina. Standard amberina is where the outer edges of the piece are red but as you look toward the center of the piece you see an increasing amount of yellow. Amberina opalescent is known, but is very rare.

Reverse Amberina occurs in a similar way to amberina, but the other way around—the yellow tones are to the outer edge of the piece. Reverse amberina opalescent is known, but is very rare.

Red, that is pure cherry red, like the red of stop lights, is a much sought after color. Highest prices are paid for true cherry red with a clear iridescence rather than the deeper, darker iridescent effects that tend to mask the overall red quality.

Red opalescent is a very unusual shade that has a faint whitish edge on red. It is exceptionally rare and quite probably not a production line item.

Brick red is a shade of red with brown tones.

Red slag is a scarce hybrid, no doubt due to poor quality control. This is a cherry red color with swirls of darker shades, possibly from the "end of the pot." At first glance, the piece may appear amethyst or blue, and it requires a very bright light shining through the piece to see the redness in the color.

Shades of White (Lightest First)

Clear is a crystal clear, colorless base glass with no acid frosting to obscure it. It has a pastel, multi-colored iridescence.

White is also a crystal, clear, colorless base glass, but the overall effect is of a frosty white coloration, created by acid treatment to the surface of the glass.

Iridized moonstone is a translucent, see-through milky effect that often has a marigold iridescence. This is a scarce, off-beat color.

Iridized milk glass (marigold on milk glass) is a dense, solid, white milk glass base with a marigold iridescence. The base glass is totally opaque.

Pearl is iridized custard glass, quite opaque and dense, with a solid cream base. The iridescence is almost clear and the effect is of pale pinks and golds. Custard glass was originally termed "ivory" by Northwood. That term describes it well.

Iridized custard glass (marigold on custard) has the same base as pearl—a cream colored custard glass—but iridized custard glass has an orange, marigold iridescence that gives a totally different color effect to pearl. Iridized custard is from Northwood.

Shades of Brown, Grey, and Yellow

Smoke can be seen as a light brown, smudgy shade (when it is a surface iridescence on clear glass) or as a gray base color with a smoky iridescence shot with pinks and purples. Some examples of the gray smoky iridescence can also be found on clear base glass. Usually, smoke is an Imperial color, though small amounts from Northwood and Fenton are found.

Smoke opalescent is exceptionally rare and undoubtedly an experimental color, or maybe even an accident. We have only seen one example of this shade in Carnival Glass.

Honey amber is a color that is very similar to marigold and could be mistaken for it. The base glass is clear but the iridescence is light butterscotch brown. Honey amber is a typical color from the United States Glass Company.

Horehound is a scarce brown shade that has been likened to "root beer" in color.

Amber is a true mid-brown typically from Imperial. It often has a stunning iridescence, shot with vivid purples and pinks. Very small amounts are known from Northwood and Fenton, both of which are lighter than the Imperial version. Note that Northwood's amber is more of a honey shade and is actually slightly paler than Northwood's horehound.

Yellow is a very scarce, but true, pale shade of yellow. Some *FOUR FLOWERS VARIANT* bowls and plates are found in this shade. There are several Westmoreland pieces, too. Yellow Opal is reported.

[1] Minnie Watson Kamm, *A Fourth Two Hundred Pattern Glass Book* (Grosse Pointe, Michigan: by author, 1950).

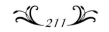

The following is a listing of most of the Carnival Glass pattern names that were ascribed by Marion Hartung. These are the names generally used by collectors today. Rose Presznick, however, originated a different set of pattern names; these are used only infrequently today, but the collector may come across some of these names from time to time. It is also quite fascinating to study the different names—Mrs. Hartung and Mrs. Presznick did not always think alike! This listing cross-references the Hartung pattern names with the Presznick pattern names. By no means are all Carnival pattern names included; many more patterns have come to light since the pioneering researchers/collectors, Hartung and Presznick, first began to record them. However, in the interest of future generations of students and collectors of Carnival Glass, we are privileged to be able to record them here.

The original list was compiled by Rosalie White of Missouri. It was continued and extended by Wily and Catherine Addis of Ohio and has recently been further extended by the authors. The list was re-issued in the December 1992 issue of the *American Carnival Glass News*, the journal of the American Carnival Glass Association (ACGA). Thanks to ACGA and President Edward Radcliff for permission to include it.

Note that Hartung names are written in italicized capitals, while Presznick names are written in regular lower case.

HARTUNG	Presznick
ACANTHUS	Parrot Tulip Swirl
ACORN	Oak Leaf and Acorn
ACORN BURRS	Acorn Burrs and Bark
AMARYLLIS	Tulip and Poppy
APPLE PANELS	Crab Apple Variant
BAMBOO BIRD	Bamboo and Bird
AUGUST FLOWERS	Daisy Panels
BASKET, N's	Bushel Basket
BASKETWEAVE AND CABLE	Basketweave and Cable Band
BEADED BULLSEYE	Beaded Medallion and Teardrop
BELLS AND BEADS	Bell Flower
BIG FISH	Fish and Flowers
BIRDS AND CHERRIES	Birds and Bough
BIRD WITH GRAPES	Cockatoo and Grapes
BLACKBERRY	Blackberry A.
BLACKBERRY BLOCK	Blackberry and Checkerboard
BLACKBERRY SPRAY	Blackberry B.
BLOSSOMS AND BAND	Apple Blossom Border
BLOSSOMTIME	Northwood's Primrose
BLUEBERRY	Blueberry
BOUQUET	Spring Flowers
BOUQUET AND LATTICE	Late Lattice
BROCADED ACORNS	Oak Leaf Brocade
BUTTERFLY AND BERRY	Butterfly and Grape
BUTTERFLY AND FERN	Butterfly and Fern
BUTTERFLY AND TULIP	Flower Pot
BUTTERFLY, N's	Butterfly and Stippled Rays
BUTTERFLIES	Fenton's Butterflies
BULLSEYE AND LEAVES	Dahlia and Oak Leaves
CAPTIVE ROSE	Battenburg Lace #2 B
CHECKERBOARD	Barred Hobstar
COLOGNE BOTTLE, CAMBRIDGE	Broken Arches, Variant
COUNTRY KITCHEN	Finecut &Daisy/Daisy &Star
CHERRY, FENTON'S	Cherries and Mums
CHERRY, N's	N. Cherry (Iridescent Cherry)
CHERRY CIRCLE	Cherries and Holly Wreath
CHRISTMAS COMPOTE	Holly Christmas Compote
COBBLESTONES	Bubbles and Peacock Eye
COIN DOT	Coin Dots
COLONIAL CARNIVAL	Colonial
COMPASS	Eight Point Star
CONCAVE DIAMONDS	Kimberly
CONCORD	Latticed Grape
CONSTELLATION	Beaded Star and Snail
CORN BOTTLE	"Ole Corn"
CORNUCOPIA	Horn of Plenty
COSMOS AND CANE	Diamond Point and Daisy
CURVED STAR	Astral Star / Cathedral
DAHLIA, NORTHWOOD's	Dahlia
DAISY CUT BELL	Near-Cut Bell
DAISIES AND DRAPE	Daisy Band and Drape
DANDELION, N's	Sunflower
DANDELION, PANELED	Dandelion Variant
DIAMOND	Diamond Band
DIAMOND AND RIB	Melon and Fan
DIAMOND OVALS	English Hob Medallion and Fan
DIVING DOLPHINS	Dolphins and Flowers
DOUBLE DOLPHINS	Dolphins Twins
DOUBLE STAR	Hobstar and Torch
DOUBLE STEM ROSE	Roses and Loops
DRAGON AND BERRY	Dragon and Strawberry
DRAPE, FOOTED	Noble Drape Vase
EASTERN STAR	Scroll Embossed &Peacock Eye
EMBROIDERED MUMS	Mums and Greek Key
ESTATE	Scroll Cable
FANCIFUL	Battenburg Lace - C
FANCY, N's	Mabel
FARMYARD	Busy Chickens
FEATHER AND HEART	Heart Band and Herringbone
FEATHER STITCH	Briar Medallion / Coin Dot
FEATHERS	Poplar Tree
FEATHERED SERPENT	Feathered Scroll
FENTONIA	Diamond and Cable
FIELDFLOWER	Sunflower and Wheat
FINE CUT AND ROSES	Floral and Diamond Point
FISHERMAN'S MUG	Cattails and Fish
FISHSCALE AND BEADS	Honeycomb Collar
FLORAL AND GRAPE	Floral and Grapevine
FLORAL AND WHEAT	Floral and Wheat Spray
FLOWERING DILL	Michigan Beauty
FLOWERS AND SPADES	Spear Medallion and Flowers
FLOWERS, FENTON'S	Aurora
FOOTED SHELL	Ribbed Shell
FOUR FLOWERS	Stippled Posy and Pods
FOUR SEVENTY FOUR	Mayflower
FROLICKING BEARS	Bears Tumbler
FRUIT LUSTRE	Late Embossed Fruits
GARDEN MUMS	Shasta Daisy
GOD AND HOME	Constitution
GOLDEN HARVEST	Harvest Time
GOOSEBERRY SPRAY	Gooseberry Garland
GRAPE, FENTON'S	Embossed Grape
GRAPE LEAVES, N's	Wild Grapes
GRAPEVINE LATTICE	Grapevine Diamonds
HARVEST FLOWER	Sunflower / Wheat / Clover
HATTIE	Busy Lizzie
HEADDRESS	Indian Rose
HEARTS AND FLOWERS	Battenburg Lace #1
HOBNAIL SPITTOON	Stippled Dot Cuspidor
HOBSTAR BAND	(Arched) Hobstar
HOBSTAR, CARNIVAL	Hobstar
HOBSTAR AND FEATHER ROSEBOWL	Intaglio Mazie
HOBSTAR AND FRUIT	Four Fruit and Hobstar
HOLLY, CARNIVAL	Holly and Berry

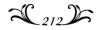

HOLLY, PANELED	Holly Star	*RAYS AND RIBBONS*	Ribbons and Rays Stippled
HOLLY SPRIG	Holly Spray	*RIBBON TIE*	Comet
HONEYCOMB AND CLOVER	Honeycomb &Four Leaf Clover	*RIPPLE*	Ripple Threads
HORSES' HEADS	Horse Medallions	*ROBIN*	Robin Red Breast
ILLUSION	Fenton's Arabic	*ROSALIND*	Drape and Tie
INVERTED COIN DOT	Polka Dot	*ROSE AND GREEK KEY*	LaBelle Rose Wreath
INVERTED FEATHER	Feather and Hobstar	*ROSE GARDEN*	Rose Marie
IRIS	Old Fashion Flag	*ROSE PILLARS*	Rose Columns
IRIS, HEAVY	Iris	*ROSE SHOW*	LaBelle Rose
IRIS AND HERRINGBONE	Late Iris	*ROSETTE, N's*	Rosette and Prisms
KNOTTED BEADS	Variegated Vase	*ROUND-UP*	Egyptian Band
LATTICE AND DAISY	Daisy and Lattice Band	*ROYALTY*	Queen's Crown
LATTICE AND GRAPE	Lattice and Grapevine	*RUFFLES AND RINGS*	Carnation and Pleats
LEAF AND BEADS	Stippled Leaf and Beads	*RUSTIC*	Maryland
LEAF CHAIN	Leaf Medallion	*SAILBOATS*	Sailboat and Windmill
LEAF RAYS	Cactus Leaf Rays	*SAILING SHIP*	The Dutchman
LEAF SWIRL	Oak Leaf	*SCALE BAND*	Two Band
LEAF TIERS	Stippled Leaf	*SCALES*	Looped Petals
LILY OF THE VALLEY	Banded Lily of the Valley	*SCROLL EMBOSSED*	Peacock Eye
LITTLE FISHES	Sea Lanes	*SEACOAST*	Maine Coast
LITTLE FLOWERS	Stippled Diamond and Flower	*SEAFOAM*	Beaded Star and Snail
LITTLE STARS	Stippled Clematis	*SEAWEED*	Stippled leaf and Scroll
LOUISA	Irish Lace	*SHELL, CARNIVAL*	Shell and Sand
LUSTRE FLUTE	Waffle Band	*SIX PETALS*	Christmas Rose and Poppy
MANY FRUITS	Multi Fruits and Flowers	*SODA GOLD*	Soda Gold / Spider Web
MARY ANN	Cordelia	*SPRINGTIME*	Butterfly and Cable
MAYAN	Coral Medallion	*STAR AND FILE*	Finecut and Star
MIKADO	(Interior of Cherries and Mums)	*STAR OF DAVID AND BOWS*	Star of David medallion
MILADY	Paneled Batchelor Buttons	*STARFISH*	Stippled Starfish Medallion
MY LADY'S POWDER JAR	Lucilea	*STIPPLED FLOWER*	Stippled Cosmos
NAUTILUS	Argonaut Shell	*STORK AND RUSHES*	Heron and Rushes
NU-ART PLATE	Nu-Art Currier and Ives	*STRAWBERRY SCROLL*	Strawberry and Scroll Band
OCTAGON	Princess Lace	*SWAN, CARNIVAL*	Nesting Swan
OKLAHOMA	Strawberry and Fan Variant	*SWIRL*	Wide Swirl
OPEN ROSE	Rose and Ruffles	*TARGET*	Loops and Columns
ORANGE PEEL	Stippled Orange	*TEN MUMS*	Chrysanthemum Wreath
ORANGE TREE ORCHARD	Orange Tree and Cable	*THISTLE, FENTON'S*	Christmas Cactus
ORANGE TREE SMALL	Orange Tree Variant	*TIGER LILY*	Amaryllis / Tiger Lily
ORANGE TREE VARIANT	Orange Tree and Scroll	*TOMAHAWK*	Big Chief Tomahawk
PARLOR PANELS	Lilith	*TORNADO*	Tadpole
PEACH, N's	Peach	*TREEBARK*	Fisherman's Net
PEACH AND PEAR	Apple and Pear	*TREETRUNK*	Killarney
PEACOCK	Peacock / The Fluffy Bird	*TROUT AND FLY*	Fish and Flowers
PEACOCK LAMP	Peacock Fantail	*TWINS*	Horseshoe Curve
PEACOCK, N's	Peacock on Fence	*TWO FLOWERS*	Dogwood and Marsh Lily
PEACOCK TAIL	Flowering Almonds	*TWO FRUITS*	Apple and Pear
PEOPLES' VASE	First Thanksgiving	*VINEYARD*	Peacock Eye and Grape
PERFECTION	Beaded Jewel and Leaf	*VINTAGE*	Grape Delight
PERSIAN GARDEN	Fan and Arch	*WATER LILY*	Magnolia and Poinsettia
PETALS	Stippled Dahlia	*WATERLILY AND CATTAILS*	Cattails and Waterlily
PINE CONE	Pine Cone Wreath	*WHIRLING LEAVES*	Leaf Pinwheel and Star Flower
PLAID	Granny's Gingham	*WIDE PANEL EPERGNE*	Colonial Epergne
POINSETTIA	Poinsettia and Lattice / The Christmas Plate	*WILD BERRY*	Autumn
PONY	Pony Rosette	*WILD ROSE, N's*	Shell and Wild Rose
POPPY, N's	Stippled Poppy / Poppy Scroll	*WILD ROSE SYRUP*	Wild Rose and Fleur de Lis
POPPY SHOW	LaBelle Poppy	*WILD STRAWBERRY, N's*	Strawberry
POPPY SHOW VASE	Poppy Delight	*WINDMILL, MARIGOLD*	Windmill Medallion
PRIMROSE	LaBelle Elaine	*WINE AND ROSES*	Cabbage Rose and Grape
PRISM AND DAISY BAND	Eyelet Band and Plaits	*WISHBONE*	Melinda
PULLED LOOP	Loop and Column	*WISTERIA*	Wisteria and Lattice
QUILL	Feather and Scroll	*WOODPECKER*	Hummingbird
QUESTION MARKS	Fantasy	*WREATH OF ROSES*	American Beauty Roses
RAINDROPS	Teardrops	*WREATHED CHERRY*	Cherry Wreathed
RAMBLER ROSE	Field Rose	*ZIPPERED LOOP LAMP*	Emaline
RASPBERRY	Blackberry and Checkerboard		

Bibliography

Adams, Steven. *The Arts and Crafts Movement*. Hertfordshire, England: Apple Press Ltd., 1987.

Archer, Margaret, and Douglas Archer. *Imperial Glass*. Paducah, Kentucky: Collector Books, 1990.

Audsley, G.A. and Audsley, M.A. *Victorian Patterns and Designs*. New York City: Dover Publications Inc., 1988.

Audsley, W. & G. *Designs and Patterns from Historic Ornament*. New York City: Dover Publications Inc., 1968.

Australian Carnival Enthusiasts Association Inc. *Carnival Glass of Australia*. Australia: Australian Carnival Glass Enthusiasts Association, 1988.

Barta, Dale, Diane Barta, and Helen M Rose. *Czechoslovakian Glass and Collectibles*. Paducah, Kentucky: Collector Books, 1992.

Battie, David, and Simon Cottle. *Sotheby's Concise Encyclopedia of Glass*. London, England: Conran Octopus, 1991.

Burns, Carl O. *Northwood's Carnival Glass*. Gas City, Indiana: L-W Book Sales, 1994.

———. *Imperial Carnival Glass*. Paducah, Kentucky: Collector Books, 1996.

Butler Brothers. Catalog facsimile *Our Drummer 1908-1931*. San Diego and Southern California Carnival Glass Clubs, 1994.

Cooke, Frederick. *Glass*. London, England: Bell and Hyman, 1986.

Cosentino, Geraldine, and Regina Stewart. *Carnival Glass*. Racine, Wisconsin: Western Publishing Company, Inc., 1976.

Crane, Walter. *Of the Decorative Illustration of Books Old and New*. London, England: George Bell and Sons, 1972.

Dore, Helen. *William Morris*. London, England: Hamlyn, 1996.

Doty, David, and Joan Doty. *Carnival Glass Appointment Calendar*. Chicago, Illinois: PageWorks, 1994 and 1995.

Dresser, Dr. Christopher. *Studies in Design*. London, England: Studio Editions, 1988.

Edwards, Bill. *Standard Encyclopedia of Carnival Glass*. Paducah, Kentucky: Collector Books, 1996.

Faulkner, Norman. *Glass India*. Calgary, Canada: by author (Video) 1994.

Freeman, Larry. *Iridescent Glass*. Watkins Glen, New York: Century House. 1956, 1964.

Gillow, Norah. *William Morris: Designs and Patterns*. London, England: Bracken Books, 1988.

Grafton, Carol Belanger. *A Treasury of Art Nouveau Design and Ornament*. New York City: Dover Publications Inc., 1980.

Grasset, Eugene. *Art Nouveau Floral Designs*. London, England: Bracken Books, 1988.

Hajdamach, Charles R. *British Glass. 1800-1914*. Suffolk, England: Antique Collectors' Club Ltd., 1993.

Hand, Sherman. *Colors in Carnival Glass*. Four book set. Scottsville, New York: by author, 1968-72.

Hand, Sherman. *The Collectors' Encyclopedia of Carnival Glass*. Paducah, Kentucky: Collector Books, 1978.

Hartung, Marion T. *Carnival Glass, Books 1-10*. Emporia, Kansas: by author, 1960-73.

Heacock, William. *Fenton, the First Twenty Five Years*. Marietta, Ohio: O-Val Advertising Corp., 1978.

Heacock, William, James Measell, and Berry Wiggins. *Harry Northwood. The Early Years*. Marietta, Ohio: Antique Publications, 1990.

———. *Harry Northwood. The Wheeling Years*. Marietta, Ohio: Antique Publications, 1991.

———. *Dugan/Diamond. The Story of Indiana, Pennsylvania, Glass*. Marietta, Ohio: Antique Publications, 1993.

Heart of America Carnival Glass Association Inc. *Educational Series I*. Kansas City, Kansas. Heart of America Carnival Glass Association, 1990.

———. *Educational Series II*. Kansas City, Kansas. Heart of America Carnival Glass Association, 1992.

———. *Educational Series III*. Kansas City, Kansas. Heart of America Carnival Glass Association, 1996.

Imperial Glass Company. *General Catalog. 1909*. Facsimile reprint. No date.

Jennings, Steve, and Karen Jennings. *A Catalog Reprint of Dugan Glass Company and H. Northwood Co., Glass manufacturers*. Jennings Design Company. No date.

Jervis, Simon. *Dictionary of Design and Designers*. Middlesex, England: Penguin, 1984.

Jones, Owen. *The Grammar of Ornament*. New York City: Dover Publications Inc., 1987.

Kamm, Minnie Watson. *Pattern Glass Pitchers. Vols. I - VIII*. Grosse Pointe, Michigan: by author, 1939-54.

Karhula-Iittala Kuvasto Katalog P. 1922. Karhulan Lasimuseo. Iittalan Lasimuseo, Finland, 1981.

Karhula Osakeyhtio Katalog A. 1932. Kuvasto P. 1934. Nakoispainos: Finland.

Klamkin, Marian. *The Collectors' Guide to Carnival Glass*. New York: Hawthorn, 1976.

Kock, Jan and Torben Sode. *Glass, Glassbeads and Glassmakers in Northern India*. Vanlose, Denmark: Thot Print, no date.

Lee Manufacturing Company. *Lee's 1911 Catalog*. Lee Manufacturing, 1911.

Lee, Ruth Webb. *Early American Pressed Glass*. Framlingham Centre, Massachusetts: by author, 1933.

Lilley, A.E.V. and Midgley. *Plant Form and Design:* London, England: Chapman and Hall, 1916.

Maeda, Taiji. *Japanese Decorative Design*. Tokyo: Japan Travel Bureau, 1957.

McDermot, Catherine. *Essential Design*. London, England: Bloomsbury, 1992.

McGee, Marie. *Millersburg Glass. As I Know It*. Marietta, Ohio: The Glass Press, Inc., 1995.

Moore, Donald. *The Shape of Things in Carnival Glass*. Alameda, California: by author, 1987.

Moore, Donald. *Carnival Glass: A Collection of Writings*. Alameda, California: by author, 1987.

Mordini, Tom and Sharon. *Carnival Glass Auction Price Report*. Freeport, Illinois: by authors, 1984 - 1997.

National Imperial Glass Collectors' Society. *Imperial Glass Encyclopedia. Volume I*. Marietta, Ohio: The Glass Press, Inc., 1995.

———. *Imperial Glass Encyclopedia. Volume II*. Marietta, Ohio: The Glass Press, Inc., 1997.

Olson, O. Joe. *God and Home. Carnival Glass Superstar*. Kansas City, Missouri: by author, 1976.

Owens, Richard, E. *Carnival Glass Tumblers*. La Habra, California: by author, 1975.

Paul, Tessa. *The Art of Louis Comfort Tiffany*. Avenel, New Jersey: Crescent Books, 1987.

Paulsson, Ulla-Carin, Patricia Soderberg, and Gunnar Lersjo. *Eda Glasbruk*. Varmland, Sweden: ABF, 1985.

Pavitt, William Thomas, and Kate Pavitt. *The Book of Talismans*. London, England: William Rider and Son Ltd., 1922.

Petrie, Flinders. *Decorative Symbols and Motifs for Artists and Craftspeople*. New York City: Dover Publications Inc., 1986.

Poulson, Christine. *William Morris*. Secaucus, New Jersey: Chartwell Books, 1989.

Prakash, K. *Authentic Folk Designs from India*. New York City: Dover Publications, 1995.

Quintin-Baxendale, Marion. *Carnival Glass Worldwide*. Cornwall, England: Carnivalia Publications, 1983.

Riihimaen Lasi Oy. Kuvasto-Hinnasto P. 1939. Nakoispainos: Finland. 1993.

Resnick, John D. *The Encyclopedia of Carnival Glass Lettered Pieces*. Nevada City, California: by author, 1989.

Revi, Albert Christian. *Nineteenth Century Glass: Its Genesis and Development*. Atglen, Pennsylvania: Schiffer Publishing Ltd., 1967.

Ross, Richard, and Wilma Ross. *Imperial Glass*. Des Moines, Iowa: Wallace-Homestead, 1971.

Sears Roebuck and Co., Ltd., *The Great Price Maker, 1908 Catalog* (facsimile). Nutfield, Illinois: DBI Books, Inc., 1971.

Sato, Tomoko, and Toshio Watanabe. *Japan and Britain: An Aesthetic Dialogue 1850-1930*. London, England: Lund Humphries Publishers Ltd., 1991.

Tait, Hugh. *Five Thousand Years of Glass*. London, England: British Museum Press, 1991.

Tana, Pradumna and Rosalba. *Traditional Designs from India*. New York City: Dover Publications Inc., 1981.

Truitt, Robert, and Deborah Truitt. *Collectible Bohemian Glass 1880-1940*. Kensington, Maryland: B & D Glass, 1995.

Turner, Mark and Hoskins, Lesley. *Home Decorating Sourcebook*. London, England: Crescent Books, 1995.

Verneuil, M.P., et al. *Art Nouveau Floral Ornament in Color*. New York City: Dover Publications Inc., 1976.

Whitley, Cecil. *The World of Enameled Carnival Glass Tumblers*. By author, 1985.

Whittick, Arnold. *Symbols, Signs and their Meaning and Uses in Design*. London, England: Leonard Hill, 1971.

Wilhide, Elizabeth. *William Morris: Decor and Design*. London, England: Pavilion Books Ltd., 1994.

Wilson, Chas West. *Westmoreland Glass*. Paducah, Kentucky: Collector Books, 1996.

Index

References to illustrations are noted in parenthesis and preceded by "illus".

Pattern Index

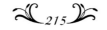

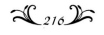